MOUS
Word 2000
Exam Prep

D0572063

Carol Cram
Jennifer A. Duffy
Marie L. Swanson

 CORIOLIS

MOUS Word 2000 Exam Prep

The Coriolis Group, LLC
14455 N. Hayden Road, Suite 220
Scottsdale, Arizona 85260

480/483-0192
FAX 480/483-0193
http://www.coriolis.com

Library of Congress Cataloging-in-Publication Data

Swanson, Marie, L.
    MOUS Word 2000 exam prep / by Marie L. Swanson, Carol Cram, and
    Jennifer A. Duffy.
        p. cm.
    Includes index.
    ISBN 1-57610-481-8
    1. Microsoft Word--Examinations--Study guides. 2. Electronic data processing
personnel--Examinations--Study guides. I. Title: Microsoft office user specialist
Word 2000 exam prep. II. Cram, Carol M. III. Duffy, Jennifer A. IV. Title.

Z52.5M52 S86 2000
652.5'5369'076--dc21

                                    00-023981

Printed in the United States of America
10 9 8 7 6 5 4 3 2 1

President, CEO
Keith Weiskamp

Publisher
Steve Sayre

Acquisitions Editor
Jeff Kellum

Marketing Manager
Cynthia Caldwell

Product Managers
Sharon Sanchez McCarson
Rebecca VanEsselstine

Production Editors
Kim Eoff
Catherine G. DiMassa

Editorial Assistant
Hilary Long

Cover Design
Jesse Dunn

Layout Design
Joseph Lee
April Nielsen

CD-ROM Developer
Robert Clarfield

⊚ CORIOLIS™

14455 North Hayden Road • Suite 220 • Scottsdale, Arizona 85260

Coriolis: The Smartest Way To Get Certified™

To help you reach your goals, we've listened to readers like you, and we've designed our entire product line around you and the way you like to study, learn, and master challenging subjects.

In addition to our highly popular *Exam Cram* and *Exam Prep* books, we offer several other products to help you pass certification exams. Our *Practice Tests* and *Flash Cards* are designed to make your studying fun and productive. Our *Audio Reviews* have received rave reviews from our customers— and they're the perfect way to make the most of your drive time!

The newest way to get certified is the *Exam Cram Personal Trainer* —a highly interactive, personalized self-study course based on the best-selling *Exam Cram* series. It's the first certification-specific product to completely link a customizable learning tool, exclusive *Exam Cram* content, and multiple testing techniques so you can study what, how, and when you want.

Exam Cram Insider —a biweekly newsletter containing the latest in certification news, study tips, and announcements from Certification Insider Press—gives you an ongoing look at the hottest certification programs. (To subscribe, send an email to **eci@coriolis.com** and type "subscribe insider" in the body of the email.) We also sponsor the Certified Crammer Society and the Coriolis Help Center—two other resources that will help you get certified even faster!

Help us continue to provide the very best certification study materials possible. Write us or email us at **cipq@coriolis.com** and let us know how our books have helped you study. Tell us about new features that you'd like us to add. Send us a story about how we've helped you; if we use it in one of our books, we'll send you an official Coriolis shirt!

Good luck with your certification exam and your career. Thank you for allowing us to help you achieve your goals.

Keith Weiskamp
President and CEO

Preface

Welcome to *MOUS Word 2000 Exam Prep.* This highly visual book offers users a comprehensive hands-on introduction to Microsoft Word 2000 and also serves as an excellent reference for future use.

▶ Organization and Coverage

This text contains sixteen units that cover basic to advanced Word skills. In these units, you learn how to edit and format documents, work with tables, add graphics, create Web pages, merge documents, create charts and forms, and customize Word.

▶ About this Approach

What makes this approach so effective at teaching software skills? It's quite simple. Each skill is presented on two facing pages, with the step-by-step instructions on the left page, and large screen illustrations on the right. You can focus on a single skill without having to turn the page. This unique design makes information extremely accessible and easy to absorb, and provides a great reference.

Each unit, or "information display," contains the following elements:

Each 2-page spread focuses on a single skill.

Clear step-by-step directions explain how to complete the specific task. When you follow the numbered steps, you quickly learn how each procedure is performed and what the results will be.

Concise text that introduces the basic principles discussed in the lesson. Procedures are easier to learn when concepts fit into a framework.

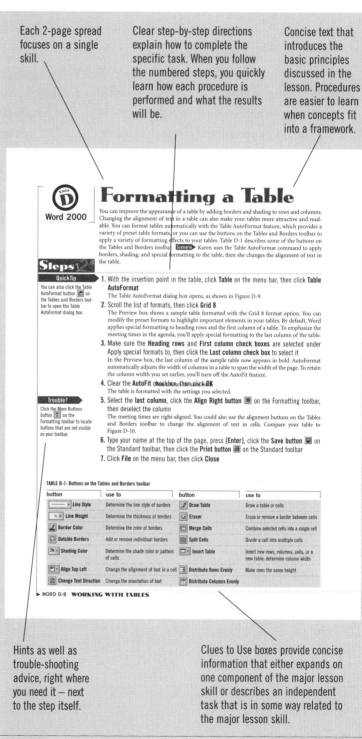

Hints as well as trouble-shooting advice, right where you need it — next to the step itself.

Clues to Use boxes provide concise information that either expands on one component of the major lesson skill or describes an independent task that is in some way related to the major lesson skill.

Every lesson features large-size, two-color representations of what your screen should look like after completing the numbered steps.

Features

The two-page lesson format featured in this book provides the new user with a powerful learning experience. Additionally, this book contains the following features:

▶ MOUS Certification Coverage
Each unit opener has a ⌊MOUS⌋ next to it to indicate where Microsoft Office User Specialist (MOUS) skills are covered. This book thoroughly prepares you to learn the skills needed to pass the Word Core and Expert 2000 exams.

▶ End of Unit Material
Each unit concludes with a Concepts Review that tests your understanding of what you learned in the unit. The Concepts Review is followed by a Skills Review, which provides you with additional hands-on practice of the skills. The Visual Workshops that follow the Skills Review helps you develop critical thinking skills. You are shown completed Web pages or screens and are asked to recreate them from scratch.

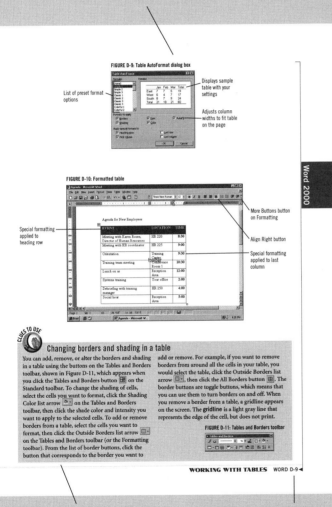

FIGURE D-9: Table AutoFormat dialog box

List of preset format options

Displays sample table with your settings

Adjusts column widths to fit table on the page

FIGURE D-10: Formatted table

Special formatting applied to heading row

Agenda for New Employees

More Buttons button on Formatting

Align Right button

Special formatting applied to last column

Changing borders and shading in a table

You can add, remove, or alter the borders and shading in a table using the buttons on the Tables and Borders toolbar, shown in Figure D-11, which appears when you click the Tables and Borders button 🔲 on the Standard toolbar. To change the shading of cells, select the cells you want to format, click the Shading Color list arrow on the Tables and Borders toolbar, then click the shade color and intensity you want to apply to the selected cells. To add or remove borders from a table, select the cells you want to format, then click the Outside Borders list arrow on the Tables and Borders toolbar (or the Formatting toolbar). From the list of border buttons, click the button that corresponds to the border you want to

add or remove. For example, if you want to remove borders from around all the cells in your table, you would select the table, click the Outside Borders list arrow, then click the All Borders button. The border buttons are toggle buttons, which means that you can use them to turn borders on and off. When you remove a border from a table, a gridline appears on the screen. The gridline is a light gray line that represents the edge of the cell, but does not print.

FIGURE D-11: Tables and Borders toolbar

WORKING WITH TABLES WORD D-9 ◀

Quickly accessible summaries of key terms, toolbar buttons, or keyboard alternatives connected with the lesson material. You can refer easily to this information when working on your own projects at a later time.

The page numbers are designed like a road map. WORD indicates the Word section, D indicates the fourth unit, and 9 indicates the page within the unit.

Contents At A Glance

Contents

Word 2000

Getting
Started with Word 2000

Objectives

- ► **Define word processing software**
- ► **Start Word 2000**
- ► **View the Word program window**
- ► **Create a document**
- MOUS ► **Save a document**
- MOUS ► **Preview and print a document**
- MOUS ► **Get Help**
- ► **Close a document and exit Word**

Welcome to Microsoft Word 2000. Microsoft Word is a powerful computer program that helps you create documents that communicate your ideas clearly and effectively. It includes sophisticated tools for editing text, creating tables and graphics, formatting pages, and proofing a document, to name just a few of its features. The lessons in this unit introduce you to the basic features of Word and familiarize you with the Word environment as you create a new document. Scenario ► Karen Rosen is the director of human resources at MediaLoft, a nationwide chain of bookstore cafés selling books, videos, and CDs. Karen's responsibilities include communicating with employees about company policies and benefits. She uses Word to create attractive and professional-looking documents.

Defining Word Processing Software

Microsoft Word is a full-featured word processing program. A **word processing program** is a software program that allows you to create attractive and professional-looking documents quickly and easily. Word processing offers many advantages over typing. The information you type in a word processing document is stored electronically on your computer, so it is easy to revise text and reuse it in other documents. Editing tools allow you to insert and delete text, move information from one part of a document to another, and check spelling and grammar. In addition, you can enhance your documents by changing the appearance of text, adding lines or graphics, and creating tables. Figure A-1 illustrates some of the word processing features you can use to create and enhance your documents using Word.

Details

Word allows you to:

Enter and revise text
Using Word's editing tools, you can easily enter and delete text, insert new text in the middle of a sentence, undo a change, and find and replace text throughout a document.

Copy and move text without retyping
You can copy or move text from one part of a document to another part of the same document, or from one document to a different document.

Locate and correct spelling mistakes and errors in grammar
Word's proofreading tools identify misspelled words and grammatical errors in your documents. You can correct the mistakes yourself or allow Word to suggest a correction.

Format text and design pages
By formatting the text and pages in your document to highlight important ideas, you can create documents that convey your message more effectively to your readers. In Word you can change the size and appearance of text, create bulleted or numbered lists, apply formatting styles, and add borders and shading to words and paragraphs. You can also organize text in columns, change margins, line spacing, and paragraph alignment, and adjust tabs and indents.

Align text in rows and columns using tables
You can create tables in Word to present information in an easy-to-read grid of rows and columns. You can format the tables to emphasize important points, and use the information contained in Word tables to create charts and graphs.

Enhance the appearance of a document using images, lines, and shapes
Word's graphic tools make it easy to illustrate your documents with graphic elements. You can draw lines and shapes, add color, and insert photographs and professionally-designed images into your documents.

Use Mail Merge to personalize form letters and create mailing labels
Mail merge allows you to customize form letters when you need to send the same letter to many different people. When you perform a mail merge, you merge a standard letter with a separate list of names and addresses. Mail merges are useful for creating labels and for sending frequent correspondence to the same group of people.

FIGURE A-1: Features of a word processing document

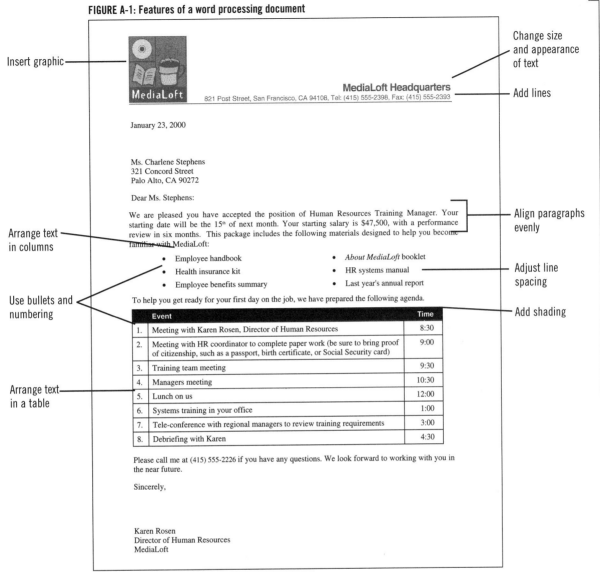

Insert graphic

Change size and appearance of text

Add lines

Arrange text in columns

Align paragraphs evenly

Adjust line spacing

Use bullets and numbering

Add shading

Arrange text in a table

Word 2000

Starting Word 2000

To start Word, you must first start Windows by turning on your computer. You can start Word on your computer by clicking the Start button on the taskbar, pointing to Programs, and then clicking Microsoft Word on the Programs menu. The Programs menu displays the list of programs installed on your computer, so you can start any program this way. Because computer systems have different setups depending on the hardware and software installed, your procedure for starting Word might be different from the one described below, especially if your computer is part of a network. See your instructor or technical support person if you need assistance. **Scenario** MediaLoft has just installed Word 2000 on the computers in the Human Resources department. Karen starts Word to familiarize herself with the program.

Steps

1. Make sure Windows is open, then click the **Start button** 🏁Start on the taskbar
The Start menu appears on the desktop.

2. Point to **Programs** on the Start menu
The Programs menu opens, as shown in Figure A-2. Your list of programs will depend on the programs installed on your computer.

Trouble?
If an Office Assistant dialog balloon appears, click Start using Microsoft Word.

3. Click **Microsoft Word** on the Programs menu
When you start Word, the **Word program window** opens in the most recently used view. **Views** are different ways of displaying a document in Word. Figure A-3 shows the Word program window in Normal view. The lessons in this unit assume you are using Normal view. The Office Assistant may also appear in your program window. The **Office Assistant** is an animated character that appears periodically to provide tips as you work in Word.

QuickTip
An indented button indicates that a feature is turned on.

4. Click the **Normal View button** ▤ in the lower-left corner of the program window if it is not already indented, as shown in Figure A-3
The document window changes to Normal view. The blinking vertical line | at the left edge of the document window is called the **insertion point.** It indicates where text will appear when you begin typing. When you start Word, you can enter text and create a new document right away.

5. Move the mouse pointer around in the Word program window
The mouse pointer changes shape depending on where it is in the Word program window. When the mouse pointer is in the document window in Normal view, the pointer changes to an **I-beam** I. Table A-1 describes other Word mouse pointers.

Trouble?
If the Office Assistant does not appear, continue with Step 8.

6. If the Office Assistant appears in your program window, move the pointer over the Office Assistant, then click the **right mouse button**
Right-clicking displays a pop-up menu of commands related to the item you click. You can choose to hide the Office Assistant until you want to get help with Word.

7. Click **Hide** on the pop-up menu
The Office Assistant disappears from the window.

Trouble?
See your instructor or technical support person for assistance.

8. Click **Tools** on the menu bar, click **Customize**, click the **Options tab** in the Customize dialog box, click **Reset my usage data** to restore the default settings, click **Yes** in the alert box, then click **Close**
You'll learn about restoring default settings for toolbars and menus in the next lesson.

FIGURE A-2: Starting Word from the desktop

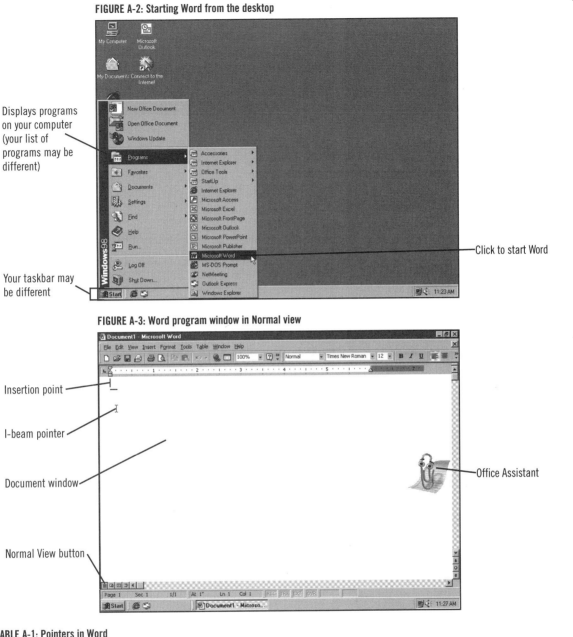

Displays programs on your computer (your list of programs may be different)

Click to start Word

Your taskbar may be different

FIGURE A-3: Word program window in Normal view

Insertion point

I-beam pointer

Document window

Office Assistant

Normal View button

TABLE A-1: Pointers in Word

pointer	description
I	Appears in the document window when working in Normal, Web Layout, and Outline views; use to move the insertion point in the document, or to select text to edit
I≡	Appears in the document window when working in Print Layout view; use to move the insertion point in the document or to select text to edit
↖	Appears when you point to a menu, toolbar, ruler, status bar, or other areas that are not part of the document window; use to click a button, menu command, or other element of the Word program window
↗	Appears when you point to the left edge of a line of text; use to select a line or lines of text
↖?	Appears when you click the What's This command on the Help menu; click this pointer over text to view the format settings applied to the text, or click an element of the Word program window or a dialog box to view information about that tool, option, or feature

Viewing the Word Program Window

Word 2000

When you start Word, the Word program window opens with a new, blank document in the document window. Refer to your screen and Figure A-4 as you locate the elements of the Word program window described below.

Trouble?

If your Word program window does not fill your screen, click the Maximize button on the title bar.

 The **title bar** displays the name of the document and the name of the program. Until you save the document and give it a name, its temporary name is Document1.

The **menu bar** lists the names of the menus that contain Word commands. Clicking a menu name displays a list of commands from which you can choose. When you open a menu, you may at first see a short list of commonly used commands. After the menu remains open for a few seconds, additional commands appear on the menu. Menus stay open until you point to another menu, click outside the menu, or press [Esc].

The **toolbar** contains buttons for the most frequently used commands. Clicking buttons on a toolbar is often faster than using menu commands. By default, there are actually two toolbars in this row. The **Standard toolbar** (on the left) contains buttons for the most commonly used operational commands, such as opening, saving, and printing documents. The **Formatting toolbar** (on the right) contains buttons for the most frequently used formatting commands, such as changing font type and size, applying bold to text, or aligning text. Not all the buttons on the Standard and Formatting toolbars are visible on the screen. To view other buttons, click the **More Buttons button** at the right end of each toolbar. Throughout the lessons in this book, you will need to remember to click the More Buttons button if a button you are instructed to click is not visible on your screen. When you use a button from the More Buttons list, Word adds it to your visible toolbar. That's why each user's toolbars look unique. You can return your toolbars to their original state by resetting your usage data. Be sure to read the Clues to Use in this lesson to learn more about working with Word's toolbars. Word also includes toolbars related to other features, such as a toolbar that contains drawing tools.

 The **horizontal ruler** displays tab settings, left and right paragraph indents, and document margins.

 The **document window** is the area where you type text and format and organize the content of your documents. The blinking insertion point is the location where text appears when you type.

 The **vertical and horizontal scroll bars** display the relative position of the text displayed in the document window. You use the scroll bars and **scroll boxes** to view different parts of your document.

 The **view buttons**, which appear in the horizontal scroll bar, allow you to display the document in one of four views: Normal, Web Layout, Print Layout, and Outline. Each view offers features that are useful for working on different types of documents.

 The **status bar** displays the current page number, section number, total number of pages in the document, and the position of the insertion point (in inches, in lines, and in columns, from the upper-left corner of the document).

 ScreenTips appear when you place the pointer over a toolbar button or some other element of the Word program window. A ScreenTip is a label that identifies the name of the button or feature.

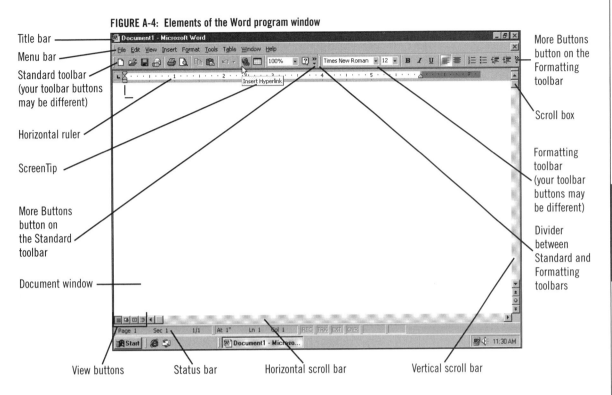

FIGURE A-4: Elements of the Word program window

Title bar

Menu bar

Standard toolbar (your toolbar buttons may be different)

Horizontal ruler

ScreenTip

More Buttons button on the Standard toolbar

Document window

More Buttons button on the Formatting toolbar

Scroll box

Formatting toolbar (your toolbar buttons may be different)

Divider between Standard and Formatting toolbars

View buttons

Status bar

Horizontal scroll bar

Vertical scroll bar

Personalized toolbars and menus in Word 2000

Word toolbars and menus modify themselves to your working style. The Standard and Formatting toolbars you see when you first start Word include the most frequently used buttons. To locate a button not visible on a toolbar, click the More Buttons button ⟩⟩ on the Standard or Formatting toolbar to see the list of additional toolbar buttons. As you work, Word adds the buttons you use to the visible toolbars, and moves the buttons you haven't used in a while to the More Buttons list. Similarly, Word menus adjust to your work habits, so that the commands you use most often automatically appear on shortened menus. Click the double arrow at the bottom of a menu to view additional menu commands. You can return toolbars and menus to their default settings by clicking Tools on the menu bar, then clicking Customize. On the Options tab in the Customize dialog box, click Reset my usage data. An alert box or the Office Assistant appears asking if you are sure you want to do this. Click Yes, then click Close in the Customize dialog box. Resetting your usage data erases changes made automatically to your menus and toolbars. It does not affect the options you set yourself. The lessons in this book assume you are using personalized menus and toolbars, but you can also turn off this feature if you'd like, so that your Standard and Formatting toolbars appear on separate rows, and your menus display the full list of commands. To turn off these features, remove the checks from the Standard and Formatting toolbars share one row and the Menus show recently used commands first checkboxes in the Customize dialog box, then click Close.

Word 2000

Creating a Document

You can begin a new document by simply typing text in the document window. Entering text with a word processor is different from typing with a typewriter. When you reach the end of a line as you type with Word, the insertion point moves to the next line. This feature is called **wordwrap**. You need to press [Enter] only when you want to insert a new line or start a new paragraph. After typing text, you can edit it by inserting new text or by deleting text you want to remove. When you insert or delete text, Word adjusts the spacing of the existing text. Scenario ▶ Karen uses Word to type a letter offering an internship to Alice Anderson. She begins her letter with the date, then types the inside address, salutation, body, and closing.

Trouble?

If you type the wrong letter, press [Backspace] to erase the incorrect letter, then type again.

▶ **1.** Type **today's date**, starting with the month (for example, January 21, 2000)

As you type the space after the name of the month, notice that Word's AutoComplete feature displays today's date. You can ignore AutoComplete for now and continue typing the date.

2. Press **[Enter]** four times

The first time you press [Enter], the insertion point moves to the start of the next line. Each time you press [Enter] again, you create blank lines.

3. Type the following text, pressing **[Enter]** after each line as indicated:

Ms. Alice Anderson [Enter]
456 Goodview Lane [Enter]
Palo Alto, CA 90272 [Enter] [Enter]
Dear Alice: [Enter] [Enter]

If you see the Office Assistant, click Cancel in the Office Assistant dialog balloon. If you see a wavy, red line under words it means that these words are not in Word's dictionary and might be misspelled. You can ignore the wavy lines for now. Don't worry if you make typing errors. You can fix them after you finish typing the letter.

QuickTip

Word processing programs have made it unnecessary to type two spaces after a period. Typing one space provides enough space after a period to separate sentences because the space is automatically adjusted by the word processing software.

▶ **4.** Type the following, pressing **[Enter]** twice at the end of the paragraph as indicated:

We are pleased to offer you an internship at MediaLoft. Your experience with Microsoft Office was a major factor in deciding to hire you. Please call my office at (415) 555-2221 to discuss the details. We look forward to working with you this year. [Enter] [Enter]

5. Type **Sincerely**, press **[Enter]** four times, then type your name

Your letter should resemble Figure A-5. Don't be concerned if your text wraps differently than the text shown in the figure. Text wrapping can depend on your monitor or printer. Now that you have finished typing the letter, you can edit it by inserting and deleting text as necessary.

6. Position the pointer I after the word **an** (but before the space) in the first sentence, then click to place the insertion point

The insertion point is now located between the words "an" and "internship" in the first sentence. Anything you type will be added to the document here.

QuickTip

If your typing overwrites existing text, double-click OVR in the status bar to switch back to Insert mode. See your instructor or technical support person for assistance.

▶ **7.** Press **[Backspace]**, press **[Spacebar]**, then type **professional**

Pressing [Backspace] removes the character before the insertion point.

8. Place the insertion point between **2** and **1** in the third sentence, press **[Delete]** to remove the character **1**, then type **6**

Pressing [Delete] removes the character after the insertion point. Fix your other typing mistakes using [Backspace] or [Delete], then compare your document to Figure A-6. You'll learn how to save your new document in the next lesson.

FIGURE A-5: Text in a Word document

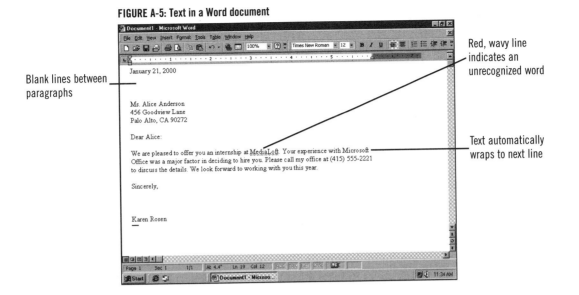

Blank lines between paragraphs

Red, wavy line indicates an unrecognized word

Text automatically wraps to next line

FIGURE A-6: Edited document

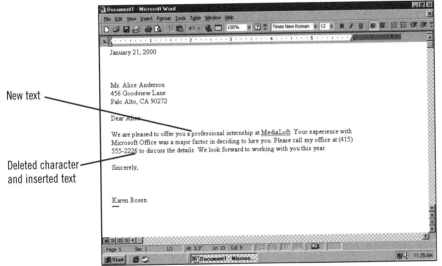

New text

Deleted character and inserted text

CLUES TO USE

Working with AutoCorrect

Certain kinds of spelling or typographical errors are automatically corrected as you type. This feature is called **AutoCorrect**. For example, Word corrects some common spelling mistakes (such as typing "adn" instead of "and") as soon as you type the first space or punctuation mark after the word. Similarly, if you type two uppercase letters in a row, the second character is automatically changed to lowercase as you continue typing (except in a state's abbreviation, such as "WA"). If Word makes a correction that you do not want to use, click the Undo button on the Standard toolbar. If you type a word that is not in Word's dictionary, the word is underlined with a red, wavy line to indicate it may be misspelled. If you make a possible grammatical error, the error is underlined with a green, wavy line. Right-click red- or green-underlined text to display a pop-up menu of correction options, then click a correction to accept it and remove the underlining.

Word 2000

Saving a Document

When you create a document, the text you enter and the changes you make are only temporarily stored in your computer. To store a document permanently so that you can retrieve and edit it in the future, you must **save** your document to your computer's internal hard disk or to a floppy disk. Documents are saved as **files** on your computer. When you save a document you give it a name, called a **filename**. It's helpful to give your documents brief filenames that describe the contents of the document. It's also a good idea to save your work soon after starting. After saving a document for the first time, save it again every 10 or 15 minutes and always save before printing. When you save after making changes, the document file is updated to reflect your latest revisions. You can save a document using the Save button on the Standard toolbar or the Save command on the File menu. **Scenario** Karen saves her letter to Alice Anderson with the filename Intern Offer Letter.

Steps

1. Insert your Project Disk in the appropriate drive, then click the **Save button** 📖 on the Standard toolbar

    The first time you save a document the Save As dialog box opens, as shown in Figure A-7. In this dialog box, you assign a name to the document (replacing the default filename) and indicate the location where you want the file to be stored. The default filename is based on the first few words of the document, in this case today's date.

2. Type **Intern Offer Letter** in the File name text box

    The name of the current drive or folder appears in the Save in list box. You want to save the file to your Project Disk.

QuickTip

This book assumes your Project Disk is in drive A. Substitute the correct drive if this is not the case. See your instructor or technical support person for assistance.

3. Click the **Save in list arrow**, then click the drive that contains your Project Disk

    Your Save As dialog box should resemble Figure A-8.

4. Click **Save**

    The document is saved with the name "Intern Offer Letter" on your Project Disk. Notice that the new name of the document appears in the title bar. Depending on your computer's settings in Windows Explorer, the filename in your title bar may include the DOC extension after the period. All Word documents automatically include this extension to help you distinguish Word documents from other files on your disks. Once you save a document as a file, you can continue to work on it in Word, or you can close it. If you continue to work on a file, you should save it again every 10 or 15 minutes and before you close it.

Using the AutoRecover feature

The AutoRecover feature in Word automatically saves your document every few minutes in a temporary file, so that all your work is not lost in case of an interruption to power or some other problem that abruptly stops Word. If Word shuts down unexpectedly, a temporary version of the document you were working on opens automatically the next time you start Word. You can then save the temporary document with a filename and continue to work on it. AutoRecover is not a substitute for using the Save command frequently, so be sure to save a new document right away and to save often. To change how often AutoRecover saves a document, click Tools on the menu bar, click Options, change the number of minutes on the Save tab, then click OK.

FIGURE A-7: Save As dialog box

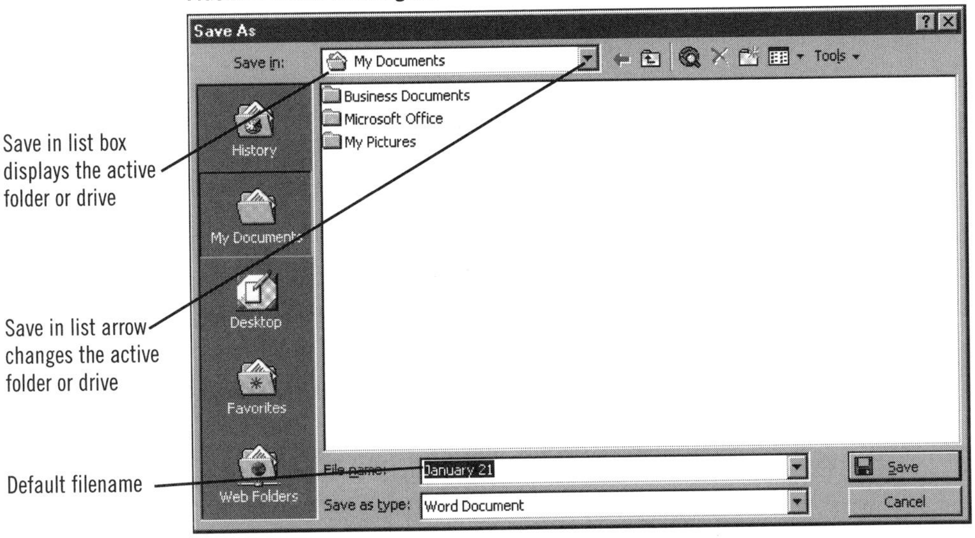

Save As
Save in:
My Documents
Tools
Business Documents
Microsoft Office
My Pictures
History
My Documents
Desktop
Favorites
Web Folders
File name:
January 21
Save as type:
Word Document
Save
Cancel
Save in list box displays the active folder or drive
Save in list arrow changes the active folder or drive
Default filename

FIGURE A-8: File to be saved to the A drive

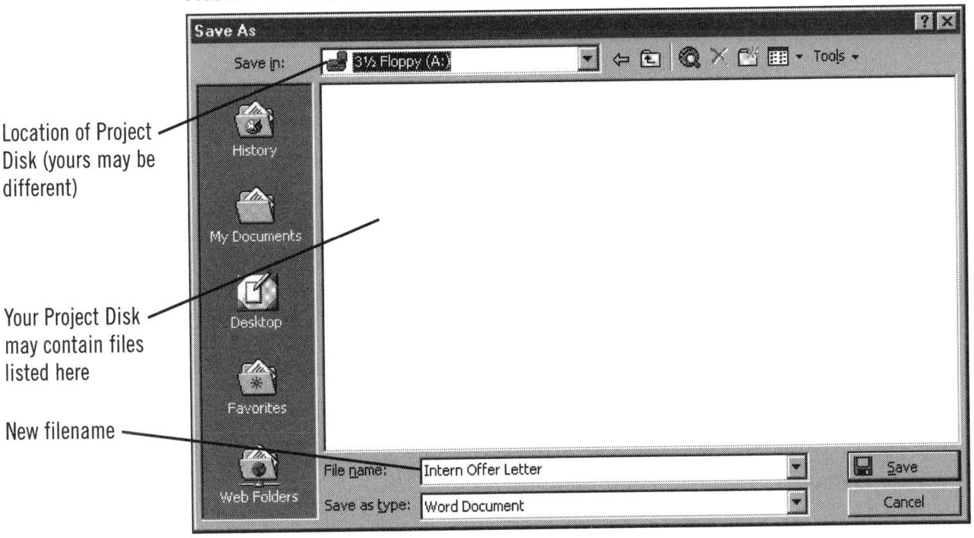

Save As
Save in:
3½ Floppy (A:)
Tools
History
My Documents
Desktop
Favorites
Web Folders
File name:
Intern Offer Letter
Save as type:
Word Document
Save
Cancel
Location of Project Disk (yours may be different)
Your Project Disk may contain files listed here
New filename

Previewing and Printing a Document

After saving your document, you can quickly print it by clicking the Print button on the Standard toolbar. When you use the Print button, you print the document using the default print settings. To print a specific page of a document or to choose other printing options, use the Print command on the File menu. Before printing, however, it is good practice to preview the document to see exactly what it will look like when it is printed. When you preview a document you can magnify the page to make it easier to read the text. **Scenario** Karen previews, then prints her letter.

Steps

Trouble?

If 🔍 does not appear on your Standard toolbar, click the More Buttons button ⏩ to view additional toolbar buttons.

1. Click the **Print Preview button** 🔍 on the Standard toolbar

The document appears in the Print Preview window as it will look when it is printed, as shown in Figure A-9.

2. Move the pointer over the page until it changes to 🔍, then click the letter

Clicking with 🔍 magnifies the document in the Print Preview window, allowing you to read the text. When the document is magnified the pointer changes to 🔍. Clicking with 🔍 reduces the size of the document in the Print Preview window.

QuickTip

Click the Print button 🖨 on the Print Preview toolbar to print the document directly from Print Preview.

3. Examine your letter for mistakes, then click the **Close Preview button** Close on the Print Preview toolbar

Print Preview closes and the letter appears in the document window. After fixing any mistakes you noticed in Print Preview, you are ready to print your document. You should always save a document right before printing it.

4. Click **File** on the menu bar, then click **Save**

Any changes you made to the document since the last time you saved it are saved. You can also click the Save button 🖫 on the Standard toolbar or press [Ctrl][S] to save changes.

Trouble?

If you are not connected to a printer, ask your instructor or technical support person for assistance.

5. Click **File** on the menu bar, then click **Print**

The Print dialog box opens, as shown in Figure A-10. The settings in your Print dialog box might be different, depending on your printer. Table A-2 describes some of the options in the Print dialog box.

6. Click **OK**

Clicking OK closes the Print dialog box and prints your document. You can also use the Print button 🖨 on the Standard toolbar to print the document using the default settings.

TABLE A-2: Options in the Print dialog box

print option	use to
Printer Name	Change the current printer
Properties	Display the printer's Properties dialog box; use it to change settings for the size or type of paper in your printer, the orientation of the paper, the resolution you want your printer to use, and other printer properties
Page range	Indicate what pages of a document to print
Copies	Specify the number of copies to print, and whether or not you want the copies to be collated
Zoom	Specify the number of pages you want to print on each sheet of paper
Print what	Select which aspect of a document to print, such as the document itself (the default) or other associated text
Print	Specify the portion of the document you want to print

FIGURE A-9: Print Preview window

Magnifier button

Zoom list arrow changes the size of the document in the window

Close Preview button

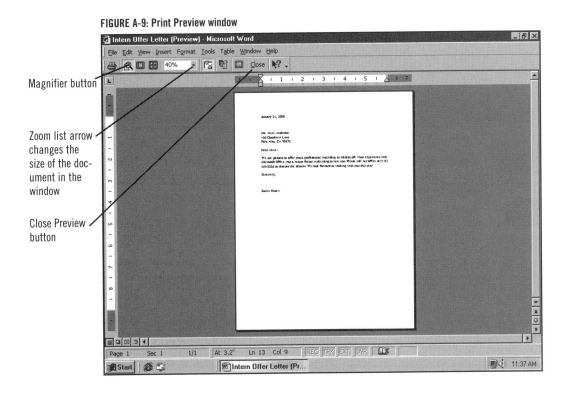

FIGURE A-10: Print dialog box

Opens the Properties dialog box for the printer

Default printer (your printer may be different)

Select the range of pages to print here

Changes the number of copies to print

Prints the document

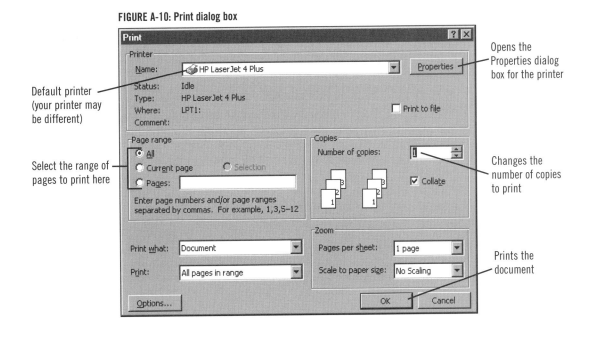

Word 2000

Getting Help

Word includes an extensive Help system that provides information and instructions about Word features and commands. You can use Help to get as little or as much information as you need, from quick definitions of unfamiliar terms to detailed steps for completing a procedure. The **Office Assistant**, an animated character that provides tips while you are working in Word, is one way to get help. You can also use the Office Assistant to display Help information and discover new features. You can also use the commands on the Help menu, described in Table A-3. Scenario ► Karen uses Help to learn about previewing a document.

Trouble?

If the Help window opens instead of the Office Assistant, someone turned the Office Assistant off on your computer. Click the Close button in the Help window, click Help on the menu bar, click Show the Office Assistant, then repeat Step 1.

1. Click the **Microsoft Word Help button** 🔲 on the Standard toolbar
   The Office Assistant appears, as shown in Figure A-11. Your assistant may look different. In the Office Assistant dialog ballon, you can enter key words or whole questions for which you would like more information.

2. Type **preview documents**, then click **Search**
   The Office Assistant displays topics related to previewing documents.

3. Click **Preview a document before printing**
   The Microsoft Word Help window opens, as shown in Figure A-12. Read the information on previewing a document before you continue. The underlined text in the Help window indicates a link to a related topic.

4. Place the pointer over the underlined topic **edit text in print preview** until the pointer changes to 🖑, then click
   A new Help window opens displaying the steps for editing text in print preview.

5. Click the **Magnifier button** 🔍 in the Help window
   A pop-up description of this button opens. Read the description before you continue.

6. Click the description to close it, then click the **Show button** 🔲 on the Help window toolbar
   The Help window expands and displays the Contents, Answer Wizard, and Index tabs. These tabs offer additional methods for searching and accessing Help topics.

7. Click the **Close button** in the Help window to return to Word

8. Click **Help** on the menu bar, then click **Hide the Office Assistant**
   Selecting Hide the Office Assistant hides it temporarily; it will reappear later to give you tips. To turn off the Office Assistant completely, right-click the Assistant, click Options, and deselect the Use the Office Assistant checkbox.

Using the Contents, Index, and Answer Wizard tabs to get Help

The Contents, Index, and Answer Wizard tabs offer different methods for searching Word's Help system. Use the Contents tab as you would use a table of contents in a book. Scroll through the list of general topics to find the topic that best relates to the topic that interests you, then click the plus sign next to each closed book icon to display a list of subtopics in that topic. Click a subtopic to display information about it in the Help window. The Answer Wizard tab works like the Office Assistant: type a question (or even just the name of the feature you want to learn about), then click Search to display information about your question in the Help window. Use the Index tab to search for topics that relate to a keyword. Type your keyword in the first box, click Search, then double-click the keyword in the second box that best describes your topic. In the third box, click the topic you want to view in the Help window.

FIGURE A-11: Word's Office Assistant

Microsoft Word Help button

Help topics (your list of topics may be different)

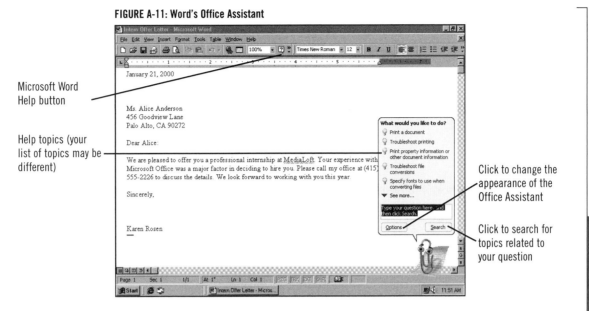

Click to change the appearance of the Office Assistant

Click to search for topics related to your question

FIGURE A-12: Microsoft Word Help window

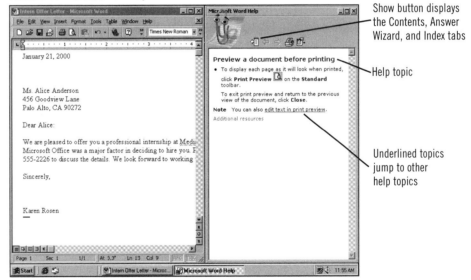

Show button displays the Contents, Answer Wizard, and Index tabs

Help topic

Underlined topics jump to other help topics

TABLE A-3: Help menu options

help menu option	function
Microsoft Word Help	Opens the Office Assistant if the Office Assistant is turned on; opens the Microsoft Word Help window if the Office Assistant is turned off
Show/Hide the Office Assistant	Opens/closes the Office Assistant
What's This?	Changes the mouse pointer to ; click a button or menu option to view a brief explanation
Office on the Web	Connects to Microsoft's Web site, where you can find additional information and articles; you must be connected to the Internet to use this option
About Microsoft Word	Provides the version and Product ID of Word

Word 2000

Word 2000

Closing a Document and Exiting Word

After you save your work on a document, you can close the document. Closing a document removes the document window from the Word program window, but it does not close Word. You should save and close all open documents before exiting Word. Exiting Word closes all open files and the Word program window. You can use the Close and Exit commands on the File menu to close a document and exit Word, or you can use the Close buttons on the menu bar and title bar, as shown in Figure A-13. Table A-4 describes the Close and Exit commands. Scenario▶ Karen closes her letter and then exits Word.

Steps

QuickTip

You can also close a document by clicking the Close Window button on the menu bar.

▶ **1.** Click **File** on the menu bar, then click **Close**

If you saved your document before closing it, the document window closes immediately. If you did not save your changes before closing it, an alert box or the Office Assistant opens, asking if you want to save your changes.

2. Click **Yes**, if necessary

The Word program window remains open, as shown in Figure A-14. After you close a document you can use the menus and toolbars to create a new document or to open an existing Word document, or you can exit Word.

QuickTip

You can also exit Word by clicking the Close button on the title bar.

▶ **3.** Click **File** on the menu bar, then click **Exit**

The Word program window closes.

TABLE A-4: The Close and Exit commands

command	function
Close	Closes the current document; leaves Word open so that you can open another document or use Help
Exit	Closes all open Word files; closes the Word program window and returns you to the Windows desktop

FIGURE A-13: Closing the document and program windows

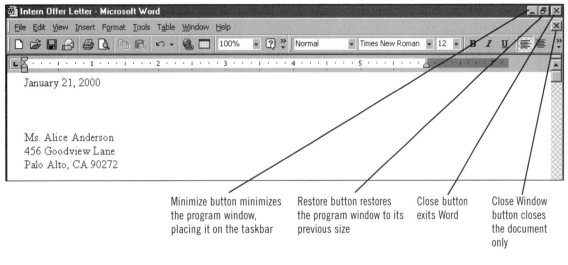

Minimize button minimizes the program window, placing it on the taskbar

Restore button restores the program window to its previous size

Close button exits Word

Close Window button closes the document only

FIGURE A-14: Word program window with no documents open

Practice

▶ Concepts Review

Label each element of the Word program window shown in Figure A-15.

FIGURE A-15

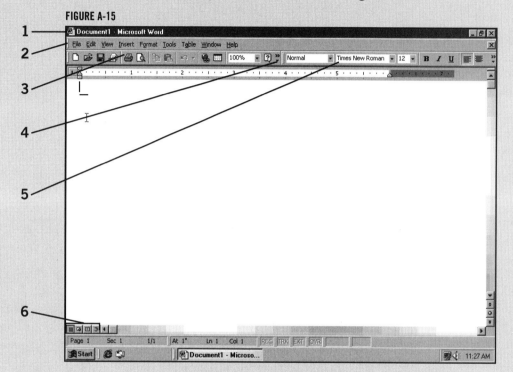

Match each term with the statement that describes it.

7. **Standard toolbar**
8. **Formatting toolbar**
9. **Document window**
10. **Ruler**
11. **Status bar**
12. **AutoCorrect**
13. **More Buttons button**
14. **Office Assistant**

a. Changes the spelling of misspelled words as you type
b. Identifies the location of the insertion point
c. Contains buttons for commands such as Save and Print
d. The part of the Word program window in which you enter text
e. Displays tab settings and paragraph and document margins
f. Provides tips and information about using Word
g. Contains buttons for commands that change the appearance of text
h. Displays buttons not currently visible on the toolbar

Select the best answer from the list of choices.

15. How is word processing different from typing with a typewriter?
   a. Word processors automatically adjust the spacing between characters
   b. Word processors use word wrap
   c. Word processors allow you to enter new text in the middle of a sentence
   d. All of the above

16. To view a document as it will look when printed, you
   a. Click View on the menu bar, then click Document Map.
   b. Click the Normal View button on the horizontal scroll bar.
   c. Click the Print Preview button on the Standard toolbar.
   d. Click File on the menu bar, then click Print.

17. You can get Help in any of the following ways, except
   a. Clicking Help on the menu bar.
   b. Double-clicking anywhere in the document window.
   c. Clicking the Microsoft Word Help button on the Standard toolbar.
   d. Viewing topics on the Contents tab.

18. The Close command on the File menu
   a. Closes the document without saving changes.
   b. If you have made changes to the document, asks if you want to save them, then closes the document.
   c. Closes all open Word documents.
   d. Closes Word without saving any changes.

19. To close the Word program window, you must
   a. Click the Close Window button on the menu bar.
   b. Click the Exit button on the Standard toolbar.
   c. Click File on the menu bar, then click Exit.
   d. Click File on the menu bar, then click Close.

20. The Standard toolbar does not include
   a. The Print button.
   b. The More Buttons button.
   c. The Bold button.
   d. The Save button.

Word 2000

▶ Skills Review

1. Start Word 2000.
a. Click the Start button on the Windows taskbar.
b. Click Microsoft Word on the Programs menu.
c. Click the Normal View button if necessary.
d. Hide the Office Assistant if it appears.
e. Reset your usage data to return your toolbars and menus to the default settings. (*Hint*: Click Tools on the menu bar, click Customize, click the Options tab in the Customize dialog box, click Reset my usage data, click Yes, then click Close.

2. View the Word program window.
a. Identify as many elements of the Word program window as you can.
b. Click each menu and drag the pointer through all the commands on each menu.
c. Point to each button on the toolbars and read the ScreenTips.
d. Click the More Buttons buttons on the Standard and Formatting toolbars and read the ScreenTips for the buttons on the More Buttons lists.

3. Create a document.
a. Begin a short letter to your local newspaper. Type today's date.
b. In the inside address, type "Editor," the name of the paper, a street address, and the city, state, and ZIP code. Make up the information if you don't know it.
c. For a salutation, type "To Whom It May Concern:" (If the Office Assistant appears, click Cancel.)
d. In the body of the letter, state that you are interested in a career in journalism, and mention that you have strong Word 2000 skills. Request an informational interview with the editors to learn more about working for newpapers.
e. For a closing, type "Sincerly," press [Enter] four times, then type your name. (Notice that Word corrects your typing for you.)
f. Insert the sentence "I can be reached at 555-3030." after the last sentence in your letter.
g. Correct any spelling and grammatical mistakes you made as you typed the letter. (*Hint*: Use the [Backspace] or [Delete] key to correct your typing.)
h. Using the [Backspace] key, change the inside address to:
Ms. Alexandra Thomas
Hamilton Transcript
35 Conval Street
Hamilton, NH 02468
i. Using the [Delete] key, change the salutation to "Dear Ms. Thomas:"

4. Save a document.
a. Click File on the menu bar, then click Save.
b. Save the document on your Project Disk with the filename "Information Letter."
c. Change the date on the letter to tomorrow's date.
d. Save your changes to the letter.

5. **Preview and print a document.**
   a. Click the Print Preview button on the Standard toolbar.
   b. Click to zoom in on the document in Print Preview, then proofread the letter.
   c. Click to zoom out on the document and then close Print Preview.
   d. Print a copy of the letter using the default print settings. (*Hint:* Don't forget to save the document before you print it.)

6. **Get Help.**
   a. Click the Microsoft Word Help button on the Standard toolbar.
   b. Type "Print" in the Office Assistant dialog balloon, then click Search.
   c. Click Print a document, and read about printing more than one copy at a time. (*Hint:* Click "See More" in the dialog balloon if necessary.)
   d. Click the Show button, then type "How do I print a help topic?" on the Answer Wizard tab.
   e. Read about printing a help topic, then close the Help window.
   f. Hide the Office Assistant.

7. **Close a document and exit Word.**
   a. Close the Information Letter document, saving your changes if necessary.
   b. Exit Word.

▶ Visual Workshop

Using the skills you learned in this unit, create the document shown in Figure A-16. Save it on your Project Disk with the file name "Acceptance Letter," then print a copy of the letter.

FIGURE A-16

April 2, 2000

Mr. David Matthews
Management Systems Enterprises
Human Resources Department
128 Technology Drive
Needham, MA 02128

Dear Mr. Matthews:

Thank you for offering me the systems coordinator position in your department. I am writing to accept this position under the terms you described in your letter. I am eager to put my Microsoft Office experience to practical use at Management Systems Enterprises.

Again, thank you for your offer. I look forward to working with you and your team.

Sincerely,

Your Name

Editing
and Proofing Documents

Objectives

- ▶ Plan a document
- MOUS ▶ Open and save a new document
- MOUS ▶ Select and replace text
- MOUS ▶ Understand the Office Clipboard
- MOUS ▶ Move text
- MOUS ▶ Copy text
- MOUS ▶ Check spelling and grammar
- MOUS ▶ Create AutoCorrect entries
- MOUS ▶ Find and replace text

Word's editing and proofing tools make it easy to edit and fine-tune your documents. In this unit, you will learn a variety of techniques for copying and moving text and for replacing specific occurrences of text throughout a document. You will also use Word's proofing tools to find and correct misspelled words and grammatical errors. To begin, you'll create a new document by saving an existing document with a new name, leaving the original unchanged. Scenario▶ Karen Rosen wants to write a letter to the woman she just hired to be the new training manager at MediaLoft, confirming the terms of her employment. She bases this letter on a similar letter she wrote to another recently hired employee.

Planning a Document

It is important to plan a document before you create it. Planning a document involves determining the purpose of the document, identifying its audience, developing the content, organizing the content logically, and then deciding the tone the document should take to achieve its purpose. The **tone** of a document is the way it "sounds." It affects how someone feels while reading it. A document's tone should match its audience and purpose. For example, the tone of an invitation to a company picnic is different from the tone of a letter requesting payment for an overdue invoice. Planning a document also involves thinking about its visual appearance. You want the layout and design of a document to complement its purpose, audience, content, organization, and tone. For example, you would never design a business letter to look like a newspaper article. Scenario Karen plans her letter to MediaLoft's new training manager. She jots down her ideas as shown in Figure B-1.

Details

In planning her letter Karen is careful to:

Identify the audience and purpose of the document
The audience for this letter is the new training manager. Its purpose is to welcome her to MediaLoft and to confirm the terms of her employment.

Choose the information and important points to cover in the document
If you later want to add or remove information from a document, you can easily insert and delete text. Karen wants to confirm the new training manager's title, responsibilities, and salary in the letter. She also wants to mention why MediaLoft decided to offer her the position, and to include several enclosures.

Decide how the information will be organized
If you decide to rearrange the structure of your document later, you can use Word's editing features to move, copy, and cut text. Because the information about the position is most important, Karen decides to present it first, followed by a list of enclosures.

Choose the tone of the document
You can edit your documents until you achieve exactly the tone you want. The document is being sent to a new employee, so Karen plans to use a businesslike tone that is welcoming and enthusiastic. She wants the new training manager to be excited about her new job and to feel comfortable with her decision to work at MediaLoft.

Plan the layout and design of the document
Planning the layout of a document involves thinking about its overall appearance: selecting the fonts to use, organizing text under headings, sketching ideas for tables and lists, and planning to include lines and shading to highlight important points and help to organize content, among many other formatting options. If you change your mind about the format of a document, you can make adjustments later. Karen wants to use a simple business letter format for her document.

FIGURE B-1: Document plan

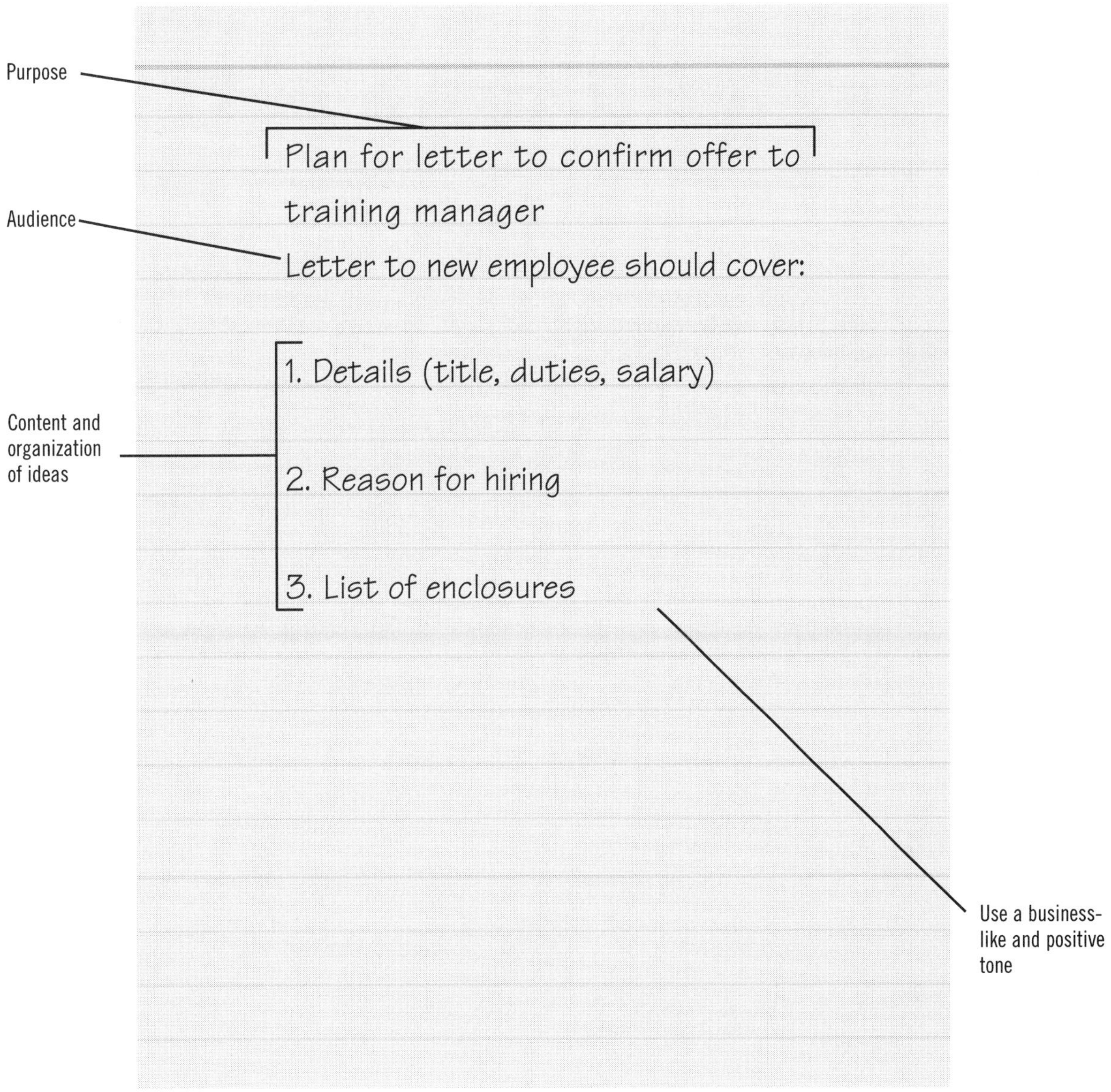

Purpose
Plan for letter to confirm offer to training manager
Audience
Letter to new employee should cover:
1. Details (title, duties, salary)
Content and organization of ideas
2. Reason for hiring
3. List of enclosures
Use a business-like and positive tone

Word 2000

CLUES TO USE

Creating new documents using wizards and templates

Word includes wizards and templates that help you create a variety of professionally designed documents, including resumes, memos, faxes, letters, and other publications. **Document wizards** are interactive coaches that guide you through the process of creating a document, prompting you to enter information and to choose the design and appearance of a document. **Templates** are pre-formatted documents that contain placeholder text that you replace with your own words. Either method gives you a great head start in developing attractive and effective documents, because wizards and templates offer formatting options that fit many common purposes and tones, such as a professional memo. All you do is provide the text. To create such a document, click File on the menu bar, then click New. In the New dialog box, click the tab containing the type of document you want to create, then double-click the icon for the wizard or template you want to use.

Opening and Saving a New Document

Word 2000

To save time and effort, you can use text from an existing document as the basis for another similar document. When you want to work in an existing document, you must first **open** it, that is, display it in the document window. Using the Save As command, you can save the open document with a different name to create a new document that is a copy. You can then edit the new document without changing the original. **Scenario** Karen wants to use a letter she wrote to a new intern at MediaLoft as the basis for her letter to the new training manager. To preserve the contents of the original document, she creates a new document by saving it with a new name.

Steps

1. Start **Word**, click **Tools** on the menu bar, click **Customize**, click the **Options tab** in the Customize dialog box, click **Reset my usage data** to restore the default settings, click **Yes** in the alert box, then click **Close**

QuickTip

You can also click File on the menu bar, then click Open, or press [Ctrl][O] to display the Open dialog box.

2. Insert your Project Disk in the appropriate drive, then click the **Open button** 📂 on the Standard toolbar
The Open dialog box opens, as shown in Figure B-2. You use this dialog box to navigate the drives and folders on your computer to locate the file you want to open. The Look in list box displays the current drive or folder. You can click the Look in list arrow to display a list of other drives and folders on your computer, or use the buttons in the dialog box to navigate to a different location or to change the way files and folders are displayed in the Open dialog box. Table B-1 describes the function of the buttons in this dialog box.

3. Click the **Up One Level button** 🗁 until you see the drive containing your Project Disk listed in the center of the dialog box

QuickTip

A fast way to open a document is to double-click a filename in the Open dialog box.

4. Double-click the drive containing your Project Disk to display its contents
The files on your Project Disk appear in the Open dialog box, as shown in Figure B-3.

5. Click the filename **WD B-1** in the Open dialog box, then click **Open**
The file opens in the document window. The filename WD B-1 appears in the title bar.

QuickTip

To create a new folder within the current folder, click the Create New Folder button 📁, type a name for the folder, then click OK.

6. Click **File** on the menu bar, then click **Save As**
The Save As dialog box opens. By saving the file with a new name, you create a new file that is identical to the original file. Changes you make to the new file will not affect the original file.

7. Navigate to the drive or folder where you store your project files (if necessary), type **Training Manager Letter** in the File name text box, then click **Save**
The original document closes and the Training Manager Letter file is displayed in the document window, ready for you to edit. Note the name of the new document appears in the title bar.

Save command vs. Save As command

The Save and the Save As commands are different in important ways. Use the Save command the first time you want to name a new document and store it permanently on a disk. When you save a document for the first time, the Save command displays the Save As dialog box, in which you name your document. Using the Save command after naming a file writes your latest changes to the document file on the disk. The Save As command has a different purpose. Use the Save As command to create a new document that is a copy of an existing document. Using Save As allows you to make changes in a copy of a document while leaving the original intact.

FIGURE B-2: Open dialog box

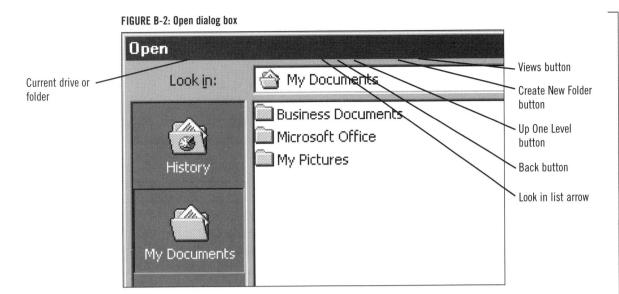

Current drive or folder

Look in: My Documents

Business Documents
Microsoft Office
My Pictures

History

My Documents

Views button
Create New Folder button
Up One Level button
Back button
Look in list arrow

FIGURE B-3: Document file to open

Open

Look in: 3½ Floppy (A:) — Tools ▾

WD B-1
WD B-2
WD B-3
WD B-4

History

My Documents

Desktop

Favorites

Web Folders

File name:

Files of type: All Word Documents

Open

Cancel

Document file to open (your list of files may differ)

Drive containing your Project Disk (yours may differ)

TABLE B-1: Open dialog box buttons

button	function
⇐ Back	Navigates to the previously active folder or drive; the ScreenTip for this button displays the name of the previously active folder or drive
⬆ Up One Level	Navigates to the next highest folder in the folder hierarchy (to the folder or drive that contains the current folder)
🔍 Search the Web	Connects to the World Wide Web to locate a file
✕ Delete	Deletes the currently selected file
📁 Create New Folder	Creates a new folder in the current drive or folder
▦ Views	Changes the way file information is displayed in the Open dialog box; click to scroll through each view—List, Details, Properties, and Preview—or click the list arrow to choose a view

Selecting and Replacing Text

Most Word operations require that you **select** text before editing or formatting it. You can select text by clicking before the text you want to select and dragging the mouse pointer across it, or you can use the selection bar to select lines of text. The **selection bar** is the blank area to the left of text. When you click in the selection bar you can select a line, several lines, a paragraph, or the entire document. Table B-2 describes different ways to select text. When you select text and start typing, the text you type replaces the text you selected. **Scenario** Karen revises her letter by selecting the text she wants to change and replacing it with new text.

Steps

QuickTip

You can click anywhere in the document window to deselect text.

1. Click at the start of the text **January 23, 2000** and drag the mouse pointer over the date to select it
   The date is selected, as shown in Figure B-4.

2. Type **today's date**
   The text you type replaces the selected text.

3. Click before **Alice** in the inside address, drag over **Anderson** to select the entire name, then type **Charlene Stephens**

4. Place the pointer in the **selection bar** to the left of the **second line** in the inside address, when the pointer changes to ⌐⧸ click to select the entire line of text, then type **321 Concordia Street**
   Clicking once in the selection bar selects a line of text.

5. Double-click **Alice** in the salutation, then type **Charlene**
   Double-clicking a word selects the word.

6. Select **a professional internship** in the first sentence, then type **the position of Human Resources Training Manager**

Trouble?

Click the down arrow at the bottom of the vertical scroll bar to display text that is not currently visible in the document window.

7. Select and replace text in the letter using the following table as a guide:

select:	type:
an intern	the training manager
assisting the training manager and myself on a variety of projects	developing and implementing a corporate-wide training program
9.25 per hour	47,500 per year

8. Click the **Save button** 🖫 on the Standard toolbar
   The changes you made to the letter are saved. Compare your document with Figure B-5.

CLUES TO USE

Reversing and repeating changes

Word keeps track of the operations you perform in a document so that you can reverse and repeat any action (with the exception of saving, opening, closing, and printing documents). You can repeat the last action by clicking Edit on the menu bar, and then clicking the Repeat command. The name of the Repeat command changes to reflect your most recent action. You can also press [F4] to repeat the last action. In addition, clicking the Undo button 🖙 reverses the most recent change you've made. To reverse a series of changes, click the Undo list arrow 🖙 ▾ and scroll through the list of actions to find the last action you want to undo. Click the action and Word reverses all the changes you've made to that point. If you decide to keep a change you just reversed, click the Redo button 🖰. To reverse a series of changes, click the Redo list arrow 🖰 ▾ and click the last change you want to reverse.

FIGURE B-4: Selected text

Selected text ——————

Selection bar ——————

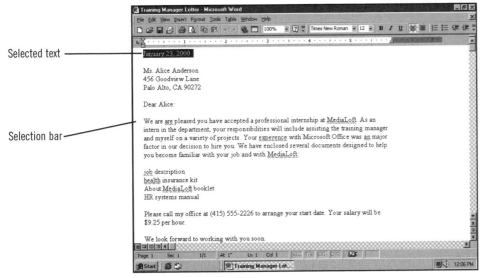

FIGURE B-5: Edited letter

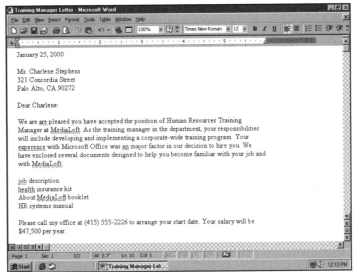

TABLE B-2: Mouse selection techniques

to select	do this
A word	Double-click the word
A sentence	Press and hold [Ctrl], then click the sentence
A paragraph	Triple-click the paragraph, or double-click the selection bar next to the paragraph
A line of text	Click the selection bar next to the line
An entire document	Press and hold [Ctrl], then click anywhere in the selection bar, or triple-click the selection bar
A vertical block of text	Press and hold [Alt], then drag through the text
A large amount of text	Place the insertion point at the beginning of the text, press and hold [Shift], then click the end of the text

Understanding the Office Clipboard

The **Clipboard** is a temporary area in the computer's memory for storing text and graphics that you want to reuse. When you use an Office program such as Word, you use the **Office Clipboard**, which can hold up to 12 items. You can place text or graphics on the Clipboard by selecting the text or graphic and using either the Copy or the Cut command on the Edit menu or the Copy or Cut button on the Standard toolbar. When you **cut** text, you remove it from the document and place it on the Clipboard. When you **copy** text, you place a copy of the text on the Clipboard without removing the original text from the document. After you place an item on the Clipboard it is available for you to **paste**, or insert, into a document using the Paste command. You can paste it into a new location in the same document, or into a different document. Table B-3 describes the commands on the Edit menu that work with the Clipboard. Figure B-6 illustrates how you can use the Office Clipboard to reuse text and graphics from one document in other documents.

It is important to understand the following about the Office Clipboard:

 Like a physical paper clipboard, the Office Clipboard allows you to place multiple items on it. In Word (and in other Office programs), you can place up to 12 items on the Clipboard.

 Each item you place on the Clipboard can be pasted into a document an unlimited number of times. When you paste an item from the Clipboard, the item remains on the Clipboard until you exceed 12 items and choose to replace it with another item.

 The Clipboard toolbar holds the items copied or cut to the Office Clipboard. You can view the Clipboard toolbar by clicking View on the menu bar, pointing to Toolbars, and then clicking Clipboard. It also appears automatically whenever you cut or copy multiple selections. The Clipboard toolbar is shown in Figure B-7.

 You can review the contents of each item on the Clipboard toolbar by pointing to the item. When you point to an item, a ScreenTip displays its contents.

 To paste an item from the Office Clipboard toolbar, you click the item on the Clipboard to paste it to the location of the insertion point in a document. You can also use the Paste command or the Paste button on the Standard toolbar to paste the most recent item you collected.

 The Office Clipboard is available in all Office applications, so you can use it to paste text and graphics that you have cut or copied from other Office programs into a Word document, and vice versa. For example, you can use the Office Clipboard to insert a spreadsheet or chart created in Excel or a graphic from a PowerPoint presentation into your Word documents.

 Items remain on the Office Clipboard until you close all open Office applications.

TABLE B-3: The Edit menu Clipboard commands

command	description
Cut	Removes the selected text or graphic from the document and places it on the Clipboard
Copy	Copies the selected text or graphic to the Clipboard; the selection remains in the document
Paste	Inserts the last item you cut or copied at the insertion point in the document
Paste Special	Inserts an item created in another Office program (such as a spreadsheet or a picture) in a document; you can create a link so that changes to the source file are reflected in the document or embed objects so that you can edit the object in its original program

FIGURE B-6: Using the Office Clipboard

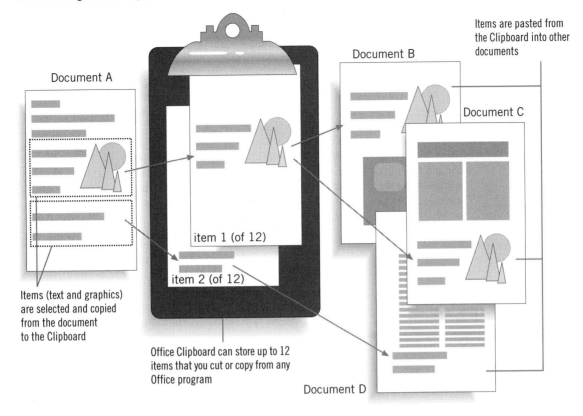

Document A

Document B

Items are pasted from the Clipboard into other documents

Document C

item 1 (of 12)

item 2 (of 12)

Items (text and graphics) are selected and copied from the document to the Clipboard

Office Clipboard can store up to 12 items that you cut or copy from any Office program

Document D

FIGURE B-7: Clipboard toolbar

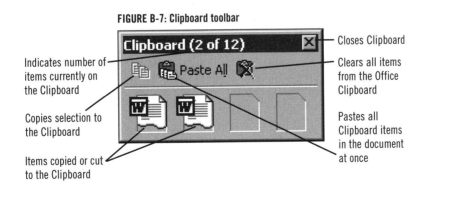

Indicates number of items currently on the Clipboard

Copies selection to the Clipboard

Items copied or cut to the Clipboard

Closes Clipboard

Clears all items from the Office Clipboard

Pastes all Clipboard items in the document at once

Moving Text

You can move text from its current location to a new location in the same document or to a different document. Before you move text, you must select it. To **move** text, use the Cut command or the Cut button to place the text on the Clipboard, then use the Paste command or the Paste button to insert the text from the Clipboard in a new location. You can also move text by selecting it and dragging it to a new location using the mouse. When you drag text, however, it is not placed on the Clipboard. Dragging is a great way to move text when both the text and its new location are visible in the document window at the same time. **Scenario** Karen reorganizes her letter by moving text using both the cut-and-paste and dragging methods. To begin, she displays the Clipboard toolbar.

1. Click **View** on the menu bar, point to **Toolbars**, then click **Clipboard**
   The Clipboard toolbar appears in the document window.

Trouble?

If the Clipboard toolbar is in your way, click the toolbar title bar, then drag it to a different location.

2. If the Clipboard toolbar contains items, click the **Clear Clipboard button** 🔳 to empty the Clipboard of previously collected items

3. Select the sentence that begins **Please call...**
   You may need to click the up or down arrows on the vertical scroll bar to display text that is not visible in the document window.

QuickTip

Click the More Buttons button 》 on the Standard toolbar to locate buttons that are not visible on your screen.

4. Click the **Cut button** ✂ on the Standard toolbar
   The sentence is removed from the document and placed on the Clipboard, as shown in Figure B-8. You can also click Edit on the menu bar, then click Cut, or press [Ctrl][X] to cut text.

5. Place the insertion point at the end of the third sentence in the first body paragraph (after the space between **you.** and **We**)

QuickTip

You can also click Edit on the menu bar, then click Paste, or press [Ctrl][V] to paste text.

6. Click the **Paste button** 📋 on the Standard toolbar
   The sentence is inserted in the first paragraph.

7. Select **Human Resources** in the first sentence, then press and hold the mouse button over the selected text until the pointer changes to ⬚ (do not release the mouse button)

Trouble?

If you make a mistake, click the Undo button 🔙 on the Standard toolbar, then repeat Steps 8 and 9.

8. Drag the pointer's vertical line in front of the word **department** in the next sentence, as shown in Figure B-9

9. Release the mouse button
   The text is moved from its original location in the first sentence to its new location in the second sentence.

10. Click anywhere in the document window to deselect the text, then click the **Save button** 💾 on the Standard toolbar
    Compare your letter to Figure B-10.

Working with multiple documents

If you want to copy or cut text from one document and paste it into another, it is easiest to work with both documents open in the program window at the same time. To open multiple documents, you can open one document and then open subsequent documents one by one, or you can open several documents at once by holding [Ctrl] as you click the filename of each document you want to open in the Open dialog box, and then clicking Open. To move between open documents in the document window, click Window on the menu bar, then click the filename of the document you want to display. You can also view multiple documents at once in the program window, by clicking Window on the menu bar, and then clicking Arrange All. All the open documents will appear on the screen, each in its own program window. To activate a document, click its program window. With multiple documents open, you can easily copy and move text between documents by selecting the text you want to copy or move in one document, and then pasting it in another document. To quickly save or close all open documents at the same time, press and hold [Shift] as you click File on the menu bar, then click Save All or Close All.

FIGURE B-8: Cut item on the Clipboard toolbar

Item cut from letter

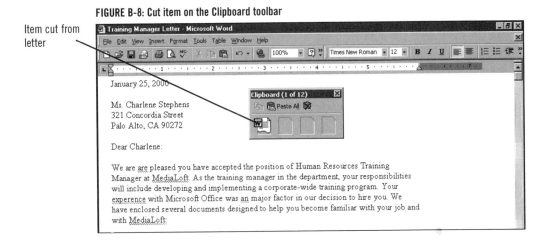

FIGURE B-9: Dragging to move text

New location for text

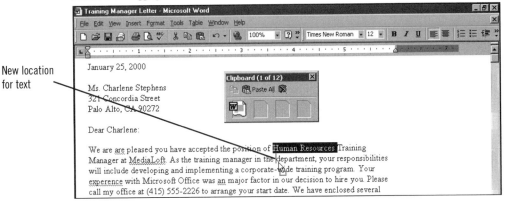

FIGURE B-10: Moved text in document

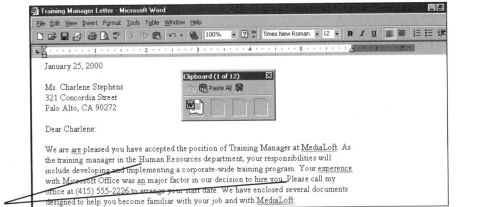

Moved text

Copying Text

Copying text is similar to moving text, except that when you copy text it remains in its original location. A copy of the text is placed on the Clipboard, available to be pasted in the same document or in another document. Before you copy text you must select it. To copy text to the Clipboard you can use the Copy command on the Edit menu or the Copy button on the Standard toolbar or the Clipboard toolbar. You can also copy text by selecting it and pressing [Ctrl] while you drag it to a new location. When you copy text by dragging it, the selection does not get copied to the Clipboard. **Scenario** Karen further edits her letter by copying text from one location in the document to another.

QuickTip

You can also click 🖺 on the Clipboard toolbar to copy text to the Clipboard.

▶ **1.** Select **Training Manager** in the first sentence, then click the **Copy button** 🖺 on the Standard toolbar
The selected text is copied to the Clipboard. You want to place a copy of this text in front of "job description" in the list.

2. Place the insertion point in front of **job description** in the list, then click the **Paste button** 🖺 on the Standard toolbar
"Training Manager" is inserted before "job description." Note that Word automatically inserts a space between "Manager" and "job." "Training Manager" also remains on the Clipboard.

3. Select **Human Resources department** in the second sentence, click **Edit** on the menu bar, then click **Copy**
The selected text is copied to the Clipboard, as shown in Figure B-11. You want to paste the text "Human Resources department" at the end of the last sentence in the first paragraph.

4. Place the insertion point after **MediaLoft** but before the **colon (:)** in the last sentence of the first paragraph, type **'s**, then press **[Spacebar]**

5. Move the pointer over the items on the Clipboard toolbar until you find **Human Resources department**, then click to paste it at the insertion point
The text is pasted at the end of the sentence.

6. Select **HR** in the list, then click **Human Resources department** on the Clipboard toolbar
The pasted text replaces the selected text in the document.

7. Select **MediaLoft** in the first sentence, press and hold **[Ctrl]**, then press and hold the mouse button over the selected text until the pointer changes to 🖺

QuickTip

Click the Undo button 🖺 on the Standard toolbar if you make a mistake, then try again.

▶ **8.** Drag the pointer in front of **health insurance kit** in the list to position the pointer's vertical line in front of **health**, release the mouse button, release **[Ctrl]**, then deselect the text
Pressing [Ctrl] while you drag selected text copies the text to a new location. Compare your document with Figure B-12.

9. Click the **Close button** on the Clipboard toolbar, then click the **Save button** 🖺 on the Standard toolbar

FIGURE B-11: Copying to and from the Clipboard toolbar

Text copied to the Clipboard

Item placed on Clipboard

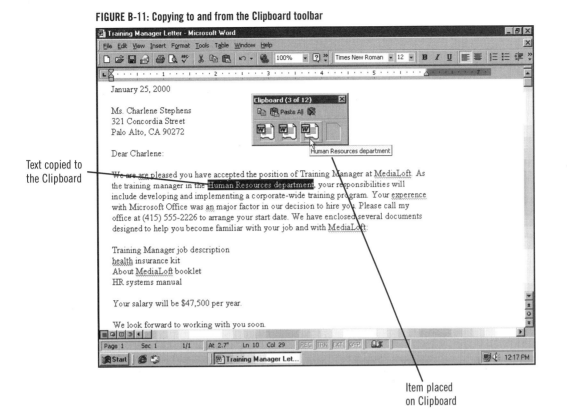

FIGURE B-12: Copied text

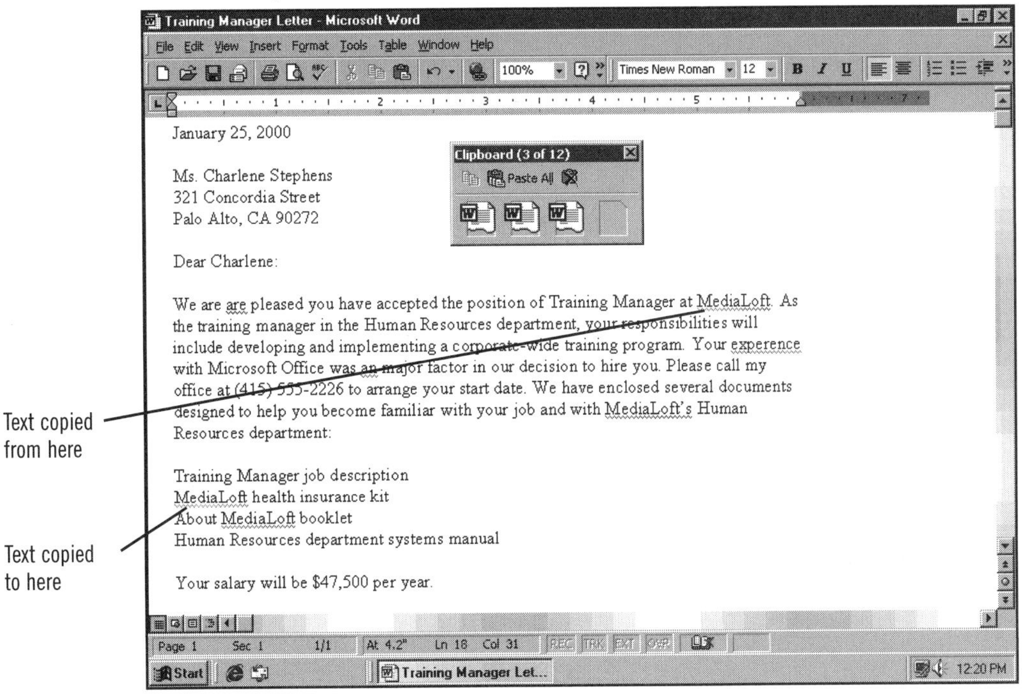

Text copied from here

Text copied to here

Checking Spelling and Grammar

You can use Word's Spelling, Grammar, and AutoCorrect features to help you identify and correct mistakes in your document. **AutoCorrect** automatically corrects commonly misspelled words as you type. Word also underlines possible spelling and grammatical errors as you type. Words that are not in Word's dictionary are underlined with a red, wavy line. Possible grammatical errors are underlined with a green, wavy line. When you finish creating a document, you can use Word's Spelling and Grammar command to review and correct misspelled words, as well as grammatical errors such as punctuation, sentence fragments, or subject-verb agreement. Although the Spelling and Grammar command catches most errors, there are certain errors it will not find, such as homonyms. For example, if you typed "here" and you meant to use "hear," Word will not identify this as an error. Ultimately, you are still responsible for proofreading your work. **Scenario** Karen uses the Spelling and Grammar command to search her document for errors. Before searching the document, she sets AutoCorrect to ignore the word "MediaLoft," which she knows is not in Word's dictionary because it is underlined in red in her document.

Steps

Trouble?

If "MediaLoft" is not under-lined, click Tools on the menu bar, click Options, click the Spelling & Grammar tab, click Recheck Document, click Yes, click OK, then continue with Step 1.

1. Right-click **MediaLoft** in the first sentence to open a pop-up menu
   This pop-up menu includes a suggestion for correcting the spelling ("Media Loft") as well as commands for ignoring Word's suggestion and for adding the word to Word's dictionary. Note that Word's suggested correction is wrong in this case.

2. Click **Ignore All** on the pop-up menu, right-click **MediaLoft's**, then click **Ignore All**
   Clicking Ignore All tells Word to ignore all instances of "MediaLoft" and "MediaLoft's" in the current document, and removes the red, wavy lines under these words.

Trouble?

If a word is identified as misspelled, click Ignore to ignore it, or click the correct spelling in the Suggestions list, then click Change.

3. Press **[Ctrl][Home]** to move the insertion point to the top of the document, then click the **Spelling and Grammar button** 📝 on the Standard toolbar
   The Spelling and Grammar dialog box opens. The dialog box indicates that the word "are" is repeated, as shown in Figure B-13. You want to delete the second occurrence of the word.

4. Click **Delete**
   The second "are" is deleted from the document. Next, "experence" is identified as misspelled. The correct spelling is selected in the Suggestions list.

Trouble?

Click the Office Assistant button ❓ in the Spelling and Grammar dialog box if the Office Assistant does not open.

5. Click **Change**
   The correctly spelled word replaces the misspelled word. Next, the Spelling and Grammar dialog box suggests using the word "a" in place of "an." The Office Assistant displays an explanation of the rule that applies to this error, as shown in Figure B-14.

6. Read the explanation, then click **Change**
   The word "a" is substituted for the incorrect word "an." If you made other errors in your document, you may need to correct them. When Spelling and Grammar check is complete, the dialog box closes.

7. When a message box opens saying the Spelling and Grammar check is complete, click **OK** to close it, then proofread the letter for other errors

8. Press **[Ctrl][Home]**, then click the **Save button** 💾 on the Standard toolbar

FIGURE B-13: Spelling and Grammar dialog box

Error in the document

Ignores this occurrence

Ignores all occurrences

Adds this word to the dictionary so that it is not identified as misspelled in the future

Repeated word

Deletes repeated word

Office Assistant button provides an explanation of grammar errors

Creates an AutoCorrect entry for this occurrence

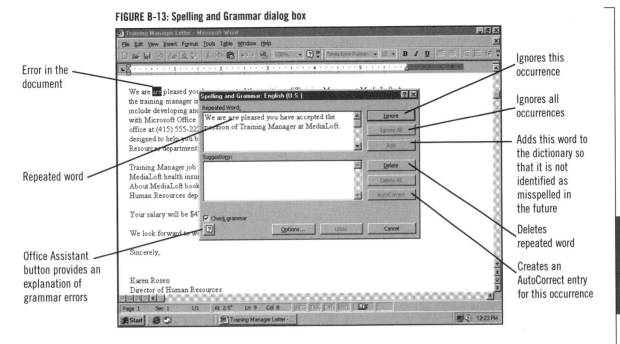

FIGURE B-14: Grammar explanation

Accepts this change

Office Assistant button

Read this explanation to understand the error

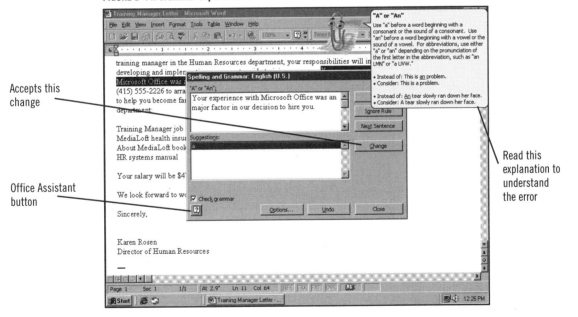

Using the Thesaurus

You can use Word's Thesaurus to look up synonyms for overused or awkward words in your document. For some words, you can also look up antonyms. To use the Thesaurus, select the word for which you want to find a synonym, click Tools on the menu bar, point to Language, then click Thesaurus. In the Thesaurus dialog box, select the synonym you want to use in your document, then click Replace.

Creating and Using AutoCorrect Entries

While AutoCorrect automatically corrects hundreds of commonly misspelled words, you can also create your own AutoCorrect entries to help you work more efficiently. You can create entries for text you use frequently, such as your name, title, or the name of your company, or you can create entries for words you often misspell that Word does not correct for you. For example, you could create an AutoCorrect entry for your initials, so that each time you typed your initials Word would automatically insert your name into your document. **Scenario** Karen types "MediaLoft" many times every day. To save time, she creates an AutoCorrect entry that inserts "MediaLoft" whenever she types the abbreviation "ml".

1. Click **Tools** on the menu bar, then click **AutoCorrect**

The AutoCorrect dialog box opens, as shown in Figure B-15. The AutoCorrect tab displays the list of existing AutoCorrect entries. Use the tab to enter new text you want to be automatically corrected (such as an abbreviation or a misspelled word) and the text you want to be automatically inserted in its place.

2. Type **ml** in the Replace text box

3. Press **[Tab]** to move the insertion point to the With text box, then type **MediaLoft**

4. Click **Add**, then click **OK**

Word adds the new AutoCorrect entry to the list of AutoCorrect entries. Every time you type "ml" in a document, Word will replace it with "MediaLoft."

5. Press **[Ctrl] [End]** to place the insertion point at the end of the document, then type **ml [Spacebar]**

"MediaLoft" is inserted after you press [Spacebar], as shown in Figure B-16.

6. Press **[Ctrl] [Home]**, then click the **Save button** 📁 on the Standard toolbar

Creating AutoCorrect exceptions

There are some situations when you do not want Word to automatically correct what it assumes to be a mistake. For example, AutoCorrect automatically capitalizes the first character you type after typing a period. However, when you type the abbreviation "Cal." (for California) in the middle of a sentence, you do not want AutoCorrect to capitalize the next character. To avoid this, you can create an AutoCorrect exception. Create an AutoCorrect exception by clicking Tools on the menu bar, clicking AutoCorrect, then clicking Exceptions. In the AutoCorrect Exceptions dialog box, click the tab that includes the type of AutoCorrect exception you want to create: First Letter, Initial Caps, or Other Corrections. Type the text you do not want automatically corrected in the text box on the tab, click Add, then click Close. You can later remove an exception by deleting it from the list of exceptions in the AutoCorrect dialog box.

FIGURE B-15: AutoCorrect dialog box

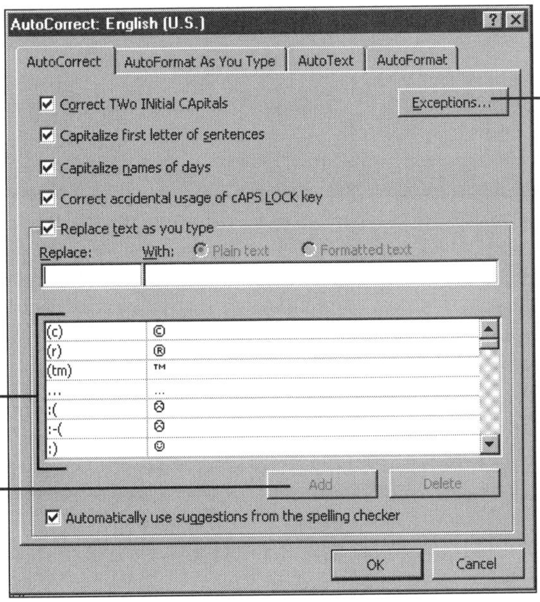

Use to create an AutoCorrect exception

List of existing AutoCorrect entries

This button changes to "Replace" if the AutoCorrect entry already exists

FIGURE B-16: Inserted AutoCorrect entry

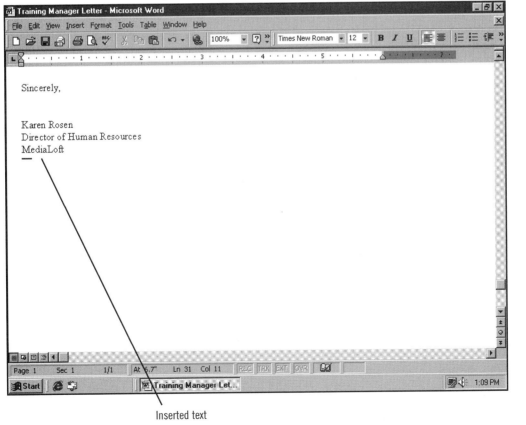

Inserted text

Unit B

Finding and Replacing Text

Sometimes you need to replace text throughout a document. In a long document, doing this manually would be time-consuming and prone to error. For example, suppose you just finished writing an announcement of a new beverage for the MediaLoft café, when the marketing department decides that the product name should change from "ChocoShakes" to "CocoShakes". Rather than having to find, select, and replace each instance of "ChocoShakes" in your document, it would be much easier to use the Replace command to search for and replace "ChocoShakes" throughout the document automatically. You have the option to review and replace each occurrence one at a time (so that you can decide in each case whether or not to make the substitution), or you can perform a global replace. A **global replace** changes all occurrences at once. You can also use Word's Find command to locate text in a document. ▶ Scenario Karen decides to use the term "position" instead of "job" in her letter. She uses the Replace command to change "job" to "position" throughout the document. When she is finished, she saves, prints, and closes the document.

Steps

1. Click Edit on the menu bar, click Replace, then click More in the Find and Replace dialog box if necessary

The Find and Replace dialog box opens, as shown in Figure B-17. Clicking More in the Find and Replace dialog box reveals additional options for narrowing a search and replace. Table B-4 describes the search options available in the Find and Replace dialog box.

2. Type job in the Find what text box

This text will be replaced.

3. Press [Tab] to move the insertion point to the Replace with text box, then type position

QuickTip

If you want to review each occurrence before replacing it, click Find Next.

4. Click Replace All

Clicking Replace All changes all occurrences of "job" to "position" in the document. A message box or balloon reports that two replacements were made.

5. Click OK to close the message box or click to close the message balloon, then click Close

The dialog box closes. Compare your document to Figure B-18.

6. Click Edit on the menu bar, click Find, type Karen Rosen in the Find what text box, click Find Next, then click Cancel

"Karen Rosen" is selected in the document.

7. Type your name, click the Save button 🖫 on the Standard toolbar, then click the Print button 🖨 on the Standard toolbar

A copy of the document prints.

8. Click File on the menu bar, click Close, click File on the menu bar, then click Exit

The documents and Word close.

CLUES TO USE

Replacing text in Overtype mode

Word's Overtype feature allows you to type over existing text without selecting it first. When you work in Overtype mode, Word replaces the existing text with any new text you type. You can turn on Overtype mode by double-clicking the OVR box on the status bar (it appears in light gray when Overtype is off, and in black when Overtype is on). On some keyboards you can also turn on Overtype by pressing [Insert]. To turn off Overtype mode, double-click the OVR box in the status bar again, or press [Insert].

FIGURE B-17: Find and Replace dialog box

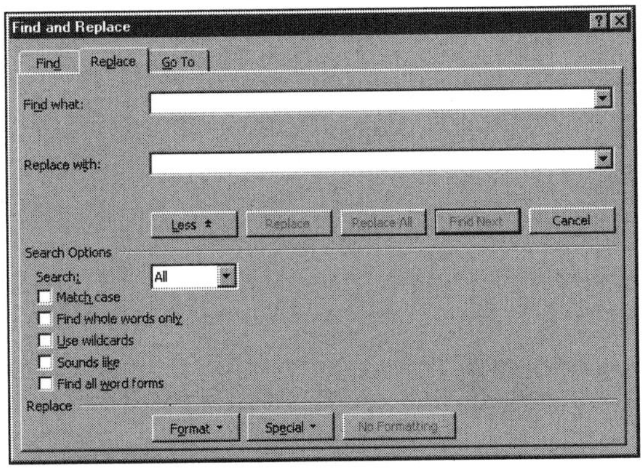

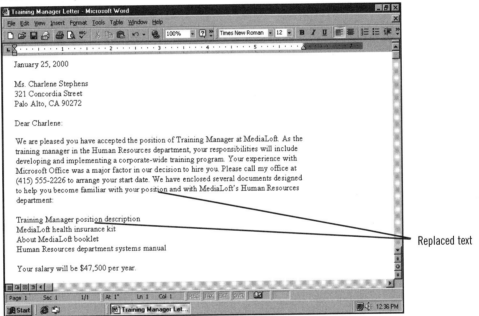

FIGURE B-18: Completed document

Replaced text

TABLE B-4: Search options in the Find and Replace dialog box

search option	use to
Search	Specify the direction of the search from the current location of the insertion point: Down, Up, or All
Match case	Locate only exact matches for the uppercase and lowercase letters entered in the Find what text box; select to find "President" but not "president"
Find whole words only	Locate only words that are complete and not part of a larger word; select to locate "Asia" but not "Asian"
Use wildcards	Search for a string of characters by using wildcards; select to enter "c*t" to find "cat" and "coat"
Sounds like	Locate words that sound like the text in the Find what text box, but have different spellings; select to find "their" and "there" and "they're"
Find all word forms	Find and replace all forms of a word; for example, specify "find" in the Find what text box to locate "find," "finds," "found," and "finding" and replace each with the comparable form of the replacement word

Practice

► Concepts Review

Label each element of the Open dialog box shown in Figure B-19.

FIGURE B-19

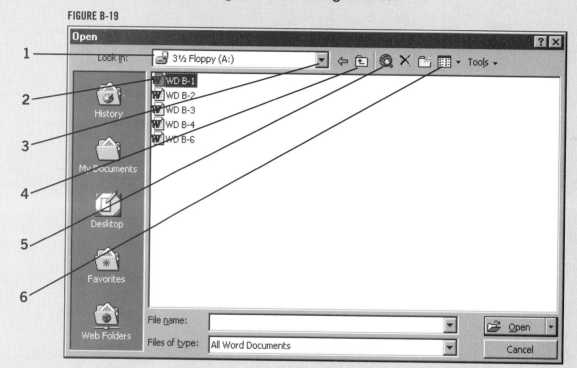

Match each command with the statement that describes it.

7. Copy   **a.** Removes text from a document and places it on the Clipboard

8. Paste   **b.** Reviews a document for spelling, punctuation, and usage errors

9. Spelling and Grammar   **c.** Suggests synonyms and antonyms

10. Thesaurus   **d.** Creates a new document while saving the original document

11. Cut   **e.** Places text on the Clipboard without removing it from the document

12. Replace   **f.** Embeds or links an item created in another Office program in a document

13. Save As   **g.** Locates and replaces occurrences of text in a document

14. Paste Special   **h.** Inserts text from the Clipboard in a document

Select the best answer from the list of choices.

15. To place text on the Clipboard, you must first
   - **a.** Select the text.
   - **b.** Click the Cut button.
   - **c.** Click the Paste button.
   - **d.** Click the Copy button.

16. **How many times can you paste an item from the Clipboard into a document?**
    a. An unlimited number of times
    b. Twice
    c. 12 times
    d. Once

17. **Which of the following statements best describes the selection bar?**
    a. The selection bar is the empty area to the right of text in the document window.
    b. To display the selection bar, you must click View on the menu bar, then click Selection Bar.
    c. The selection bar contains up to 12 items that you have copied or pasted to the Clipboard.
    d. The selection bar is the empty area to the left of text in the document window.

18. **Which option is NOT available in the Spelling and Grammar dialog box when a spelling error is identified?**
    a. Choose a suggested spelling
    b. Add an AutoCorrect entry
    c. Select a synonym for the word
    d. Add the word to the dictionary

19. **The Spelling and Grammar feature does not**
    a. Explain grammatical errors.
    b. Suggest revisions to make a sentence correct.
    c. Automatically correct all misspelled words.
    d. Check for words that are repeated.

20. **Which of the following is not true about the AutoCorrect feature?**
    a. AutoCorrect corrects commonly misspelled words as you type them.
    b. Words underlined with a wavy line indicate possible spelling or grammatical errors.
    c. You can create AutoCorrect entries.
    d. AutoCorrect corrects common grammatical errors as you type them.

21. **Using the Find and Replace commands, you can do all of the following *except***
    a. Locate all the different forms of a word in a document.
    b. Search the document for specified text in a certain direction only.
    c. Substitute all occurrences of a word with another word.
    d. Search for all uses of the passive voice in your document.

▶ Skills Review

1. **Open and save a new document.**
   a. Start Word.
   b. Open the file WD B-2 from your Project Disk and save it as "Road Map."

2. **Select and replace text.**
   a. Select the date and replace it with today's date.
   b. Select "Wing" in the inside address and replace it with "Carroll."
   c. Select "Wing" in the salutation, then use the Repeat Typing command to replace the name with "Carroll."
   d. Select the street address and replace it with "280 Technology Drive."
   e. Select the line after the street address and delete it.
   f. Undo the deletion, then select "8B" and replace it with "555."

3. **Move text.**
   a. Display the Clipboard toolbar.
   b. Use the cut-and-paste method to move the last two sentences of the first body paragraph to the end of the second body paragraph.
   c. Use the drag method to move the last sentence of the last body paragraph in front of the second sentence in the first body paragraph.

4. **Copy text.**
   a. Copy "Open Roads, Inc." from the first sentence to under "Your Name" in the signature block.
   b. Copy "Open Roads" in the first sentence to in front of "package" in the third sentence.
   c. Close the Clipboard toolbar.

5. **Check spelling and grammar.**

   a. Press [Ctrl][Home], then click the Spelling and Grammar button.

   b. Correct the spelling and grammatical errors in the letter.

   c. Use the Thesaurus to find a substitution for "contact" in the last paragraph, then replace "contact." If the Thesaurus is not installed on your computer, substitute a word of your own.

6. **Create and use AutoCorrect entries.**

   a. Create an AutoCorrect entry for "Account Representative." Use the abbreviation "ar."

   b. Insert a blank line after "Your Name," type "ar," then press [Spacebar].

7. **Find and replace text.**

   a. Press [Ctrl][Home], then use the Replace command to replace all occurrences of "Inc." with "Intl."

   b. Double-click "OVR" in the status bar, place the insertion point in front of "Your Name," then type your name.

   c. Double-click "OVR" in the status bar again to turn Overtype mode off, save your changes, then print the document.

   d. Close the document and exit Word.

▶ Visual Workshop

Create the letter shown in Figure B-20, using the Contemporary Letter template. Save it as "Lakeside Letter" on your Project Disk, then print a copy of the letter.

FIGURE B-20

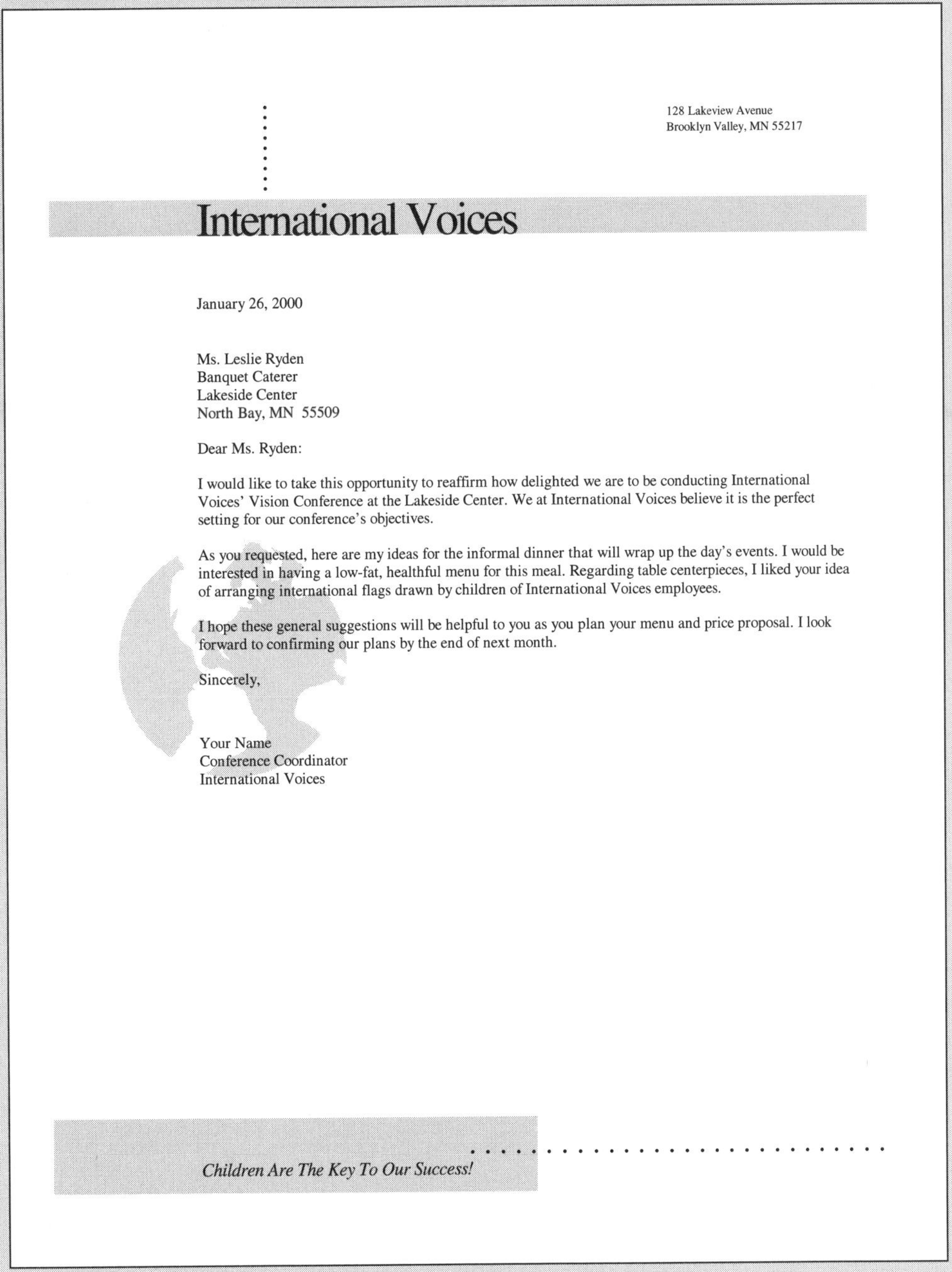

128 Lakeview Avenue
Brooklyn Valley, MN 55217

International Voices

January 26, 2000

Ms. Leslie Ryden
Banquet Caterer
Lakeside Center
North Bay, MN 55509

Dear Ms. Ryden:

I would like to take this opportunity to reaffirm how delighted we are to be conducting International Voices' Vision Conference at the Lakeside Center. We at International Voices believe it is the perfect setting for our conference's objectives.

As you requested, here are my ideas for the informal dinner that will wrap up the day's events. I would be interested in having a low-fat, healthful menu for this meal. Regarding table centerpieces, I liked your idea of arranging international flags drawn by children of International Voices employees.

I hope these general suggestions will be helpful to you as you plan your menu and price proposal. I look forward to confirming our plans by the end of next month.

Sincerely,

Your Name
Conference Coordinator
International Voices

Children Are The Key To Our Success!

Formatting
a Document

Objectives

- ► **Change fonts and font sizes**
- ► **Apply font effects**
- ► **Change paragraph alignment**
- ► **Indent paragraphs**
- ► **Change line spacing**
- ► **Change paragraph spacing**
- ► **Align text with tabs**
- ► **Create bulleted and numbered lists**
- ► **Apply borders and shading**

Without some formatting, even a simple document could be almost impossible to read. You can highlight important words or improve the look of a document by changing its typeface or the size of its words. You can organize ideas and add structure to a document by changing the spacing, indentation, and alignment of text in paragraphs. Formatting a document makes it easier to read and easier to understand. Scenario Karen Rosen has drafted a description of the orientation packet for new MediaLoft employees. Before distributing the document to her colleagues, she formats the text and paragraphs to improve the document's organization and to emphasize important topics.

Changing Fonts and Font Sizes

One of the easiest ways to change the appearance of a document is to change its font. A **font** is a family of characters, which includes letters, numbers, and punctuation, with the same typeface or design. A font can be basic, with clean, simple lines, or more stylized, with a lot of curlicues or a definite "theme." The font you choose affects the tone of your document: stylized fonts can add a note of flamboyance, formality, or sleekness to a document, while a more traditional font can "feel" businesslike or scholarly. You can also change the size of text in your documents by increasing or decreasing the **font size**. Fonts are measured in points (pts). A **point** is ½ of an inch. The bigger the number of points, the larger the size of the font. To quickly change fonts and font size, select the text you want to format, then use the buttons on the Formatting toolbar. **Scenario** Karen changes the font and font size of the title and headings in her document, so that readers can quickly find the information they need.

Steps

1. Start **Word**, click **Tools** on the menu bar, click **Customize**, click the **Options tab** in the Customize dialog box, click **Reset my usage data** to restore the default settings, click **Yes** in the alert box, then click **Close**

2. Open the file **WD C-1** from your Project Disk, then save it as **Orientation Packet**
   The document opens in Normal view. The name of the font used in the document appears in the Font list box on the Formatting toolbar, and the font size appears next to it in the Font Size list box. The document is formatted in 12 point Times New Roman.

3. Select the title **New Employee Orientation Packet**, then click the **Font list arrow** on the Formatting toolbar
   The Font list opens with Times New Roman selected, as shown in Figure C-1. The name of each font is formatted in the font so you can see what it looks like. Use the scroll box in the list to view the fonts available on your computer. Fonts you have used recently appear at the top of the list.

4. Click **Arial**
   The font of the selected text changes to Arial. Arial is a font that is commonly used in headings. Titles and headings often appear in a font different from that document's body text.

5. Click the **Font Size list arrow** on the Formatting toolbar, then click **18**
   The size of the title increases to 18 points. The headings should also be formatted in the Arial font.

6. Select the heading **Offer Letter**, click the **Font list arrow**, click **Arial**, click the **Font Size list arrow**, then click **14**
   The heading is formatted in 14 point Arial. Headings in a document are usually larger than body text, but smaller than the title. You'll format each heading in the document in the same way.

7. Click the **down scroll arrow** at the bottom of the vertical scroll bar until the heading **Employee Handbook** appears at the top of your screen
   The Orientation Packet document contains more text than will fit in the document window. **Scrolling** allows you to navigate a document to display the text you want to read or edit in the document window.

8. Select the heading **Employee Handbook**, change the font to **Arial**, change the font size to **14**, then change the font and font size to 14 point Arial (scrolling as needed) for each of the following headings: **Health Insurance Kit**, **Employee Benefits Summary**, and **About MediaLoft © booklet**

9. Deselect the text, then click the **Save button** 🖫 on the Standard toolbar
   Compare your document to Figure C-2.

FIGURE C-1: Font list

Formatting toolbar (yours may differ)

Your font list may be different

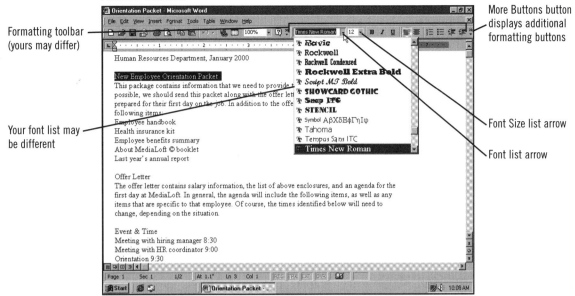

More Buttons button displays additional formatting buttons

Font Size list arrow

Font list arrow

FIGURE C-2: Formatted document

Text formatted in 14 point Arial

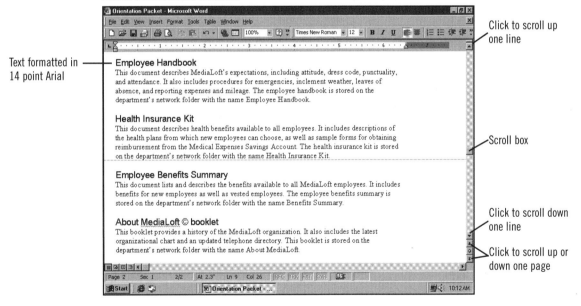

Click to scroll up one line

Scroll box

Click to scroll down one line

Click to scroll up or down one page

Scrolling a document

If your document contains more text than will fit in the document window, you need to scroll the document to display the text you want to read or edit. Scrolling changes the position of the document window relative to the document text. You can scroll up or down in a document. Scroll one line at a time by clicking the arrows at the top and bottom of the vertical scroll bar, or scroll one document window at a time by clicking the scroll bar above or below the scroll box. If you want to scroll the document one page at a time, click the up or down double-arrows at the bottom of the scroll bar. You can also drag the scroll box to a new location in the scroll bar to move to a specific page in the document.

Word 2000

Applying Font Effects

You can emphasize words and ideas in a document by changing the font style, such as making text darker (called **bold**) or slanted (called **italics**). Buttons for these and other font effects, including underlining and changing font color, are on the Formatting toolbar. You can also use the Font command on the Format menu to apply additional special effects to text, such as superscripting it (raising text above the line) or adding a shadow. ▶Scenario Karen applies font effects to emphasize important elements in her document, and to italicize the title of the About MediaLoft booklet.

1. Drag the **scroll box** to the top of the vertical scroll bar
   The top of the document appears in the document window.

QuickTip

You can also underline text by clicking the Underline button 🄤 on the Formatting toolbar.

2. Select **New Employee Orientation Packet**, click the **Bold button** 🄱 on the Formatting toolbar, then deselect the text
   Applying bold to the text makes each character fatter, creating a darker appearance.

3. Select **About MediaLoft** in the list under the first body paragraph, then click the **Italic button** 🄘 on the Formatting toolbar
   The title of the booklet appears in italics. Next you want to apply the superscript effect to the copyright symbol.

QuickTip

Use the Character Spacing tab in the Font dialog box to expand or condense the amount of space between characters, adjust the width or scale of characters, raise or lower characters, and adjust kerning (the spacing between standard character combinations). Formatting character spacing can dramatically affect the appearance of text.

4. Select © (the copyright symbol) after About MediaLoft, click **Format** on the menu bar, then click **Font**
   The Font dialog box opens as shown in Figure C-3. You can use the Font tab to apply many different effects to text, including shadow, superscript, and subscript. You can also change the font, font size, style, and color of text on this tab, and select the style of underline you want to apply to the selected text. Using the Font dialog box, you can apply multiple font effects to text at once. The Preview box on the Font tab displays the combined effects you have chosen for the selected text.

5. Click the **Superscript** check box, click **OK**, then deselect the text
   The copyright symbol is superscripted—formatted in a smaller font size and raised above the line of text.

6. Select **Event & Time** at the top of the list below the second body paragraph, click **Format** on the menu bar, then click **Font**

7. Click **Bold Italic** in the Font style list, click the **Underline style list arrow**, click **Words only**, then click the **Small caps** check box
   The text appears in the Preview box formatted in bold, italic, small caps, with the words (not the spaces between them) underlined. When you change text to small caps, the characters change to uppercase, with the capital letters two points larger than lowercase letters.

8. Click **OK**, deselect the text, then click the **Save button** 🖫 on the Standard toolbar
   Compare your document to Figure C-4.

Adding color to text

When you want to use color to add visual interest in a document, you can highlight, or apply a transparent layer of color to text, or you can change the color of the text itself. To highlight text, click the Highlight button 🖉 on the Formatting toolbar and then drag the Highlighter pointer over the text you want to highlight. You can change the highlight color by clicking the Highlight list arrow and then clicking a new color. To turn off the Highlighter pointer, simply click the Highlight button again. If you want to change the color of the characters themselves, select the text you want to color, click the Font Color list arrow 🄰▾ on the Formatting toolbar, and then click a new color.

FIGURE C-3: Font dialog box

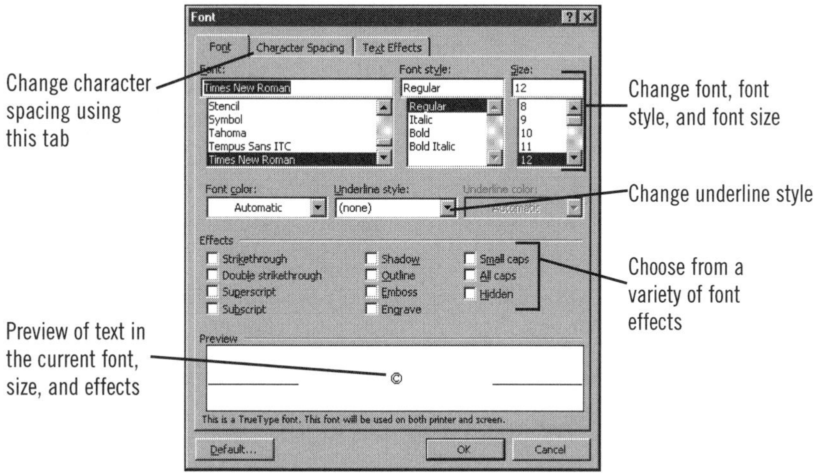

Change character spacing using this tab

Change font, font style, and font size

Change underline style

Choose from a variety of font effects

Preview of text in the current font, size, and effects

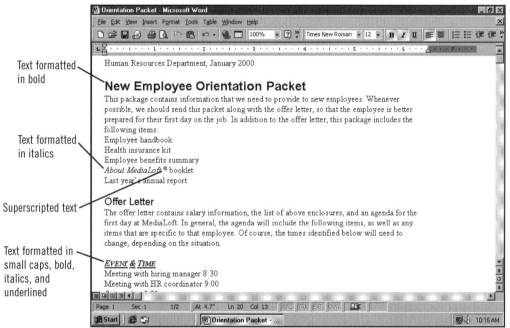

FIGURE C-4: Completed font formatting

Text formatted in bold

Text formatted in italics

Superscripted text

Text formatted in small caps, bold, italics, and underlined

Serif vs. sans serif fonts

Fonts can be divided into two types: serif and sans serif. A **serif font**, such as Times New Roman, has a small stroke, or a **serif**, at the ends of its characters, as shown in Figure C-5. Serif fonts are typically used in business documents, such as letters and resumes, and as the body text in books and other publications. Fonts without serifs, such as Arial, are known as **sans serif fonts**. Sans serif fonts are often used for headings in a document, or as the main font in other types of publications, such as flyers, brochures, and business cards. In a longer document, serif fonts can be easier to read than sans serif fonts.

FIGURE C-5: Serif vs. sans serif fonts

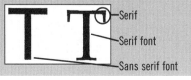

Serif
Serif font
Sans serif font

Word 2000

Changing Paragraph Alignment

Another way to change the appearance of text in a document is to change the alignment of paragraphs. Paragraphs are aligned relative to the margins in a document. **Margins** are the blank areas between the edge of the text and the edge of the page. By default, text is **left-aligned**, or flush with the left margin. However, you can also **center** a paragraph between margins or **right-align** a paragraph so that its right edge is even with the right margin. You can also **justify** a paragraph so that both the left and right edges are evenly aligned. These paragraph alignment options are available on the Formatting toolbar or with the Paragraph command on the Format menu. When you format a paragraph, Word applies your formatting changes to the paragraph that contains the insertion point. If you wish to format multiple paragraphs, you must first select the paragraphs you want to format. Scenario▶ Karen varies the alignment of paragraphs in her document to make it easier to read.

Steps

Trouble?

Click the More Buttons button ▷ on the Formatting toolbar to locate buttons that are not visible on your Formatting toolbar.

1. Select the first line of the document, **Human Resources Department, January 2000**, then click the **Align Right button** ▤ on the Formatting toolbar
   The text is aligned with the right margin.

2. In the first line, place the insertion point after the comma after **Department**, press **[Backspace]** to remove the comma, then press **[Enter]**
   The new paragraph is also right-aligned, as shown in Figure C-6. When you press [Enter] in the middle of a paragraph, the new paragraph "inherits" the paragraph formatting of the original paragraph.

3. Select **New Employee Orientation Packet**, then click the **Center button** ▤ on the Formatting toolbar
   The title is centered evenly between the left and right margins. If you change the margins, this text will always remain centered relative to the margins.

4. Scroll down to locate the paragraph that begins **I would like to share ...**, place the insertion point in the paragraph, then click the **Justify button** ▤ on the Formatting toolbar
   Word adjusts the spacing between words of the paragraph so that each line in the paragraph is the same length, and flush with both the left and right margins. Justifying paragraphs eliminates the ragged right edge, and can make your documents look neater.

5. Click the **Save button** ▤ on the Standard toolbar
   Compare your document to Figure C-7.

CLUES TO USE

Using the FormatPainter to copy formatting

You can use Word's FormatPainter to copy text or paragraph formatting to other text that you want to format the same way. This feature is especially useful when you want to copy multiple effects at once. To use the Format Painter, select the text whose formatting you want to copy, then click the FormatPainter button ◁ on the Standard toolbar. When the pointer changes to ▵, simply select the text you want to format. The new formatting is automatically applied. If you want to copy the formatting to multiple locations, double-click the FormatPainter button so that the FormatPainter pointer remains active. To turn off the FormatPainter, click the FormatPainter button again.

FIGURE C-6: Right-aligned text

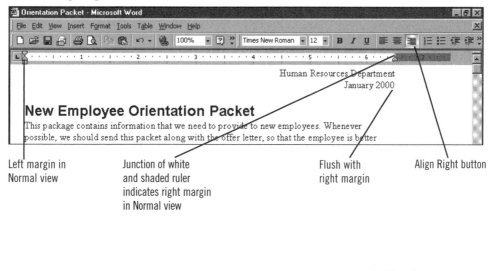

Left margin in Normal view

Junction of white and shaded ruler indicates right margin in Normal view

Flush with right margin

Align Right button

Justify button

FIGURE C-7: Justified text

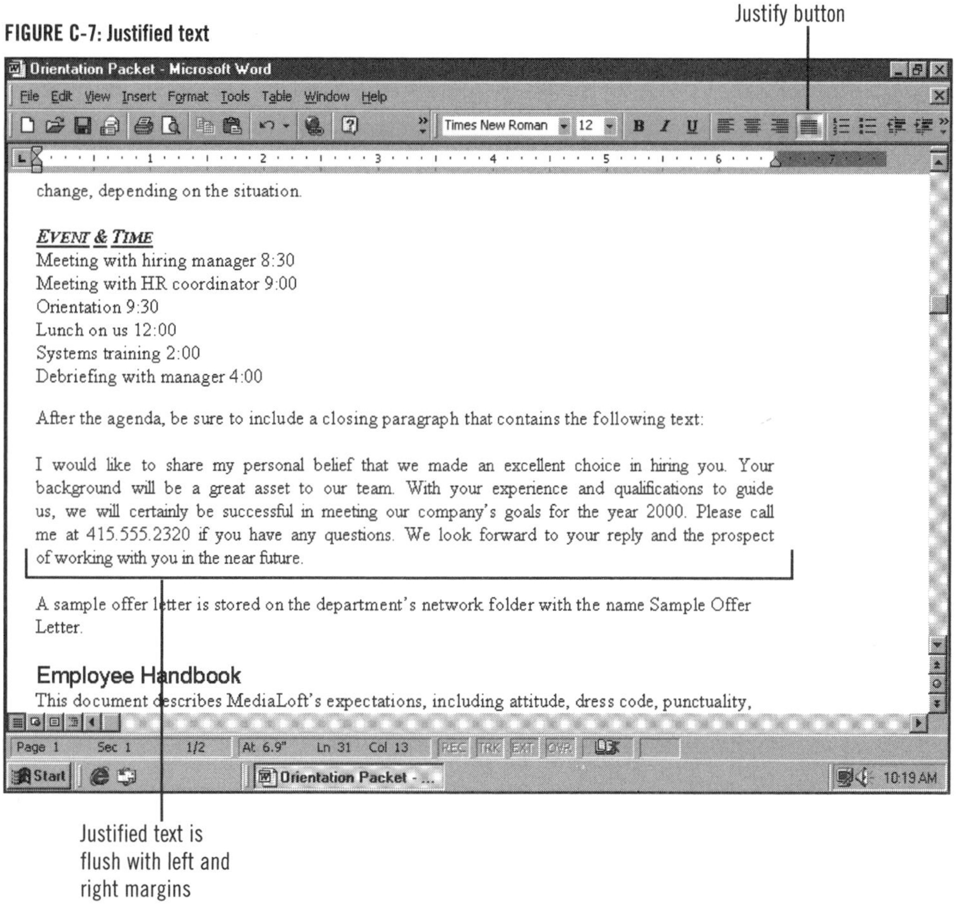

Justified text is flush with left and right margins

Unit C
Word 2000

Indenting Paragraphs

One way to visually structure a document is to change the indentation of individual paragraphs. When you **indent** text you change the width of the lines in the paragraph. You can modify the indentation from the right or left margins (or both) or you can indent just the first line of a paragraph and leave the remaining lines aligned with the left margin. **Indent markers** on the horizontal ruler show the indent settings for the paragraph that contains the insertion point. You can also drag the indent markers to change a paragraph's indentation. Dragging the Left Indent marker indents an entire paragraph, dragging the First Line Indent marker indents only the first line of the paragraph, and dragging the Right Indent marker indents a paragraph from the right margin. You can also use the Formatting toolbar or the Paragraph command on the Format menu to change a paragraph's indentation. **Scenario** Karen indents several paragraphs to help clarify the structure of her document. She uses the buttons on the Formatting toolbar and the indent markers on the horizontal ruler.

Steps

QuickTip

To indent text with extra precision, click Format on the menu bar, click Paragraph, then enter the amount you want to indent in the Paragraph dialog box.

1. Scroll to the top of the document, select the **five lines** in the list under the first body paragraph (beginning with **Employee handbook**), click the **Increase Indent button** on the Formatting toolbar twice, then deselect the text
   Each time you click the Increase Indent button, Word indents the left edge of the text ½ inch from the left margin. Notice that the indent markers on the ruler reflect the indentation, as shown in Figure C-8. (To see the indent markers, place the insertion point in the indented paragraphs.) You can decrease the indentation just as easily.

2. Select the same **five lines**, then click the **Decrease Indent button** on the Formatting toolbar once
   The text moves ½ inch to the left. The indent markers on the ruler also move ½ inch to the left. The indent markers indicate how much the selected text is indented. You can also drag the indent markers to change indentation.

Trouble?

Be sure to drag the Left Indent marker, not the First Line Indent marker or the Hanging Indent marker. Click the Undo button if you make a mistake, then redo the step.

3. Scroll down to locate the paragraph that begins **I would like to share ...**, place the insertion point in the paragraph, then drag the **Left Indent marker** to the ¾" mark on the horizontal ruler, as shown in Figure C-9
   Dragging the Left Indent marker indents all the lines in the paragraph. The left edge of the paragraph is aligned with the ¾" mark on the ruler. You can also use the indent markers to indent text from the right.

4. With the insertion point in the same paragraph drag the **Right Indent marker** to the 5¾" mark on the horizontal ruler
   The right edge of the paragraph is indented ¾" from the right margin. You can also indent only the first line of a paragraph by dragging the First Line Indent marker.

5. Scroll to the top of the document, place the insertion point in the first body paragraph that begins **This package contains ...**, then drag the **First Line Indent marker** to the ½" mark on the horizontal ruler, as shown in Figure C-10
   Dragging the First Line Indent marker indents only the first line of text in a paragraph.

6. Place the insertion point in the **paragraph** directly below each heading in the document (except "Event & Time"), then drag the **First Line Indent marker** to the ½" mark on the horizontal ruler so that the first line in each paragraph is indented ½"

7. Click the **Save button** on the Standard toolbar

FIGURE C-8: Indented list

First Line Indent marker

Hanging Indent marker

Left Indent marker

Indented text

Decrease Indent button

Increase Indent button

Right Indent marker

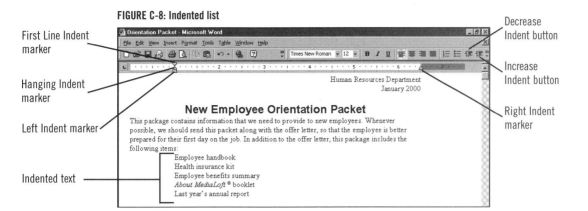

FIGURE C-9: Dragging Left Indent marker

Left Indent marker being dragged to change indent

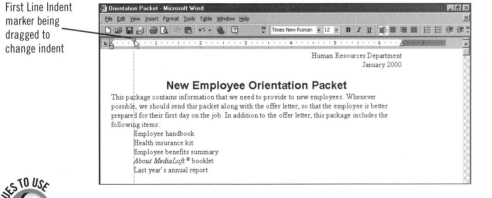

FIGURE C-10: Dragging First Line Indent marker

First Line Indent marker being dragged to change indent

Using hanging indent paragraph formatting

Sometimes you want a paragraph formatted so that the first line of the paragraph is not indented as much as the text in the remaining lines. This formatting is known as a **hanging indent**, shown in Figure C-11. Notice the arrangement of the indent markers on the horizontal ruler and the indentation of the first and remaining lines of the paragraph. You can create a hanging indent by dragging the Hanging Indent marker on the horizontal ruler or by pressing [Ctrl] [T].

FIGURE C-11: Hanging indent

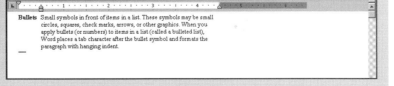

Changing Line Spacing

Another way to make a document easier to read is to increase the amount of spacing between lines. For example, thesis papers or draft versions of documents are often double-spaced to allow space for readers to add written comments. Increase line spacing whenever you want to give a more "open" feel to a document. You use the Paragraph command on the Format menu to change line spacing. Table C-1 describes several keyboard shortcuts for formatting paragraphs. Scenario> Karen wants to provide space for comments from her colleagues, so she increases the line spacing in the document.

Steps

1. Scroll to the top of the document, then place the insertion point in the first body paragraph that begins **This package contains ...**

2. Click **Format** on the menu bar, then click **Paragraph**
   The Paragraph dialog box opens with the Indents and Spacing tab displayed, as shown in Figure C-12. On this tab you can change the amount of space between lines. You can also change other paragraph format settings, including alignment and indentation.

3. Click the **Line spacing list arrow**, click **1.5 lines**, then click **OK**
   The space between the lines increases to one and a half lines.

4. Scroll down to locate the indented paragraph that begins **I would like to share ...**, then place the insertion point in the paragraph

5. Click **Format** on the menu bar, click **Paragraph**, click the **Line spacing list arrow**, click **Double**, then click **OK**
   The space between the lines of the paragraph doubles, as shown in Figure C-13.

6. Click the **Save button** 🖫 on the Standard toolbar

TABLE C-1: Keyboard shortcuts for aligning text and changing line spacing

to	press	to	press
Left-align text	[Ctrl] [L]	Format text with 1.5 line spacing	[Ctrl] [5]
Center text	[Ctrl] [E]	Single-space text	[Ctrl] [1]
Right-align text	[Ctrl] [R]	Double-space text	[Ctrl] [2]
Justify text	[Ctrl] [J]		

FIGURE C-12: Paragraph dialog box

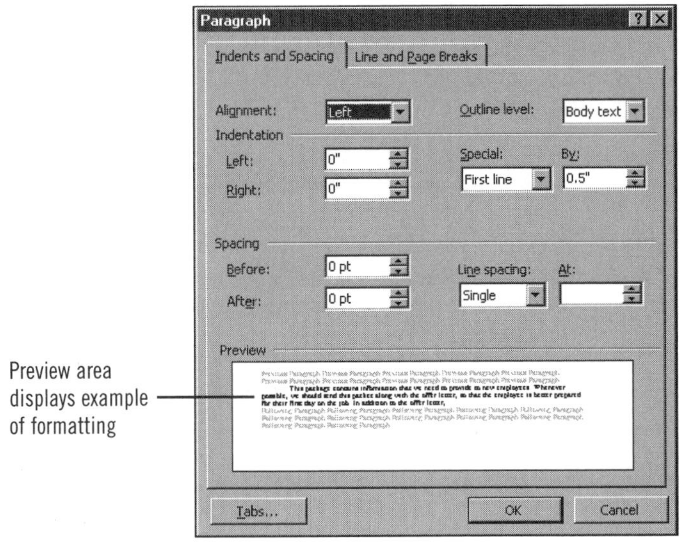

Preview area displays example of formatting

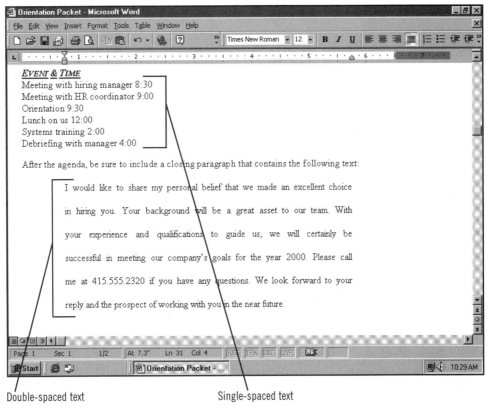

FIGURE C-13: New line spacing in a document

Double-spaced text

Single-spaced text

Changing Paragraph Spacing

In the same way increasing line spacing can make a document easier to read, adding space between paragraphs can help to visually organize the content of your document. Spacing between lines and paragraphs is measured in points. Because you can set the number of points you want, adjusting paragraph spacing is a much more precise way to format than simply inserting blank lines between paragraphs. **Scenario▶** Karen increases the paragraph spacing between headings and body text to make the document more readable.

Steps

1. Scroll to the top of the document, select **New Employee Orientation Packet**, click **Format** on the menu bar, then click **Paragraph**
   The Paragraph dialog box opens with the Indents and Spacing tab displayed. You can use this tab to change the amount of space between paragraphs. You want to increase the amount of space after the title.

2. Click the **After up arrow** twice, then click **OK**
   The space after the paragraph is increased to 12 points. Clicking the Before or After arrows increases or decreases the amount of space above or below a paragraph. Each time you click an up or down arrow, the spacing changes by 6 points. You can also type the specific number of points you want in the Before and After text boxes.

3. Select the **five lines** in the list that follows the first body paragraph, click **Format** on the menu bar, then click **Paragraph**

4. Double-click **0** in the **Before text box**, type **3**, press **[Tab]** to move the insertion point to the **After text box**, then type **3**
   Your Paragraph dialog box should resemble Figure C-14.

5. Click **OK**, then deselect the text
   The space before and after each paragraph in the list increases by 3 points, as shown in Figure C-15.

6. Select the heading **Offer Letter**, click **Format** on the menu bar, click **Paragraph**, click the **After up arrow** once, then click **OK**
   The space between the heading and the paragraph below it increases by 6 points. The other headings should also be formatted with 6 points of space after.

QuickTip
You can press [F4] to repeat the last command.

7. Place the insertion point in each remaining **heading** in the document (except "Event & Time"), then format each heading with 6 points of space after it

8. Click the **Save button** 🖫 on the Standard toolbar

FIGURE C-14: Paragraph spacing in Paragraph dialog box

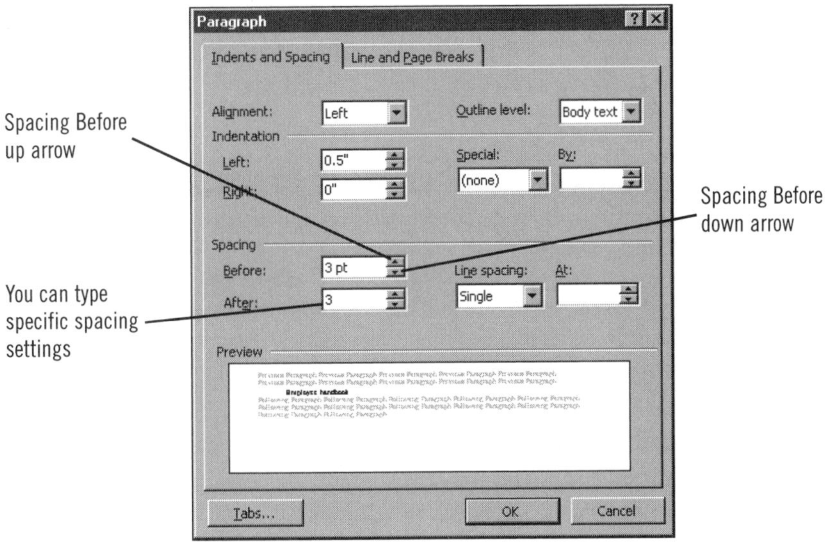

Spacing Before up arrow

You can type specific spacing settings

Spacing Before down arrow

FIGURE C-15: Increased paragraph spacing

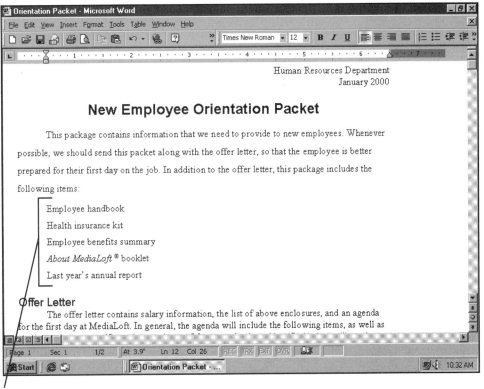

Increased space before and after paragraphs

Aligning Text with Tabs

Word 2000

Numerical information (such as tables of financial results) is often easier to read when you align the text with tabs. A **tab** is used to position text at a specific location in the document. You should use tabs rather than the Spacebar to vertically align your text because tabs are more accurate, faster, and easier to change. When you press [Tab] in a document, the insertion point moves to the next tab stop. A **tab stop** is a predefined position in the document to which you can align tabbed text. By default, tab stops are located at every ½" from the left margin, but you can also create and modify tab stops. Table C-2 describes the five types of tabs. Scenario Karen uses tabs to align the meeting times listed in the agenda.

> **QuickTip**
>
> Click the Show/Hide button ¶ on the Standard toolbar to reveal tab symbols (→), paragraph marks (¶), and spaces between characters (•) in your document. Click it again to hide the symbols.

1. Scroll to locate the heading **Event & Time**, place the insertion point in front of **Time**, then press **[Tab]**

Pressing [Tab] moves the word "Time" to the next default tab stop at the 1" mark on the horizontal ruler. You can also set your own tab stops.

2. At the left end of the horizontal ruler be sure the **Left Tab icon** ⌊ is active, as shown in Figure C-16, then click the **5" mark** on the ruler

If the Left Tab icon is not visible in the tab indicator at the left end of the ruler, click the tab indicator until the Left Tab icon appears. Clicking the ruler moves the tab stop to the 5" mark, and the tabbed text "Time" moves to the new location as shown in Figure C-16. To align the meeting times under this heading, you need to create a tab stop for each line in the agenda. To do this you'll use the Tabs command.

> **QuickTip**
>
> You can also adjust the location of a tab stop by dragging the tab marker to a new location on the ruler.

3. Select the **six lines** under the heading **Event & Time**, click **Format** on the menu bar, then click **Tabs**

The Tabs dialog box opens. You can use this dialog box to set tab stop position and alignment and to set **tab leaders** (lines or dots that appear in front of the tabbed text). You can also use the Tabs command to clear tabs. You'll set right-aligned tabs with leaders.

4. Type **5.3** in the Tab stop position text box, click the **Right option button**, then click the **2.... option button**

Your Tabs dialog box should resemble Figure C-17.

5. Click **Set** to create the tab setting, then click **OK**

A new right tab marker appears on the ruler just after the 5¼" mark. You'll insert tabs in front of each of the meeting times.

6. Place the insertion point in front of **8:30** in the first line of the agenda, then press **[Tab]**

The time "8:30" is right-aligned with the 5.3" tab stop with a dotted tab leader in front of it.

> **QuickTip**
>
> You can remove a tab stop by dragging it off the ruler.

7. Place the insertion point in front of each remaining **time** in the agenda, then press **[Tab]**

The times right-align at 5.3".

8. Select **&** in the Event & Time heading, then press **[Delete]**

9. Click the **Save button** 🖫 on the Standard toolbar

Compare your document to Figure C-18. To see the right-aligned tab marker, place the insertion point in the agenda.

FIGURE C-16: Setting a tab stop on the ruler

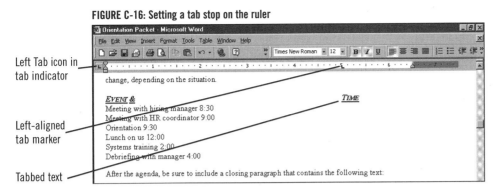

Left Tab icon in tab indicator

Left-aligned tab marker

Tabbed text

FIGURE C-17: Tabs dialog box

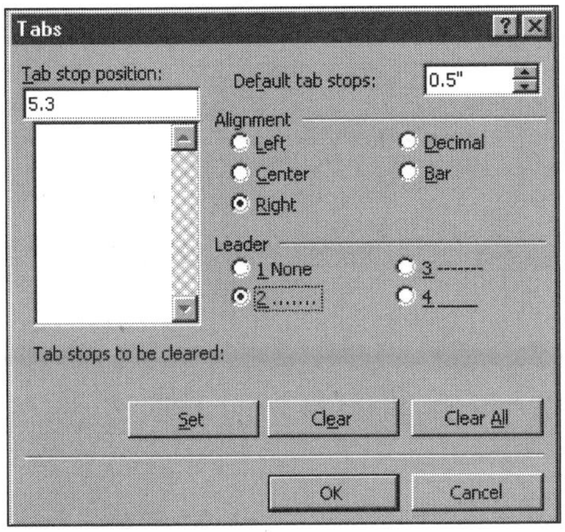

FIGURE C-18: Right-aligned tabs with tab leaders

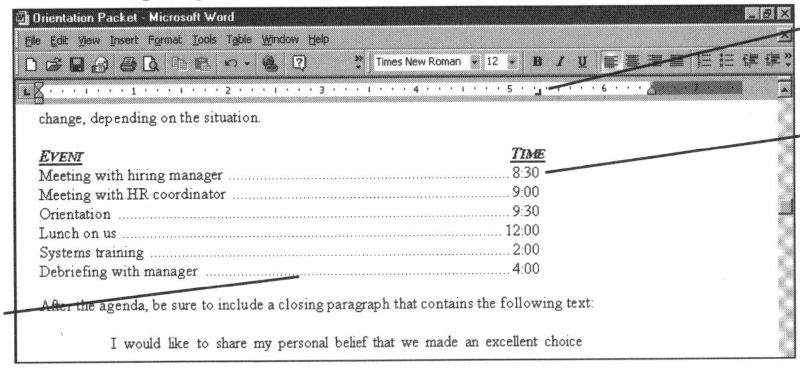

Right-aligned tab marker

Right-aligned tabbed text

Tab leader

TABLE C-2: Types of tabs

alignment	description	tab indicator
Left	Text left-aligns at the tab stop and extends to the right	
Center	Text aligns at the middle of the tab stop, extending an equal distance to the left and right	
Right	Text right-aligns at the tab stop and extends to the left	
Decimal	Text aligns at the decimal point: text before the decimal point extends to the left, and the text after the decimal point extends to the right (used to align numbers)	
Bar	Inserts a vertical bar at the tab position	

Creating Bulleted and Numbered Lists

In a bulleted list, a **bullet**—a small symbol such as a circle or square—precedes each paragraph in the list. Using the Bullets button on the Formatting toolbar, you can insert a bullet in front of each item in a list. When you want to show items in a sequence, a numbered list best reflects the order or priority of the items. To create a simple numbered list, you can use the Numbering button on the Formatting toolbar. You can also use the Bullets and Numbering command on the Format menu to specify additional bullet and numbering formatting options. Scenario►Karen draws attention to the lists in her document by formatting them with bullets and numbers.

Steps

1. Scroll to the top of the document, select the **five lines** in the list under the first body paragraph, then click the **Bullets button** 📋 on the Formatting toolbar
   A bullet appears in front of each item in the list.

2. With the list still selected, click **Format** on the menu bar, then click **Bullets and Numbering**
   The Bullets and Numbering dialog box opens with the Bulleted tab displayed, as shown in Figure C-19. In this dialog box, you can choose from seven different bullet styles. Do not be concerned if your bullet styles are different from those shown in the figure. You can customize your styles to use whatever bullet characters you prefer.

3. Click the **check mark box**, then click **OK**
   The bullet character changes to a small check mark.

4. Scroll to the agenda under the "Event Time" heading, select the **six lines** in the agenda, then click the **Numbering button** 📋 on the Formatting toolbar
   The agenda becomes a numbered list. You can also change the format of a numbered list in the Bullets and Numbering dialog box.

5. Make sure the six lines of the agenda are selected, then right-click the **agenda**
   A pop-up menu appears.

6. Click **Bullets and Numbering** on the pop-up menu, then click the **Numbered tab** in the dialog box, if it is not already displayed
   The Numbered tab in the Bullets and Numbering dialog box displays additional numbering options.

7. In the first row, click the **uppercase Roman numeral box**, then click **OK**
   The numbers in the list change to Roman numerals.

8. Deselect the text, then click the **Save button** 💾 on the Standard toolbar
   Compare your document to Figure C-20.

Creating outline style numbered lists

You can create a simple outline style numbered list by applying an outline numbering scheme from the Outline Numbered tab in the Bullets and Numbering dialog box to a list. To create a new outline, choose a numbering scheme (one that does not include headings), then type your outline, pressing [Enter] after each item in the list. After you have applied an outline numbering scheme to a list, you can increase or decrease the indentation of individual paragraphs to change their level of importance in the outline. For example, to demote an item to a lower level in the outline, click in the paragraph, then click the Increase Indent button on the Formatting toolbar. To promote an item to a higher level, click the Decrease Indent button. You can choose to format outline style numbered lists with a combination of letters and numbers, numbers alone, or bullets, or you can create a custom outline style.

FIGURE C-19: Bullets and Numbering dialog box

Current bullet style

None

Click if you want to display a different bullet style

FIGURE C-20: Bulleted and numbered lists

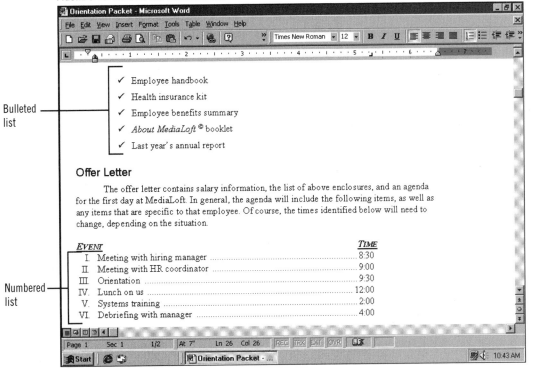

Bulleted list

- ✓ Employee handbook
- ✓ Health insurance kit
- ✓ Employee benefits summary
- ✓ *About MediaLoft* ® booklet
- ✓ Last year's annual report

Offer Letter

The offer letter contains salary information, the list of above enclosures, and an agenda for the first day at MediaLoft. In general, the agenda will include the following items, as well as any items that are specific to that employee. Of course, the times identified below will need to change, depending on the situation.

EVENT	*TIME*
I. Meeting with hiring manager	8:30
II. Meeting with HR coordinator	9:00
III. Orientation	9:30
IV. Lunch on us	12:00
V. Systems training	2:00
VI. Debriefing with manager	4:00

Numbered list

Applying Borders and Shading

Borders and shading add visual interest to text. **Borders** are lines you can add to the top, bottom, or sides of paragraphs. Preset border settings make it easy to create a box around a paragraph. **Shading** is a transparent color or pattern you apply to a paragraph. With the Tables and Borders toolbar you can apply the borders and shading options you use most often, or you can use the Borders and Shading command on the Format menu to select from additional border and shading options. When you use the Tables and Borders toolbar, Word displays the document in Print Layout view. **Views** are different ways of displaying a document in the document window. Each view provides different features that are especially helpful in different phases of working on a document. Table C-3 describes different views in Word. You can change the document view by clicking the view buttons to the left of the horizontal scroll bar. [Scenario] Karen uses borders to emphasize the headings and adds shading to draw attention to the closing paragraph.

Steps

Trouble?

Click the More Buttons button [»] on the Standard toolbar to locate buttons that are not displayed on your Standard toolbar. Click Cancel if the Office Assistant appears.

1. Place the insertion point in the paragraph that begins **I would like to share...**, then click the **Tables and Borders button** [⊞] on the Standard toolbar
   The Tables and Borders toolbar appears, and the document switches to Print Layout view.

2. Click the **Shading Color list arrow** [⯆▾] on the Tables and Borders toolbar, then click the **Gray 20% box**, as shown in Figure C-21
   A transparent gray rectangle covers the paragraph.

3. Scroll to the top of the document, click the **Line Style list arrow** [———▾] on the Tables and Borders toolbar, then click the **Thick/Thin style** (thick line on top, thin line below) on the Line Style list
   The Thick/Thin line style is now the active line style. It remains in effect for all the borders you create until you change the style again. The pointer also changes to [✐]. To apply a border you need to turn off the pointer.

Trouble?

If a box appears, click the Undo button [↶], click the text, then click [▦] again.

4. Click the **Draw Table button** [✐] on the Tables and Borders toolbar to turn off the pointer, then select **New Employee Orientation Packet**

5. Click the **Outside Border list arrow** [▦▾] on the Tables and Borders toolbar, then click the **Top Border button** [▦]
   A border of a Thick/Thin line appears above the selected text. You'll change to a new line style before adding a border under the selected text.

6. With the text still selected, click the **Line Style list arrow**, click the **Thin/Thick style** (thin line on top, thick line below), then click [✐] to turn off the pointer

7. Click the **Top Border list arrow** [▦▾] on the Tables and Borders toolbar, click the **Bottom Border button** [▦] on the menu that appears, then deselect the text
   A border appears below the title, as shown in Figure C-22.

8. Click the **Close button** on the Tables and Borders toolbar, place the insertion point in front of **Human Resources Department** at the top of the document, type your name, then press **[Enter]**

9. Click the **Save button** [▤] on the Standard toolbar, then click the **Print button** [▤] on the Standard toolbar

10. Close the document, then exit Word

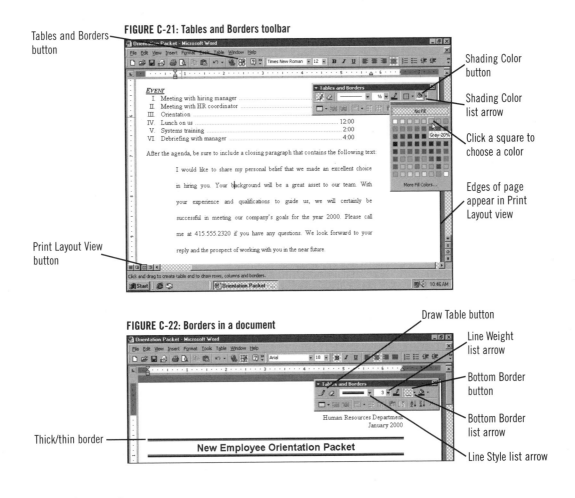

FIGURE C-21: Tables and Borders toolbar

Tables and Borders button

Shading Color button

Shading Color list arrow

Click a square to choose a color

Edges of page appear in Print Layout view

Print Layout View button

FIGURE C-22: Borders in a document

Draw Table button

Line Weight list arrow

Bottom Border button

Bottom Border list arrow

Line Style list arrow

Thick/thin border

New Employee Orientation Packet

TABLE C-3: Word document views

view	displays	use to
Normal	A simple layout view of the document	Type, edit and format text quickly
Print Layout	The document as it will appear when printed on paper, along with the horizontal and vertical rulers	Edit and view the exact placement of text and graphics on the page, adjust margins, and work with columns and tables
Outline	Selected levels of headings and body text	View major headings and organize ideas in outline format
Web Layout	The document as a Web page	Create a Web page

CLUES TO USE

Adding borders and shading with the Borders and Shading command

The Tables and Borders toolbar includes the most frequently used border and shading options. However, for even more border and shading options use the Borders and Shading command on the Format menu to display the Borders and Shading dialog box. In this dialog box, you can use the Borders tab to select preset box, shadow, and 3-D borders, or design a border of your own using the many line, color, and spacing options available on this tab. Borders can be as simple or as complex as you like. On the Shading tab, you can select a shade pattern, including stripes, checkerboards and grids, and choose the color of the pattern and its background. You can also create a custom shade color and adjust the intensity of the shading you apply to text. Use the Apply to list arrow on both tabs to choose to apply borders or shading to the selected text or to paragraphs.

Practice

► Concepts Review

Label each of the formatting elements shown in Figure C-23.

FIGURE C-23

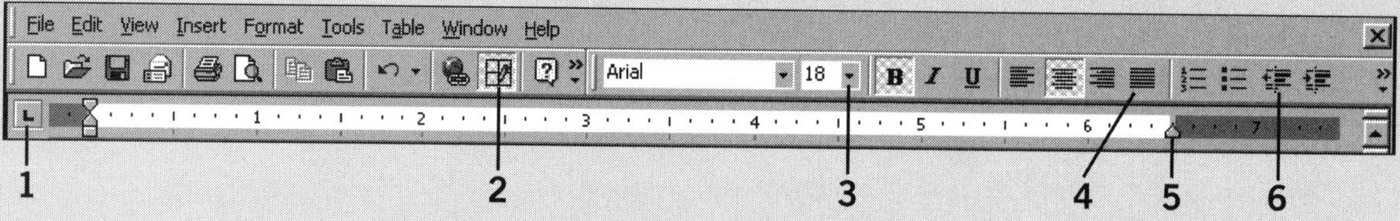

1 2 3 4 5 6

Match each term with the statement that describes it.

7. Font
8. Bold
9. Hanging indent
10. Tab stop
11. Justified

a. A style that makes text appear darker
b. A set of characters of a specific design
c. Both the left and right edges of a paragraph are evenly aligned
d. The first line of a paragraph is closer to the left margin than the remaining lines
e. A set location in the document to which you can align text

Select the best answer from the list of choices.

12. Which paragraph formatting feature is not available on the Formatting toolbar?
   a. Borders
   b. Line spacing
   c. Decrease indentation
   d. Paragraph alignment

13. Which view would you use to best see the margins on a page?
   a. Web Layout
   b. Outline
   c. Print Layout
   d. Normal

14. Which of the following statements about tabs is not true?
   a. Tabs are a more accurate way to align text than spaces.
   b. You can use the Tab command on the Format menu to set tab stops.
   c. You can use the horizontal ruler to create a tab leader.
   d. You can use the horizontal ruler to set tab stops.

15. Which button on the Tables and Borders toolbar do you click when you want to apply shading to text?
   a. You cannot apply shading with a button
   b. Shading
   c. Borders and Shading
   d. Borders

▶ Skills Review

1. Change fonts and font sizes.

a. Start Word, open the file WD C-2 from your Project Disk, and save it as "Press Release."

b. Format "Press Release" in 26 point Arial Black.

c. Format the second line of text in 20 point Arial.

d. In the second sentence, format "RoadMap" in Arial.

e. Format all occurrences of "Open Roads, Inc." in Arial.

2. Apply font effects.

a. Format the heading, "Package Delivery Company ..." in bold.

b. In the first body paragraph, format "RoadMap" in bold italics with an underline.

c. Use the Format Painter to apply the same formatting to "RoadMap" in the second body paragraph.

d. Apply superscript formatting to the copyright symbol after the first occurrence of "RoadMap."

e. Format the first occurrence of "Open Roads, Inc." in bold, and apply the All caps effect.

f. Apply the same formatting to all occurrences of "Open Roads, Inc."

3. Change paragraph alignment.

a. Center "Press Release" and "Package Delivery Company ...".

b. Justify the remaining paragraphs in the document.

c. Type your name and today's date at the bottom of the document, then right-align your name and the date.

4. Indent paragraphs.

a. Drag the First Line Indent marker to indent the first line in the first and second body paragraphs ½".

b. Indent the three lines after the first body paragraph one inch.

c. With the insertion point in the last body paragraph, drag the Left Indent marker to the ½" mark on the horizontal ruler.

d. Right-indent the last body paragraph ½" from the right margin.

5. Change line spacing.

a. Change the line spacing of the body text (not the headings) to 1.5.

b. Change the line spacing of the last body paragraph to single-spacing.

6. Change paragraph spacing.

a. Format "Press Release" with 12 points of space before and 3 points of space after.

b. Format "Package Delivery Company ..." with 18 points of space before and 6 points of space after.

c. Format the first body paragraph with 6 points of space after.

7. Align text with tabs.

a. Near the bottom, insert a blank line after "Typical shipping prices:".

b. Press [Tab], type "Weight," press [Tab], type "Cost," then press [Enter].

c. Press [Tab], type "Under 1 lb," press [Tab], type "5.25," then press [Enter].

d. Press [Tab], type "1 - 10 lbs," press [Tab], then type "10.75." Do not press [Enter].

e. Select all three lines of the list and place a left-aligned tab stop at the 2" mark.

f. With the same three lines selected, click the tab alignment indicator at the left end of the ruler until you see the decimal tab marker, then place a decimal-aligned tab stop at the 4.5" mark.

    g. Press [Enter] at the end of the last item in the list, press [Tab], type "More than 10 lbs," press [Tab], then type "14.50."

    h. Remove the decimal tab stop from the first line in the table, then set a new left-aligned tab stop at the 4⅜" mark.

    i. Select the next three lines of the table, and format the 4.5" tab stop to have a dotted leader.

    j. Underline each word in the first line of the table.

8. Create bulleted and numbered lists.

    a. Number the three-line list under the first body paragraph.

    b. Apply bullets to the list, then change the bullets to another bullet style.

9. Apply borders and shading.

    a. Apply a thin double line above and below "Press Release."

    b. Apply 15% gray shading to the last paragraph.

    c. Save your changes to the document, print the document, and exit Word.

► Visual Workshop

Create the flyer shown in Figure C-24 and save it as "Kids Flyer" on your Project Disk. Use 16 point Garamond for the font and change the font size of the heading to 24 points. Adjust the character spacing of the heading text to expand it and change the scale to 150%. (*Hint*: Use the Character Spacing tab in the Font dialog box.) For the contact information, use a 3 point box border. (*Hint*: Use the Borders and Shading command.) Print a copy of the completed flyer.

FIGURE C-24

COMPANIES FOR KIDS
NEEDS YOUR HELP!

COMPANIES FOR KIDS is a non-profit community program that collects toys, clothing, and books for children in local shelters. We depend largely on local businesses to help fund our efforts.

Each weekend **COMPANIES FOR KIDS** sends out corporate teams to collect clothing, books, and toys from the community. Your company may also choose to help our children in any of the following ways:

❖ Provide a monetary donation.

❖ Assemble teams to sort or collect clothing and toys.

❖ Send individuals to spend time with children in local shelters.

We look forward to your company's participation and support in this valuable community program.

Contact: Your Name

Fundraising Coordinator

COMPANIES FOR KIDS

(415) 555-2020

Working
with Tables

Objectives

- [MOUS] ▶ **Create a table**
- [MOUS] ▶ **Adjust table rows and columns**
- [MOUS] ▶ **Add and delete rows and columns**
- [MOUS] ▶ **Format a table**
- [MOUS] ▶ **Calculate data in a table**
- [MOUS] ▶ **Sort a table**
- [MOUS] ▶ **Draw a table**
- [MOUS] ▶ **Split and merge cells**

A **table** is text that is arranged in a grid of rows and columns. With Word, you can create a table from scratch or you can convert existing text into a table. Once you have created a table, you can easily modify it, sort and calculate the data in it, and quickly make it attractive using a preset table format. You can also build tables by drawing rows and columns exactly where you want them. Tables are an excellent tool for displaying data that is typically found in lists or columns. **Scenario** Karen Rosen needs to create an agenda for a new employee, a record of earned vacation days, and a record of employee absences. She decides to format this information in tables to make the documents attractive and easy to use.

Creating a Table

In a **table**, text is arranged in a grid of rows and columns that is divided by borders. A **column** in a table is text arranged vertically. A **row** is text arranged horizontally. The intersection of a column and a row is called a **cell**. **Borders** surround each cell to help you see the structure of the table. You can create an empty table and then add text to it, or you can convert existing text into a table. When you create a new, blank table, you specify the number of rows and columns you want your table to include. Once the table is created, you can enter information in it. To create a blank table, you can use the Insert Table button on the Standard toolbar, or the Insert Table command on the Table menu. You can later change the structure of the table by adding and deleting rows and columns. Scenario ▶ Karen creates a table for tracking employee attendance in a new document. As she works, she adds rows to the table.

Steps 123

1. Start **Word**, click **Tools** on the menu bar, click **Customize**, click the **Options tab** in the Customize dialog box, click **Reset my usage data** to restore default settings, click **Yes** in the alert box, then click **Close**

2. Click the **Print Layout View button** ▣ on the horizontal scroll bar
The document displays in Print Layout view and the I-beam pointer changes to I⁼

3. Type **Agenda for New Employees**, then press **[Enter]** twice

4. Click the **Insert Table button** ▣ on the Standard toolbar
A grid opens. You use this grid to indicate the number of rows and columns you want the new table to contain.

5. Click the **second box** in the last row of the grid to select four rows and two columns, as shown in Figure D-1
A blank table containing four rows and two columns appears in the document.

6. Type **EVENT** in the first cell, then press **[Tab]**
Pressing [Tab] moves the insertion point to the next cell in the row.

7. Type **TIME**, press **[Tab]**, type **Meeting with Karen Rosen, Director of Human Resources**, press **[Tab]**, type **8:30**, then press **[Tab]**
Pressing [Tab] at the end of a row moves the insertion point to the next cell in the next row.

8. Type the following text in the table, pressing **[Tab]** to move from cell to cell
Meeting with HR coordinator   9:00
Orientation   9:30

9. Press **[Tab]**
Pressing [Tab] with the insertion point in the last cell of a table creates a new blank row at the end of the table, as shown in Figure D-2.

10. Type the following text in the table, pressing **[Tab]** to move from cell to cell, and to add new rows

Lunch on us	**12:00**
Systems training	**2:00**
Tele-conference with regional managers	**3:00**
Debriefing with training manager	**4:00**

11. Click the **Save button** ▣ on the Standard toolbar, then save the document with the filename **Agenda** to your Project Disk
Compare your table to Figure D-3.

FIGURE D-1: Creating a table

Your toolbars may differ

Insert Table button

Indicates 4 rows and 2 columns

More Buttons button on Standard toolbar

Drag the lower-right corner of grid to expand number of rows and columns

4 x 2 Table

Agenda for New Employees

FIGURE D-2: New row

Column

Row

New row

Agenda for New Employees

EVENT	TIME
Meeting with Karen Rosen, Director of Human Resources	8:30
Meeting with HR coordinator	9:00
Orientation	9:30

Cell

Border

FIGURE D-3: Text in a table

Agenda for New Employees

EVENT	TIME
Meeting with Karen Rosen, Director of Human Resources	8:30
Meeting with HR coordinator	9:00
Orientation	9:30
Lunch on us	12:00
Systems training	2:00
Tele-conference with regional managers	3:00
Debriefing with training manager	4:00

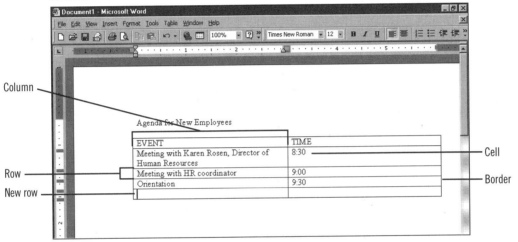

CLUES TO USE

Converting text to a table

Sometimes it is easier to enter text in your document and convert it into a table than to create a blank table and enter the text in the cells. The text you intend to convert to a table must be formatted with tabs, commas, or paragraph marks so that Word can interpret the formatting and create the table. You can create a table based on existing text by selecting the text and then using the Insert Table button on the Standard toolbar or the Convert Text to Table command on the Table menu. In the Convert Text to Table dialog box, you can specify the number of rows and columns you want in your table, along with other table formatting options.

Adjusting Table Rows and Columns

Once you create a table, you can easily adjust the size of rows, columns, and individual cells to make your tables easier to read. You can adjust the size of rows and columns by dragging the borders, by using the AutoFit command on the Table menu to resize columns and rows automatically, or by specifying the column width and row height you want using the Table Properties command on the Table menu. **Scenario** Karen adjusts the height of the rows and the width of the columns in her table.

Trouble?

If the width of only one cell in the column changes when you adjust the column width, deselect the cell, then click the Undo button ↶ on the Standard toolbar. If you want to adjust the width of the entire column, make sure no cells are selected.

1. Position the pointer over the **right border of the first column** until the pointer changes to ◄||►, then drag the border to the **2¼" mark** on the horizontal ruler
   The first column narrows and the second column widens as shown in Figure D-5. In some cells, the text in the first column wraps onto a second line. Moving the border for the first column resulted in the second column becoming too wide for the text. You can adjust the width of a column to fit the text by double-clicking the column border.

2. Position the pointer over the **right border of the second column** until the pointer changes to ◄||►, then double-click
   The second column automatically adjusts to fit the text. You can also adjust the table so that all rows are the same height. First you need to select the entire table.

3. Click anywhere in the table, then click the **Table Select icon** ⊞ that appears at the upper-left corner of the table
   The entire table is selected. You can also select a whole table by clicking Table on the menu bar, pointing to Select, and then clicking Table.

4. Click **Table** on the menu bar, point to **AutoFit**, click **Distribute Rows Evenly**, then deselect the table
   All the rows in the table are the same height, as shown in Figure D-6. If you had wanted to make all the columns the same width, you would have clicked Distribute Columns Evenly on the AutoFit menu. You can also use the commands on this menu to adjust the size of columns and rows to fit the text or the document window.

5. Click the **Save button** 💾 on the Standard toolbar

Setting table properties

You can use the Table Properties command to change the structure and format of the tables you create. This command is especially useful when you want to set a specific row height or column width, or when you want to change the alignment of a table on the page. To open the Table Properties dialog box, click Table on the menu bar, then click Table Properties. On the Row, Column, and Cell tabs you can specify an exact height and width for the columns, rows, and cells selected in your table. You can also change the vertical alignment of text in cells on the Cells tab. To change a table's alignment on the page, choose the alignment you want on the Table tab, shown in Figure D-4. You can also specify the width of the table on this tab and set text wrapping options, if any.

FIGURE D-4: Table Properties dialog box

Select table alignment

FIGURE D-5: Resized columns

Table Select icon

Dragging a column border adjusts the column width

Drag to adjust size of all the rows and columns

FIGURE D-6: Resized rows and columns

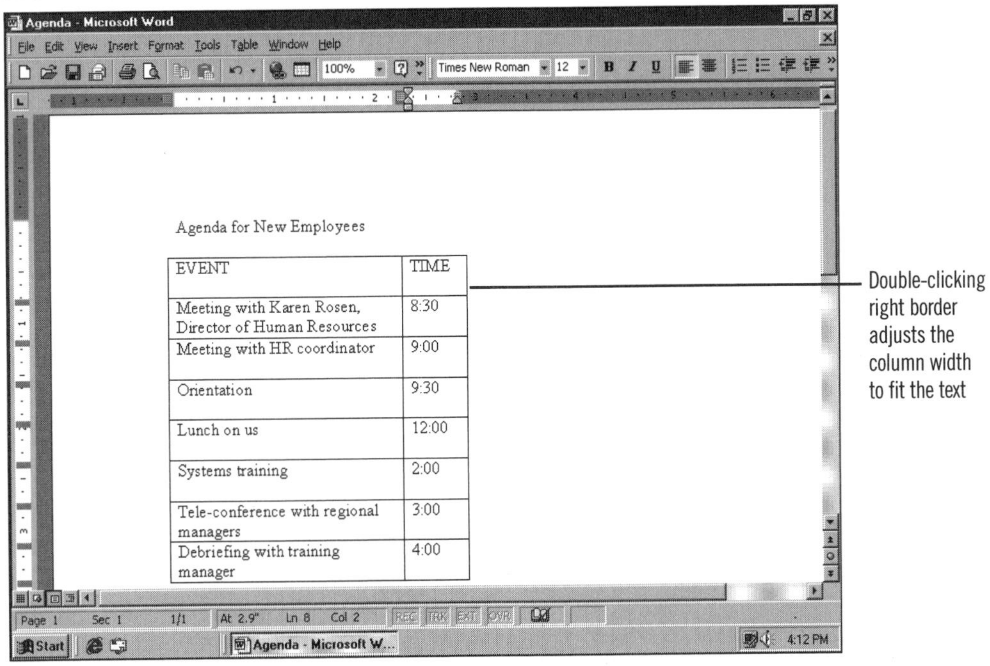

Double-clicking right border adjusts the column width to fit the text

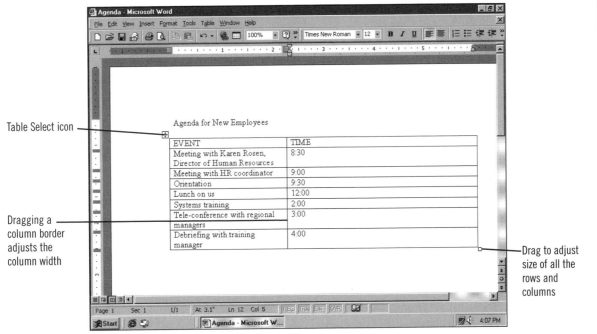

Unit D

Word 2000

Adding and Deleting Rows and Columns

As you add or remove information in a table, you may need to change the number of rows or columns. You can quickly add or delete rows and columns using the commands on the Table menu or the commands on the pop-up menu for tables. Before you add or delete rows and columns, you must select an existing row or column in the table to indicate where you want to add or remove cells. The easiest way to select a row or column is to use the selection bar. Each row, column, and cell in a table has its own selection bar. Click to the left of a cell or a row to select the whole row, or click above a column to select a whole column. You can also click and drag to select cells, columns, or rows. **Scenario** Karen adds new rows for new agenda events to the table, and deletes an unnecessary row. She also adds a column to identify the location of each event.

Steps

QuickTip

You can also select a row or column by clicking Table on the menu bar, pointing to Select, and then clicking Row or Column.

QuickTip

To quickly delete a row or column, select it, then press [Shift][Delete] or [Ctrl][X]. You can also click Table on the menu bar, point to Delete, then click Rows or Columns. To remove only the text from a selected row or column, press [Delete].

QuickTip

To insert a new column at the right end of a table, place the insertion point in the last column, click Table on the menu bar, click Insert, then click Columns to the Right. You can also use the Insert command to insert rows above or below the selected cell.

1. Click the **selection bar** to the left of the **Lunch on us row** to select it, then click the **Insert Rows button** on the Standard toolbar
   A new blank row appears above the row you selected, as shown in Figure D-7. Notice that the Insert Table button changes to the Insert Rows button when a row is selected. If you had selected a column, the button would have changed to the Insert Columns button.
2. In the first cell of the new blank row, type **Training team meeting,** press **[Tab]**, then type **10:30**
3. Select the **Tele-conference row**, right-click, then click **Delete Rows** on the pop-up menu
   The selected row is deleted.
4. Place the insertion point in **the last row**, click **Table** on the menu bar, point to **Insert**, click **Rows Below**, type **Social hour**, press **[Tab]**, then type **5:00**
5. Select the entire **second column** in the table, then click the **Insert Columns button** on the Standard toolbar
   A new blank column appears between the first and second columns. Word places the insertion point in the first cell of the new column when you begin typing.
6. Type **LOCATION**
   The column width adjusts to fit the text.
7. Press [↓], then type the following in the remaining cells in the column:
   HR 220 [↓]
   HR 225 [↓]
   Training Center [↓]
   Conference Room 1 [↓]
   Reception Area [↓]
   Your office [↓]
   HR 250 [↓]
   Reception Area
   Compare your document to Figure D-8.
8. Click the **Save button** on the Standard toolbar

FIGURE D-7: Inserted row

Insert Rows button

New row

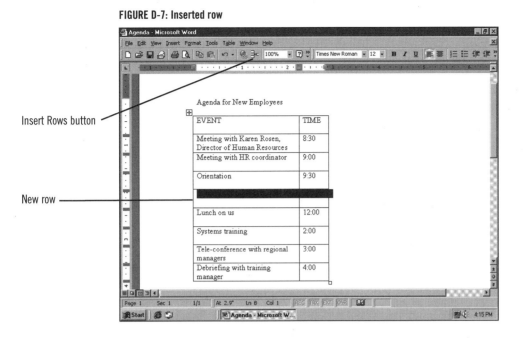

FIGURE D-8: Edited table

Inserted column

Added row

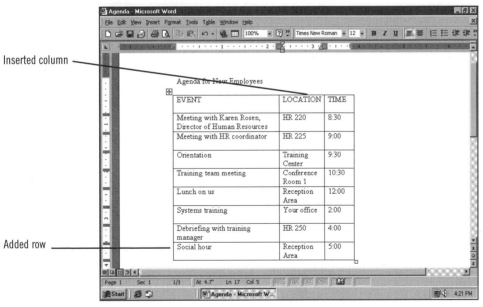

Copying and moving columns and rows

You can use the same techniques to copy and move columns and rows that you use to copy and move text in a document. Be sure to select the entire row or column you want to copy or move, then click the Cut or Copy buttons to place the selection on the Clipboard. Place the insertion point in the location you want to insert the row or column in the table, then click the Paste button. You can also copy or move rows or columns by clicking and dragging them. Again, select the rows or columns you want to copy or move, click and hold the mouse over the selection until the pointer changes, then drag the selection to the new location in the table and release the mouse button.

Word 2000

Formatting a Table

You can improve the appearance of a table by adding borders and shading to rows and columns. Changing the alignment of text in a table can also make your tables more attractive and readable. You can format tables automatically with the Table AutoFormat feature, which provides a variety of preset table formats, or you can use the buttons on the Tables and Borders toolbar to apply a variety of formatting effects to your tables. Table D-1 describes some of the buttons on the Tables and Borders toolbar. **Scenario** Karen uses the Table AutoFormat command to apply borders, shading, and special formatting to the table, then she changes the alignment of text in the table.

Steps

QuickTip

You can also click the Table AutoFormat button on the Tables and Borders toolbar to open the Table AutoFormat dialog box.

1. **With the insertion point in the table, click Table on the menu bar, then click Table AutoFormat**
   The Table AutoFormat dialog box opens, as shown in Figure D-9.

2. **Scroll the list of formats, then click Grid 8**
   The Preview box shows a sample table formatted with the Grid 8 format option. You can modify the preset formats to highlight important elements in your tables. By default, Word applies special formatting to heading rows and the first column of a table. To emphasize the meeting times in the agenda, you'll apply special formatting to the last column of the table.

3. **Make sure the Heading rows and First column check boxes are selected under Apply special formats to, then click the Last column check box to select it**
   In the Preview box, the last column of the sample table now appears in bold. AutoFormat automatically adjusts the width of columns in a table to span the width of the page. To retain the column width you set earlier, you'll turn off the AutoFit feature.

4. **Clear the AutoFit checkbox, then click OK**
   The table is formatted with the settings you selected.

Trouble?

Click the More Buttons button on the Formatting toolbar to locate buttons that are not visible on your toolbar.

5. **Select the last column, click the Align Right button on the Formatting toolbar, then deselect the column**
   The meeting times are right-aligned. You could also use the alignment buttons on the Tables and Borders toolbar to change the alignment of text in cells. Compare your table to Figure D-10.

6. **Type your name at the top of the page, press [Enter], click the Save button on the Standard toolbar, then click the Print button on the Standard toolbar**

7. **Click File on the menu bar, then click Close**

TABLE D-1: Buttons on the Tables and Borders toolbar

button	use to	button	use to
Line Style	Determine the line style of borders	Draw Table	Draw a table or cells
Line Weight	Determine the thickness of borders	Eraser	Erase or remove a border between cells
Border Color	Determine the color of borders	Merge Cells	Combine selected cells into a single cell
Outside Borders	Add or remove individual borders	Split Cells	Divide a cell into multiple cells
Shading Color	Determine the shade color or pattern of cells	Insert Table	Insert new rows, columns, cells, or a new table; determine column width
Align Top Left	Change the alignment of text in a cell	Distribute Rows Evenly	Make rows the same height
Change Text Direction	Change the orientation of text	Distribute Columns Evenly	Make columns the same width

FIGURE D-9: Table AutoFormat dialog box

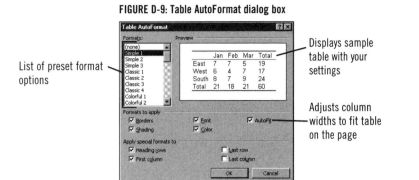

List of preset format options

Displays sample table with your settings

Adjusts column widths to fit table on the page

FIGURE D-10: Formatted table

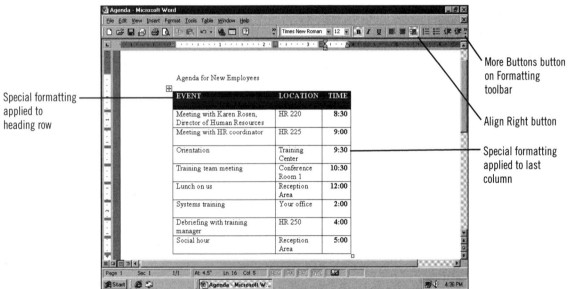

Special formatting applied to heading row

More Buttons button on Formatting toolbar

Align Right button

Special formatting applied to last column

Changing borders and shading in a table

You can add, remove, or alter the borders and shading in a table using the buttons on the Tables and Borders toolbar, shown in Figure D-11, which appears when you click the Tables and Borders button 🔲 on the Standard toolbar. To change the shading of cells, select the cells you want to format, click the Shading Color list arrow 🔲 ▾ on the Tables and Borders toolbar, then click the shade color and intensity you want to apply to the selected cells. To add or remove borders from a table, select the cells you want to format, then click the Outside Borders list arrow 🔲 ▾ on the Tables and Borders toolbar (or the Formatting toolbar). From the list of border buttons, click the button that corresponds to the border you want to

add or remove. For example, if you want to remove borders from around all the cells in your table, you would select the table, click the Outside Borders list arrow 🔲 ▾, then click the All Borders button 🞖. The border buttons are toggle buttons, which means that you can use them to turn borders on and off. When you remove a border from a table, a gridline appears on the screen. The **gridline** is a light gray line that represents the edge of the cell, but does not print.

FIGURE D-11: Tables and Borders toolbar

Calculating Data in a Table

The Formula command allows you to perform calculations using the numbers in a table. For example, you might want to add the numbers in a row or column to display a total in your table. Word includes built-in formulas that make it easy to quickly perform standard calculations (such as totals or averages). Table D-2 describes several of these formulas. You can also enter your own formulas in a table. To do this, you refer to cells in the table using cell references. A **cell reference** identifies a cell's position in the table. Each cell reference contains a letter (A, B, C….) to identify its column and a number (1, 2, 3….) to identify its row. For example, the cell reference for the first cell in the first row of a table is A1, the second cell in the first row is B1, and so on, as shown in Figure D-12. You can create formulas to multiply, divide, add, and subtract the values of cells. When you change the numbers in a table, you can easily recalculate values associated with those numbers. Scenario▶ Karen has created a table for tracking employee attendance that includes columns for the number of vacation days allowed, taken, and remaining. To calculate each employee's remaining vacation days, she enters a formula in each cell of the Remaining column. She then edits data in the table and updates the associated calculation.

Steps

1. Open the file **WD D-1** from your Project Disk, save it with the filename **Department Attendance**, then place the insertion point in the first blank cell in the Remaining column

2. Click **Table** on the menu bar, then click **Formula**
   The Formula dialog box opens, as shown in Figure D-13. Based on the location of the insertion point, Word suggests a formula in the Formula text box—in this case, the built-in SUM formula. Word also suggests which cells to use in the calculation—in this case, the cells to the left of the selected cell. Because you do not want to add the numbers in the Allowed and Taken columns, as Word has suggested, you need to enter a new formula to calculate the remaining vacation days.

3. In the Formula text box, select **=SUM(LEFT)**, then press **[Delete]**
   You must type an equal sign, "=", to indicate that the text that follows it is a formula. You want to enter a formula that subtracts the number of vacation days taken from the number allowed.

QuickTip

Use a plus sign (+) to represent addition; a minus sign (-) for subtraction; an asterisk (*) for multiplication; and a slash (/) for division.

4. Type **=D2 – E2**, then click **OK**
   The dialog box closes and 16 appears in the current cell. This is the difference between the value in the fourth column, second row (cell D2) and the fifth column, second row (cell E2).

5. Press **[↓]**, to move the insertion point to **cell F3** (the last cell in the third row), then repeat Steps 2 through 4 using **=D3 – E3** as the formula
   The cells D3 and E3 are the third cells in the fourth and fifth columns. To calculate the other values in the Remaining column, you need to insert a similar formula in each of the empty cells.

6. Press **[↓]**, repeat Steps 2 through 4 using **=D4 – E4** as the formula, then enter the formula for each remaining cell, using **=D5 – E5** and **=D6 – E6** as the formulas

7. Select **7** in cell E6 (the last cell of the fifth column), then type **14**
   If you change a number that is part of a formula, you need to recalculate the formula.

8. Press **[Tab]** to move to the next cell, then press **[F9]**
   Pressing [F9] updates the calculation in the selected cell. "10" now appears in cell E7, as shown in Figure D-14.

9. Deselect the text, then click the **Save button** 🖫 on the Standard toolbar

FIGURE D-12: Cell references in a table

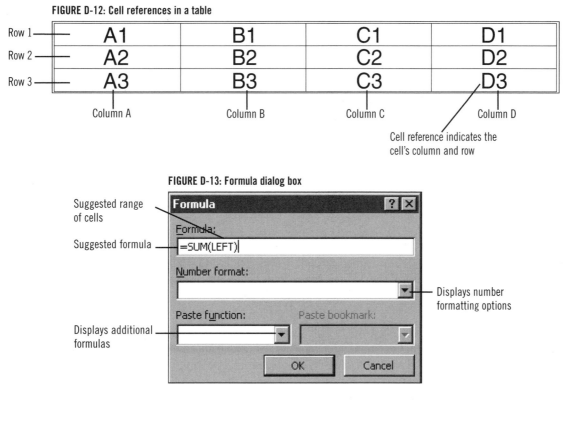

Row 1 — | A1 | B1 | C1 | D1 |
Row 2 — | A2 | B2 | C2 | D2 |
Row 3 — | A3 | B3 | C3 | D3 |

Column A   Column B   Column C   Column D

Cell reference indicates the
cell's column and row

FIGURE D-13: Formula dialog box

Suggested range of cells

Suggested formula

Formula

Formula:
=SUM(LEFT)

Number format:

Paste function: Paste bookmark:

OK   Cancel

Displays number formatting options

Displays additional formulas

FIGURE D-14: Calculated cells in a table

Department Attendance - Microsoft Word

File Edit View Insert Format Tools Table Window Help

Times New Roman ▾ 12 ▾ B I U

Last Name	First Name	Staff/Hourly	Allowed	Taken	Remaining
Rosen	Karen	Staff	24	8	16
Meister	Henry	Hourly	15	10	5
Buchanan	Tricia	Hourly	12	12	0
Ortez	Miranda	Staff	21	15	6
Williams	David	Staff	24	14	10

Updated calculation

TABLE D-2: Table functions

function	description
Average	Calculates the sum of specified cells, then divides the sum by the number of cells included in the calculation
Count	Displays the number of cells in a specified range of cells
Product	Multiplies the values in specified cells
Sum	Totals the values of cells above or to the left of the current cell

Word 2000

Sorting a Table

Sometimes information in a table is easier to interpret if the rows are **sorted**, that is, arranged in a logical order or sequence. For example, you might sort a department telephone directory by last name, or sort an employee list by date hired. To sort the rows of a table, you must first determine the column (or columns) by which you want to sort. You can sort by a single column or by multiple columns. When you sort by multiple columns, you must select primary, secondary, and sometimes tertiary sort criteria. The primary sort criterion is the first column by which you want to sort. After that, rows are sorted by the additional columns you specify. For example, if you sort an employee list first by a column that contains department names and second by a column that contains employee names, the rows with the same department name would be grouped together, and within those groups employees would be listed alphabetically. For each column, you can sort in ascending or descending order. Sorting in **ascending order** (the default) arranges rows alphabetically (from A to Z) if the sort column contains text, and from smallest to largest if the sort column contains numbers. **Descending order** is the reverse: text is arranged from Z to A and numbers from largest to smallest. Once you group rows by sorting them, you can use the Split Table command on the Table menu to divide a table in two if you wish. Scenario Karen sorts the table so that staff and hourly employees are grouped together in the list, and so that employees are listed alphabetically within those groups. She then splits the table to create separate tables for staff and hourly employees.

Steps

QuickTip

You can also click the Sort Ascending ⬆ or Sort Descending ⬇ buttons on the Tables and Borders toolbar to sort a table by the selected column.

QuickTip

You can also sort lists and paragraphs by selecting them, clicking Table on the menu bar, and then clicking Sort.

1. Place the insertion point anywhere in the table

You do not need to select the table to sort the entire table, although you do need to select specific rows if you intend to sort only part of a table.

2. Click **Table** on the menu bar, then click **Sort**

The Sort dialog box opens, as shown in Figure D-15. In this dialog box, you specify how you want your table sorted. The Sort by drop-down list includes all the columns in the table. You want to sort the table by the information in the Staff/Hourly column, the third column.

3. Click the **Sort by list arrow**, then click **Column 3**

You want the staff (which begins with "S") employees to appear before the hourly (which begins with "H") employees in your table, so you must change the sort order to descending, since "S" falls after "H" in the alphabet.

4. Click the **Descending option button** in the Sort by section

The rows will be sorted in descending order by the text in the third column. So that the employees are listed alphabetically in each group, you also have to specify the column and sort order of the second sort criterion.

5. Click the **Then by list arrow**, then click **Column 1**

Within the Staff and Hourly groups, the rows will be sorted alphabetically by the text in the first column. Your table includes a row of column headings (the first row) that you do not want included in the sort.

6. Click the **Header row option button**, click **OK**, then deselect the table

The table is sorted based first on the values in the Staff/Hourly column, and then by the values in the Last Name column, as shown in Figure D-16. The first row of the table (containing the column headings) is not included in the sort. Now that the table is sorted, you can split the table into two separate tables.

7. Place the insertion point in the **Tricia Buchanan row**, click **Table** on the menu bar, then click **Split Table**

The table is divided into two tables separated by a blank line, as shown in Figure D-17.

8. Click the **Save button** 🖫 on the Standard toolbar

FIGURE D-15: Sort dialog box

Sort
Sort by
Column 1
Type: Text
Ascending
Descending
Then by
Type: Text
Ascending
Descending
Then by
Type: Text
Ascending
Descending
My list has
Header row
No header row
OK
Cancel
Options...
Displays the type of data in the column, such as dates, numbers and text
Displays columns for sorting
Clicking this option prevents the first row from being sorted

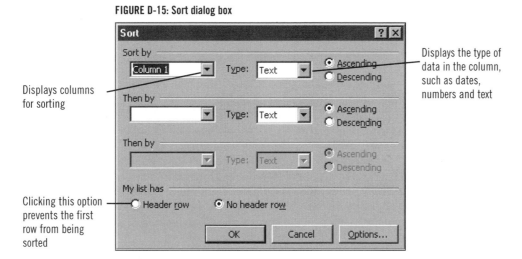

FIGURE D-16: Sorted table

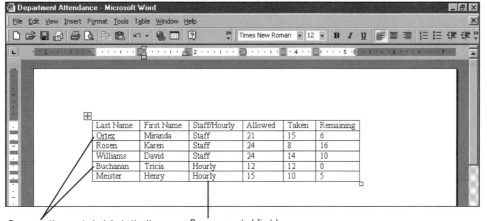

Department Attendance - Microsoft Word
Rows are then sorted alphabetically within each group
Rows are sorted first by Staff/Hourly in descending order

Last Name	First Name	Staff/Hourly	Allowed	Taken	Remaining
Ortez	Miranda	Staff	21	15	6
Rosen	Karen	Staff	24	8	16
Williams	David	Staff	24	14	10
Buchanan	Tricia	Hourly	12	12	0
Meister	Henry	Hourly	15	10	5

FIGURE D-17: Split table

Department Attendance - Microsoft Word
Splitting a table adds a blank line between the two new tables

Last Name	First Name	Staff/Hourly	Allowed	Taken	Remaining
Ortez	Miranda	Staff	21	15	6
Rosen	Karen	Staff	24	8	16
Williams	David	Staff	24	14	10

Buchanan	Tricia	Hourly	12	12	0
Meister	Henry	Hourly	15	10	5

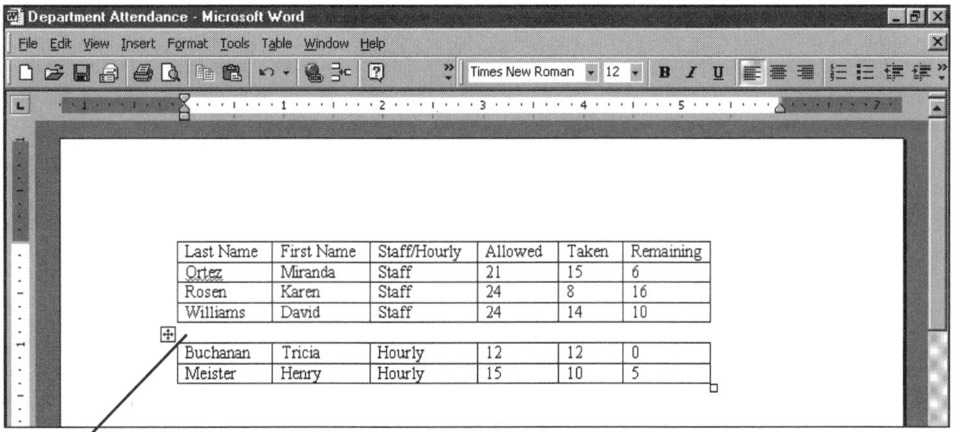

Word 2000

Drawing a Table

Sometimes you may not want your table to contain the same number of cells in each row or column. For example, you might need only one cell in the header row or an extra cell in the last column to display an important total. Word's Draw Table feature allows you to customize your tables by drawing cells exactly where you want them. `Scenario` Karen uses the Draw Table feature to create a table to help her keep track of employees' vacation days and personal days.

Steps

QuickTip

If the Office Assistant opens, click Cancel.

Trouble?

Move the Tables and Borders toolbar by clicking its title bar and dragging it if it blocks the area in which you want to work.

QuickTip

If you want to remove a line you drew in a table, click the Eraser button on the Tables and Borders toolbar, then click and drag along the line you want to erase.

1. Click the **Tables and Borders button** on the Standard toolbar
   The Tables and Borders toolbar is displayed, as shown in Figure D-17. Notice that the Draw Table button on the Tables and Borders toolbar is indented and the pointer has changed to the Pencil pointer. You use this pointer to draw a new table.

2. Click the **Down scroll arrow** until you see mostly blank space on your screen
   You'll draw a new table in this blank space in your document.

3. Place the pointer at the **left margin** near the 2" mark on the vertical ruler, click and drag down and to the right to create a cell about 4" wide and 3" high, then release the mouse button
   As you drag, dotted lines that represent the cell border appear. Use the vertical and horizontal rulers as guides for determining the size of the cell. The first cell you draw using the Pencil pointer represents the outside border of the table. Next, you'll create smaller cells within the first cell.

4. Click the **left border** of the cell about ½" below the top, drag the pointer straight across to the **right border**, then release the mouse button
   You created a row. Next you'll create a column in the table.

5. Click the **new line** about 1" from the left border of the table, drag to the **bottom border** of the table, then release the mouse button
   Compare your table with Figure D-19.

6. Keeping the top row intact, draw a line that splits the **right column** in half
   The table now has three columns in the second row. The first row is a single column. Next, you'll add more rows to the table.

7. Draw **four lines** across the **second row** to create five new rows, each about ½" high

8. Click the **Draw Table button** on the Tables and Borders toolbar to deactivate the Pencil pointer

9. Place the insertion point in the first row, type **Allowable Absences**, press **[Tab]** twice, type **Vacation Days**, press **[Tab]**, then type **Personal Days**
   Compare the structure of your table to the table shown in Figure D-20. In the next lesson you will use the Tables and Borders toolbar to modify the structure of the table and to format it.

10. Click the **Save button** on the Standard toolbar

Rotating text in a table

When a column heading is much wider than the contents of the other cells in the column, you can improve the appearance of the table by displaying the column heading vertically (rather than horizontally) in a cell. To rotate text in a cell, select the text, then click the Change Text Direction button on the Tables and Borders toolbar. Click the button once to rotate the text 90°. Click the button again to change the direction of the vertical text, or to rotate it another 180°. Click the button a third time to return the text to its horizontal position.

FIGURE D-18: Tables and Borders toolbar

Draw Table button ——

Dragging and clicking the Pencil pointer creates lines and cells in a table

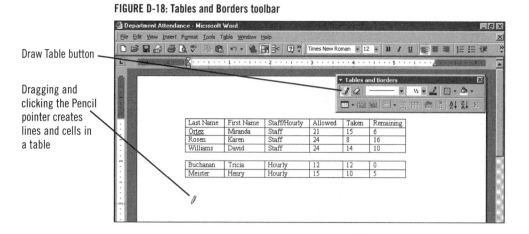

FIGURE D-19: New column

Draw a line from here...

...to here

Turns Pencil pointer on and off

Eraser button removes lines/cell boundaries

FIGURE D-20: New rows and columns in a table

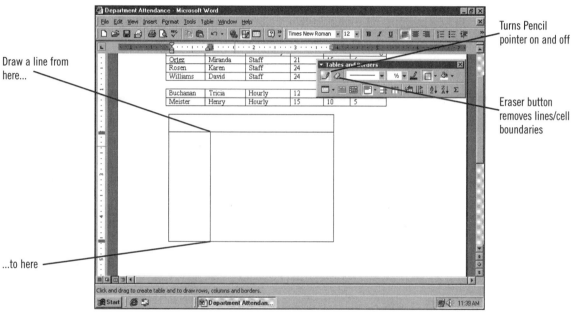

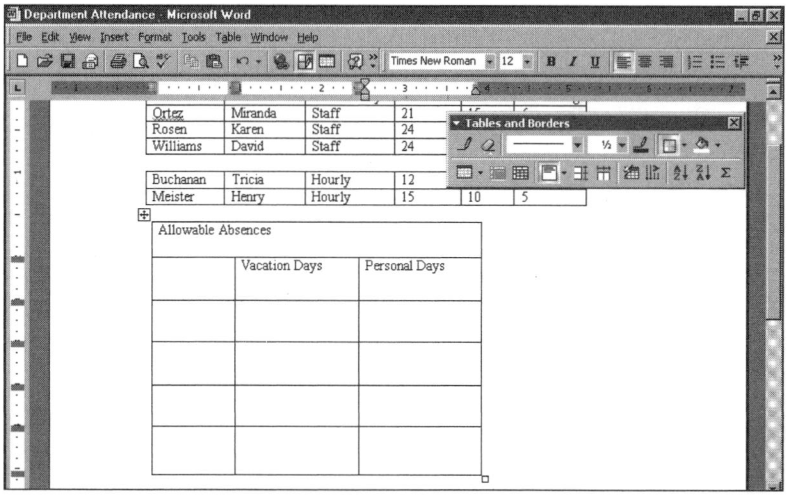

Splitting and Merging Cells

You can also use the buttons on the Tables and Borders toolbar to modify the structure of a table. In addition to adding or deleting rows and columns, you can change the structure of a table by merging or splitting cells. When you **merge cells**, you combine two or more cells to create one larger cell. When you **split cells** you divide a single cell to create two or more separate cells. Scenario To create additional columns in the table, Karen splits existing cells. She also merges two cells to create a single cell. After completing the structure of her table, she adds text, formats the table, and prints her document.

Steps

1. Select the **8 cells** below the headings in the second and third columns (cells B3 to C6), then click the **Split Cells button** on the Tables and Borders toolbar
   The Split Cells dialog box opens, as shown in Figure D-21. You can split selected cells into rows or columns or both. You'll split the two columns into four columns.

Trouble?

If the border between cells B2 and C2 is not aligned with the border between cells C3 and D3, adjust the width of the columns in the second row.

2. Make sure the Number of columns text box displays **4**, click **OK**, then deselect the cells
   The columns are evenly divided into four smaller columns, as shown in Figure D-22.

3. Type **Earned** in cell B3, press **[Tab]**, type **Taken**, press **[Tab]**, type **Earned**, press **[Tab]**, then type **Taken**

4. Click the **Table Select icon** at the upper-left corner of the table to select the table, then click the **Distribute Rows Evenly button** on the Tables and Borders toolbar
   The rows are now all the same height. You can merge cells that you want to combine.

QuickTip

You can also click Table on the menu bar, then click Merge Cells to combine cells, or click Split Cells to divide cells.

5. Deselect the table, select **cells A2** and **A3** (the first two blank cells in the first column), click the **Merge Cells button** on the Tables and Border toolbar, then type **Name**
   The two cells merge to become one cell.

6. Press **[↓]**, type **Miranda Ortez**, press **[↓]**, type **Karen Rosen**, press **[↓]**, then type **David Williams**

7. Select the entire table, click the **Align Top Left list arrow** on the Tables and Borders toolbar, click the **Align Center Left button**, then click in the table
   The text in each cell is left-aligned, but centered vertically.

8. Click the **Table AutoFormat button** on the Tables and Borders toolbar, scroll to the bottom of the Formats list in the Table AutoFormat dialog box, click **Elegant**, then click **OK**
   Compare your table to Figure D-23.

9. Close the Tables and Borders toolbar, type your name at the bottom of the document, click the **Save button** on the Standard toolbar, then click the **Print button** on the Standard toolbar

10. Click **File** on the menu bar, then click **Exit**

FIGURE D-21: Split Cells dialog box

Split Cells button

Merge Cells button

Alignment list arrow

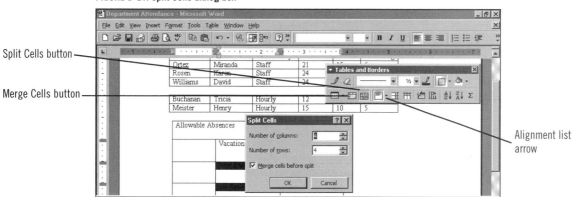

FIGURE D-22: Split cells in a table

Table Select icon

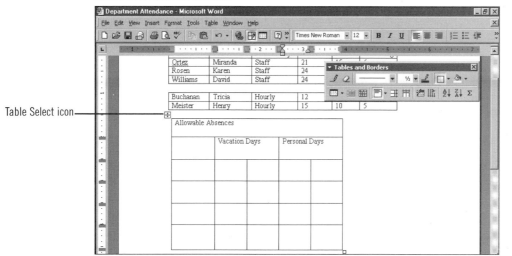

FIGURE D-23: Completed table

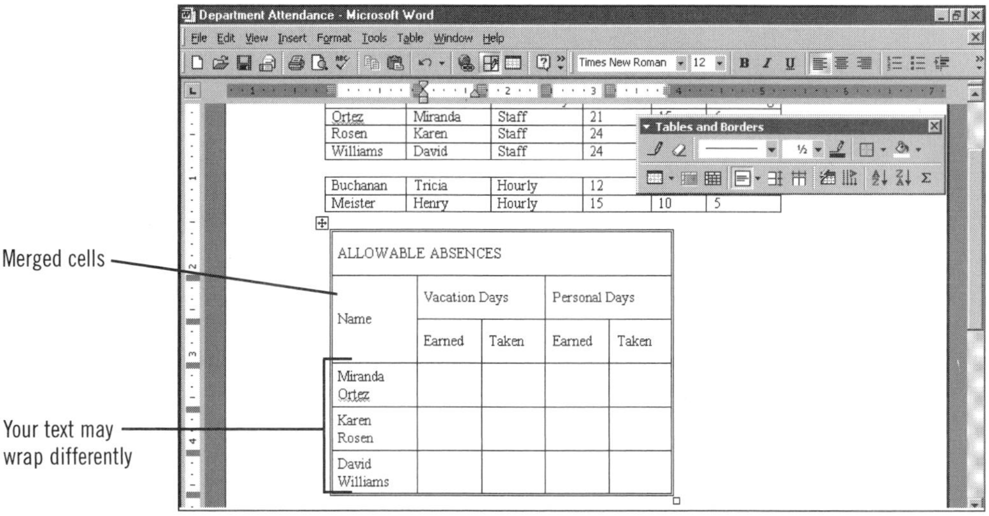

Merged cells

Your text may wrap differently

Practice

► Concepts Review

Label each element of the toolbar shown in Figure D-24.

FIGURE D-24

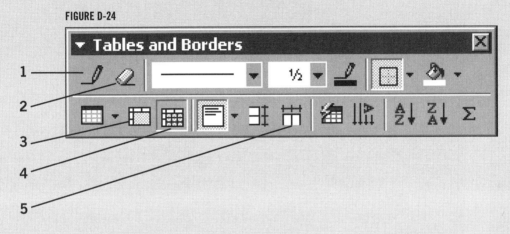

Match each term with the statement that describes it.

6. Gridline
7. Table AutoFormat
8. B3
9. Cell
10. Descending order
11. Ascending order

a. A cell reference
b. Adds borders and shading to tables
c. A non-printing cell boundary
d. Organizes text from Z to A
e. Organizes text from A to Z
f. The intersection of a row and a column

Select the best answer from the list of choices.

12. Which of the following is NOT a way to create a table in Word?
    a. Click Table on the menu bar, then click Table AutoFormat
    b. Click the Insert Table button and drag to select the number of rows and columns you want
    c. Click the Tables and Borders button, then drag the Pencil pointer
    d. Select tabbed text and click the Insert Table button

13. Which statement best describes the commands on the pop-up menu that displays when you right-click a table?
    a. The pop-up menu contains the command you use to insert calculations in a table
    b. The pop-up menu contains the commands you are likely to use most often when working in a table
    c. The pop-up menu contains Table AutoFormat commands you can use to design a table
    d. The pop-up menu contains only the commands found on the Table menu

14. **Which statement best describes how to delete only the text inside a row?**
    a. Select the row, then press [Shift][Delete]
    b. With the insertion point in the row, click Table on the menu bar, click Delete Cells, then click Delete Entire Row
    c. Select the row, then click the Cut button
    d. Select the row, then press [Delete]

15. **To break a table into two separate tables, you**
    a. Create a new blank table below the table you want to separate, move the text to the new table, then delete the blank rows from the first table.
    b. Click the Split Cells button.
    c. Click Table on the menu bar, then click Split Table.
    d. Insert a new row and erase its borders.

16. **To add a new blank row to the bottom of a table, you**
    a. Place the insertion point in the last row, then press [Shift] [↓].
    b. Select the last row, click Table on the menu bar, then click Split Cells.
    c. Place the insertion point in the last cell of the last row, then press [Tab].
    d. Place the insertion point in the last row, click Table on the menu bar, click Insert, then click Rows Above.

17. **Which of the following does NOT adjust the width of a column?**
    a. Specifying a column width on the Column tab in the Table Properties dialog box
    b. Clicking the Right Border button
    c. Dragging a column border
    d. Double-clicking the right border of a column

18. **Which of the following is NOT true of the Table AutoFormat command?**
    a. You can sort by column or row
    b. You can apply special formatting to the last row
    c. You can see an example of the format in the Table AutoFormat dialog box
    d. You can apply special formatting to the last column

19. **Which of the following is a valid cell reference for the first cell in the third column?**
    a. 3A   c. 1C
    b. A3   d. C1

20. **Which of the following is NOT true about sorting rows in a table?**
    a. You can choose the order in which you want rows sorted
    b. You can sort a table by more than one column
    c. You can specify not to sort the header row
    d. The Sort command always sorts all the rows in a table

► Skills Review

1. Create a table.

a. Start Word, type your name at the top of the new document, then press [Enter] twice.

b. Use the Insert Table button to create a table that contains 4 rows and 3 columns.

c. Enter the following text in the table:

N	New	Create a new document
O	Open	Open a document
D	Delete	Clear selected text
S	Save	Save a document

d. Add two new rows to the bottom of the table and enter the following text:

Y	Repeat	Redo the last action
Z	Undo	Undo the last action

e. Save the document as "Quick Reference" to your Project Disk.

2. Adjust table rows and columns

a. Adjust the width of the first two columns to fit the text.

b. Drag the right border of the last column to the 2½" inch mark on the horizontal ruler.

c. Select the entire table, and distribute the rows evenly.

d. Center the table on the page, then save your changes to the table.

3. Add and delete rows and columns.

a. Add a new row to the bottom of the table.

b. Type "P," press [Tab], type "Print," press [Tab], then type "Print the current document."

c. Delete the third row of the table.

d. Move the last row so that it becomes the fourth row.

e. Insert a new column between the first and second columns.

f. With the first row selected, insert a new first row at the top of the table.

g. In the first cell of the new row, type "CTRL+," press [Tab], type "Menu," press [Tab], type "Command," press [Tab], then type "To do this."

h. In the new second column, type "File" in the first four cells in the Menu column.

i. Type "Edit" in the remaining cells in the Menu column.

j. Save your changes to the table.

4. Format a table.

a. Display the Tables and Borders toolbar. (*Hint*: Click the Tables and Borders button on the Standard toolbar.)

b. Format the table in the Grid 3 preset format.

c. Change the shade color of the first row to Lavender. (*Hint*: Use the Shading Color list arrow on the Tables and Borders toolbar.)

d. Format the text in the top row in bold.

e. Add inside horizontal borders to the table. (*Hint*: Select the table, click the Outside Borders list arrow, then click the Inside Horizontal Border button.)

f. Center the text in the first 3 columns of the table.

g. Save and print the table, then close the document.

5. **Calculate data in a table.**
   a. Open the file WD D-2 from your Project Disk and save it as "Travel Details."
   b. Type your name at the top of the document, then press [Enter] twice.
   c. In the second cell in the Expense Total column, enter a formula that calculates the sum of the values of the cells to the left. In the Formula dialog box, click the Number format list arrow, then click 0.00.
   d. Repeat Step 5c for the remaining cells in the Expense Total column.
   e. Replace the Transportation value in the January column with "122.00".
   f. Update the transportation calculation in the Expense Total column.
   g. Save your changes.

6. **Sort a table.**
   a. Sort the table in descending order by the values in the Expense Total column.
   b. Sort the table alphabetically by the Expenses column, making sure not to include the heading row in the sort.
   c. Apply the Classic 2 preset format, then save your changes.

7. **Draw a table.**
   a. Insert several blank lines under the Travel Details table, then use the Pencil pointer to draw a cell 2" high and 3" wide.
   b. Draw three lines to create four rows each about ½" high, within the outside border of the new table.
   c. Add a vertical line to divide the four rows into two columns.
   d. Enter the following text in the table:
      Agenda
      8:30   Opening Ceremonies
      10:00
      12:00   Group Luncheon
   e. Save your changes.

8. **Split and merge cells.**
   a. Split the empty cell in the third row into two columns, then enter the following in the two new cells: Meeting A for Advisors; Meeting B for Committee Members.
   b. Merge the cells in the first row.
   c. Adjust the width of the first column so that it is about ½" wide.
   d. Adjust the width of the second and third columns in the third row so that they are about the same size.
   e. Center the text vertically and horizontally within each cell. (*Hint*: Use the Tables and Borders toolbar to align the text.)
   f. Change the direction of the times listed in the first column, so that the text is vertically aligned from bottom to top.
   g. Format the table using the Colorful 2 preset format, then center the table on the page.
   h. Save, print, close the document, and exit Word.

▶ Visual Workshop

Create the table shown in Figure D-25 and save it as "Activity Prices" on your Project Disk. Be sure to align the text and the table as shown in the figure. (*Hint*: Make each row ½" high and use the List 7 preset format.)

FIGURE D-25

Your Name
Extreme Fitness

Activity	Price	Sales	Total
Aerobic Classes	$15.00	89	$1335.00
Basketball	$7.00	152	$1064.00
Racquetball	$10.00	214	$2140.00
Swimming	$10.00	345	$3450.00
Total for 2000		800	$7989.00

Formatting

Pages

Objectives

- ▶ **Change document margins**
- ▶ **Create headers and footers**
- ▶ **Modify headers and footers**
- ▶ **Insert page numbers**
- ▶ **Insert page breaks**
- ▶ **Create sections**
- ▶ **Create columns**
- ▶ **Balance columns**

In addition to formatting text and paragraphs, you can format the pages of your documents. Page formatting includes determining the size and orientation of the paper as well as setting the document margins. In a multiple page document you can also create headers and footers, add page numbers, insert breaks to control the flow of text, and arrange text in columns. **Scenario** Alice Wegman is the marketing manager at MediaLoft. Alice knows that people who belong to book groups tend to buy a lot of books. Alice wants to interest MediaLoft customers in reading and buying more books, so she creates a newsletter promoting book groups that she intends to distribute in MediaLoft stores. She uses Word's page formatting features to make her newsletter attractive and easy to read.

Changing Document Margins

In a document, the blank area between the edge of the text and the edge of a page is called the **margin**. When you create a new document, it contains preset default margins. You can adjust a document's margins to change the appearance of the document or to manipulate the amount of text on a page. To adjust margins, you can change the settings on the Margins tab of the Page Setup dialog box, or you can use the rulers. Scenario➤ Alice plans for her newsletter to be a four-page document. She has already written and edited the text and completed most of the font formatting. Now she needs to format the pages. She begins by opening the document and changing the default margins.

Steps 1 2 3 4

1. Start **Word**, open the file **WD E-1** from your Project Disk, then save it as **Book News**
The file opens in Print Layout view, which displays the text as it will appear on a printed page.

2. Click **File** on the menu bar, click **Page Setup**, then click the **Margins tab** if necessary
The Page Setup dialog box opens, as shown in Figure E-1. You can use this dialog box to set the document margins, to change the paper size and orientation of your document, to change the paper source on your printer, and to set other page layout options. You want to change the size of all four document margins.

3. Click the **Top down arrow** three times until .7" appears, then click the **Bottom down arrow** three times until .7" appears
Notice that the margins change in the Preview area of the Page Setup dialog box.

4. Click the **Left down arrow** until .7" appears, then click the **Right down arrow** until .7" appears
On the Margins tab, you can choose to add a **gutter** to your document to allow extra space for a binding at the top or on the left side of a page. You can also create facing pages. **Facing pages** are the left and right pages of a double-sided document, such as a book or a magazine. Documents with facing pages have **mirror margins**—inside and outside margins that are a mirror image of each other—rather than left and right margins. For this brief newsletter, you'll use left and right margin settings.

5. Click **OK**
All four document margins change to .7".

6. Click the **Print Preview button** 🔍 on the Standard toolbar, then click the **One Page button** ▣ on the Print Preview toolbar if necessary
The first page appears in Print Preview. Note that you can also change a document's margins in Print Preview (or in Print Layout view) by dragging the edges of the rulers. You want to see the new margin settings applied to the whole document.

7. Click the **Multiple Pages button** ▦ on the Print Preview toolbar, select **2x3 Pages** (third box in the bottom row) on the grid that appears, then click
Six pages of the document display in the Print Preview window.

8. Click ▦, select **1x2 Pages** (second box in the top row), then click
The first two pages of the document appear side by side in Print Preview, as shown in Figure E-2. You can scroll down to see the other pages of the document.

9. Scroll to see the other pages in the document, click **Close** on the Print Preview toolbar, then click the **Save button** 💾 on the Standard toolbar

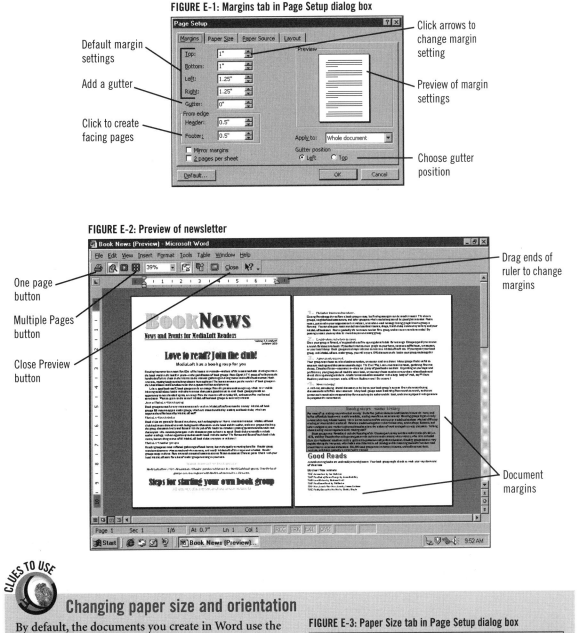

FIGURE E-1: Margins tab in Page Setup dialog box

Default margin settings

Add a gutter

Click to create facing pages

Click arrows to change margin setting

Preview of margin settings

Choose gutter position

FIGURE E-2: Preview of newsletter

One page button

Multiple Pages button

Close Preview button

Drag ends of ruler to change margins

Document margins

Changing paper size and orientation

By default, the documents you create in Word use the standard 8 ½ x 11" paper size with a portrait orientation. **Portrait** orientation means that a page is taller than it is wide. Using the Paper Size tab in the Page Setup dialog box shown in Figure E-3, you can change the orientation of a page to **landscape**, so that it is wider than it is tall. On this tab you can also select a different paper size, such as legal or envelope, or you can create a custom paper size. To change the page orientation, click the option button for the orientation that you want, portrait or landscape. To change the paper size, select a predefined paper size or type custom measurements.

FIGURE E-3: Paper Size tab in Page Setup dialog box

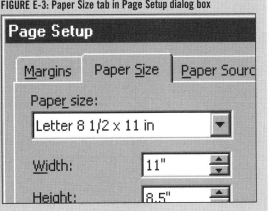

Creating Headers and Footers

In multiple page documents, the top or bottom of every page typically contains information, such as a page number, title, author's name, or graphic element, that appears on every page. A **header** is text that appears at the top of every page of a document. A **footer** is text that appears at the bottom of every page. You create headers and footers by opening the headers and footers areas from the View menu and then inserting text or graphics in the header or footer area. **Scenario** Alice adds a footer that includes text and a border to her newsletter.

1. Click **View** on the menu bar, then click **Header and Footer**

The Header area opens and the document text is dimmed, as shown in Figure E-4. The Header and Footer toolbar also opens. The Header and Footer toolbar includes buttons for inserting standard text into headers and footers and for navigating between headers and footers in a document. In a later lesson you'll add a page number to the header, but first you want to create a footer for the newsletter.

2. Click the **Switch Between Header and Footer button** 🖹 on the Header and Footer toolbar

The insertion point moves to the Footer area. Any text or formatting you add to the Footer area will appear at the bottom of every page in your document.

3. Type **Books Music Videos Cafe**, then press **[Spacebar]**

Pressing [Spacebar] adds an accent to "Café". You can format text in headers and footers just as you would format text in the document.

4. Select **Books Music Videos Café**, click the **Font list arrow** on the Formatting toolbar, click **Arial**, click the **Font Size list arrow**, click **14**, click the **Bold button** 🅱, then click the **Center button**

The text in the Footer area is centered. You can also use the tab stops displayed on the ruler for the Header and Footer areas to align text. A center tab stop and a right tab stop for Header and Footer areas are set by default. If you change the margins in a document, you need to adjust the tab stops in the Header and Footer areas to match the new margin settings. Next you want to add a border that will set your footer off from the rest of the text.

5. Click the footer text to deselect it, click **Format** on the menu bar, click **Borders and Shading**, click the **Borders tab** if necessary, click the **Custom box** in the Setting area, make sure the **top line** is selected in the Style list, make sure the color is set to **Automatic**, click the **Width list arrow**, click the **1 ½ pt line**, click the **Top border button** in the Preview area, make sure **Paragraph** is selected in the Apply to list box, compare your dialog box to Figure E-5, then click **OK**

A thin line spans the top of the footer.

6. Click **Close** on the Header and Footer toolbar, then scroll to the bottom of page 1

Closing the Header and Footer toolbar closes the Header and Footer areas. The footer you created appears at the bottom of the page, as shown in Figure E-6. The footer text is dimmed.

7. Click the **Print Preview button** 🔍 on the Standard toolbar, then scroll down to see the footer at the bottom of every page

8. Click **Close** on the Print Preview toolbar, then save your changes

FIGURE E-4: Header area

Your toolbars may differ

Header area is open

Document is dimmed and cannot be edited

Tab stops for header are set for default document margins

Header and Footer toolbar

Switch Between Header and Footer button

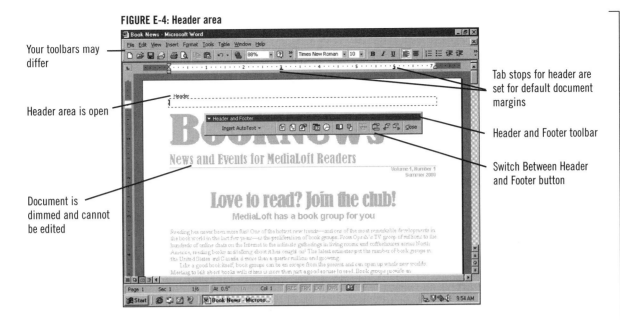

FIGURE E-5: Borders and Shading dialog box

Top border button

Border applied to whole paragraph

Top border only should be present

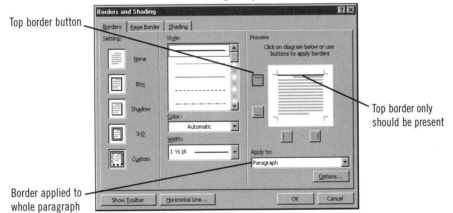

FIGURE E-6: Footer in the document

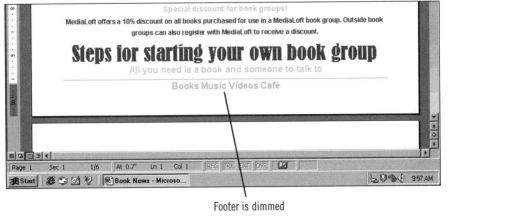

Footer is dimmed

Word 2000

Modifying Headers and Footers

If you want to change the text or formatting in a header or footer, you must first open the Header and Footer areas. You can use the Header and Footer command on the View menu to open headers and footers, or, when you are working in Print Layout view, you can double-click the area you want to edit. **Scenario** Alice decides the footer would look better if it included a graphic element between the words. She inserts a small circle symbol between the words in the footer to give the newsletter more style.

Steps

QuickTip

To specify the distance of the header or footer from the edge of the page, change the Header and Footer settings on the Margins tab in the Page Setup dialog box.

1. Position the ⌖ pointer over the footer at the bottom of the first page, then double-click
The Footer area opens. You can now edit the footer.

2. Place the insertion point between Books and Music in the Footer area, click Insert on the menu bar, then click Symbol
The Symbol dialog box opens, as shown in Figure E-7. In addition to keyboard characters, many fonts include symbols. You can click the Font list arrow in the Symbol dialog box to see the fonts on your computer that include symbols. **Symbols** are special characters, such as bullets, foreign language characters, and simple graphics that you can insert into a document. A trademark symbol ™, a function symbol f, and a paragraph mark ¶ are just a few examples of the kinds of symbols you can add.

QuickTip

When you click a symbol, it enlarges so you can see it better.

3. Make sure Symbol appears in the Font list box, then click the circle symbol, then click Insert
The circle symbol is added to the footer between "Books" and "Music".

QuickTip

Be sure to click two times slowly. Do not double-click.

4. Click two times between Music and Videos in the footer, click Insert, click two times between and Videos and Café, then click Insert

5. Click Close in the Symbol dialog box, then use the [Spacebar] to add a space before or after each symbol as needed, so that there is a single space between each side of the symbol and the words
Compare your document with Figure E-8.

6. Click Close on the Header and Footer toolbar, scroll to the bottom of the page to see your changes to the footer, then save your changes

Creating headers and footers for specific pages

Sometimes you will not want headers and footers to appear on the first page of a document, for example, a title page. Alternatively, you may want to include different information in the header or footer for the first page. Sometimes you will also want to create different headers and footers for facing pages. For example, if you were formatting the pages of a book, you might want the title of the book to appear at the top of every left (or even-numbered) page, and the title of the current chapter to appear at the top of every right (or odd-numbered) page. You can easily create different odd and even or different first page headers and footers using the Layout tab in the Page Setup dialog box. Click File on the menu bar, click Page Setup, then click the Layout tab. On the Layout tab, select the Different odd and even check box or the Different first page check box (or both), then click OK. When you open headers and footers, you will have different header and footer areas for each option you selected (for example, a First Page header area, an Odd Page header area, and an Even Page header area). You must enter text in each area where you want a header or footer to appear. You can use the Show Previous, Show Next, and Switch Between Header and Footer buttons on the Header and Footer toolbar to navigate between the different header and footer areas in your document.

FIGURE E-7: Symbol dialog box

Special Characters tab contains typographical characters

Symbols for selected font

Click to select a different font

Circle symbol

Click to insert selected symbol at insertion point

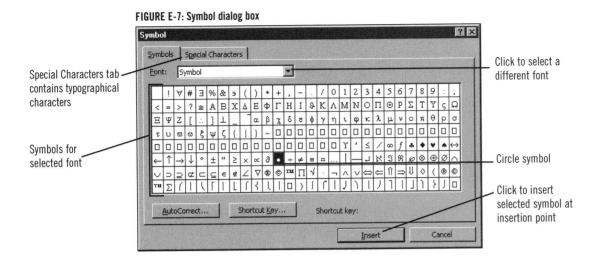

FIGURE E-8: Symbols added to footer

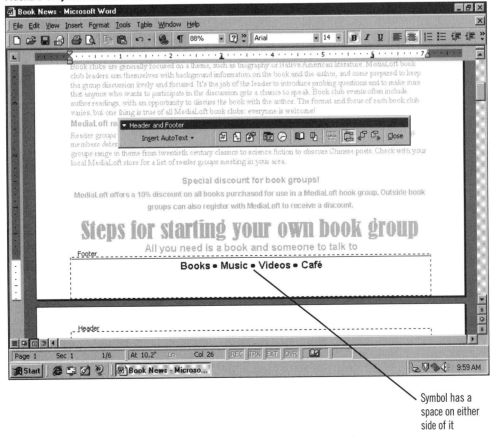

Symbol has a space on either side of it

Inserting Page Numbers

You can add page numbers to your documents by inserting a page number field in the header or footer. A **field** is an instruction or code that serves as a placeholder for information that changes, such as a page number. When you insert page numbers in a document, Word automatically numbers each page for you. You can use the Page Numbers command on the Insert menu to add a page number field to a header or footer automatically, or you can open headers and footers and then use the buttons on the Header and Footer toolbar to insert page numbers. Using the Page Numbers command, you can also change the number format of your page numbers (for example, to Roman numerals), and you can start your page numbering with a number other than 1. Scenario Alice wants to include a page number at the top of every page of her newsletter except the first page. She uses the Page Numbers command on the Insert menu to add page numbers to her newsletter.

Steps

1. Press **[Ctrl][Home]**, click **Insert** on the menu bar, then click **Page Numbers**
   The Page Numbers dialog box opens, as shown in Figure E-9. You can use the options in the Page Numbers dialog box to specify the position and the alignment of page numbers in the document. You want to add page numbers to the header.

QuickTip

To change or modify the number format of your page numbers, or to start numbering your document with a number other than 1, click Format in the Page Numbers dialog box, or click the Format Page Number button on the Header and Footer toolbar, then select from the options in the Page Number Format dialog box.

2. Click the **Position list arrow**, then click **Top of Page (Header)**
   The Preview box shows the page number right-aligned in the upper-right corner of the page. Because the finished newsletter will be folded so that pages 2 and 3 appear next to each other, you want the page numbers to be located on the outside edges of each page in the document.

3. Click the **Alignment list arrow**, then click **Outside**
   The Preview box shows two pages, each with a page number in the outside corner at the top. Since the masthead for the newsletter is at the top of the first page, you don't want the page number to appear on the first page.

4. Click the **Show number on first page check box** to deselect it, then click **OK**

5. Scroll down to see the top of page 2
   The number "2" appears in the header at the top of page 2, as shown in Figure E-10.

6. Click the **Print Preview button** on the Standard toolbar
   The first two pages of the document appear in the Print Preview window. Notice that there is no page number on the first page and that the footer is also gone. When you deselect the Show number on first page check box in the Page Numbers dialog box, Word creates a different header and footer for the first page. The header and footer on the first page remain blank until you enter text in the First Page header and/or footer areas. You still want the footer to appear on the first page.

QuickTip

To remove page numbers from a document, open headers and footers, then delete the page number field.

7. Click **Close** on the Print Preview toolbar, scroll to the bottom of page 2, double-click the **footer** to open the Footer area, use the selection bar to select **Books • Music • Videos • Café**, then click the **Copy button** on the Standard toolbar
   The footer text is copied to the Clipboard.

8. Scroll up to the bottom of page 1, click in the **First Page Footer area**, click the **Paste button** on the Standard toolbar, then press **[Delete]** to remove the extra paragraph that was added
   The text is copied to the footer for the first page. Be sure your footer matches the one shown in Figure E-11.

9. Click **Close** on the Header and Footer toolbar, click , scroll the document to see the page numbers and footers on all pages, close Print Preview, then save your changes

FIGURE E-9: Page Numbers dialog box

Click to change alignment

Clear to hide page number on first page

Click to select header or footer location

Preview of page number position on page

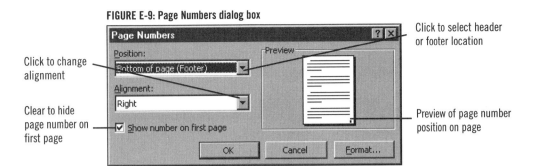

FIGURE E-10: Page number in header

Footer area on first page is empty

Page number in header

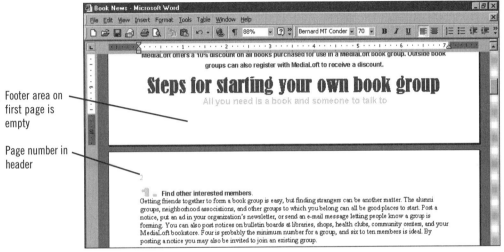

Steps for starting your own book group

All you need is a book and someone to talk to

1. Find other interested members.

Getting friends together to form a book group is easy, but finding strangers can be another matter. The alumni groups, neighborhood associations, and other groups to which you belong can all be good places to start. Post a notice, put an ad in your organization's newsletter, or send an e-mail message letting people know a group is forming. You can also post notices on bulletin boards at libraries, shops, health clubs, community centers, and your MediaLoft bookstore. Four is probably the minimum number for a group, and six to ten members is ideal. By posting a notice you may also be invited to join an existing group.

FIGURE E-11: First page footer

Text and formatting copied to first page footer

Books • Music • Videos • Café

Inserting the date and time into a document

You can easily insert the current date and time into your document in a variety of formats using the Date and Time command on the Insert menu. The date and time information is linked to your computer's clock, so the information should always be current. To add the current date or time to a document, click Insert on the menu bar, then click Date and Time. In the Date and Time dialog box, select the date and time format you want to use from the list of available formats. If you want to insert the date and time as a field that will be updated automatically when you open or print a document, select the Update automatically check box. If you want the current date and time to remain in the document as static text, clear the Update automatically check box. Click OK to insert the date and time at the location of the insertion point. You can also use the Insert Date and Insert Time buttons on the Header and Footer toolbar to insert the current date and time into a header or footer.

Inserting Page Breaks

When the amount of text in a document fills a page, Word automatically inserts a **page break**, a separator that forces text after the break to appear on the next page. As you type, Word inserts a **soft page break** when you reach the end of a page, which allows you to continue typing on the next page. You can also manually insert a page break, sometimes called a **hard page break**, into a document to force text to begin on a new page. ▶Scenario▶ Alice is planning for the finished newsletter to be four pages long. Before arranging the text on the pages, she inserts page breaks at the location she wants each page of the newsletter to begin.

Steps

QuickTip

Page breaks, section breaks, and column breaks are always visible in Normal view.

▶ **1.** Click the **Show/Hide ¶ button** ¶ on the Standard toolbar to display nonprinting characters in the document if necessary
The nonprinting paragraph, space, and tab marks appear in the document. Displaying the formatting marks embedded in the document can make it easier to insert and view some of the changes you make to a document. These marks display on the screen but do not print.

QuickTip

If the heading flows onto two lines, select the heading, then reduce the font size until the heading fits on one line.

▶ **2.** Scroll to the heading **Steps for starting your own book group**
You want this article to appear at the top of page 2 in the newsletter, so you'll insert a page break before the heading.

3. Place the insertion point in front of **Steps**, click **Insert** on the menu bar, then click **Break**
The Break dialog box opens, as shown in Figure E-12.

4. Make sure the **Page break option button** is selected, then click **OK**
Word inserts a hard page break before the heading and moves all the text after the break to the beginning of the next page, as shown in Figure E-13. The page break appears on the screen as a dotted line.

5. Scroll down to the heading **Good Reads**, then place the insertion point in front of **Good**
You want the "Good Reads" list to start at the top of a new page.

Trouble?

If pressing [Ctrl][Enter] creates more than one hard page break, press [Backspace] to delete the unwanted hard page breaks.

▶ **6.** Press and hold **[Ctrl]**, then press **[Enter]**
Pressing [Ctrl][Enter] inserts a hard page break and the "Good Reads" list moves to the next page.

7. Scroll to the end of the "Good Reads" list on page 4, place the insertion point in front of **MediaLoft Headquarters**, then press **[Ctrl][Enter]**
The text after "MediaLoft Headquarters" is forced onto the next page.

8. View the document in Print Preview, then save your changes

FIGURE E-12: Break dialog box

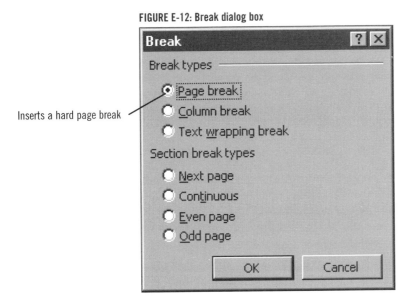

Inserts a hard page break

FIGURE E-13: Page break in document

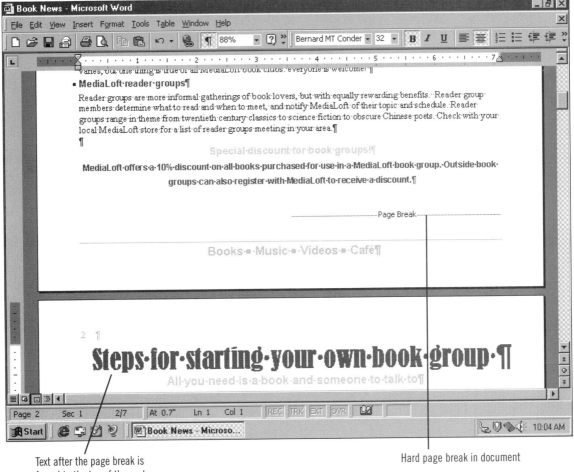

Text after the page break is forced to the top of the next page

Hard page break in document

Word 2000

Creating Sections

Each new blank document is one section by default, but you can easily divide a document into more than one section in order to apply different page layout formats to different parts of the document. A **section** is a part of a document that is separated from the rest of the document by **section breaks**. Dividing a document into sections allows you to apply different formats to individual sections of the document. Format options include margins, columns, headers and footers, page size and orientation, page numbering, and other page layout options. Scenario Alice wants to format some of the text in the newsletter in columns. She inserts section breaks to divide the document into sections so she can easily apply different formats to different sections.

Trouble?

Adjust your zoom level as necessary to complete the steps.

1. **Press [Ctrl][Home], click the Zoom list arrow on the Standard toolbar, then click 75%**
   You plan to format the "Love to Read" article in two columns, so you'll insert a section break at the top and the bottom of the article.

2. **Click in front of Reading at the beginning of the first paragraph in the "Love to Read" article, click Insert on the menu bar, then click Break**
   The Break dialog box opens. You can use this dialog box to insert section breaks. You want to insert a continuous section break to begin a new section on the same page, at the location of the insertion point.

Trouble?

If you delete a section break or a paragraph mark by mistake, click the Undo button 🔄 on the Standard toolbar. Deleting a section break or a paragraph mark changes the formatting of the section or paragraph to the formatting of the previous section or paragraph.

3. **Click the Continuous option button, then click OK**
   Word inserts a continuous section break (shown as a dotted double line) before "Reading", as shown in Figure E-14. When you insert a section break at the start of a paragraph, Word places the section break at the end of the previous paragraph. A section break stores the formatting information for the preceding section just as a paragraph mark stores formatting for the preceding paragraph. Next you want to insert another section break at the end of the article.

4. **Scroll down to the end of the article, place the insertion point in front of the paragraph mark ¶ between the article and "Special discount", click Insert on the menu bar, click Break, click the Continuous option button, then click OK**
   Word adds a continuous section break between the end of the article and the "Special discount" information. You continue to create sections because you want to apply different formats to different parts of the newsletter.

5. **Scroll to the top of page 2, place the insertion point in front of Steps, click Insert on the menu bar, click Break, click the Continuous option button, then click OK**
   Word adds a continuous section break before the "Steps" article.

6. **Scroll to the bottom of the "Steps" article, then insert a continuous section break in front of the first paragraph mark under the article**

7. **Scroll to the "Good Reads" heading at the top of page 3, click in front of Good, then insert a continuous section break, then save your changes**
   Word adds a continuous section break before the "Good Reads" list, as shown in Figure E-15. Notice that the document has six sections. You are ready to apply different formats to some sections.

FIGURE E-14: Section break in document

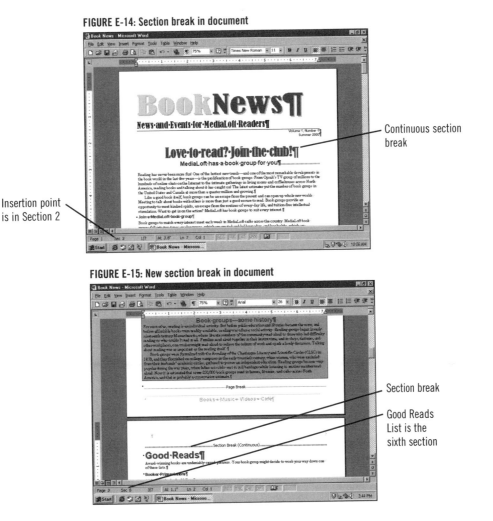

Continuous section break

Insertion point is in Section 2

FIGURE E-15: New section break in document

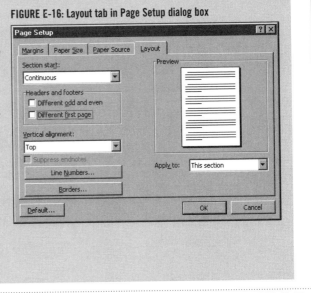

Section break

Good Reads List is the sixth section

CLUES TO USE

Aligning text vertically on a page

By default, Word vertically aligns the first paragraph of text on a page with the top margin, but you can change the vertical alignment of text to center it between the top and bottom margins, justify it between the top and bottom margins, or align it with the bottom margin. This is especially useful for pages that are not filled with text, such as the title page of a report. You can change the vertical alignment of all the text in a document, or you can change the vertical alignment of a single section. To change vertical alignment, place the insertion point in the text you want to align, click File on the menu bar, click Page Setup, then click the Layout tab in the Page Setup dialog box, as shown in Figure E-16. Click the Apply to list arrow and select the part of the document whose alignment you want to change. Then click the Vertical alignment list arrow and select the alignment you want: Top, Center, Justified, or Bottom.

FIGURE E-16: Layout tab in Page Setup dialog box

Word 2000

Creating Columns

Newspapers and magazines arrange text in columns to make it easier to read and to enable more text to fit on a page. Text that is formatted in **newspaper columns** flows from one column to the next column. In a new Word document, text is arranged in one column that spans the width of the page, but you can create any number of columns. You can apply column formatting to a section, to the whole document, or to selected text. You can create standard size columns using the Columns button on the Standard toolbar, or you can use the Columns command on the Format menu to create columns and to customize the width and appearance of columns. **Scenario** Alice formats several sections in her document in newspaper columns. She varies the number of columns between sections to highlight different articles and make the newsletter interesting to look at and read.

Steps

1. Click **Edit** on the menu bar, then click **Go To**
   The Find and Replace dialog box opens. You can use the Go To command to navigate quickly to a page, section, or other element in a document. Table E-1 describes some ways to navigate quickly through longer documents.

2. Click **Section** in the Go to what list box, type **2** in the Enter section number text box, click **Go To**, then click **Close**
   Notice that the insertion point moved to the beginning of Section 2 (the "Love to Read" article), as indicated on the status bar.

QuickTip
You can also create columns by clicking Format on the menu bar, clicking Columns, and then selecting the number of columns in the Columns dialog box.

3. Click the **Columns button** on the Standard toolbar, select **2 Columns** in the grid that appears, then click
   The section is formatted in two columns, as shown in Figure E-17.

4. Press **[Ctrl][G]** to open the Find and Replace dialog box, select **2** and type **4** in the Enter section number text box, click **Go To**, then click **Close**

5. Click , select **2 Columns** on the grid that appears, then click
   The section is formatted in two columns. You want the heading and subheading for the article to span the width of the page, so you'll change the headings to be one column.

6. Select **Steps for starting your own book group** and **All you need is a book and someone to talk to** including the paragraph marks, click , select **1 Column** in the grid that appears, click, then deselect the text
   A new section break appears after the heading, as shown in Figure E-18. Section breaks are automatically inserted wherever you apply page layout options that affect only part of a document. Next you'll format the text in Section 7.

7. Press **[Ctrl][G]**, select **4** and type **7** in the Enter section number text box, click **Go To**, click **Close**, click , select **4 Columns** in the grid that appears, then click
   The text in the section is formatted in four columns. However, the page would look better if the columns were wider, with less white space between them and divided by lines.

QuickTip
You can also change column width by dragging the column markers on the horizontal ruler.

8. With the insertion point in Section 7, click **Format** on the menu bar, then click **Columns**
   The Columns dialog box opens, as shown in Figure E-19. You can use the Columns dialog box to change the number of columns, adjust the width and spacing of columns, create columns of unequal width, and add lines between columns.

9. Click the **Equal column width check box** to select it, click the **Spacing down arrow** twice until .3 appears, click the **Line between check box** to select it, click **OK**, then save your changes
   Now the columns are wider with lines between them. All the text now fits on four pages.

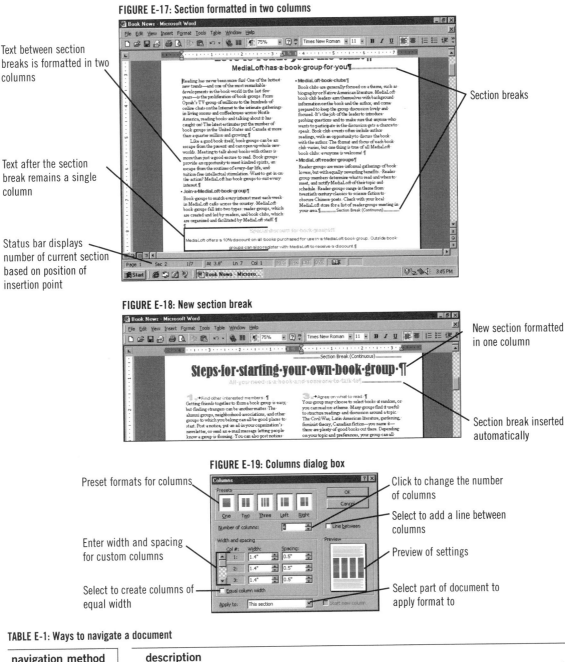

FIGURE E-17: Section formatted in two columns

Text between section breaks is formatted in two columns

Section breaks

Text after the section break remains a single column

Status bar displays number of current section based on position of insertion point

FIGURE E-18: New section break

New section formatted in one column

Section break inserted automatically

FIGURE E-19: Columns dialog box

Preset formats for columns

Click to change the number of columns

Select to add a line between columns

Enter width and spacing for custom columns

Preview of settings

Select to create columns of equal width

Select part of document to apply format to

TABLE E-1: Ways to navigate a document

navigation method	description
Go To command	Use the Go To command on the Edit menu to go to a specific item in a document, such as a page, section, line, footnote, bookmark, table, or heading
Browse by object	Click the Select Browse Object button on the vertical scroll bar to open a menu of objects by which you can browse through a document, including pages, sections, tables, graphics, and fields; click the item you want to browse by, then click the Previous Page or Next Page buttons on the scroll bar to continue browsing
Document map	Click the Document Map button on the Standard toolbar to display a list of the headings in a document in the Document Map pane; click a heading in the Document Map to jump to the corresponding heading in the document
Hyperlinks	Click a text or image hyperlink to jump to the file, Web page, or location in the same document to which the hyperlink is connected

Balancing Columns

Text that is formatted in newspaper columns wraps from the bottom of one column to the top of the next. When the text does not fill all the columns on a page, you may end up with a page that has columns of unequal length. You can balance the length of unequal columns by inserting a continuous section break at the end of the last column. Another way to control the flow of text in columns is to insert a **column break**, which forces the text after the break to move to the top of the next column. Scenario▶ Before finishing her newsletter, Alice adjusts the text flow in the columns on pages 3 and 4 by inserting continuous section breaks and column breaks to balance the columns.

Steps

1. Scroll to page 3, click the **Zoom list arrow** on the Standard toolbar, then click **Whole Page**
   The columns on page 3 are unequal in length. You can balance the columns by inserting a section break at the end of the fourth column.

Trouble?

Be sure to place the insertion point before the page break. Adjust your zoom level as necessary to complete the steps.

2. Place the insertion point at the bottom of the fourth column (click at the end of the last line of text), click **Insert** on the menu bar, click **Break**, click the **Continuous** option button, then click **OK**
   The columns on page 3 automatically adjust to become roughly the same length, and the page break moves to below the columns, as shown in Figure E-20.

3. Scroll to page 4, click the **Zoom list arrow** on the Standard toolbar, click **50%**, then place the insertion point in front of **MediaLoft Book Club Events**
   The page will look better if this text appears at the top of the next column, so you'll insert a column break.

4. Click **Insert** on the menu bar, then click **Break**
   The Break dialog box opens.

QuickTip

When a page has a column break, inserting a continuous section break will not balance the columns on that page.

5. Click the **Column break option button**, then click **OK**
   The text moves to the top of the second column and a column break appears at the bottom of the first column, as shown in Figure E-21. You have finished formatting the newsletter. Before printing, you'll view it in Print Preview.

6. Click the **Print Preview button** 📖 on the Standard toolbar
   Pages 3 and 4 display in Print Preview.

7. Scroll up to view pages 1 and 2, click **Close** on the Print Preview toolbar, press **[Ctrl][End]** to move the insertion point to the end of the document, press **[Enter]** twice, then type your name

8. Save your changes, print the document, close the document, then exit Word

CLUES TO USE

Adding hyphenation

Another way to control text flow in a document is to use hyphenation. **Hyphens** are short dashes used to break words that appear at the end of a line. Hyphenating text eliminates the gaps that often appear in justified paragraphs and reduces ragged right edges in unjustified text. You can insert hyphens manually or you can use the hyphenation feature to hyphenate a document quickly and automatically. To hyphenate a document automatically, click Tools on the menu bar, point to Language, then click Hyphenation. In the Hyphenation dialog box, select the Automatically hyphenate document check box, then set a value in the Hyphenation zone. This zone is the distance between the margin and the end of the last word in a line. The narrower the hyphenation zone, the greater the number of hyphenated words. Click OK to turn on automatic hyphenation.

FIGURE E-20: Balanced columns

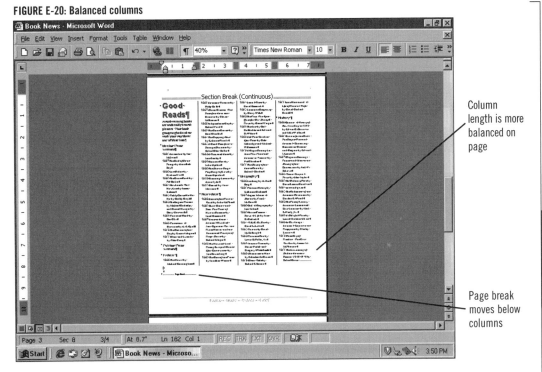

Column length is more balanced on page

Page break moves below columns

FIGURE E-21: Column break

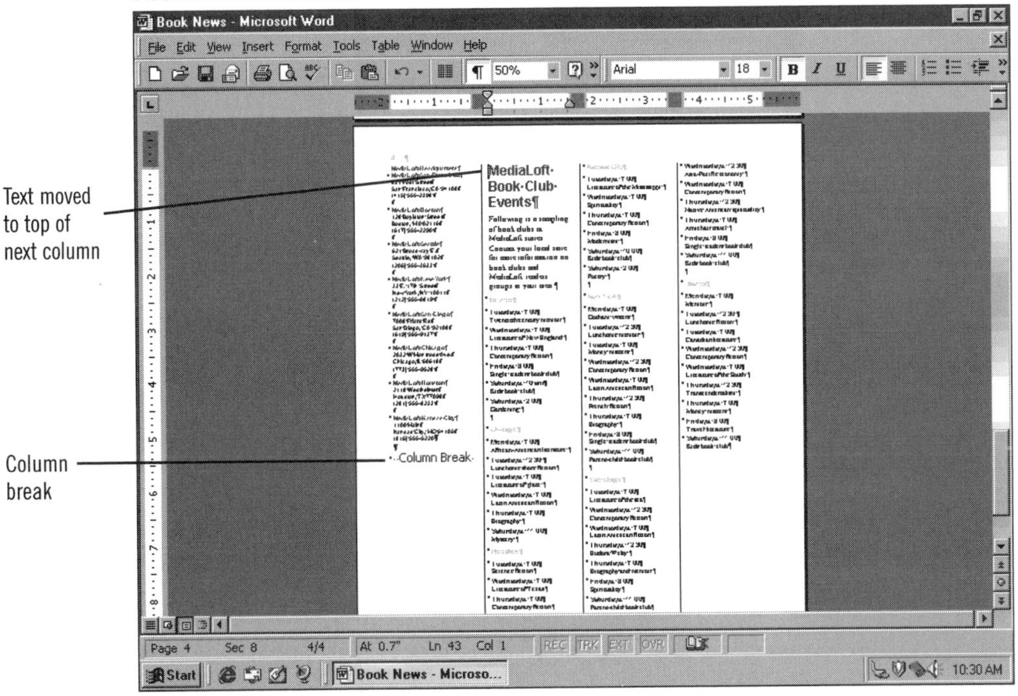

Text moved to top of next column

Column break

Practice

► Concepts Review

Label each element shown in Figure E-22.

FIGURE E-22

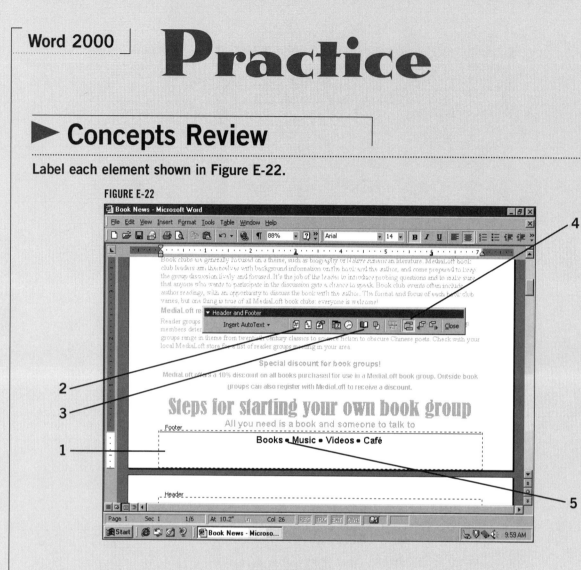

Match each term with the statement that describes it.

6. Footer
7. Header
8. Portrait orientation
9. Section
10. Margin
11. Landscape orientation

a. A part of a document that can be formatted differently (such as in columns) from the rest of the document
b. The white space between the edge of the text and the edge of the page
c. A page that is wider than it is tall
d. Text that appears at the top of every page in a document
e. Text that appears at the bottom of every page in a document
f. A page that is taller than it is wide

Select the best answer from the list of choices.

12. Which of the following options is not available in the Page Setup dialog box?
    a. Select the page orientation
    b. Adjust the tab settings for a header and footer
    c. Add a gutter
    d. Adjust the margins for the top, bottom, left, and right edges of a document

13. **When you decrease the size of all margins in a document**
    a. You change the orientation of the paper.
    b. You decrease the amount of text that will fit on the page.
    c. The amount of text that will fit on the page does not change.
    d. You increase the amount of text that will fit on the page

14. **Which of the following is not true about headers and footers?**
    a. You can edit document text while you are working in headers and footers
    b. You can insert fields in a header or footer
    c. You can create a different header or footer for the first page
    d. Clicking View and then clicking Header and Footer displays the Header and Footer toolbar

15. **The easiest way to balance column length on a page is to**
    a. Insert a continuous section break at the end of the page.
    b. Insert column breaks.
    c. Adjust the spacing between columns.
    d. Change the number of columns on the page.

16. **Pressing [Ctrl][Enter] inserts a**
    a. Column break.
    b. Hard page break.
    c. Continuous section break.
    d. Soft page break.

17. **To open headers and footers you**
    a. Click the Show Next button on the Header and Footer toolbar.
    b. Double-click one of the headers or footers.
    c. Click the Show Previous button on the Header and Footer toolbar.
    d. Click the Switch Between Header and Footer button on the Header and Footer toolbar.

18. **A document with mirror margins always has**
    a. A gutter.
    b. Right and left margins.
    c. Outside and inside margins.
    d. An even number of pages.

19. **Which of the following is not a way to insert page numbers in a header or footer?**
    a. Click Insert on the menu bar, then click Page Numbers
    b. Click the Insert Page Number button on the Header and Footer toolbar
    c. Click Page X of Y on the Insert AutoText menu
    d. Click the Numbering button on the Formatting toolbar

20. **To create a document that is 8½ inches high and 11 inches wide**
    a. Change the width and height settings on the Paper Size tab in the Page Setup dialog box.
    b. Adjust the document margins on the Margins tab in the Page Setup dialog box.
    c. Change the vertical alignment on the Layout tab in the Page Setup dialog box.
    d. Select landscape orientation on the Paper Size tab in the Page Setup dialog box.

► Skills Review

1. Change document margins.
a. Start Word and open the document WD E-2 from your Project Disk. Save the document as "Mountain Travel".
b. Change the document margins to the following settings:

Top   1.3"
Bottom   1.3"
Left   1"
Right   1"

c. View all four pages of the document in Print Preview, then return to Print Layout view.

2. Create headers and footers.
a. Open headers and footers.
b. On the horizontal ruler, drag the right tab stop to align with the right margin at the 6½" mark. Drag the center tab stop to the 3 ¼" mark.
c. In the header, type "Mountain Travel Executive Summary", click before the text, then press [Tab].
d. Format the header text in 11 point Arial, then bold the text.
e. Add a 1 pt. black border under the header text, making sure to apply the border to the paragraph.
f. Switch to the footer, then adjust the tab stops in the footer to correspond with the new margins you created in Step 1.
g. Press [Tab] twice, then insert today's date using the Date and Time command on the Insert menu. Select any date format you like, and deselect the Update automatically check box in the Date and Time dialog box if necessary.
h. Close headers and footers, then view the document in Print Preview.

3. Modify headers and footers.
a. Double-click the header to open the Header area.
b. Click between "Travel" and "Executive" in the header, then use the Symbol command on the Insert menu to open the Symbol dialog box.
c. Click the Font list arrow and select the Almanac MT font.
d. In the second row, click the Sun symbol (12th from the left), then click Insert. (*Hint*: If the Almanac MT font is not installed on your computer, insert a symbol of your choice.)
e. Close the Symbol dialog box. Add a space before and after the symbol as needed.
f. Select the symbol in the header and change the font size to 36.

4. Insert page numbers.
a. Switch to the Footer area.
b. Click the Format Page Number button on the Headers and Footers toolbar, change the number format to lower-case Roman numerals, then click OK.
c. Click the Insert Page Number button on the Header and Footer toolbar.
d. Close headers and footers.
e. View the page numbers in Print Preview.

5. Insert page breaks.
a. Use the Go To command to navigate to the top of page 3.
b. Scroll up, then insert a page break before the heading "Communications".

6. Create sections.
a. Use the Go To command to navigate to the top of page 1.
b. On the first page, insert a next page section break before "Finance".

c. Click inside the first section, then change the vertical alignment of the first section to center. (*Hint*: Use the Layout tab in the Page Setup dialog box.)

7. Create columns.

a. Click in Section 2.

b. Using the Columns button, format Section 2 in two columns.

c. Using the Columns command, change the spacing between the columns to .4". Make sure the new columns are of equal width.

d. Add a line between the columns.

e. View all five pages of the document in Print Preview.

8. Balance columns.

a. Hyphenate the document using the automatic hyphenation feature. (*Hint*: Click Tools on the menu bar, point to Language, then click Hyphenation.)

b. On page 3, insert a continuous section break before the page break to balance the columns.

c. Balance the columns on page 5.

d. Type your name at the bottom of the title page before the section break, then preview the document. Make any necessary adjustments so that the text flows smoothly between columns and from page to page.

e. Save your changes, print the document, then close it and exit Word.

Word 2000

► Visual Workshop

Open the file WD E-6 on your Project Disk and save it as "Miller Street". Format the file as shown in Figure E-23. (*Hint:* Set the right and left margins to 6".) Add your name to the bottom of the list of artists, save the file, then print a copy.

FIGURE E-23

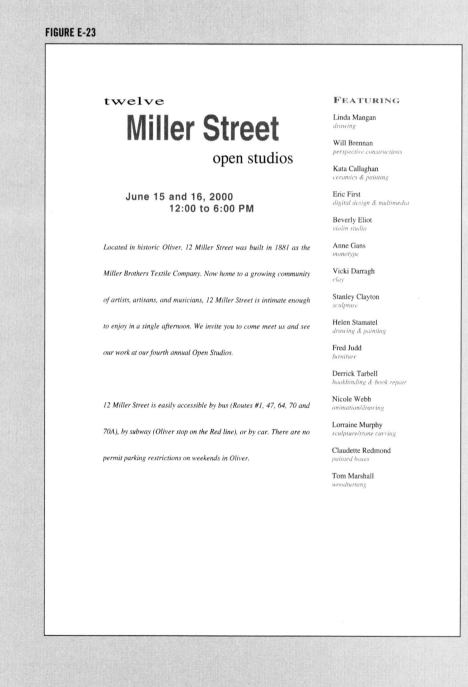

Adding

Graphics

Objectives

- MOUS ► **Insert clip art graphics**
- ► **Wrap text around graphics**
- ► **Move and resize graphics**
- MOUS ► **Insert pictures from files**
- MOUS ► **Draw AutoShapes**
- MOUS ► **Insert text boxes**
- MOUS ► **Draw lines**
- MOUS ► **Create WordArt**
- MOUS ► **Use Click and Type**

By adding graphics to a document you can create dramatic effects. Graphics can illustrate a point, break up the monotony of large blocks of text, and make your documents visually interesting. Word provides many built-in graphic images, called clip art, that you can add to your documents. You can also insert graphics that are created in other programs. You can also use the drawing feature in Word to create your own graphics. Scenario➤ The marketing department at MediaLoft sponsors a variety of in-store events to encourage customers to visit MediaLoft and browse. Alice Wegman needs to create several flyers to advertise upcoming events at the San Francisco store. She uses clip art and Word's drawing features to make her flyers colorful and appealing.

Word 2000

Inserting Clip Art

Adding clip art to your documents is a fun way to illustrate your ideas and create documents that have a powerful effect. **Clip art** is a collection of graphic images that you can insert in documents. Clip art files are stored in the Microsoft ClipGallery, which is a library of pictures, recorded sounds, and motion clips that comes with Word and is shared by all Office applications. Clip art images in the ClipGallery are organized in categories. You can browse the ClipGallery by category to find a clip art image (or "clip") that meets your needs, or you can perform a search to locate all the clips that match a keyword or topic. If you are connected to the Internet, you can also download clip art from Clips Online, a Microsoft Web site for ClipGallery users, into your ClipGallery. ▶Scenario Alice has begun working on a flyer advertising readings for children at MediaLoft. To give the flyer some personality, she illustrates it with clip art.

Steps

QuickTip

To return personalized toolbars and menus to the default settings, click Tools on the menu bar, click Customize, click Reset my usage data on the Options tab, click Yes, then click Close.

1. Start **Word**, open the file **WD F-1** from your Project Disk, then save it as **Readings Flyer**
The document opens in Print Layout view.

2. Scroll down, then click in front of **Wednesday**
You want to insert a clip art image near Wednesday.

3. Click **Insert** on the menu bar, point to **Picture**, then click **Clip Art**
The ClipGallery opens, which displays the pictures, sounds, and motion clips that are available with Word. You can also click the Insert Clip Art button 🖾 on the Drawing toolbar to open the ClipGallery.

Trouble?

If the categories do not display on your Picture tab, click the All Categories button 🏛 on the ClipGallery toolbar.

4. Click the **Pictures tab** if necessary
The clip art pictures are organized in categories. Word includes many default categories, but you can add your own categories to the ClipGallery as well. You can scroll to see all the categories in your ClipGallery.

5. Click the **Cartoons** category
The clips in the Cartoons category appear on the Pictures tab, as shown in Figure F-1.

6. Click the **owl clip** in the top row
A menu with four buttons appears when you select a clip art image. You can use this menu to insert the selected clip, preview it, add it to another category, or search for similar clips.

QuickTip

You can also drag a clip from the ClipGallery into a document to insert it.

7. Click the **Insert Clip button** 🖾
The clip is inserted in the document at the location of the insertion point. The ClipGallery remains open, which is useful if you want to insert more than one clip art image into a document. Some of the clips in your ClipGallery may be stored on your Office 2000 CD. When you click the Insert Clip button, if a message appears saying the file is stored on a disc, insert your Office 2000 CD, then click Retry.

8. Click the **Close button** on the ClipGallery title bar
The owl image appears in the document at the location of the insertion point, as shown in Figure F-2. Notice that the image is larger than you want it to be and that it displaced the text when it was inserted. When you insert an image, it is part of the line of text in which it was inserted (an **inline** graphic). To allow graphics to be placed near text without being part of a line of text, you must apply text wrapping to the graphic. You will learn how to wrap text around graphic objects in the next lesson.

9. Click the **Save button** 🖫 on the Standard toolbar

FIGURE F-1: Cartoons clips in Microsoft ClipGallery

ClipGallery toolbar

Click to show all categories

Tab containing sound clips

Owl clip

Click to find clips online

Tab containing motion clips

Clips in Cartoons category

FIGURE F-2: Clip art image in the document

Your toolbars may differ

Clip art image inserted at location of insertion point

Text is displaced by graphic when graphic is inserted

Graphic is part of same line of text as "Wednesday"

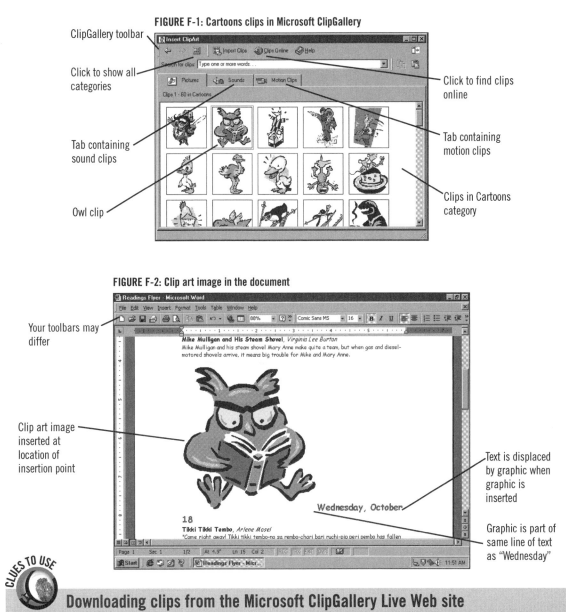

Downloading clips from the Microsoft ClipGallery Live Web site

For an even broader range of clips to illustrate your documents, you can download images from the ClipGallery Live Web site. To get clips from the Microsoft ClipGallery Live Web site, click the Clips Online button on the ClipGallery toolbar, then click OK. This launches your browser and connects you to the site. Once you have read and accepted the License Agreement, which specifies how you are permitted to use clips from the site, the ClipGallery Live window opens. You can view the clips by type (clip art, photos, sounds, and motions), search by keyword, or browse the clips by category. Figure F-3 shows clips found using the keyword "Australia."

FIGURE F-3: Microsoft ClipGallery Live Web site

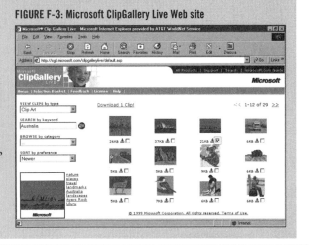

Wrapping Text Around Graphics

Word 2000 — Unit F

When positioning a graphic near text, you can specify how you would like the text to wrap around the graphic. **Wrapping** means that text flows around a graphic object rather than over it. You can choose to wrap text in a square around the object's frame, wrap it above and below the graphic object, or you can wrap it around the shape of the graphic itself. When you apply text wrapping to an inline graphic object, it becomes a **floating** graphic. You can move a floating graphic anywhere on a page. The Picture toolbar and the Format Picture dialog box contain options for wrapping text and for positioning graphics within text. ▸Scenario◂ Alice wraps the document text around the owl so that the text flows more smoothly on the page.

Trouble?

If your Picture toolbar does not open, click View on the menu bar, point to Toolbars, then click Picture. If necessary, move the toolbar by dragging its title bar to a new location.

QuickTip

The anchor symbol appears when nonprinting characters are displayed.

1. Click the **Show/Hide ¶ button** ¶ on the Standard toolbar to display nonprinting characters if necessary, then click the **owl graphic** to select it
   When a graphic is selected, squares called **sizing handles** appear on all four sides and corners of the object. Before you wrap text around an inline graphic, its sizing handles are black. When you select a graphic, the Picture toolbar also opens. The Picture toolbar includes buttons for modifying graphics.

2. Click the **Text Wrapping button** 📷 on the Picture toolbar
   A menu of text wrapping options appears.

3. Click **Square** on the menu, then scroll to see the graphic if necessary
   The text wraps to the sides of the object frame so that the graphic is set off in the text as a square, as shown in Figure F-4. The sizing handles are now white, which indicates that the graphic is a floating object. Usually the first thing you should do after inserting a graphic is to apply text wrapping to it so that it becomes a floating graphic. Notice that an anchor symbol appears in the upper-right corner of the graphic object, next to the "Wednesday" paragraph. The anchor indicates the graphic is anchored to the "Wednesday" paragraph. When a graphic object is **anchored** to a paragraph, it moves with the paragraph if the paragraph moves.

4. Click 📷, then click **Tight**
   Now the text wraps to the irregular shape of the graphic image itself. However, the image divides the lines of text, making it difficult to read. You can adjust text wrapping so that it only wraps to one side of an image.

5. Click **Format** on the menu bar, click **Picture**, then click the **Layout tab**
   The Layout tab in the Format Picture dialog box includes several Wrapping style options as well as options for aligning graphic images horizontally between the margins. You want to use the more advanced options.

6. Click **Advanced**, then click the **Text Wrapping tab**
   The Text Wrapping tab in the Advanced Layout dialog box, shown in Figure F-5, includes options for changing the wrapping style, determining which sides of the object to wrap text around, and changing the spacing between the edge of the image and the edge of the text. You want to wrap the text around the right side of the image only.

7. Click the **Right only option button** in the Wrap text area, click the **Right up arrow** in the Distance from text area once so that **.2"** displays, click **OK**, then click **OK**
   The text wraps around the right side of the image only, as shown in Figure F-6. The text, which originally fit on one page, now flows to page 2 because the graphic was added.

8. Deselect the graphic, click ¶, then save your changes

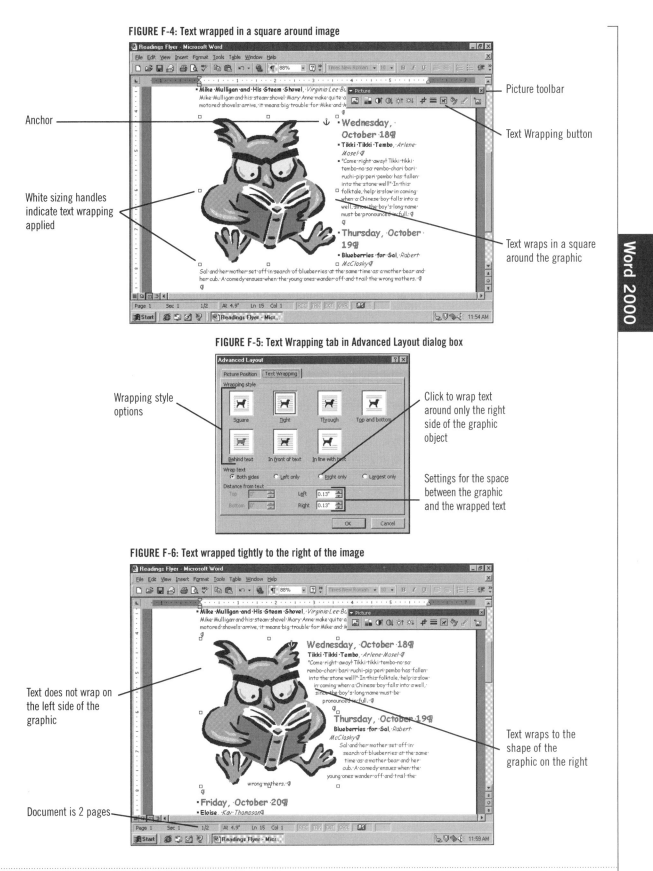

FIGURE F-4: Text wrapped in a square around image

Picture toolbar

Text Wrapping button

Anchor

White sizing handles indicate text wrapping applied

Text wraps in a square around the graphic

FIGURE F-5: Text Wrapping tab in Advanced Layout dialog box

Wrapping style options

Click to wrap text around only the right side of the graphic object

Settings for the space between the graphic and the wrapped text

FIGURE F-6: Text wrapped tightly to the right of the image

Text does not wrap on the left side of the graphic

Text wraps to the shape of the graphic on the right

Document is 2 pages

Word 2000

Moving and Resizing Graphics

After you insert a clip art image or any other graphic object in Word, you can resize it to be smaller or larger. You can change the size of a graphic object using the mouse, which allows you to see how the graphic looks as you change it, or you can use the Picture command on the Format menu, which allows you to alter precisely the size of a picture. You can also move a graphic to a new location in a document by dragging it with the mouse, or by placing it with precise measurements. ▶Scenario▶ Alice reduces the size of the clip art image she inserted and moves it to a different location in the document. She then adjusts the size and position of the image to make it work with the flow of text.

Steps

1. Click the **owl graphic** to select it

QuickTip

Dragging a side, top, or bottom sizing handle changes only the height or width of the graphic so that the object's proportions change.

2. Position the pointer over the **lower-right sizing handle**, when the pointer changes to ↖, drag up and to the left until the graphic is about **2"** wide and **2"** tall
   The size of the image is reduced, as shown in Figure F-7. Dragging a corner sizing handle changes the size of the object proportionally; in other words, its height and width are reduced or enlarged by the same percentage. Next you want to move the graphic up the page.

3. Scroll up so that "Monday" and the graphic appear in the document window
   You want to move the graphic to the left of the text "Monday". You can drag a graphic to move it.

4. With the graphic still selected, position the pointer over the graphic, when the pointer changes to ✥, drag the graphic up so its top aligns with the top of **Monday** as shown in Figure F-8, release the mouse button, then deselect the graphic
   The graphic is now located to the left of "Monday". You decide the graphic would look better if it were slightly larger.

QuickTip

You can also click Format on the menu bar, then click Picture to open the Format Picture dialog box.

5. Double click the **owl graphic**
   The Format Picture dialog box opens. You can double-click any graphic object to open the Format Picture dialog box, where you can choose from a variety of options for sizing, positioning, coloring, and wrapping text around the object.

6. Click the **Size tab**
   The Size tab allows you to enter precise measurements for a graphic. You can also enter a percentage by which you want to reduce or enlarge the graphic proportionally.

7. Select the number in the **Height text box** in the Size and rotate area, type **2.75**, then click in the **Width text box** in the Size and rotate area
   The width automatically changes to 2.64" when you click the Width text box. When the Lock aspect ratio check box is selected, you only need to enter a height or a width. Word automatically calculates the other measurement to keep the resized graphic proportional to the original.

8. Click **OK**
   The graphic is enlarged. Now you can reposition the graphic to make it work with the flow of text and make your flyer more eye-catching.

9. Drag the graphic to the left so that the right edge of the graphic frame aligns at about the **2"** mark on the horizontal ruler, then deselect the graphic
   Notice that you can position the graphic in the margin now that text wrapping is applied. Compare your flyer with Figure F-9 and make any necessary adjustments.

10. Save your changes

FIGURE F-7: Resized graphic

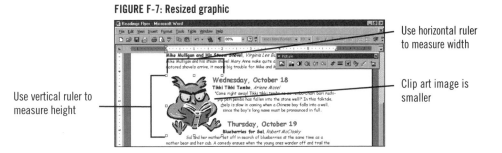

Use horizontal ruler to measure width

Use vertical ruler to measure height

Clip art image is smaller

FIGURE F-8: Owl graphic being dragged to new location

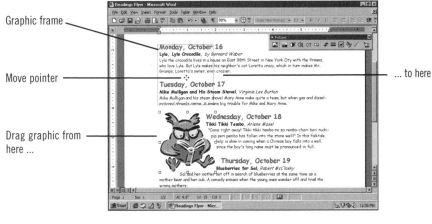

Graphic frame

Move pointer

... to here

Drag graphic from here ...

FIGURE F-9: Resized graphic moved

Graphic is moved to the left

Document is again 1 page

CLUES TO USE

Moving inline and floating graphics

When working with graphics it is important to understand that usually you will need to change an inline graphic to a floating graphic to be able to move it where you want in a document. When you insert a graphic in a document, it is automatically inserted as an inline graphic, which makes it part of the document's text. Inline graphics have black sizing handles and can only be moved to another location in the text – you can't move an inline graphic to a blank area of a page. Floating graphics, on the other hand, have white sizing handles and can be moved anywhere on a page, independent of a document's text. To change an inline graphic to a floating graphic, you must apply a text wrapping style to the graphic, *even if there is no text on the page*. To change an inline graphic to a floating graphic, use the Text Wrapping button on the Picture toolbar or double-click the graphic, click the Layout tab in the Format Picture dialog box, select a text wrapping style other than "In line with text", then click OK.

Inserting Pictures from Files

In addition to the clip art graphics that come with Word, you can insert graphics that were scanned or created in other graphics programs into your documents. Most graphics created in other programs have a bitmapped format. **Bitmapped graphics** are composed of many small dots, called **pixels**, that contain information about color and intensity. Some of the more common file extensions for bitmapped graphics are .gif, .tif, .jpg, and .bmp, but there are many others as well. You can insert graphics created in other graphics programs into your documents using the Picture, From File command on the Insert menu. Scenario Alice wants to add the MediaLoft logo to the flyer. The logo graphic was created in another graphics program, so Alice needs to insert the graphic file into the document.

Steps 123 4

1. Press **[Ctrl][End]**
   The insertion point is at the end of the document. You want to add the MediaLoft logo near the contact information.

2. Click **Insert** on the menu bar, point to **Picture**, then click **From File**
   The Insert Picture dialog box opens.

3. Use the **Look in list arrow** to locate the files stored on your Project Disk, click the file **WD F-2**, wait until the preview of the graphic file appears in the Insert Picture dialog box, then click **Insert**
   The logo graphic is inserted at the location of the insertion point. Since the logo is too big to fit on page 1, it is now on page 2. You want to reduce the size of the logo so that it will fit at the bottom of page 1.

4. Double click the **logo graphic**, then click the **Size tab** in the Format Picture dialog box
   The Size tab in the Format Picture dialog box, shown in Figure F-10, opens. You already used the Size tab to enter precise measurements to size a graphic. Now you will use it to scale graphics. You want to reduce the logo proportionally to be 20% of its current size.

5. Make sure the **Lock aspect ratio** and **Relative to original picture size check boxes** are selected in the Scale area, double-click **100** in the Height text box in the Scale area, type **20**, then click in the **Width text box**
   Because the Lock aspect ratio check box is selected, the width automatically changes to 20% when you click the Width text box. You also want to wrap the text around the graphic.

6. Click the **Layout tab**, click **Tight** in the Wrapping style area, click **OK**, then scroll down to locate the logo graphic in the document
   The logo is much smaller, but still on page 2. You'll need to drag the logo to position it to the right of the text at the bottom of page 1.

7. Select the **logo graphic** if necessary, then drag it up to the bottom of page 1 so that its right edge is even with the right margin, as shown in Figure F-11
   The text wraps to the left of the logo and the flyer is once again just one page.

8. Replace the name **Alice Wegman** with your name, then click the **Print Preview button** on the Standard toolbar
   Compare your flyer with Figure F-12.

9. Close Print Preview, save your changes, click the **Print button** on the Standard toolbar, then close the file
   A copy of the flyer prints.

FIGURE F-10: Size tab in Format Picture dialog box

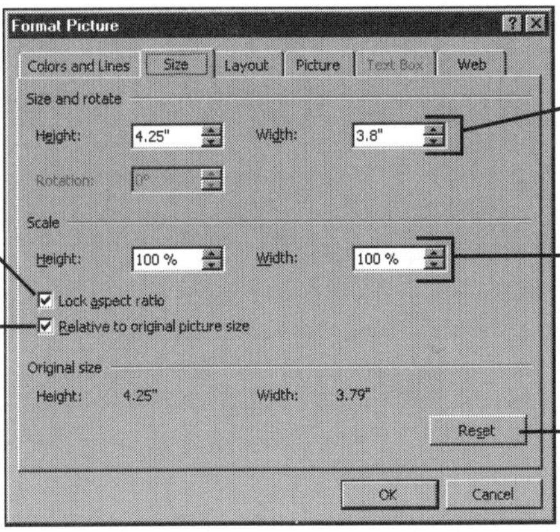

Select to keep scaled graphic proportional

Select to make scaled measurements relative to the original graphic

Set specific height and width here (your measurements may differ)

Change the scale of an object here

Click to reset image back to its original size and proportions

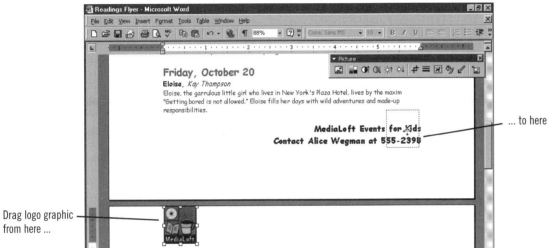

FIGURE F-11: Logo graphic being dragged to a new location

... to here

Drag logo graphic from here ...

FIGURE F-12: Completed Readings flyer

Logo graphic

Drawing AutoShapes

You are not limited to clip art and graphics created in other programs to illustrate your documents. You can also create your own graphics in Word using the drawing tools on the Drawing toolbar. The Drawing toolbar includes tools for drawing lines and shapes, as well as tools for applying color, shadows, and fills to the images you create. Using the AutoShapes button on the Drawing toolbar, you can create simple shapes quickly without having to draw them from scratch. **AutoShapes** include squares, triangles, ovals, block arrows, lightening bolts, stars, banners, and other fun designs. Once you insert a shape, you can resize it, rotate it, color it, or combine it with other shapes to create more complex graphics. Scenario▶ The marketing department has invited the author of a new book about paper sculpture for kids to demonstrate several projects at MediaLoft. Alice uses AutoShapes to make the flyer she creates for the event colorful and eye-catching.

Steps

1. Click the **New Blank Document button** 🗋 on the Standard toolbar, save the new document as **Sculpture Flyer** to your Project Disk, click the **Zoom list arrow** on the Standard toolbar, then click **Whole Page**

The blank Sculpture Flyer document appears in Print Layout view.

Trouble?

Click the More Buttons button ≫ on the Standard or Formatting toolbar to locate buttons that are not displayed on your toolbar.

2. Click the **Drawing button** 🖉 on the Standard toolbar

The Drawing toolbar appears at the bottom of the Word document window. The Drawing button is a toggle button, which means that you can use it to display or hide the Drawing toolbar. You use the buttons on the Drawing toolbar to create your own graphic images.

3. Click the **Oval button** ◯ on the Drawing toolbar

When you click an AutoShape button, the pointer changes to ╋. You drag this pointer to draw the selected AutoShape. You can use the oval tool to draw ovals and circles.

QuickTip

Pressing [Shift] while you drag with the Oval tool creates a circle.

4. Position the pointer in the middle of the page at the left margin, then drag down and to the right to create an oval that is about 6½" wide and 1¾" tall

You do not need to be very exact in your measurements as you drag. An oval appears when you release the mouse button. Like other graphic objects, you can move, resize, and wrap text around AutoShapes. You'll move the oval to the bottom of the page.

5. Position the pointer over the **oval shape**, then when the pointer changes to ↖⟶, drag the oval down so that its bottom edge is about **1"** from the bottom edge of the page

6. Click **AutoShapes** on the Drawing toolbar, point to **Stars and Banners**, then click the **Explosion 2 button** 💥 on the menu that appears

The AutoShapes menu contains the categories of lines and shapes that you can easily draw. You can point to each item on the menu to view the different AutoShapes that come with Word.

QuickTip

To check or change the exact size of a shape you draw, double-click the shape, then check the measurements on the Size tab in the Format AutoShape dialog box.

7. Click about ¼" in from the upper-left corner of the page, then drag to create a shape that is about **4"** wide and **4"** high

Compare your shapes with Figure F-13. You can move or resize your shapes if necessary so that your flyer resembles the figure. Next you want to add color to your shapes.

8. With the star shape selected, click the **Fill Color list arrow** 🖌▾ on the Drawing toolbar, click **Red** (1ˢᵗ box, 3ʳᵈ row), click the **Line Color list arrow** 🖌▾, click the **Yellow box** (3ʳᵈ box, 4ᵗʰ row), click the **Line Style button** ☰, then click the **4½ pt solid line**

The star shape is filled with red and outlined with a 4½ point yellow line.

QuickTip

When you select a new color, the active color changes.

9. Click the **oval shape**, click 🖌▾, click **Violet** (7ᵗʰ box, 3ʳᵈ row), click 🖌, click ☰, then click the **4½ pt solid line**, compare your flyer with Figure F-14 and make adjustments as needed, and save your changes

FIGURE F-13: AutoShapes in document

Drawing button

Star shape

Drawing toolbar

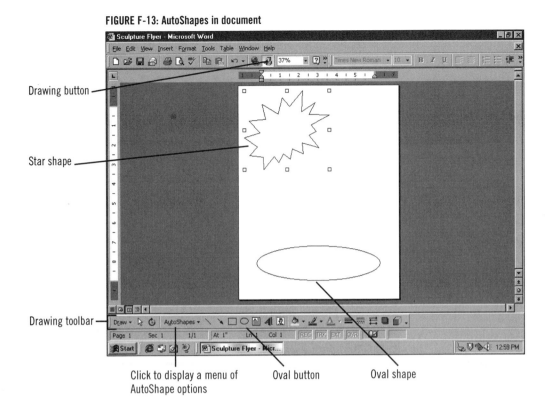

Click to display a menu of
AutoShape options

Oval button

Oval shape

FIGURE F-14: Colors applied to AutoShapes

Red fill with
yellow line

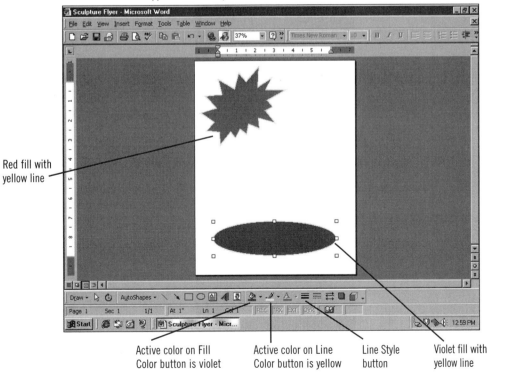

Active color on Fill
Color button is violet

Active color on Line
Color button is yellow

Line Style
button

Violet fill with
yellow line

Word 2000

Inserting Text Boxes

When you want to add text to your documents as a graphic image, you can create a text box. A **text box** is a container into which you can place text and graphics. For example, if you wanted to create a **pull quote** — decorative text in an article that you set off by wrapping the article text around it — you would place the pull quote text in a text box. You can draw a text box around existing text or graphics, or you can draw an empty text box and add text or graphics to it. Like other graphic objects, text boxes can be resized, moved, and enhanced using the tools on the Drawing toolbar. ▶Scenario Alice draws an empty text box and adds information about the event to it. She then formats the text box to make it stand out. Finally, she adds text boxes to the oval and star shapes.

Trouble?

If your Text Box toolbar does not appear, click View on the menu bar, point to Toolbars, then click Text Box.

1. Click the **Text Box button** 📰 on the Drawing toolbar, place the ✛ pointer about ½" below the left-middle of the star shape, then drag to create a text box that is about **3"** high and **5½"** wide
   When you create a text box, the Text Box toolbar appears. It contains buttons for linking text boxes, for navigating between text boxes, and for changing the direction of text in a text box. Before typing in the text box, you'll change the font and font size of the text you will type.

2. Click the **Font list arrow** on the Formatting toolbar, click **Comic Sans MS**, click the **Font Size list arrow**, then click **26**

QuickTip

To change the margins in a text box, double-click the patterned frame of the text box, click the Text Box tab in the Format Text Box dialog box, then change the margin settings.

3. Type **Paper Sculpture**, press **[Enter]** twice, then type **Maria DeLeone helps kids with projects from her new book, Paper Sculpture for Kids**
   If the text does not all fit in the text box, drag a corner of the text box to enlarge it. You can format text in a text box just as you would format text elsewhere in a document.

4. Select the text you just typed, click the **Center button** 📄 on the Formatting toolbar, select **Paper Sculpture**, click the **Bold button** **B**, click the **Font Size list arrow**, click **36**, select **Paper Sculpture for Kids**, then click the **Italic button** *I*
   Next you'll format the text box itself.

5. Select the **text box** if necessary, click the **Fill Color list arrow** 🎨▾ on the Drawing toolbar, click **Blue**, select **all the text** in the text box, click the **Font Color list arrow** A▾, click **Yellow**, click the **Line Color button** ✒, click the **Line Style button** ▤, click the **6 pt solid line**, click the **Dash Style button** ▦, click **Square Dot** (third line down), then deselect the text box
   Compare your text box with Figure F-15. You can also enter text in AutoShapes.

QuickTip

You can also create an empty text box by clicking the Text Box button, and then clicking once in the document window.

6. Right-click the **star shape**, then click **Add Text** on the pop-up menu
   The shape changes to a text box. You can add text or graphics inside the shape.

7. Change the font and font size to **24 point Comic Sans MS**, type **MediaLoft Events for Kids!**, select the text, click **B**, click ▤, click A, then deselect the graphic
   If the text does not fit in the shape, drag a corner of the shape to enlarge it.

8. Right-click the **oval shape**, click **Add Text**, change the font and font size to **26 point Comic Sans MS**, type **October 21ˢᵗ, 1:00**, press **[Enter]**, type **MediaLoft Café**, then press **[Spacebar]**
   Pressing [Spacebar] adds the accent to "Café".

9. Select the text in the oval shape, click **B**, click ▤, click A, deselect the shape, then save your changes
   Compare your flyer with Figure F-16.

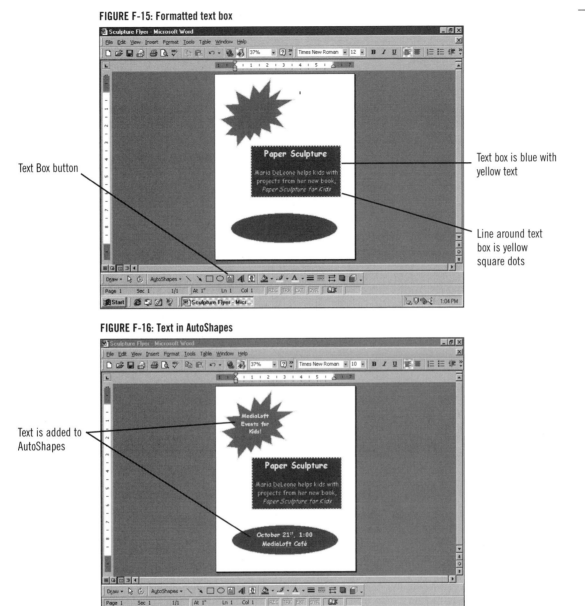

FIGURE F-15: Formatted text box

Text Box button

Text box is blue with yellow text

Line around text box is yellow square dots

FIGURE F-16: Text in AutoShapes

Text is added to AutoShapes

CLUES TO USE

Creating callouts

When you want to draw a reader's attention to a specific item in a document, you can create a callout to that item. A **callout** is a graphic object that contains text and a line that points to the item you want to call attention to. To create a callout, click AutoShapes on the Drawing toolbar, point to Callouts, then click a callout style on the menu. Position the pointer in the location you want to call out in the document, then drag the pointer to the location where you want the

callout text to appear. After you release the mouse button, type the callout text in the text box, then deselect the callout shape. You can format a callout using the tools on the Drawing toolbar. To resize a callout, select it, then drag its sizing handles. To reposition the callout text, select the callout text box, then drag it to a new location. To change the location the callout points to, select the callout line, then drag a yellow sizing handle to a new location.

Drawing Lines

Lines that you draw using the Drawing toolbar are also graphic objects. You can draw straight lines, arrows, curves, or free-form lines, and you can format lines using any of the tools on the Drawing toolbar or on the Colors and Lines tab in the Format AutoShape dialog box. ▶Scenario◀ Alice adds several decorative lines to her flyer to give it a stylish look. Before finishing her flyer, she also adds several small star shapes to enhance the finished document.

Steps

1. Click **[Ctrl][Home]**, click the **Zoom list arrow** on the Standard toolbar, then click **50%**

2. Click the **Line button** on the Drawing toolbar, position the + pointer at the inside point on the right side of the star as shown in Figure F-17, then drag the pointer to the top right corner of the page
   A straight line in the default format appears. Next you'll draw an arrow.

3. Click the **Arrow button** on the Drawing toolbar, position the + pointer at the right end of the line you just drew, then drag the pointer to the top-middle edge of the blue text box
   An arrow connects the straight line and the blue text box. When you draw an arrow, the arrowhead appears at the end of the line when you release the mouse button. Next, you'll draw another arrow to connect the blue text box with the purple oval.

4. Click , position the pointer on the bottom edge of the **blue text box** about ½" from the lower-left corner, then drag the pointer to the top-middle edge of the **purple oval**
   An arrow connects the blue text box and the purple oval. Next you'll change the line style and color of the line and the arrows.

5. Scroll so that the line and the arrows are all visible, click the **line** to select it, press and hold **[Shift]**, click the **first arrow**, then click the **second arrow**
   Pressing [Shift] while you select objects selects several objects at once. Now you can format all three lines with the same format settings.

6. Click the **Line Style button** on the Drawing toolbar, click the **6 pt solid line**, click the **Dash Style button** , click the **Square Dot** (third dash style), click the **Line Color list arrow** , click **Red**, then deselect the line and arrows
   Compare your flyer with Figure F-18. Before finishing your flyer, you'll add a few more AutoShapes to spice it up.

7. Click **AutoShapes** on the Drawing toolbar, point to **Stars and Banners**, then click the **5-Point Star button**

8. Position the pointer under the red star shape, drag to draw a 5-point star shape that is about 1/2" high and 1/2" wide, click the **Fill Color list arrow** on the Drawing toolbar, then click the **Yellow box**
   A yellow star shape appears under the red star shape.

9. Repeat step 8 to draw 6 more 5-point stars in other white areas of the flyer, right-click one of the stars, click **Add Text**, type your initials, then enlarge the star if necessary to fit your initials
   Your initials will identify the flyer as yours when you print it.

10. Preview your flyer in Print Preview, compare it to Figure F-19, save your changes, print a copy of the flyer, then close the file

QuickTip

To resize a line, drag a sizing handle. To move a line, place the pointer over the line, when the pointer changes to ⬚, drag the line to a new location.

QuickTip

Double-click the Line or Arrow buttons to draw more than one line or arrow. When you are finished, click the button again to return to the I-beam pointer.

QuickTip

You can also format lines using the Colors and Lines tab in the Format AutoShape dialog box. Double-click a line to open the Format AutoShape dialog box.

QuickTip

You can also use the Copy and Paste commands to create a copy of the graphic and then drag the copy to a new location.

FIGURE F-17: Line drawn in flyer

Draw line
from here ...   ... to here

FIGURE F-19: Completed Sculpture flyer

Your initials   5-point
in star   star
shape   AutoShape

FIGURE F-18: Formatted line and arrows

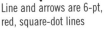

Line and arrows are 6-pt,
red, square-dot lines

CLUES TO USE

Drawing curved, freeform, and scribble lines

In addition to the straight lines and arrows that you can draw using the Line and Arrow buttons, you can also use the AutoShapes menu to draw curved, freeform, and scribble lines in your documents. Click AutoShapes on the Drawing toolbar, point to Lines, then click the Curve, Freeform, or Scribble buttons. Lines and shapes drawn using the Curve and Freeform Line tools are connected by nodes. Click the location where you want the line to begin, move the mouse pointer to draw a curved or freeform line, click to create a node, move the mouse again to create another line, and so on. When you are finished drawing the line or shape, double-click to turn off the line tool. The Scribble tool works more like a pencil on paper: to draw a line, press the mouse button, and then move the mouse pointer to draw as you would draw with a pencil. When you have finished drawing, click to turn off the Scribble tool and deselect the graphic.

Word 2000

Creating WordArt

WordArt is another powerful graphics tool that you can use to give your documents visual flair and impact. **WordArt** is a graphic object that contains specially formatted text. Text in WordArt objects is formatted in unique shapes, orientations, and patterns that you can easily modify and customize. You create WordArt using the WordArt button on the Drawing toolbar. Scenario▶ Alice needs to create a third flyer to advertise weekly musical performances in the MediaLoft Café. She creates a WordArt object to headline the flyer and to draw the attention of readers.

Steps

1. Click the **New Blank Document button** 🗋 on the Standard toolbar, save the new document as **Music Flyer** to your Project Disk, click the **Zoom list arrow** on the Standard toolbar, then click **Page Width**
   You'll insert the WordArt object at the top of the page.

2. Click the **Insert WordArt button** 🔳 on the Drawing toolbar
   The WordArt Gallery dialog box opens, as shown in Figure F-20. The WordArt Gallery displays the various styles you can choose for your WordArt text.

3. Click the second style in the third row from the top, then click **OK**
   The Edit WordArt Text dialog box opens. In this dialog box you type the text you want to format as WordArt. If desired, you can also change the font and font size of the WordArt text.

4. Type **Music at MediaLoft**, then click **OK**
   The WordArt object appears in the document with the settings you choose and the WordArt toolbar appears. The WordArt toolbar contains buttons for creating and modifying WordArt objects. It opens whenever a WordArt object is selected. You want to enlarge the WordArt object so that it spans the width of the page.

5. Position the pointer over the lower-right corner sizing handle until the pointer changes to ↖, press **[Ctrl]**, then drag down and to the right so that the object is about 2" tall and 5½" wide
   Pressing [Ctrl] while you drag to resize an object keeps the object's center fixed in place. As you drag to resize an object, it can be difficult to gauge the size of the object using the rulers. If you want to check or change the exact size of the WordArt graphic, you can select it, click the Format WordArt button 💱 on the WordArt toolbar, and then click the Size tab in the Format WordArt dialog box. The exact height and width of the selected object appear in the Size and rotate area on the Size tab. Next you'll move the WordArt object to the top of the page.

6. Position the pointer over the WordArt text, and when the pointer changes to ⁺ℛ, drag the object so that its top is about .8" from the top of the page and it is centered
   Use the rulers to help you place the object. The upper-middle sizing handle should be centered on the page and just above the top margin. Compare your document with Figure F-21 and make any necessary adjustments. Once you create, size, and position your WordArt object, it's simple to change its style, shape, color, and other formatting options to achieve the look you want.

QuickTip

To change the color of WordArt text, click the Format WordArt button 💱 on the WordArt toolbar. In the Format WordArt dialog box, select from the options on the Colors and Lines tab.

7. Click the **WordArt Same Letter Heights button** 🅰ᵃ on the WordArt toolbar
   The upper- and lower-case letters change to become the same height.

8. Click the **WordArt Gallery button** 🖼 on the WordArt toolbar, click the second style in the fourth row from the top, then click **OK**
   The WordArt changes to a new style.

9. Click the **WordArt Shape button** 🔤 on the WordArt toolbar, then click the **Double Wave 1 button** 〰 on the menu that appears
   The shape of the WordArt text changes. Compare your document with Figure F-22. You might want to experiment with several different WordArt shapes before saving the document.

10. Deselect the WordArt, then save your changes

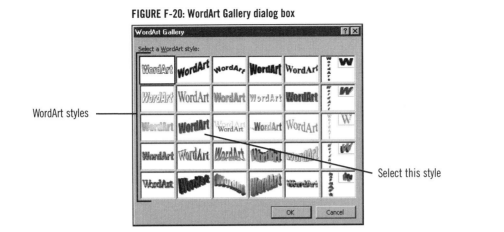

FIGURE F-20: WordArt Gallery dialog box

WordArt Gallery
Select a WordArt style:
WordArt styles
Select this style
OK
Cancel

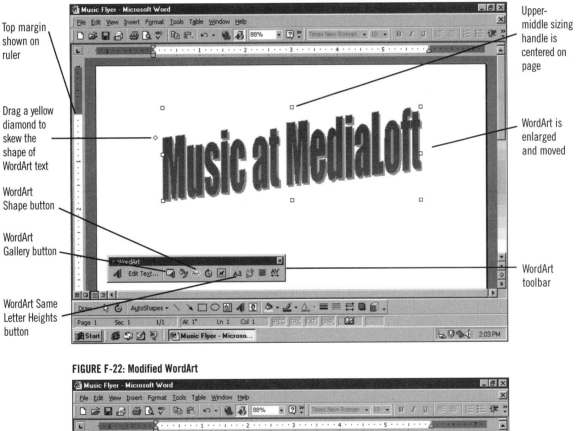

FIGURE F-21: WordArt in document

Music Flyer - Microsoft Word
Top margin shown on ruler
Drag a yellow diamond to skew the shape of WordArt text
WordArt Shape button
WordArt Gallery button
WordArt Same Letter Heights button
Upper-middle sizing handle is centered on page
WordArt is enlarged and moved
WordArt toolbar
Music at MediaLoft

FIGURE F-22: Modified WordArt

Music Flyer - Microsoft Word
WordArt is new style and shape
Music at MediaLoft

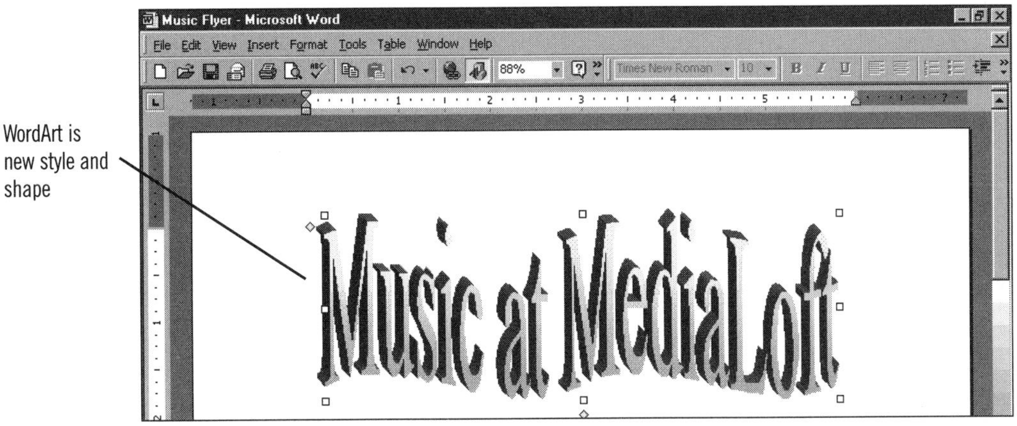

Word 2000

Using Click and Type

Word's **Click and Type** feature enables you to quickly insert text, graphics, tables, and other items in a blank area of a document without having to apply special formatting, such as alignment or indents, to the item. Double-clicking with the Click and Type pointer places the insertion point in the location where you double-clicked, and automatically applies the formatting necessary to position an item in that location. The shape of the Click and Type pointer indicates the format settings in effect for the area of the document where you want to insert an item. Table F-4 describes the different Click and Type pointers. You can use Click and Type in Print Layout or Web Layout view. ▶Scenario Alice uses Click and Type to format and enter text and clip art in her flyer.

Trouble?

If Click and Type is not turned on on your computer, click Tools on the menu bar, click Options, click the Edit tab in the Options dialog box, select the Enable click and type check box, then click OK.

1. **Click a blank area under the WordArt in the middle of the document, then slowly move the pointer over the blank area**
   Notice that the I-beam pointer changed to one of the Click and Type pointers when you clicked. Clicking once in a blank area of the screen enables the Click and Type pointer. As you move the pointer around in the document window, the pointer shape changes to indicate how text will be formatted in that area of the document. For example, the ⊥ shape indicates that text will be center-aligned.

2. **Double-click with the ⊥ pointer in the middle of the page at about the 3" mark on the horizontal ruler (about an inch below the WordArt object)**
   The insertion point is centered on the page.

3. **Click the Font list arrow on the Formatting toolbar, click Comic Sans MS, click the Font Size list arrow, click 24, click the Bold button B, type Join us every Thursday at 8:00, press [Enter], then type For an evening of music**
   The text is automatically centered on the page, as shown in Figure F-23. Notice that when you pressed [Enter], the center-aligned formatting was copied to the next paragraph.

4. **Scroll down, then double-click the ⊥ pointer about 1" below "For an evening of music"**
   The insertion point is centered on the page.

5. **Click the Insert Clip Art button 🖼 on the Drawing toolbar, click the Music category in the Clip Gallery, scroll to the bottom of the list of music clips, click the second clip in the last row (a gold and black graphic showing a guitar and a keyboard), click the Insert Clip button 📄, then close the ClipGallery**
   The clip art graphic is centered on the page. If you click to the left and right of the graphic, you'll notice the Click and Type pointer change to ⊺▤ or ▤⊺ to indicate formatting for wrapping text around a graphic.

6. **Scroll down, double-click the ⊥ pointer about 1" below the graphic, type MediaLoft Cafe, then press [Spacebar] to add the accent to Café**
   The text is center-aligned on the page.

Trouble?

If you double-click outside the margin, the Page Setup dialog box may open. If so, click Cancel, move the pointer until the ▤⊺ appears, then double-click again.

7. **Scroll down, move the pointer to the right side of the page, then double-click the ▤⊺ pointer about 1" below "MediaLoft Café"**
   The insertion point is aligned with the right margin.

8. **Click the Font Size list arrow, click 18, type MediaLoft Events, press [Enter], then type For schedules call [your name] at 555-2398.**

9. **Preview your flyer in Print Preview, compare it with Figure F-24, save your changes, print a copy of the flyer, then close the file**

FIGURE F-23: Center-aligned text

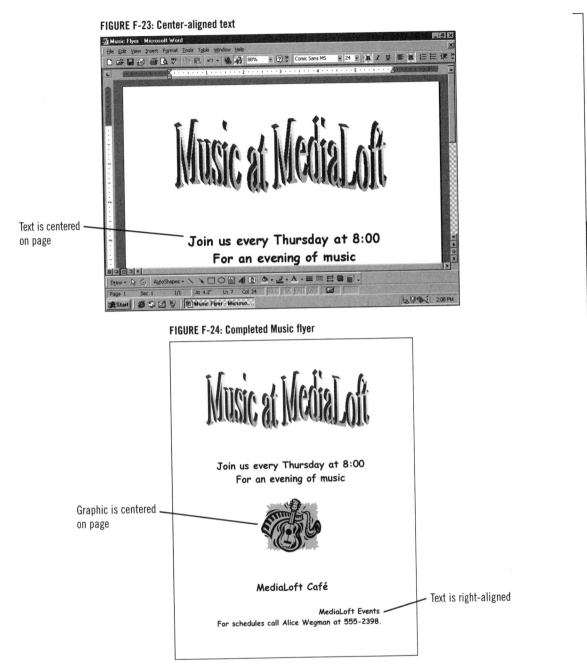

Text is centered on page

FIGURE F-24: Completed Music flyer

Graphic is centered on page

Text is right-aligned

TABLE F-1: Click and Type pointers

pointer shape	use to apply
⊥≡	A center-aligned tab stop; text that you type is centered on the page
≡I	A right-aligned tab stop; text that you type is right-aligned on the page
I≡	A left-aligned tab stop; text that you type is left-aligned on the page
I≡	A left indent
I≡■	Left text wrapping
■≡I	Right text wrapping

Practice

► Concepts Review

Label each button shown in Figure F-25.

FIGURE F-25

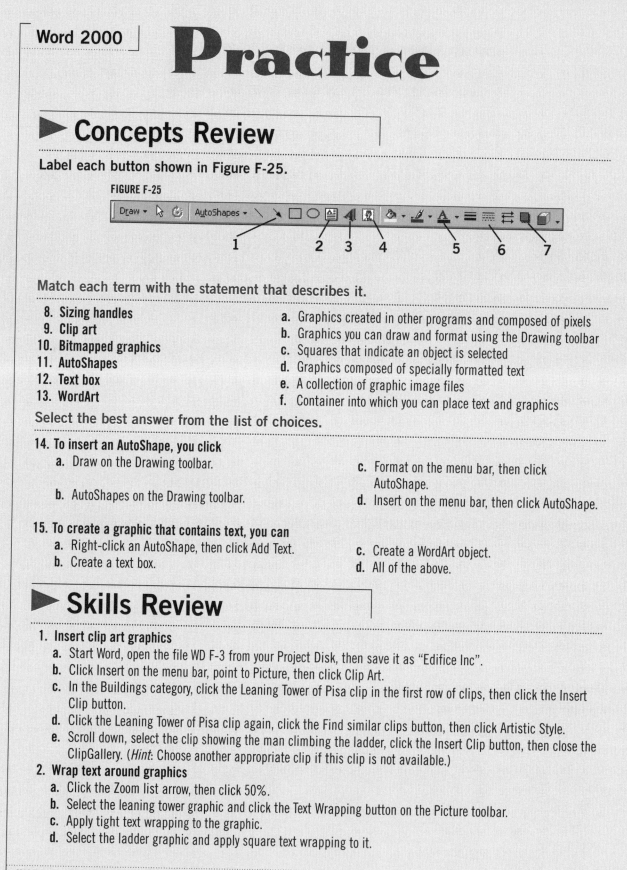

Match each term with the statement that describes it.

8. Sizing handles
9. Clip art
10. Bitmapped graphics
11. AutoShapes
12. Text box
13. WordArt

a. Graphics created in other programs and composed of pixels
b. Graphics you can draw and format using the Drawing toolbar
c. Squares that indicate an object is selected
d. Graphics composed of specially formatted text
e. A collection of graphic image files
f. Container into which you can place text and graphics

Select the best answer from the list of choices.

14. To insert an AutoShape, you click
    a. Draw on the Drawing toolbar.
    b. AutoShapes on the Drawing toolbar.
    c. Format on the menu bar, then click AutoShape.
    d. Insert on the menu bar, then click AutoShape.

15. To create a graphic that contains text, you can
    a. Right-click an AutoShape, then click Add Text.
    b. Create a text box.
    c. Create a WordArt object.
    d. All of the above.

► Skills Review

1. **Insert clip art graphics**
   a. Start Word, open the file WD F-3 from your Project Disk, then save it as "Edifice Inc".
   b. Click Insert on the menu bar, point to Picture, then click Clip Art.
   c. In the Buildings category, click the Leaning Tower of Pisa clip in the first row of clips, then click the Insert Clip button.
   d. Click the Leaning Tower of Pisa clip again, click the Find similar clips button, then click Artistic Style.
   e. Scroll down, select the clip showing the man climbing the ladder, click the Insert Clip button, then close the ClipGallery. (*Hint*: Choose another appropriate clip if this clip is not available.)
2. **Wrap text around graphics**
   a. Click the Zoom list arrow, then click 50%.
   b. Select the leaning tower graphic and click the Text Wrapping button on the Picture toolbar.
   c. Apply tight text wrapping to the graphic.
   d. Select the ladder graphic and apply square text wrapping to it.

3. **Move and resize graphics**
   a. Resize the leaning tower clip art graphic proportionally so it is about 1½" wide. (*Hint*: Change the zoom level if necessary to better see the graphic.)
   b. Resize the ladder clip art graphic proportionally so it is about 1½" wide.
   c. Move the ladder clip art graphic to the left of the heading "Safety". Adjust the position of the graphic so that the top of the graphic is aligned with the top of the "Safety" heading, the left side of the graphic is even with the left margin, and the text for the Safety section wraps smoothly around the graphic.
   d. Move the leaning tower clip art graphic to the left of the heading "Sound Construction" on the second page. (*Hint*: You can use cut and paste to move graphics from one page to another page.)
   e. Adjust the position of the graphic so that the top of the graphic is aligned with the top of the "Sound Construction" heading, the left side of the graphic is even with the left margin, and the text for the Sound Construction section wraps smoothly around the graphic.

4. **Insert pictures from files**
   a. On the first page, place the insertion point in front of "Edifice", click Insert on the menu bar, point to Picture, click From File, then insert the graphic file WD F-4 from your Project Disk.
   b. Resize the column graphic so it is about 1½" wide, then wrap the text in a square around it, adjusting the size and position of the graphic if necessary so the text wraps smoothly around it.

5. **Draw AutoShapes**
   a. Display the Drawing toolbar if necessary, click AutoShapes, point to Block Arrows, then click the Up Arrow shape.
   b. On the right side of the "Balancing the Books" section, draw an arrow that is about 2¼" tall and 1¾" wide.
   c. Adjust the position of the arrow so that the right side of the graphic object is aligned with the right margin, and the top of the arrow is aligned with the top of the "Balancing" heading, then wrap the text tightly around the arrow shape.
   d. Fill the arrow with Pale Blue fill, and apply Shadow Style 16. (*Hint*: Click the Shadow button on the Drawing toolbar. Position the pointer over a menu option to see a ScreenTip with its name.)
   e. Adjust the position of the arrow so that the text wraps smoothly around it and the shadow does not fall off the page.
   f. Scroll to the second page, click AutoShapes, point to Basic Shapes, then click the Sun shape.
   g. On the right side of the "Environment First" section, draw a sun shape that is about 2" wide and 2" tall. Align the right edge of the sun shape with the right margin.
   h. Wrap the text tightly around the sun shape so that the text only wraps to the left of the shape.
   i. Fill the sun shape with Light Yellow.

6. **Insert text boxes**
   a. Scroll to the bottom of the document, draw a text box that is about 3½" wide and 1¼" tall, and center it on the page about 1" below the last line of text.
   b. Inside the text box, type "Edifice Inc", press [Enter], type "100 Massachusetts Avenue", press [Enter], then type "Cambridge, MA 02139".
   c. Select the text, center it, and change the font size to 20.
   d. Fill the text box with Light Yellow and change the line around it to 2¼ points.
   e. Scroll to the first page, right click the arrow shape, click Add Text, type "Revenues are up 15%.", center the text, then change the font to 11 point Arial.

7. **Draw lines**
   a. Scroll to the top of the document, then draw a straight line that is 6" long above the heading "Edifice Inc".
   b. Adjust the position of the line so that it is about ½" above the heading "Edifice Inc," and centered on the page.
   c. With the line selected, click the Arrow Style button, then click the Arrow 7 style.
   d. Change the line style to a 3 pt solid line, then change the line color to Indigo.

8. Create WordArt

a. Select and cut the heading "The Cutting Edge", then click the Insert WordArt button on the Drawing toolbar.

b. Select the fourth WordArt style in the fourth row from the top, click OK, press [Ctrl][V] to paste the heading "The Cutting Edge" in the Edit WordArt Text dialog box, then click OK.

c. Resize the WordArt to be about 5" wide and 1½" tall, wrap text around the top and bottom of the WordArt object, then move it above the double-arrow line, centered on the page.

d. Click the WordArt Shape button on the WordArt toolbar and select a different shape for the WordArt.

9. Use Click and Type

a. Press [Ctrl][End], click once, position the right-align Click and Type pointer about 1" below the text box, double-click, then type your name.

b. Save the document, view it in Print Preview, make adjustments as needed, print a copy, then close the document.

▶ Visual Workshop

Create the flyer shown in Figure F-26 and save it as "Movies Flyer" to your Project Disk. Type your name on the flyer before printing it.

FIGURE F-26

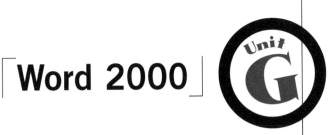

Creating
a Web Page

Objectives

▶ Plan a Web publication
[MOUS] ▶ Create a Web page
[MOUS] ▶ Apply themes
▶ Add graphics to a Web page
[MOUS] ▶ Save a document as a Web page
[MOUS] ▶ Insert hyperlinks
▶ Edit hyperlinks
[MOUS] ▶ Preview a Web page

By creating Web pages in Word, you can create online documents that others can read over the Internet or an intranet. In this unit you'll learn how to create a new Web page, apply themes and formatting to Web pages, and work with graphics on a Web page. You'll also learn how to convert an existing print document to a Web page, create and edit hyperlinks, and preview a Web page in a browser. Scenario➤ One of MediaLoft's marketing goals is to increase its presence as a retailer of CDs and other music-related products. With this in mind, Alice Wegman is creating a Web site for MediaLoft employees to keep them updated on the marketing department's efforts, as well as trends in the retail music industry. The Web site will be posted on the MediaLoft intranet site and updated as necessary.

Planning a Web Publication

A **Web page** is a document that is stored on the World Wide Web or an intranet, and viewed on a computer using a Web browser. You can create a Web page from scratch in Word, or you can convert an existing document to a Web page. Web pages often contain highlighted text or graphics called **hyperlinks** that open other Web pages when you click them. A group of associated Web pages that are linked together with hyperlinks is called a **Web site** or **Web publication**. The first page of a Web site that opens when you view the site in a browser is called the **home page**. The home page often serves as a table of contents for the Web site. Before you create a Web site, it is important to plan its content and organization. Scenario Alice's music Web site will include a home page that contains hyperlinks to the other Web pages in the Web site. Before creating the Web pages for the newsletter, Alice plans their content and organization and the tasks involved in creating them.

Details

Determine the purpose of the Web site
You can use a Web site to communicate information, collect information, or make a transaction. Alice's Web site will communicate MediaLoft's marketing program for music products to MediaLoft employees.

Sketch each Web page
Identify the information you want to include in your Web site and then sketch each page, including the links between pages. Alice identifies the documents she wants to include on the intranet site and then sketches the layout of each Web page. Her sketch is shown in Figure G-1.

Create each Web page
Create a new document and enter the Web page text, or convert an existing document to a Web page. Word includes a Web Page Wizard and templates for creating many standard types of Web pages. Alice will use a blank Web page template to create her Web site's home page, Music Notes. She will also convert an existing document to a Web page and add it to the Web site.

Format each Web page
Word includes visual themes that you can apply to any Web page. You can also create your own design for Web pages using backgrounds, lines, graphics, bullets, and other Word formatting features. Alice will select a theme and apply it to each page in her Web site to give it a cohesive look.

Save each Web page document
Web pages are saved in HTML (Hypertext Markup Language) format so that they can be viewed on the Web. Alice will use standard Word formatting features to design the layout of her Web pages before saving them in HTML format.

Format hyperlinks
Use hyperlinks to connect the pages of your Web site to each other. You can also create hyperlinks to sound and video clips, to other files on your computer, or to other Web pages. Alice will add hyperlinks linking the home page to a Web page that she creates from an existing Word document, to a Web page on the Internet, and to the MediaLoft intranet site.

View Web pages using a browser
Confirm that your Web pages are readable and correctly formatted and check that the links between Web pages work by viewing your Web site in your Web browser. Alice will use Web Page Preview to check each of her Web pages and test the links between pages.

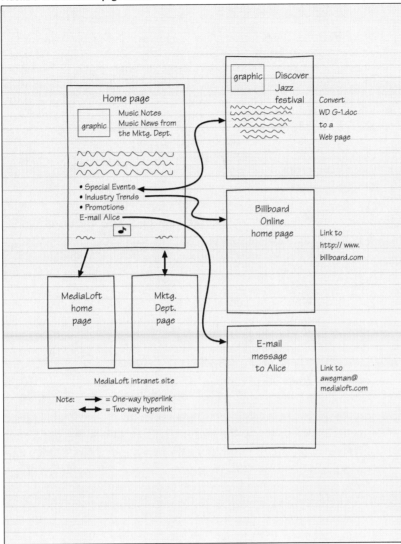

CLUES TO USE

Understanding the vocabulary of Web pages

When creating and working with Web pages, it is important to understand the following terms:

- **Home page:** the first Web page of a Web site to open when you view the site in a browser
- **Hyperlink:** highlighted text or graphic on a Web page that opens another Web page when you click it
- **Hypertext Markup Language** (HTML): the programming language used to create Web pages
- **Internet:** a communications system that connects computers and computer networks around the world

- **Intranet:** a network that connects computers in a local area and is used for internal purposes only
- **Web browser:** a software program used to access and display Web pages
- **Web page:** a document that is stored on the Web or an intranet and viewed on a computer using a Web browser
- **Web site** (or Web publication): a group of associated Web pages that are linked to each other by hyperlinks
- **World Wide Web** (the Web): a subset of the Internet that contains Web pages

Word 2000

Word 2000

Creating a Web Page

When you create a Web page in Word, you can use all the same formatting tools that you use to create and format a print document. Web page documents use **HTML** (Hypertext Markup Language) formatting. HTML places codes, or **tags**, around the elements of a Web page to describe how each element should appear when viewed with a browser. When you create a Web page in Word, Word automatically inserts the HTML tags for you. For example, when you center text on a Web page using the Center button on the Formatting toolbar, Word automatically inserts the HTML tags necessary to center the text in a Web browser. You can create a new Web page in Word using the Web pages templates in the New dialog box, or you can save an existing document as a Web page. Scenario▶ Alice begins by creating the home page for her Web site. She creates a blank Web page, enters some text, and then saves the new Web page document in HTML format.

Steps 1 2 3 4

QuickTip

To return personalized tool-bars and menus to the default settings, click Tools on the menu bar, click Customize, click Reset my usage data on the Options tab, click Yes, then click Close.

1. **Start Word, click File on the menu bar, click New, then click the General tab if necessary in the New dialog box**
   The New dialog box opens, as shown in Figure G-2. The tabs in the New dialog box include templates and wizards for creating common types of documents. You want to create a new, blank Web page.

2. **Click the Web Page icon on the General tab, then click OK**
   A blank Web page opens in Web Layout view. Text, graphics, and Web backgrounds are positioned in Web Layout view just as they would be in a Web browser. For now, notice that the New Web Page button 🔲 appears on the Standard toolbar and the Web Layout View button on the horizontal scroll bar is indented.

3. **Click the Zoom list arrow on the Standard toolbar, then click 100% if necessary**

4. **Type Music Notes, press [Enter], type Music News from the Marketing Department, press [Enter] twice, then type Our goal is to increase MediaLoft's profile as a first-rate retailer of music and music products. Check this page often for updates on trends in the retail music industry and news of MediaLoft's special promotions and events.**
   The text appears in the document window. You'll format the text in a later lesson.

QuickTip

The page title displays in the browser title bar when the Web page is published to the Web, so it is important that the page title of a Web page is descriptive of its contents.

5. **Click the Save button 🔲 on the Standard toolbar**
   The Save As dialog box opens. When you save a new Web page, Word automatically enters a page title and file name for the Web page in the Save As dialog box. You want to change the page title to indicate that it is the home page for the Music Notes Web site.

6. **Click Change Title**
   The Set Page Title dialog box opens.

7. **Click after Music Notes in the Page title text box, press [Spacebar], type Home Page, then click OK**
   The Page title changes to "Music Notes Home Page". Notice that the Save as type list box displays "Web Page" as the file type. Web pages are automatically saved in the file format—HTML—suitable for publishing a document on the Web or an intranet. You want to save the Web page with the file name "Music Notes Home" to your Project Disk.

8. **Click after Music Notes in the File name text box, press [Spacebar], type Home, then use the Save in list arrow to display the drive or folder that contains your Project Disk**
   Compare your Save As dialog box with Figure G-3.

9. **Click Save**
   The Web Page document is saved to your Project Disk.

FIGURE G-2: General tab in New dialog box

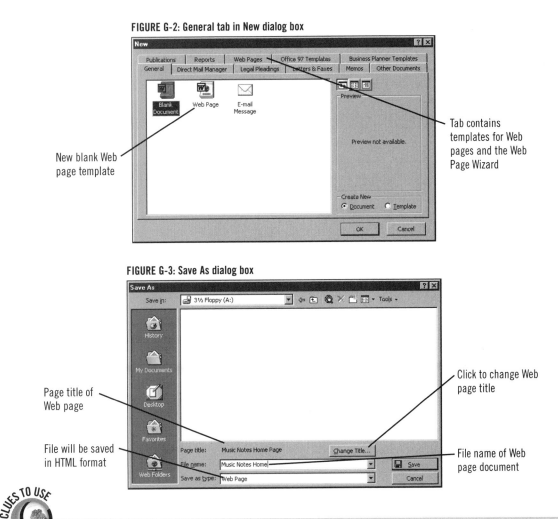

New blank Web
page template

Tab contains
templates for Web
pages and the Web
Page Wizard

FIGURE G-3: Save As dialog box

Page title of
Web page

Click to change Web
page title

File will be saved
in HTML format

File name of Web
page document

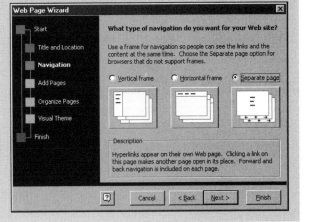

Using the Web Page Wizard

You can also use the Web Page Wizard to create
Web pages based on Word's Web page templates.
To start the Web Page Wizard, click File on the
menu bar, click New, click the Web Pages tab in
the New dialog box, then double-click the Web
Page Wizard icon. The wizard opens. Click Next,
enter a title and location for your Web site in the
first of 5 wizard dialog boxes, then click Next. In
the second dialog box, shown in Figure G-4, you
can choose to include or not include frames on
your Web pages. **Frames** contain hyperlinks and
other navigation elements that help users to navigate a group of associated Web pages. Some
browsers do not support frames, so if you are creating a Web site that will have a large audience,
you may want to create pages without frames.
Continue working through the Web Page Wizard
to add pages to the Web site, organize the pages in
the Web site, and apply a visual theme to the Web

site. When you are satisfied with your selections, click
Finish. The first Web page appears in the Word docu-
ment window. You can customize the Web pages using
Word's formatting features.

FIGURE G-4: Web Page Wizard dialog box

Word 2000

Word 2000

Applying Themes

To give to your Web site a unified look, you can apply a theme to your Web pages. A **theme** is a predefined set of design elements, colors, and fonts that you can apply to Web pages and e-mail messages to give your documents a common visual look. Themes include designs for Web backgrounds, bullets, and lines, and styles for text and hyperlinks. A **style** is a predefined set of font settings, font attributes, font colors, and paragraph formatting settings that you can apply to text to format it quickly and easily. You can apply a theme using the Theme command on the Format menu. You can apply styles to text using the Style list arrow on the Formatting toolbar. ▶Scenario Alice chooses a theme for the Music Notes Web site and applies it to the home page. She also formats the text on the home page using the styles that come with the theme.

Trouble?

Some themes may be stored on your Office 2000 CD. When you click a theme, if a message appears saying you need to install the theme, insert your Office 2000 CD, then click Install.

1. Click **Format** on the menu bar, click **Theme**, then click **Artsy** in the Choose a Theme list box

A sample of the Artsy theme appears in the Theme dialog box, as shown in Figure G-5. The theme includes a textured background, formatting for lines and bullets, and text formatting styles for headings, bulleted lists, body text, hyperlinks, and other text elements of a Web page.

2. Click **OK**

The theme is applied to the Web page. By default, the Normal style is applied to the text. To format the text with other theme formatting, you can apply styles to the text.

Trouble?

Click the More Buttons button [»] on the Formatting toolbar to locate buttons that are not visible on your toolbar.

3. Select **Music Notes**, then click the **Style list arrow** on the Formatting toolbar

A drop-down list of theme styles appears. Each style name on the drop-down list is formatted in the style itself so you can preview the style before applying it.

4. Click **Heading 1**, then deselect the text

The Heading 1 style is applied to "Music Notes". The text is now formatted in 24-point Arial with a gold font color.

5. Select **Music News from the Marketing Department**, click the **Style list arrow**, click **Heading 3**, then deselect the text

The text is formatted in purple 14-point Arial.

6. Click at the end of the last paragraph, press **[Enter]** twice, type **Special Events**, press **[Enter]**, type **Industry Trends**, press **[Enter]**, type **Promotions**, press **[Enter]** twice, select the three new lines of text, click the **Bullets button** [≡] on the Formatting toolbar, then deselect the text

The paragraphs are formatted as a bulleted list using the theme's special bullets. You also want to add a horizontal line to the Web page.

QuickTip

Double-click a line object to open the Format Horizontal Line dialog box, which you can use to change the size or alignment of a horizontal line.

7. Press **[Ctrl][End]**, click the **Tables and Borders button** [⊞] on the Standard toolbar, click the **Outside Border list arrow** [□▾] on the Tables and Borders toolbar, click the **Horizontal Line button** [≡], then close the Tables and Borders toolbar

A horizontal line formatted in the theme design is added to the Web page. Once you have applied styles to text, you can customize the formatting to suit your purposes.

8. Select **Music Notes**, click the **Font Size list arrow** on the Formatting toolbar, click **36**, click the **Bold button** [B], click the **Italic button** [I], select **Music News from the Marketing Department**, click the **Font Size list arrow**, click **18**, click [B], then deselect the text

Compare your Web page with Figure G-6.

9. Save your changes to the Web page

A folder called Music Notes Home_files is automatically created on your Project Disk when you save the formatting changes you applied to the Web page in this lesson. The folder contains all the files—such as the theme, bullets, and styles—used in the Web page.

FIGURE G-5: Artsy theme in Theme dialog box

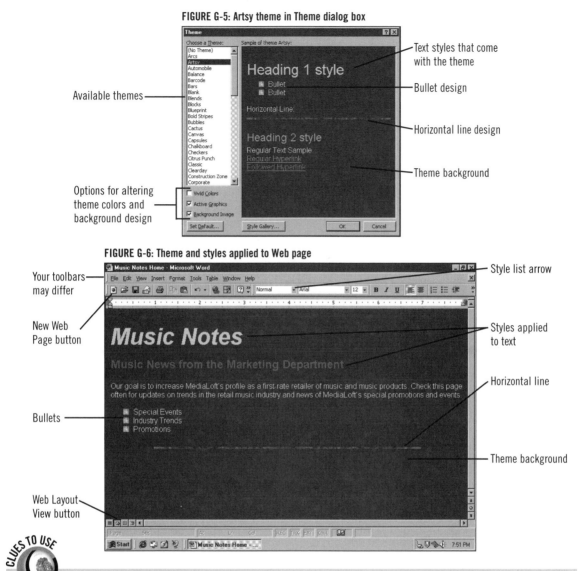

Available themes

Options for altering theme colors and background design

Text styles that come with the theme

Bullet design

Horizontal line design

Theme background

FIGURE G-6: Theme and styles applied to Web page

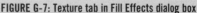

Your toolbars may differ

New Web Page button

Bullets

Web Layout View button

Style list arrow

Styles applied to text

Horizontal line

Theme background

CLUES TO USE

Adding backgrounds to Web pages

Backgrounds sit behind the text and graphics on a Web page to give your Web pages a colorful and interesting look. Word's themes include background designs, but you can also design your own backgrounds for Web pages. To add or change the background of a Web page, click Format on the menu bar, then point to Background. A color palette appears. If you want to use a solid color for a background, select a color from the palette or click More Colors to create a custom color. For more background design options, click Fill Effects on the color palette. The Fill Effects dialog box opens. The tabs in the Fill Effects dialog box allow you to choose between gradients, textures, or patterns as a background, or to select a picture file to use as a background for your Web page. Click the tab with the type of background you want, then select from the options for styles and colors on that tab. The Texture tab is shown in Figure G-7.

FIGURE G-7: Texture tab in Fill Effects dialog box

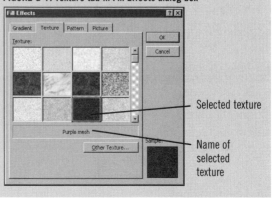

Selected texture

Name of selected texture

Adding Graphics to a Web Page

Unit G

Word 2000

You can insert clip art, bitmapped graphics, WordArt, and drawing objects into your Web pages to enhance their appearance. You can also add sound and motion clips to Web pages to create multi-media documents. When you insert a graphic object on a Web page, it is inserted as an inline graphic. To make it a floating graphic you must wrap text around it. Floating graphics align and position differently in Web Layout view than in other Word views. This is because Web browsers do not support all the same formatting options for graphics that you can use in print documents. For example, floating graphics with square text wrapping only align with the left or right side of a Web page. Using Web Layout view to position a graphic ensures that the graphic will look as you want it to when the Web page is viewed in a Web browser. ▶Scenario▶ Alice adds a clip art graphic to the Web page to make it look more interesting. For fun, she also inserts a sound clip so that people can listen to music as they read the Music Notes Web site.

Steps 1 2 3 4

1. Click at the end of **Music Notes**, click **Insert** on the menu bar, point to **Picture**, click **Clip Art**, click the **Pictures tab** if necessary, click in the **Search for clips text box**, type **CD**, press **[Enter]**, scroll down the list of CD clips, select the **black and white CD image** in the third row, click the **Insert clip button** 📷, then close the ClipGallery
   The CD graphic is inserted to the right of "Music Notes", in line with the text. Before moving the graphic, you'll change it to a floating graphic.

2. Select the **CD graphic**, double-click it, click the **Layout tab** in the Format Picture dialog box, click the **Square** wrapping style, then click **OK**
   The graphic becomes a floating graphic and automatically moves to the left side of the page. Floating graphics are right- or left-aligned on Web pages. If you want to center-align a graphic, you use an inline graphic. Next you'll resize the graphic to make it larger.

3. Position the ⬉ pointer over the **lower-right sizing handle**, then drag the sizing handle so that the graphic is about 2¼" wide
   You can use the horizontal ruler to help you resize the graphic. Notice that the graphic jumps to a fixed position in the upper-left corner of the Web page when you release the mouse button, as shown in Figure G-8. Next you'll add text to the bottom of the Web page.

4. Press **[Ctrl][End]**, click the **Style list arrow**, click **Heading 4**, click the **Bold button** 🅱 on the Formatting toolbar, then click the **Center button** ▤

5. Type **June is Jazz Month! Double-click the music icon to hear some cool jazz...**, then press **[Enter]**
   The text is formatted in the Heading 4 style, bolded, and centered on the page. You'll insert a sound clip of some jazz music at the location of the insertion point.

6. Click ▤, click **Insert** on the menu bar, point to **Picture**, click **Clip Art**, click the **Sounds tab**, click in the **Search for clips text box**, type **jazz**, then press **[Enter]**
   The jazz music clips appear on the Sounds tab.

7. Scroll down, click the **jazzy** clip in the last row, click 📷, then close the ClipGallery
   The jazzy clip is inserted below the line of text, as shown in Figure G-9. The clip remains centered because it is an inline graphic. To play a sound clip, you can double-click its icon. You must have a sound system and speakers installed on your computer to be able to play a sound file.

8. Double-click the **jazzy clip icon**, listen to the music, then save your changes to the Web page
   As the music plays, the jazzy clip icon changes to show the progress of the music clip, as shown in Figure G-10.

QuickTip
If you want to change the alignment of the floating graphic to make it right-aligned, you can double-click the graphic to open the Format Picture dialog box, and then change the horizontal alignment setting on the Layout tab.

QuickTip
If you want to position text or a floating graphic precisely on a Web page, you can create a table and insert the text and graphics in table cells.

QuickTip
If you are unable to insert or play a sound clip, read the remaining step to understand how a sound clip is played, then save your changes.

FIGURE G-8: Clip art graphic in Web page

Floating graphic is aligned on left

FIGURE G-9: Jazz clip in Web page

Inline graphic is centered on the Web page

FIGURE G-10: Jazz clip playing

Click to pause the music

Slider shows progress of music clip

Click to stop the music

Word 2000

Copying and moving Web pages

When you save a document as a Web page in HTML format, each graphic in the document is automatically converted to a GIF, JPEG, or PNG format file and placed in a supporting folder that contains all the files used in the Web page. This folder is created automatically when you create a new Web page or save a print document as a Web page. It contains the files for the graphics, backgrounds, bullets, horizontal lines, and other elements used on a Web page. The supporting folder is saved in the same location as the HTML document, and it has the same name as the HTML document file plus the suffix "files". For example, the supporting folder that was automatically created when you saved the Music Notes Home HTML file on your Project Disk is called the Music Notes

Home_files folder, and it too is located on your Project Disk. When you copy or move a Web page to a new location on your computer, you must be careful to copy all the files associated with that Web page—in other words, you must copy the supporting folder in addition to the HTML document file. If you change file locations, you might need to update the links to those graphics as well. If a browser cannot locate the graphic image files associated with a Web page, the browser will display a placeholder instead of a graphic. If you see a placeholder when you open a Web page you copied or moved, you'll know you need to go back and copy or move the supporting files associated with that Web page too, or you may need to update the graphic links.

CREATING A WEB PAGE WORD G-9 ◄

Saving a Document as a Web Page

As you learned in the preceding lessons, you can create a Web page by opening a new blank Web page, adding content, and then saving the Web page. You can also convert an existing Word document to a Web page by opening it and saving it as a Web page. When you save an existing print document as a Web page, Word saves the document as an HTML file and creates a supporting folder that contains all the files associated with the Web page. Word converts the content and formatting of the print document to HTML formatting and displays the page in Web Layout view. Web Layout view shows the document as it will look in a Web browser. Most formatting appears in a browser exactly as it appears in a print document, but some text and graphics may look different when you view them on a Web page. For example, columns are removed and graphics with certain kinds of text wrapping will change position when you convert a print document to a Web page. ▶Scenario▶ Alice wants to add a Web page about a jazz festival that MediaLoft is sponsoring to her Music Notes Web site. Rather than create the Web page from scratch, she uses a press release she wrote about the festival and saves it as a Web page. She then adjusts the formatting of the new Web page and applies the Artsy theme so that the page looks similar to the home page.

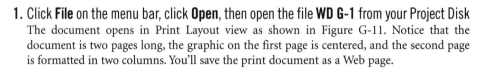

1. Click **File** on the menu bar, click **Open**, then open the file **WD G-1** from your Project Disk
The document opens in Print Layout view as shown in Figure G-11. Notice that the document is two pages long, the graphic on the first page is centered, and the second page is formatted in two columns. You'll save the print document as a Web page.

2. Click **File** on the menu bar, then click **Save as Web Page**
The Save As dialog box opens. "Discover Jazz" is the default page title and the Save as type list box displays "Web Page", indicating that the file will be saved in HTML format. You'll rename the file to match the page title.

3. Type **Discover Jazz** in the File name text box, then click **Save**
A dialog box informing you that some of the formatting features in the print document will not display in a Web browser opens as shown in Figure G-12. Specifically, the graphic with text wrapped around it in the press release will be left- or right-aligned in the Web page.

4. Click **Continue**
Word saves a copy of the document as a Web page to your Project Disk, and the document appears in Web Layout view. Notice that the graphic is now left-aligned on the Web page. If you scroll down the page, you'll also notice that there are no margins on the Web page, the document is one long page, and the text is formatted in a single column.

5. Click **Format** on the menu bar, click **Theme**, click **Artsy** in the Choose a Theme list box, then click **OK**
The Artsy theme is applied to the document. If you scroll down the page, you'll notice that text that was formerly black in the print document is now white on the Web page.

6. Scroll to the top of the page, select the **graphic**, then drag it to the upper-left corner of the Web page
The graphic jumps into place in the upper-left corner when you release the mouse button.

7. Click the **Show/Hide** ¶ button on the Standard toolbar, click in front of the first **paragraph mark** ¶ under festival, press **[Delete]** seven times, then click ¶
Compare your Web page with Figure G-13.

8. Save your changes to the Web page, then close the file
The Music Notes Home file appears in the document window.

FIGURE G-11: Discover Jazz print document in Print Layout view

Graphic is centered on the page

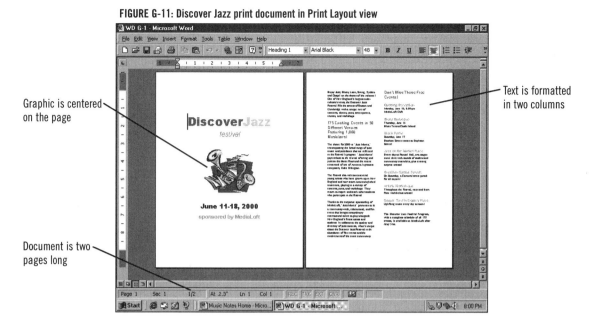

Text is formatted in two columns

Document is two pages long

FIGURE G-12: Microsoft Word dialog box

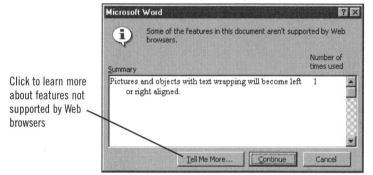

Click to learn more about features not supported by Web browsers

FIGURE G-13: Formatted Web page

Word 2000

Inserting Hyperlinks

Hyperlinks can link or "jump" to a document, to a Web page, to a different location in the current document or Web page, or to a different file, such as a multimedia file. You can also create a hyperlink to an e-mail message. When you create a hyperlink, you specify where you want to jump when the hyperlink is clicked. Text hyperlinks display in a document as colored, underlined text. You can use the Insert Hyperlink button or the Hyperlink command on the Insert menu to add hyperlinks to your documents. ▐Scenario▐ On the Music Notes home page, Alice inserts a hyperlink to the Discover Jazz festival Web page. She also inserts a hyperlink to the Billboard Online Web site on the Internet. Finally she inserts a hyperlink to her e-mail address so that MediaLoft employees can contact her with questions or suggestions.

Steps 1 2 3 4

1. Click at the end of **Special Events**, press **[Enter]**, click the **Bullets button** ▤ on the Formatting toolbar, click the **Increase indent button** ▦ twice, then type **Discover Jazz festival**

   You will create a hyperlink using this text.

2. Select **Discover Jazz festival**, then click the **Create/Edit Hyperlink button** ▦ on the Standard toolbar

   The Insert Hyperlink dialog box opens. You use this dialog box to specify the location of the file, the Web address, or the e-mail address you want to jump to when the hyperlink is clicked. You'll add a hyperlink to the Discover Jazz Web page file.

3. Click **Existing File or Web Page** in the Link to area if necessary, click **File** in the Browse for area, select the **Discover Jazz** file in the Link to File dialog box, then click **OK**

   The file name is added to the Type the file or Web page name text box. Compare your Insert Hyperlink dialog box with Figure G-14.

QuickTip

You can create a hyperlink to a graphic by selecting the graphic, then clicking the Create/Edit Hyperlink button.

4. Click **OK**

   Word automatically applies orange, underlined formatting to the "Discover Jazz festival" hyperlink. This is the text style for a hyperlink when the Artsy theme is applied. Next, you'll add another hyperlink to a Web page on the Internet.

5. Click at the end of **Industry Trends**, press **[Enter]**, click ▤, click ▦ twice, type **Billboard charts of top hits**, select the text, then click ▦

   The Insert Hyperlink dialog box opens.

QuickTip

If you don't know the URL of a Web page, you can click Browse in the Insert Hyperlink dialog box to open your browser and search the Web for the page you want.

6. Type **http://www.billboard.com/charts** in the Type the file or Web page name text box

   Compare your Insert Hyperlink dialog box with Figure G-15. You just entered the Web address, or **URL** (Uniform Resource Locator), for the Web page containing the Billboard charts of top music hits.

7. Click **OK**

   The new hyperlink appears on the Web page. Next, you'll create a hyperlink to an e-mail address.

8. Click under **Promotions**, press **[Enter]**, type **Contact Alice Wegman, Marketing Manager**, press **[Enter]**, select **Alice Wegman**, then click ▦

   The Insert Hyperlink dialog box opens.

9. Click **E-mail Address** in the Link to area, type **awegman@medialoft.com** in the E-mail address text box, then click **OK**

   "Alice Wegman" is formatted as a hyperlink, as shown in Figure G-16. You'll test your hyperlinks in a later lesson.

10. Save your changes to the Web page

FIGURE G-14: Insert Hyperlink dialog box with hyperlink to file

Creates a hyperlink to a document or Web page

File to jump to when the hyperlink is clicked

List of recently inserted links (yours will differ)

Adds a ScreenTip for the hyperlink

Text that displays as the hyperlink

Click to browse for the file to link to

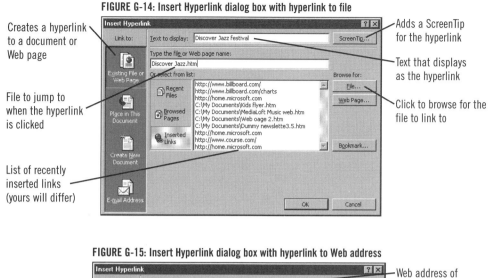

FIGURE G-15: Insert Hyperlink dialog box with hyperlink to Web address

Creates a hyperlink to a different location in the same file

Creates a new file to link to

Creates a hyperlink to an e-mail address

Web address of Billboard charts Web page

Click to browse the Internet for a Web address

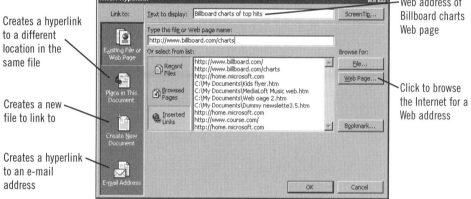

FIGURE G-16: Hyperlinks in Web page

Links to Discover Jazz festival Web page file

Links to Billboard charts of top hits Web page on the Internet

Links to e-mail message window to Alice Wegman

Editing Hyperlinks

As the information on your Web page changes, you'll need to change, update, and remove some of your hyperlinks. When you edit a hyperlink, you can change the hyperlink destination, the hyperlink text, or the ScreenTip that displays when a reader points to a hyperlink in a browser. You can easily edit or remove a hyperlink in Word using the Edit Hyperlink command. **Scenario** Alice edits the "Billboard charts" hyperlink to link to the Billboard Online home page, rather than directly to the Billboard charts of top hits Web page. She also changes the hyperlink text and adds a ScreenTip to the hyperlink.

To remove a hyperlink, right-click it, point to Hyperlink on the pop-up menu, then click Remove Hyperlink.

1. Right-click the **Billboard charts of top hits hyperlink**, point to **Hyperlink** on the pop-up menu, then click **Edit Hyperlink**

   The Edit Hyperlink dialog box opens. You'll change the destination of the hyperlink by changing the Web address to which it jumps.

2. Click at the end of the URL in the Type the file or Web page name text box, then press **[Backspace]** seven times to delete "/charts"

   The URL for the Billboard Online home page is http://www.billboard.com. You also want to change the text that displays the hyperlink.

3. Click between **Billboard** and **charts** in the Text to display text box, then type **Online—music news and**

   "Billboard Online—music news and charts of top hits" will be the hyperlink text. Before saving your edits to the hyperlink, you'll add a ScreenTip to the hyperlink.

4. Click **ScreenTip**

   The Set Hyperlink ScreenTip dialog box opens as shown in Figure G-18.

5. Type **Billboard charts and news online** in the ScreenTip text box click **OK**, click **OK** in the Edit Hyperlink dialog box, then save your changes to the Web page

   The revised hyperlink text appears in the Web page as shown in Figure G-19. The ScreenTip for the hyperlink will appear when the Web page is viewed in a browser, but it does not appear in Word. You'll preview the Web page in your browser in the next lesson.

Sending a Word document via e-mail

Another way to share information with others via the Internet or a local network is to e-mail a copy of a Word document directly from Word. To e-mail a document, open the document, then click the E-mail button on the Standard toolbar. An e-mail header opens at the top of the document window, as shown in Figure G-19. Type the e-mail addresses of the recipients in the To and Cc boxes, separated by semi-colons, or click the icons next to the To and Cc boxes to open and use your address book. When you are ready to send the file, click the Send a Copy button on the e-mail header toolbar. Word e-mails a copy of the file to the recipients using your default e-mail program.

FIGURE G-17: Document with e-mail header

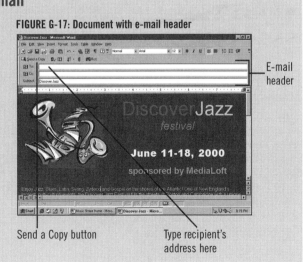

E-mail header

Send a Copy button

Type recipient's address here

FIGURE G-18: Set Hyperlink ScreenTip dialog box

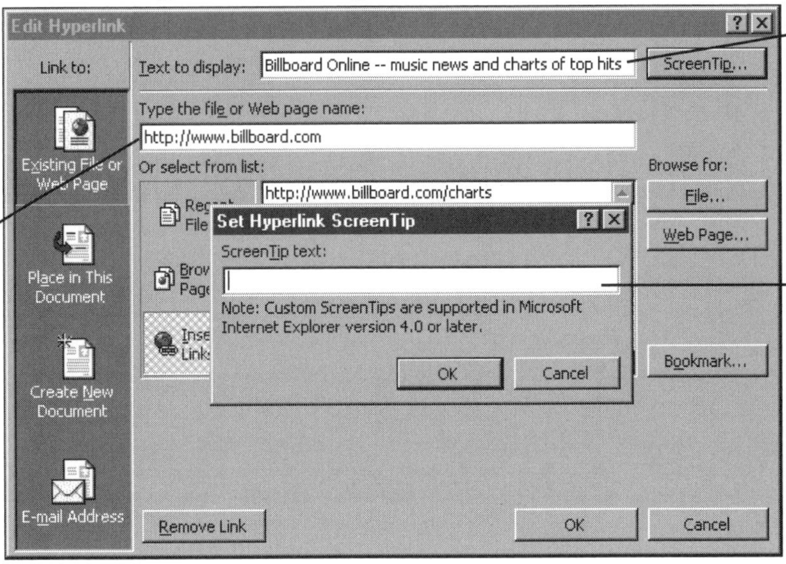

Revised hyperlink text

Revised URL

ScreenTip text will appear in the browser

FIGURE G-19: Edited hyperlink in Web page

Revised hyperlink text

Previewing a Web Page

Word's Web page preview feature allows you to see how your document will look in a browser so that you can edit it before publishing it to the Web or an intranet. When you view a document in Web page preview, Word makes a copy of the document and then opens the copy in your browser. If your browser is not open already, it opens automatically when you use Web page preview. When you view a Web page in Web page preview, you can test your hyperlinks to see if they work correctly. You can also view the HTML tags for your Web pages when the Web page is open in the browser. Scenario▶ Alice previews her Web site in her browser, tests the links, and views the HTML source code for the Web pages.

Steps 1 2 3 4

Trouble?

You must have a Web browser installed on your computer to complete this lesson. This lesson uses the Internet Explorer 5 browser. If you are using a different Web browser, your screens may not match the figures in this lesson and some features used in the lesson may not be available.

▶ **1.** Click **File** on the menu bar, then click **Web Page Preview**

The default browser opens and displays the Web page in the browser window. You may need to maximize your browser window.

2. Click the **Discover Jazz festival hyperlink**

The Discover Jazz page opens in the browser window, as shown in Figure G-20. You can scroll down the Web page to check its formatting before returning to the Music Notes home page. The browser toolbar contains buttons for navigating between Web pages.

3. Click the **Back button** ⬅ on the browser toolbar

The Music Notes home page displays in the browser window. Notice that the color of the Discover Jazz festival hyperlink has changed to olive green. The olive green color is the style for a hyperlink that has been followed when a Web page is formatted using the Artsy theme.

4. Point to the **Billboard Online hyperlink**

The ScreenTip you created for the hyperlink appears when you point to the hyperlink. If you are able to connect to the Internet, you can click the Billboard Online hyperlink to test it. The Billboard Online home page will open in your browser window. When you have finished viewing the Billboard Web site, you can click the Back button on the browser toolbar to return to the Music Notes home page. Next you'll test the e-mail hyperlink.

5. Click the **Alice Wegman hyperlink**

A new mail message to Alice Wegman opens, as shown in Figure G-21. You could type a message in the message area and click the Send button to send the message to Alice. However, you'll close the message and continue exploring your Web site in the browser.

6. Click the **Close button** on the message title bar, click **View** on the menu bar, then click **Source**

The HTML code for the Web page appears in the Music Notes Home Notepad window, as shown in Figure G-22. If you are familiar with HTML code, you can edit your Web page by changing the HTML tags in this window. Otherwise you can edit your Web pages using Word.

Trouble?

If the Edit button is not available in your browser, click the Word program button on the taskbar, then edit the document in Word.

▶ **7.** Close the Music Notes Home Notepad window, then click the **Edit button** 🖳 on the browser toolbar

The Music Notes Web page appears in the Word document window.

8. Scroll to the bottom of the page, click under the jazzy music clip, double-click with the ⫦ Click and Type pointer, then type your name

9. Save your changes to the Web page, print it, close the file, exit Word, then close your browser

You have finished your work on the Web page. Later, Alice will add a hyperlink to the marketing department Web page and the MediaLoft home page before sending her Web pages to the MediaLoft network administrator to post on the MediaLoft intranet site.

FIGURE G-20: Discover Jazz festival Web page in the browser window

Back button

Web page in browser window

Browser toolbar (your browser toolbar may be different)

Edit button in Internet Explorer

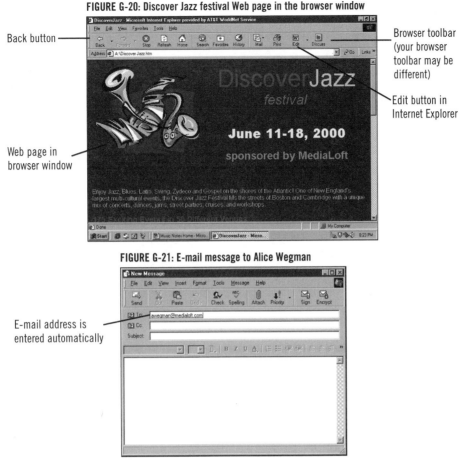

FIGURE G-21: E-mail message to Alice Wegman

E-mail address is entered automatically

FIGURE G-22: HTML source code for Web page

HTML tags

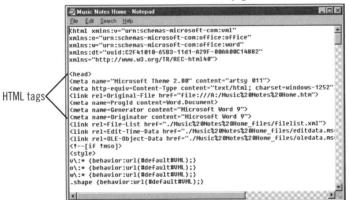

CLUES TO USE

Publishing a Web document to an intranet or the Web

To make your Web pages available on an intranet or over the Web, you need to publish (or post a copy) your Web site to a Web server. In order to post your Web site to an intranet, you must transfer the HTML files and support files to the intranet server on your local network. If you want to publish your Web site on the Internet, you can transfer the files to your Internet Service Provider (ISP), to be posted on your ISP's Web server. Check with your network administrator or your ISP for information on how to transfer your Web pages and the supporting files to the correct server.

Word 2000

Practice

► Concepts Review

Label each element shown in Figure G-23.

FIGURE G-23

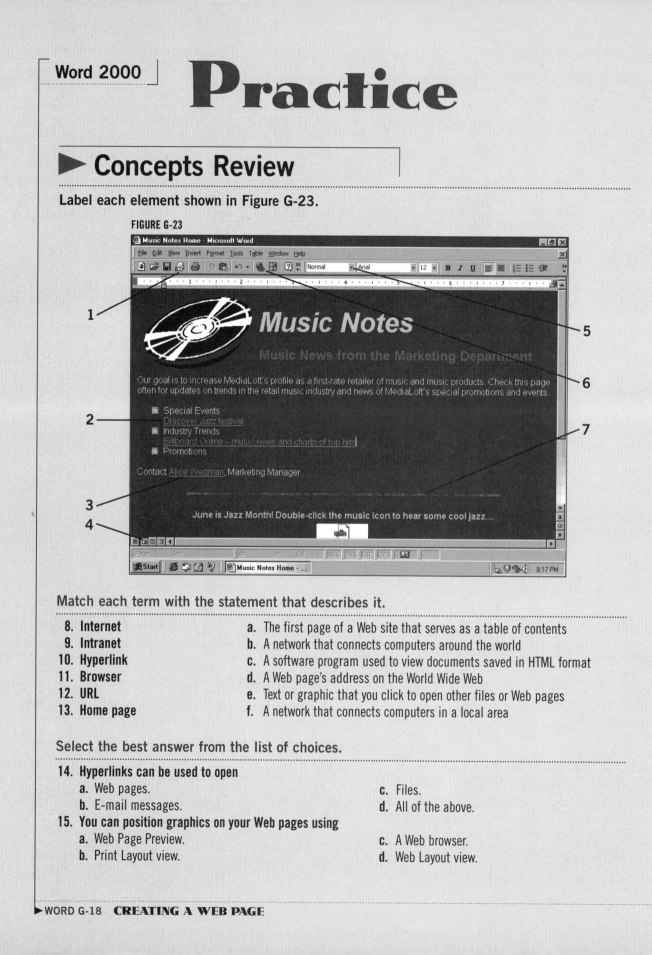

Match each term with the statement that describes it.

8. Internet
9. Intranet
10. Hyperlink
11. Browser
12. URL
13. Home page

a. The first page of a Web site that serves as a table of contents
b. A network that connects computers around the world
c. A software program used to view documents saved in HTML format
d. A Web page's address on the World Wide Web
e. Text or graphic that you click to open other files or Web pages
f. A network that connects computers in a local area

Select the best answer from the list of choices.

14. Hyperlinks can be used to open
    a. Web pages.
    b. E-mail messages.
    c. Files.
    d. All of the above.
15. You can position graphics on your Web pages using
    a. Web Page Preview.
    b. Print Layout view.
    c. A Web browser.
    d. Web Layout view.

16. **To insert a horizontal line on a Web page**
    a. Click Format on the menu bar, then click Theme.
    b. Click the Horizontal Line button on the Tables and Borders toolbar.
    c. Click the Line Style button on the Drawing toolbar.
    d. Click the Line button on the Drawing toolbar.

17. **To center a graphic on a Web page**
    a. Select the graphic, click Format on the menu bar, then click Center.
    b. Select the graphic, apply square text wrapping, then drag it to the center of the page.
    c. Select the graphic, apply square text wrapping, then click the Center button.
    d. Select the graphic, apply inline text wrapping, then click the Center button.

18. **When you save a print document as a Web page, which of the following is NOT true**
    a. The Web page has a filename and a page title.
    b. Word applies HTML tags to the document.
    c. Your browser opens.
    d. Word creates a folder in the same location as the Web page document.

19. **Web themes include designs for**
    a. Backgrounds, bullets, horizontal lines, and hyperlinks.
    b. Backgrounds, tables, hyperlinks, and bullets.
    c. Bullets, hyperlinks, headings, and frames.
    d. Bullets, horizontal lines, graphics, and headings.

20. **You can convert a print document to an HTML document in Word by**
    a. Clicking File on the menu bar, then clicking Save as Web Page.
    b. Clicking the Web Layout View button.
    c. Creating a hyperlink to the file.
    d. Clicking File on the menu bar, then clicking Web Page Preview.

► Skills Review

1. **Create a Web page**
   a. Start Word and create a new blank Web page.
   b. Type "Southeast Computer Solutions", press [Enter], type "Software training for business and home users", then press [Enter] twice.
   c. Save the new document to your Project Disk as a Web page with the page title "Southeast Home Page" and the file name "Southeast Computer Solutions".

2. **Apply themes**
   a. Apply the Straight Edge theme to the Web page.
   b. Select "Southeast Computer Solutions" and apply the Heading 1 style.
   c. Select "Software training ...." and apply the Heading 3 style.
   d. Click below the "Software training ..." subhead, type "Register now for Office 2000 courses:", then press [Enter].
   e. Type the following list, pressing [Enter] after each program name: Word, Excel, Access, PowerPoint, Internet Explorer, Publisher, FrontPage, PhotoDraw. Press [Enter] twice after "PhotoDraw".
   f. Select the list of programs and apply bullets to it.
   g. Use the Horizontal Line button on the Tables and Borders toolbar to insert a horizontal line under the bulleted list, then close the Tables and Borders toolbar.
   h. Click Format on the menu bar, point to Background, then click Fill Effects.
   i. On the Texture tab in the Fill Effects dialog box, select the Stationery texture (4th texture in top row), then click OK.

3. Add graphics to a Web page

    a. Press [Ctrl][Home], click Insert on the menu bar, point to Picture, then click Clip Art.

    b. Click the Office category on the Pictures tab, then insert the green and beige computer image in the top row (last clip in the top row).

    c. Close the ClipGallery.

    d. Drag the lower-right sizing handle to resize the graphic to be about 3" wide.

    e. Double-click the graphic.

    f. On the Layout tab in the Format Picture dialog box, set the text wrapping to square and set the horizontal alignment to right.

4. Save a document as a Web page

    a. Open the file WD G-2 from your Project Disk and scroll the document to get a feel for its content and formatting.

    b. Use the Save as Web page command to save the file as a Web page. Change the title of the page and the file name to "Southeast Fall Schedule", then click OK.

    c. Read the message about the formatting changes that will occur, then click Continue.

    d. Apply the Straight Edge theme to the Web page.

    e. Change the background to the Stationery texture.

    f. Drag the lower-right sizing handle of the graphic to resize it to be about 1" wide. Double-click the graphic, then apply the In line with text wrapping style to it.

    g. Click between the graphic and "Southeast", then press [Enter].

    h. Apply the Heading 1 style to "Southeast Computer Solutions".

    i. Center the graphic and the heading, then insert a horizontal line under the heading.

    j. Select all the text below "All courses begin September 8", including the text in the tables, then change the font size to 12.

    k. Bold the name of each software program.

5. Insert hyperlinks

    a. Click the Southeast Computer Solutions file button on the taskbar.

    b. Click under the horizontal line, type "Fall schedule", press [Enter], type "Office 2000 Certification", press [Enter], then type "Register by e-mail".

    c. Select "Fall Schedule", then click the Insert Hyperlink button.

    d. Create a hyperlink to the Southeast Fall Schedule file on your Project Disk. (*Hint*: Click File in the Browse for area.)

    e. Select "Office 2000 certification", then create a hyperlink to the URL "www.microsoft.com".

    f. Select "Register", then create a hyperlink to the e-mail address "register@southeast.com". Type "Register" in the Subject text box.

    g. Click the Southeast Fall Schedule file button on the taskbar, press [Ctrl][End], press [Enter], then type "Southeast Computer Solutions Home".

    h. Select the text, then create a hyperlink to the Southeast Computer Solutions file on your Project Disk. (*Hint*: Click the Existing File or Web Page icon in the Insert Hyperlink dialog box, then click File.)

    i. Save your changes to the file, then close it.

6. Edit hyperlinks

    a. Right-click the Register hyperlink, point to Hyperlink, then click Edit Hyperlink.

    b. Change the Text to display from "register" to your name.

    c. Click ScreenTip, then type "Send a message to Southeast Computer Solutions".

    d. Change the e-mail address to your e-mail address. If you don't have an e-mail address, type "[your name]@southeast.com". Click OK to close the Edit Hyperlink dialog box.

    e. Click in front of your name in the Web page, then type "Contact". Click after your name, then type "to register".

    f. Save your changes to the Web page.

7. **Preview a Web page**
   a. Click Web Page Preview on the File menu, then maximize your browser window if necessary.
   b. Click the Fall Schedule hyperlink.
   c. Scroll down the Southeast Fall Schedule page, then click the Southeast Computer Solutions Home hyperlink.
   d. If you can connect to the Internet, click the Office 2000 certification hyperlink to test it. Use the Back button on your browser to return to the Southeast Home Page.
   e. Click the e-mail hyperlink with your name. If you have an e-mail address, and if you can connect to the Internet to send an e-mail message, type a brief message to yourself, then send the message. Otherwise, close the mail message window.
   f. Click View on the menu bar, click Source, look at the HTML tags for the Web page, then close the Notepad window.
   g. Close the browser window to return to Word.
   h. Print a copy of the Southeast Computer Solutions file, then close the file.

Word 2000

▶ Visual Workshop

Create the Web pages shown in Figure G-24 using the files WD G-6 and WD G-7 from your Project Disk. Save the WD G-6 file with the page title and filename "Pacific Spring Flower Show". Save the WD G-7 file with the page title "Pacific Spring Flower Show Directions" and the filename "Directions". Format the Web pages using the Artsy theme, and create hyperlinks between the Web pages as shown in Figure G-24. Add your name to the Web pages before printing them.

FIGURE G-24

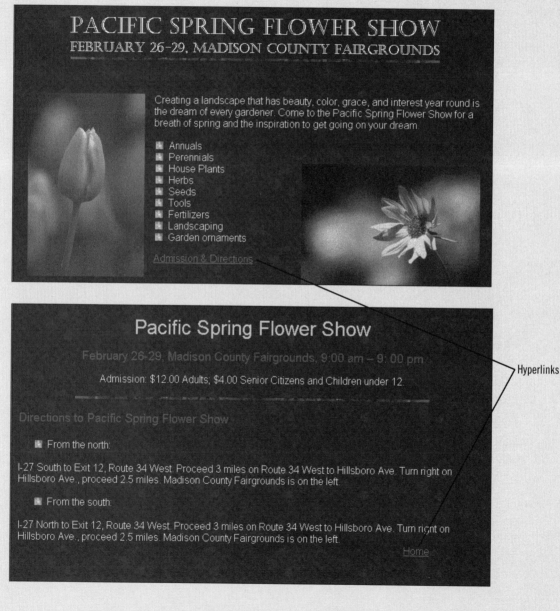

Hyperlinks

Merging

Word Documents

Objectives

► **Understand mail merge**
► **Create a main document**
► **Create a data source**
► **Enter and edit records**
► **Insert merge fields**
► **Perform a mail merge**
► **Create labels**
► **Sort records**

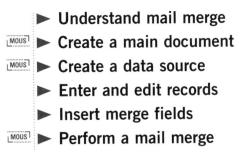

A mail merge combines a standard document, such as a form letter, with customized information, such as a recipient's name and address, to create a set of customized documents. Mail merge is widely used by companies who need to send similar documents to many individuals at once. The recipient's name and other personal information are often added to a standard document to create a more personal impression. The Word Mail Merge Helper guides you step by step through the mail merge process. ▸Scenario▸ The marketing department recently surveyed MediaLoft customers. Alice Wegman wants to write to the customers who provided especially helpful feedback. She uses the Mail Merge Helper to create a form letter, enter the customers' names and addresses, perform the mail merge, and generate a mailing label for each envelope.

Understanding Mail Merge

When you perform a mail merge, you merge a document that contains standard text with a document that contains unique data for individual people or items. Combining the two documents in a mail merge results in many customized versions of the standard document, each unique to an individual or item. Figure H-1 shows an overview of a mail merge. You can easily create form letters, mailing labels, envelopes, and other types of documents using Word's mail merge feature. **Scenario** Alice plans to produce her thank you letters using mail merge. Before beginning, she reviews the steps for merging documents using the Mail Merge Helper.

Details

Create the main document

The **main document** is the file that includes the text that will appear in every merge document. Text that appears in every version of a merge document is called **boilerplate text**. Later in the mail merge process, you will also insert merge fields into the main document to indicate where the custom information goes.

Create the data source

The **data source** is the file that contains the information, or data, that varies in each merged document. A data source is comprised of data fields and records. A **field** is a category of information—such as first name, last name, address, city, state, or ZIP code—that every merged document will contain. A **record** is a complete set of information for one individual or one item, such as one person's first name, last name, address, city, state, and ZIP code. Data source files are actually simple Word tables. Each column in the table represents one data field, such as a first name or ZIP code. The **header row** of the table contains the names of the data fields, called the **field names**, and each subsequent row in the table is a record. Each record row contains the complete set of data for one individual or one item.

Determine the fields to include in the data source

When you create a data source, you must decide what fields to include. It's important to think of and include all the fields you may need to use before you begin to enter data. For example, some addresses may include a department name or require a second line for an address, while other addresses may be very short. You can always leave a field blank if you don't need it, so it is better to use more fields rather than less fields in your data source. Each record must have the same number of data fields.

Enter the records in the data source

Once you have set up your data source and selected the fields to include, the next step is to enter the information for the records. When you perform a merge, each record is merged with the boilerplate text to create a unique document.

Insert merge fields in the main document

Merge fields are placeholders that indicate where in the main document the data from each record should be placed when the main document and the data source are merged. You must insert merge fields into the main document before performing the merge.

Perform the merge

When the main document and the data source are set up, merging the two documents is as simple as clicking a button. You can choose to merge to a new file, which will contain all the individual versions of the merged document, or to merge directly to a printer, fax, or e-mail.

FIGURE H-1: Mail Merge process

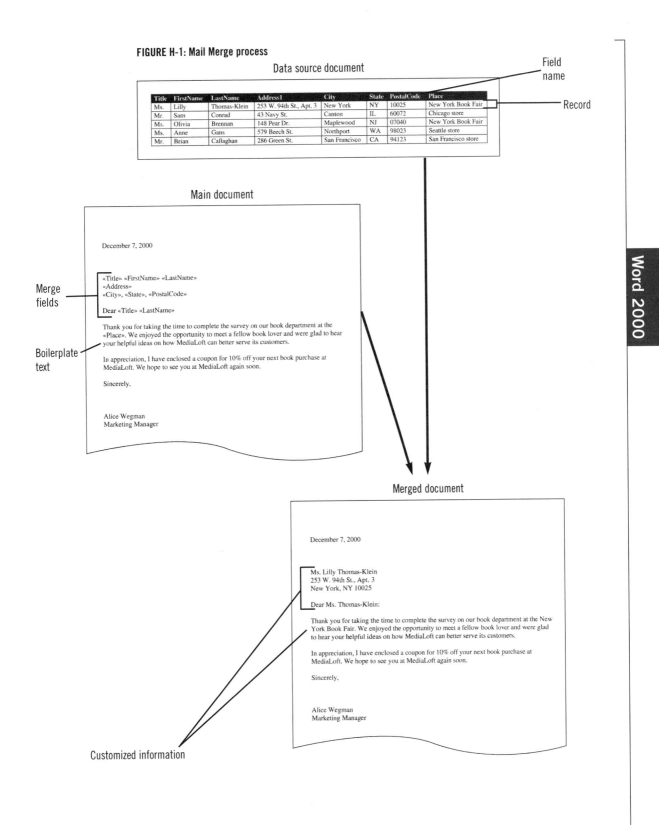

Data source document

Field name

Title	FirstName	LastName	Address1	City	State	PostalCode	Place
Ms.	Lilly	Thomas-Klein	253 W. 94th St., Apt. 3	New York	NY	10025	New York Book Fair
Mr.	Sam	Conrad	43 Navy St.	Canton	IL	60072	Chicago store
Ms.	Olivia	Brennan	148 Pear Dr.	Maplewood	NJ	07040	New York Book Fair
Ms.	Anne	Gans	579 Beech St.	Northport	WA	98023	Seattle store
Mr.	Brian	Callaghan	286 Green St.	San Francisco	CA	94123	San Francisco store

Record

Main document

December 7, 2000

Merge fields

«Title» «FirstName» «LastName»
«Address»
«City», «State», «PostalCode»

Dear «Title» «LastName»

Boilerplate text

Thank you for taking the time to complete the survey on our book department at the «Place». We enjoyed the opportunity to meet a fellow book lover and were glad to hear your helpful ideas on how MediaLoft can better serve its customers.

In appreciation, I have enclosed a coupon for 10% off your next book purchase at MediaLoft. We hope to see you at MediaLoft again soon.

Sincerely,

Alice Wegman
Marketing Manager

Merged document

December 7, 2000

Ms. Lilly Thomas-Klein
253 W. 94th St., Apt. 3
New York, NY 10025

Dear Ms. Thomas-Klein:

Thank you for taking the time to complete the survey on our book department at the New York Book Fair. We enjoyed the opportunity to meet a fellow book lover and were glad to hear your helpful ideas on how MediaLoft can better serve its customers.

In appreciation, I have enclosed a coupon for 10% off your next book purchase at MediaLoft. We hope to see you at MediaLoft again soon.

Sincerely,

Alice Wegman
Marketing Manager

Customized information

Word 2000

Creating a Main Document

The first step in performing a mail merge is to create the main document—the standard document that contains the boilerplate text. You can create a main document from scratch using the Mail Merge Helper, or you can modify an existing document and use it as the main document. You begin the mail merge process by using the Mail Merge command on the Tools menu. Scenario▶ Instead of typing the same letter to each customer, Alice will use the Mail Merge Helper to modify a standard thank you letter and merge it with a mailing list of customers. She begins by starting the Mail Merge Helper and saving an existing letter as the main document. She then modifies the boilerplate text to make the letter appropriate for the mailing.

1. Start **Word**, open the file **WD H-1** from your Project Disk, then save it as **Survey Letter Main**

The form letter opens in Print Layout view. This letter contains the boilerplate text for the main document. It's a good idea to include the word "main" in your filename so that you can easily recognize the file as the main document. You are ready to begin the mail merge process.

2. Click **Tools** on the menu bar, then click **Mail Merge**

The Mail Merge Helper dialog box opens. Instructions appear at the top of the dialog box to help guide you through the mail merge process.

3. Click **Create** in the Main Document area, then click **Form Letters**

A message box asking if you want to create a new document or use the document in the active window opens, as shown in Figure H-2. You want to use the Survey Letter Main document that is already open in your document window.

4. Click **Active Window**

The merge type and the path of the main document appear in the Mail Merge Helper dialog box, as shown in Figure H-3. Before moving on to create the data source, you'll edit the main document letter.

5. Click **Edit** in the main document area, then click **Form letter: A:\Survey Letter Main.doc**

The Mail Merge Helper dialog box closes so that you can make changes to the main document. The Mail Merge toolbar also opens. The Mail Merge toolbar appears in the document window of the main document when you are setting up a mail merge. You'll insert today's date at the top of the letter.

6. Click **Insert** on the menu bar, click **Date and Time**, click the **third date format** in the list of available formats, make sure the **Update automatically check box** is cleared, click **OK**, then press **[Enter]** five times

Today's date appears at the top of the letter. Clearing the Update Automatically check box ensures that the date is inserted in the document as a static date. In other words, the date will not be updated each time you save or print the document.

7. Scroll down, select **Alice Wegman** in the closing, type your name, then click the **Save button** on the Standard toolbar

The edited main document appears as shown in Figure H-4. Once you have edited the main document, you are ready to resume the mail merge process. You'll create a data source for the mail merge in the next lesson.

FIGURE H-2: Mail merge message box regarding the main document

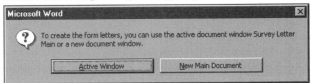

FIGURE H-3: Mail Merge Helper dialog box

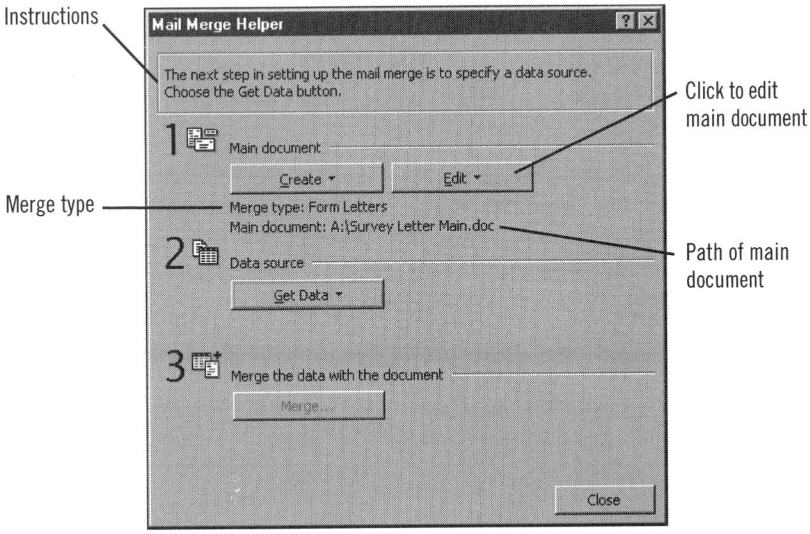

Instructions

Merge type

Click to edit
main document

Path of main
document

FIGURE H-4: Main document with Mail Merge toolbar

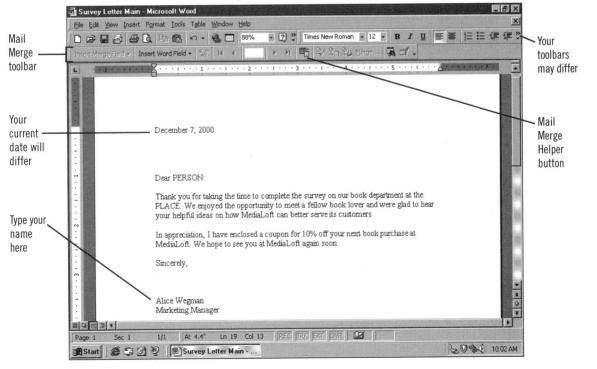

Mail
Merge
toolbar

Your
current
date will
differ

Type your
name
here

Your
toolbars
may differ

Mail
Merge
Helper
button

Word 2000

Creating a Data Source

Once you have specified a main document, you are ready to create a data source. The **data source document** contains the information that will differ in each version of the merged document. The data source document is actually a table that contains the fields to be used in a mail merge and the records for each individual document you want to create. The first row of the table is a header row that contains a field name in each column. A **field** is a specific item of data, such as a first name or a ZIP code. The remaining rows of the table contain the records for the mail merge. A **record** is the specific data for an individual or item. When setting up a mail merge, you can create a new data source or you can specify an existing data source that already contains the field names and the records you want to use in your mail merge. **Scenario** Alice creates a new data source for her mail merge. She includes fields for each customer's name, address, and place the customer filled out the survey. She begins by specifying the fields the data source will contain. Later she will enter the records.

1. Click the **Mail Merge Helper button** 📧 on the Mail Merge toolbar
The Mail Merge Helper dialog box opens with instructions for specifying the data source. Since a data source can be used with more than one main document, you want to design your data source to be flexible.

QuickTip

If you remove a field name by mistake, immediately click Add Field Name to restore it.

2. Click **Get Data** in Data Source area, then click **Create Data Source**
The Create Data Source dialog box opens, as shown in Figure H-5. The Field names in header row list box includes a list of commonly used field names. You can use each field name as is, or you can add or remove a field name from the list. The more field names you use in a record, the more flexibility you have. For example, having the title, first name, and last name fields gives you the option of addressing someone informally by using their first name, or formally by using their title and last name. You'll use some of the field names for your data source, but first you must remove the field names you don't want to use.

3. Click **JobTitle** in the Field names in header row list box, then click **Remove Field Name**
The JobTitle field is removed from the list. It will not be included in the data source.

4. Repeat Step 3 to remove the following field names: **Company, Address2, Country, HomePhone, WorkPhone**
The fields are removed from the header row list. The remaining fields are for the title, name, and address of customers. In addition to using the field names in the Field names in header row list box, you can add your own field names to create new fields. You want to add one field to your data source for the location the customer filled out the survey.

QuickTip

Field names must start with a letter, contain no spaces, and be unique within the same data source document. They can be up to 40 characters long.

5. Type **Place** in the Field name text box, then click **Add Field Name**
"Place" is added to the header row list. After adding all the fields you want to include in your data source, you are ready to save the data source file.

6. Click **OK**
The Save As dialog box opens. It's a good idea to include the word "Data" in your file name so that you can easily recognize the file as the data source file.

7. Type **Survey Data**, make sure the Save in list box displays the location of your Project Disk, then click **Save**
When you click Save, a message box reminding you that the data source contains no records opens, as shown in Figure H-6. In this message box, you can choose to edit the data source or edit the main document. You'll add records to the data source in the next lesson.

Help and instructions

Type new field name here

Click to remove selected field name

Field names

Click to move field names up or down in the list

Word 2000

Changing the order of field names

The order of field names in the data source does not matter, but it is convenient to arrange the field names in a logical order to make it easier to enter records in a data source document. To change the order of field names, select the field name that you want to move in the Field names in header row list box, then click the Up or Down arrows to reposition the field name where you want it in the list.

Entering and Editing Records

Once you have created the fields for your data source, you are ready to add records. Records contain the information related to each individual or each item. You use the Data Form dialog box to add or edit records in a data source quickly. The Data Form dialog box shows a form that includes text boxes corresponding to the field names in the data source. **Scenario** Alice enters the names and addresses of the customers who provided especially helpful feedback. She also enters information about where they completed the survey.

Steps

1. Click Edit Data Source in the Mail merge message box

The Data Form dialog box opens. The fields included in the dialog box are the fields you specified when you created the data source document. You enter each record you want to include in the data source in this dialog box.

2. Type Ms. in the Title field, then press [Tab]

"Ms." appears in the Title field and the insertion point moves to the FirstName field. Note that you must add a period after the title if you want it to appear in your letter. Pressing [Tab] moves the insertion point to the next field.

> **QuickTip**
>
> You can enter as many characters as you need to in the text boxes in the Data Form dialog box.

3. Type Lilly, press [Tab], type Thomas, press [Tab], type 253 W. 94th St., Apt. 3, press [Tab], type New York, press [Tab], type NY, press [Tab], type 10025, press [Tab], then type New York Book Fair

Compare your Data Form dialog box with the one shown in Figure H-7.

4. Click OK

Clicking OK closes the Data Form dialog box. You can add additional records to a data source at any time.

5. Click the Edit Data Source button 📋 **on the Mail Merge toolbar**

The Data Form dialog box opens showing the first record added. You'll add four new records.

> **Trouble?**
>
> If you clicked Add New after adding the last record, click Delete to delete the empty record.

6. Click Add New, then enter the following 4 records, pressing [Tab] to move from field to field and pressing Add New at the end of each record:

Title	FirstName	LastName	Address1	City	State	PostalCode	Place
Mr.	Sam	Conrad	43 Navy St.	Canton	IL	60072	Chicago store
Ms.	Olivia	Brennan	148 Pear Dr.	Maplewood	NJ	07040	New York Book Fair
Ms.	Anne	Gans	579 Beech St.	Northport	WA	98023	Seattle store
Mr.	Brian	Callaghan	286 Green St.	San Francisco	CA	94123	San Francisco store

Next, you need to review and save the changes to the data source document.

7. Click View Source

The Survey Data document showing the data records in table format appears in the document, as shown in Figure H-8. The Database toolbar also appears in the document window. Each field name in the header row of the table corresponds to a field in the Data Form dialog box. You can add or change records using this view, or you can click the Data Form button 📋 on the Database toolbar to open the Data Form dialog box. Table H-1 describes some of the buttons on the Database toolbar. You notice a mistake in the first record.

> **QuickTip**
>
> If you need your name on the printed solutions, change "Brian Callaghan" to your name.

8. In the first record, click after Thomas, then type -Klein

The data in the LastName field for the first record changes to "Thomas-Klein".

9. Save your changes to the Survey Data file, then close it

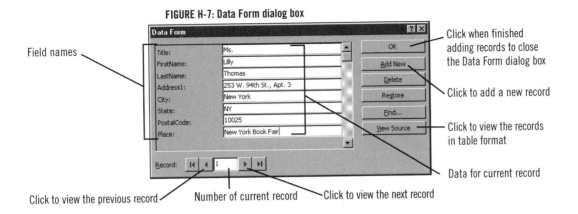

FIGURE H-7: Data Form dialog box

Field names

Title:	Ms.
FirstName:	Lilly
LastName:	Thomas
Address1:	253 W. 94th St., Apt. 3
City:	New York
State:	NY
PostalCode:	10025
Place:	New York Book Fair

Record: 1

Click when finished adding records to close the Data Form dialog box

Click to add a new record

Click to view the records in table format

Data for current record

Click to view the previous record   Number of current record   Click to view the next record

FIGURE H-8: Data records in table format

Database toolbar

Field names

Records

Title	FirstName	LastName	Address1	City	State	PostalCode	Place
Ms.	Lilly	Thomas	253 W. 94th St., Apt. 3	New York	NY	10025	New York Book Fair
Mr.	Sam	Conrad	43 Navy St.	Canton	IL	60072	Chicago store
Ms.	Olivia	Brennan	148 Pear Dr.	Maplewood	NJ	07040	New York Book Fair
Ms.	Anne	Gans	579 Beech St.	Northport	WA	98023	Seattle store
Mr.	Brian	Callaghan	286 Green St.	San Francisco	CA	94123	San Francisco store

TABLE H-1: Database toolbar buttons

button	name	use to
	Data Form	Open the Data Form dialog box to enter a new record or edit an existing record in the data source
	Manage Fields	Open the Manage Fields dialog box to add, remove, or rename fields in the data source
	Add New Record	Add a new record to the data source table
	Delete Record	Delete a record from the data source table
	Sort Ascending	Sort the records in the data source in ascending order
	Sort Descending	Sort the records in the data source in descending order
	Find Record	Search for a record in the data source
	Mail Merge Main Document	Switch to the main document

Inserting Merge Fields

Once you have selected the field names to include in your data source, the next step is to insert merge fields in the main document. The **merge fields** are placeholders that indicate where data from the data source should be inserted during the merge. You insert merge fields in the main document using the Insert Merge Field button on the Mail Merge toolbar. Table H-2 describes some of the other buttons on the Mail Merge toolbar. Inserting merge fields in the main document is the last step before performing the actual merge. Scenario➤ Alice inserts the merge fields in her main document. She uses the merge fields to create the inside address for the letters, a personalized salutation, and customized information inside the body of the letter.

Trouble?

Click the More Buttons button 🔢 to locate buttons that are not visible on your toolbars.

1. Click the **Show/Hide button** ¶ on the Standard toolbar to display nonprinting characters if necessary

You'll insert merge fields for the inside address above the salutation in the letter.

2. Click the blank line above Dear PERSON, then click the **Insert Merge Field button** on the Mail Merge toolbar

A list of the field names you selected for the data source appears.

3. Click **Title**

The Title merge field is inserted in the document, surrounded by chevrons (<< and >>). The chevrons distinguish merge fields from the rest of the text in the main document. Note that you must use the Insert Merge Field button to insert merge fields in a main document. You cannot just type chevrons around a field name.

4. Press **[Spacebar]**, click the **Insert Merge Field button**, click **FirstName**, press **[Spacebar]**, click the **Insert Merge Field button**, then click **LastName**

You must press [Spacebar] between merge fields if you want a space to appear between the data in the merged documents.

5. Press **[Enter]**, insert the **Address1 merge field,** press **[Enter]**, insert the **City merge field**, type **,** (a comma), press **[Spacebar]**, insert the **State merge field**, press **[Spacebar]**, insert the **PostalCode merge field**, then press **[Enter]** twice

Be careful to insert proper punctuation, spacing, and blank paragraphs when you insert merge fields.

6. Double-click **PERSON** in the salutation, insert the **Title merge field**, press **[Spacebar]**, then insert the **LastName merge field**

The Title merge field replaces the selected text. It can sometimes be useful to add placeholder text when you create a main document to later help you position the merge fields.

7. Select **PLACE** in the first sentence, insert the **Place merge field**, then click ¶

Compare your document to that shown in Figure H-9 and make any necessary adjustments.

8. Save your changes to the main document

FIGURE H-9: Main document with merge fields

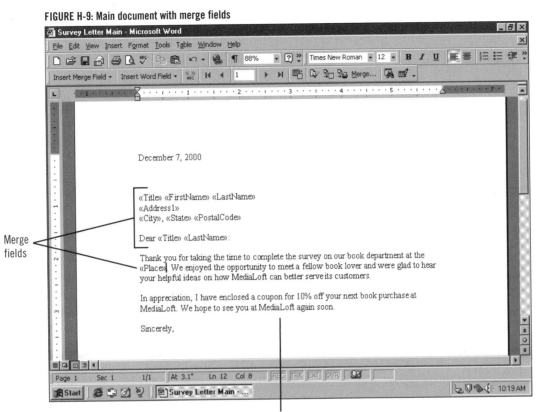

Merge fields

Boilerplate text

TABLE H-2: Mail Merge toolbar buttons

button	name	use to
««»» ABC	View Merged Data	Switch between viewing the main document with merge fields and with merged data
I◀	First Record	Go to the first record in a merged document
◀	Previous Record	Go to the previous record in a merged document
1	Go to Record	Go to a specific record in a merged document
▶	Next Record	Go to the next record in a merged document
▶I	Last Record	Go to the last record in a merged document
	Mail Merge Helper	Open the Mail Merge Helper dialog box
	Check for Errors	Check for errors in merged documents
	Merge to New Document	Merge to a new document and display the merged documents on-screen
	Merge to Printer	Print merged documents without reviewing them
Merge...	Start Mail Merge	Open the Merge dialog box
	Find Record	Search for a record in the merged documents
	Edit Data Source	Edit the data source document

Performing a Mail Merge

Once your data source is complete and you have inserted merge fields in the main document, performing the actual mail merge is as simple as clicking a button. When you perform the merge, you can choose to merge to a separate file, to a printer, to a fax, or to e-mail addresses. You can also choose to merge all the records or just certain records. Although merging to a separate file requires more disk space, it allows you to review and edit your merged documents before printing or sending them. **Scenario** Alice merges the letter to a separate file so that she can view the results of the mail merge and make any necessary adjustments before printing the letters.

Steps 1 2 3 4

QuickTip

To merge to a file quickly, click the Merge to New Document button on the Mail Merge toolbar. To merge to a printer quickly, click the Merge to Printer button.

1. Click the **Mail Merge Helper button** 🖳 on the Mail Merge toolbar
The Mail Merge Helper dialog box opens showing instructions for merging the documents.

2. Click **Merge**
The Merge dialog box opens as shown in Figure H-10. You can use this dialog box to select the destination for the merge, the specific records to be merged, and other merge options. If you have a large data source, you might identify a few records to merge to a new document. You would then review the merged records to be sure the merge fields appear in the main document as you expect them to and with proper spacing and punctuation. After reviewing the sample merged records, you could make changes to your main document if necessary before merging all the records. Since your source file is small, you'll merge all the records to a new document.

3. Click **Merge**
The main document and the data source are merged to a new document called Form Letters1, as shown in Figure H-11. The document contains five letters, each addressed to a different person. Each letter in the document is separated by a section break, which you can see when you view the document in Normal view or display non-printing characters in Print Layout view.

QuickTip

If you notice an error in an individual's merge fields, you should make the change in the data source, save the change, and then perform the merge again. This way the next time you use that data source file, the information will be up-to-date.

4. Scroll down and read each letter
The letters each include the custom information you entered in the data source. If you wanted to, you could edit an individual letter in the merged document file to customize it further. Note that any changes you make to the customized data in the merged document file are not made to the data source file.

5. Click **File** on the menu bar, then click **Save**
The Save As dialog box opens. If you have a very large data source you may decide not to save the merged file since merged files can take up quite a bit of disk space. Once the main document file and the data source file are created it is simple to merge the files any time you need the merged document. Since your merged file is small, you'll save it with a new file name before printing it.

6. Type **Survey Letter Merged**, make sure the location of your Project Disk is displayed in the Save in list box, then click **Save**
The document containing the merged letters is saved with the file name "Survey Letter Merged". You can now print the letters.

7. Click **File** on the menu bar, click **Print**, click the **Current Page option button** in the Print range area in the Print dialog box, then click **OK**
The first of five letters prints.

8. Close all open Word files, saving changes when prompted

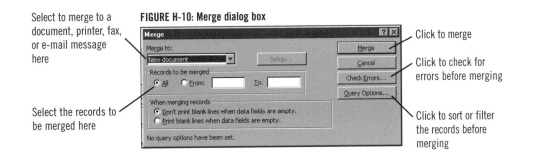

Select to merge to a document, printer, fax, or e-mail message here

FIGURE H-10: Merge dialog box

Click to merge

Click to check for errors before merging

Select the records to be merged here

Click to sort or filter the records before merging

FIGURE H-11: Merged documents

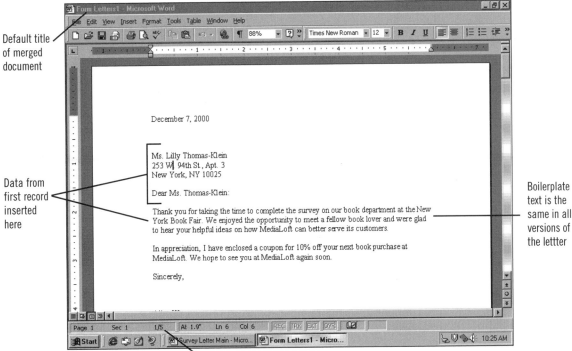

Default title of merged document

Data from first record inserted here

December 7, 2000

Ms. Lilly Thomas-Klein
253 W 94th St., Apt. 3
New York, NY 10025

Dear Ms. Thomas-Klein:

Thank you for taking the time to complete the survey on our book department at the New York Book Fair. We enjoyed the opportunity to meet a fellow book lover and were glad to hear your helpful ideas on how MediaLoft can better serve its customers.

In appreciation, I have enclosed a coupon for 10% off your next book purchase at MediaLoft. We hope to see you at MediaLoft again soon.

Sincerely,

Boilerplate text is the same in all versions of the lettter

Document is five pages long

Previewing merged documents

It's a good idea to preview a merge document before performing the merge to make sure that the printed documents will appear as you want them to. To preview a merged document, click in the main document, then click the View Merged Data button on the Mail Merge toolbar. The data from the first record in the data source appears in place of the merge fields in the main document window, and it appears just as it will in the printed document. Check the document to make sure that the merge fields, punctuation, and spacing all appear in the preview as you want them to

appear in the final merge. To view the data from other records, you can click the arrow buttons , , , , on the Mail Merge toolbar, or type a record number in the Go to Record box on the Mail Merge toolbar. To make adjustments to the main document, click the View Merged Data button again to view the merge fields in the main document, make the necessary adjustments, then save the main document. The View Merged Data button is a toggle button. You can use it to switch between viewing the merge fields and previewing the merged data.

Word 2000

Steps

Creating Labels

You can also use a data source to create labels or print envelopes for a mailing. To create labels or print envelopes, you must create a new main document, attach the existing data source, select the format for your labels or envelopes, and then merge the files. Word includes many standard formats for labels, envelopes, post cards, nametags, disk labels, and other types of label documents that you can create using a mail merge. **Scenario** Alice wants to create labels to mail the merged letters. She creates a new main document for the labels and attaches the data source.

1. Click the **New Blank Document button** 🗋 on the Standard toolbar, click **Tools** on the menu bar, then click **Mail Merge**
   The Mail Merge Helper dialog box opens. You'll create a new main document for the mailing labels.

Trouble?

The number following the filename "Document" will differ depending on the number of files you have opened during this session of Word.

2. Click **Create**, click **Mailing Labels**, then click **New Main Document**
   The merge type and a temporary name for the main document, Document4, appear in the Mail Merge Helper dialog box.

3. Click **Get Data**, then click **Open Data Source**
   The Open Data Source dialog box opens. You'll use the Survey Data data source document you created earlier.

4. Make sure the location of your Project Disk is displayed in the Look in list box, click the **Survey Data** file, then click **Open**
   A message box opens, prompting you to finish setting up your main document.

5. Click **Set Up Main Document**
   The Label Options dialog box opens, as shown in Figure H-12. You use this dialog box to select a standard format for your labels and specify options for printing the labels. The default brand name Avery standard appears in the Label products list box. The Product number box lists the many standard types of Avery labels for mailings, name badges, diskettes, file folders, post cards, business cards, and other types of label documents. You need to select the product number for the labels you plan to use.

6. Scroll down the Product number list box, then click **5161 – Address**
   The type, height, width, and paper size specifications for Avery 5161 – Address labels appear in the Label information area of the dialog box.

7. Click **OK**
   The Create Labels dialog box opens. In this dialog box, you insert the merge fields for the labels.

8. Click **Insert Merge Field** in the Create Labels dialog box, click **Title**, press **[Spacebar]**, then enter the remaining merge fields, spacing, and punctuation as shown in Figure H-13
   Be careful to enter the punctuation and spacing accurately so that your labels are punctuated properly when you perform the merge.

9. Click **OK**
   The Mail Merge Helper dialog box displays the file name and location of the data source and the merge options in effect.

10. Click **Close**
    The label main document with the merge fields inserted appears in the document window. You'll sort the records to be merged and perform the merge in the next lesson.

FIGURE H-12: Label Options dialog box

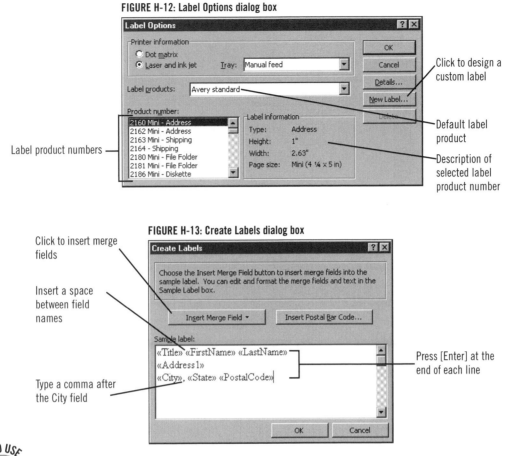

Label product numbers

Click to design a custom label

Default label product

Description of selected label product number

FIGURE H-13: Create Labels dialog box

Click to insert merge fields

Insert a space between field names

Type a comma after the City field

Press [Enter] at the end of each line

CLUES TO USE

Printing envelopes and labels

You don't need to perform a mail merge to print envelopes and labels in Word. You can easily format and print individual envelopes and labels using the Envelopes and Labels command on the Tools menu. The Envelopes and Labels dialog box includes an Envelopes tab and a Labels tab. On the Envelopes tab, shown in Figure H-14, type the recipient's address in the Delivery address box and the return address in the Return address box. Before printing the envelope, click Options to open the Envelope Options dialog box, where you can select an envelope size, format the font and position of the text on the envelope, and set the printing options. Click OK to close the dialog box. When you are ready to print the envelope, insert an envelope in your printer as shown in the Feed area on the Envelopes tab, then click Print. You can also print an individual label. On the Labels tab in the Envelopes and Labels dialog box, type the address for the label in the Address box, click Options to select the label product number in the Label Options dialog box, click OK, then click Print.

FIGURE H-14: Envelopes tab in Envelopes and Labels dialog box

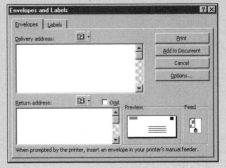

Word 2000

Sorting Records

You can determine the order in which Word merges the records in a data source by sorting the records. When you **sort** records, you arrange them in a logical order or sequence. For example, you might sort the records of a mailing list by last name or by ZIP code. You can sort the records in a data source by setting a query option. In the query option, you indicate the criteria (or fields) by which you want to sort, and then choose to sort the records in either ascending or descending order. You can sort a data source by a single field or by multiple fields. When you set a query option, you can also apply a **filter** to the records, or select a specific set of records to merge. Scenario▶ All bulk mailings at MediaLoft must be sorted in ZIP code order. Alice sorts the records in the data source so that the labels merge in ZIP code order. She then merges and prints the labels.

Steps

1. Click **Tools** on the menu bar, then click **Mail Merge**
   The Mail Merge Helper dialog box opens. You'll sort the records before performing the merge.

2. Click **Query Options,** then click the **Sort Records tab**
   The Sort Records tab in the Query Options dialog box contains options for sorting the records in a data source.

3. Click the **Sort by list arrow**, scroll down the list of field names, then click **PostalCode**
   Compare your Sort Records tab with Figure H-15. You can sort by more than one criteria if you want. Since you are using a small data source, it is sufficient to sort the labels by ZIP code.

4. Click **OK**
   The list of Options in effect in the Mail Merge Helper dialog box now includes a note that query options have been set. You are ready to perform the merge.

5. Click **Merge**
   The Merge dialog box opens with the default options in effect. You'll merge all the records.

QuickTip

If you want to see the borders around the labels, click Table on the menu bar, then click Show Gridlines.

6. Click **Merge**
   The records are merged to a new document in ZIP code order as shown in Figure H-16. The temporary name of the new document is Labels2. The labels are arranged in the document in a Word table. You may or may not be able to see the table borders depending on your table settings. Now that the labels are in a new Word document, you can format them as you wish.

7. Click **Edit** on the menu bar, click **Select All**, click the **Font Size list arrow** on the Formatting toolbar, click **14**, click the **Bold button** **B**, then deselect the labels
   The labels are formatted in 14-point bold text. To make formatting changes that affect only the fields in a document, apply the formatting changes to the merge fields in the main document. Before applying formatting, select the merge field by clicking and dragging over the chevrons and field name. Do not make formatting changes to the data source document because those changes will be lost when the merge is performed. You can now save the labels.

8. Click **File** on the menu bar, click **Save**, save the file with the filename **Survey Labels Zip Code Merge** to your Project Disk, then click the **Print button** 🖨 on the Standard toolbar
   The labels print. If you want to print the labels on label paper, you should use Avery 6151–Address label paper.

9. Close the file, save the label main document file with the file name **Survey Labels Main** to your Project Disk, close the file, then exit Word
   The sort options you specified for the data source are saved along with the main document file. When you open the data source file, the records will be sorted in ZIP code order.

FIGURE H-15: Sort Records tab in Query Options dialog box

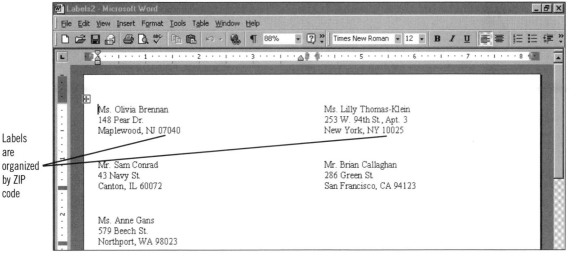

Sort in ascending order by postal code

FIGURE H-16: Merged labels in zip code order

Labels are organized by ZIP code

Filtering the records to be merged

Sometimes you do not want to send a document to all the individuals in a data source. For example, you might want to send a letter to only those customers who live in California. Using the Filter Records tab in the Query Options dialog box shown in Figure H-17, you can apply a **filter** to the records so that only the records that meet the criteria you specify merge. To filter records, click the Field list arrow on the Filter Records tab, select a data field, click the Comparison list arrow, then select a comparison phrase. A comparison phrase indicates how a field should be evaluated in relation to the criteria you enter in the Compare to text box. For example, to filter for the records of people living in California, you would select the field name "State" in the Field list box, select the phrase "Equal to"

in the Comparison list box, then type "CA" (the abbreviation for California) in the Compare to text box. You can specify up to six filter criteria on the Filter Records tab. When you finish setting filter criteria, click OK.

FIGURE H-17: Filter Records tab in Query Options dialog box

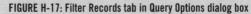

Practice

► Concepts Review

Label each element shown in the main document window in Figure H-18.

FIGURE H-18

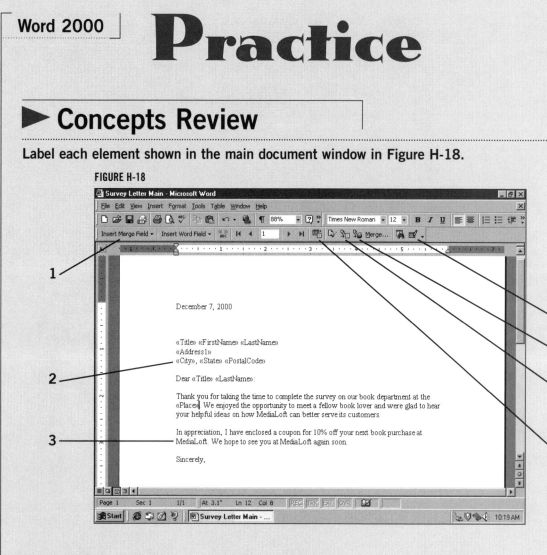

Match each term with the statement that describes it.

8.	Data source	a.	The text that is the same for each version of a merged document
9.	Record	b.	A file that contains the customized information that differs in each merged document
10.	Merge field	c.	A category of information in a data source
11.	Main document	d.	The entire collection of data related to an item or individual
12.	Boilerplate text	e.	Criteria used to select a group of records to be merged
13.	Filter	f.	A command used to show the data source in table format
14.	View Source	g.	A file that contains the standard text for all versions of the merged document
15.	Field	h.	The placeholder inserted into a main document to show where the customized data should be merged

Select the best answer from the list of choices.

16. **Which statement best describes a benefit of showing records in table format?**
    a. You can add or delete records from the data source.
    b. You can view one data record at a time.
    c. You can edit the merged document.
    d. You can add merge fields to the main document.

17. **Which of the following tasks cannot be accomplished using the Query Options dialog box?**
    a. Select records to be included in the merge operation.
    b. Save query specifications for future merge operations.
    c. Select fields to be included in the merge operation.
    d. Sort records by fields in ascending or descending order.

18. **To set up a mail merge, you must first**
    a. Click Tools on the menu bar, then click Merge Documents.
    b. Click Tools on the menu bar, then click Mail Merge.
    c. Click View on the menu bar, point to Toolbars, then click Mail Merge.
    d. Insert merge fields in a document.

19. **To place merge fields in a document**
    a. Click the Manage Fields button on the Database toolbar.
    b. Click the Insert Merge Field button on the Mail Merge toolbar.
    c. Click the New Merge Field button on the Mail Merge toolbar.
    d. Insert chevron symbols around the field names in the main document.

20. **The header row of a data source contains**
    a. Filters.
    b. Boilerplate text.
    c. Field names.
    d. Records.

▶ Skills Review

1. **Create a main document**
    a. Start Word, open the file WD H-2 from your Project Disk, then save it as "Ideas Main".
    b. Open the Mail Merge Helper dialog box by clicking Tools on the menu bar, then clicking Mail Merge.
    c. Click Create, then create a form letter main document using the Ideas Main document in the active window.
    d. Click Edit, then type your name in the From line of the memo. Click the Subject placeholder, then type "NEWSLETTER IDEAS".
    e. Save your changes to the main document.

Word 2000

2. Create a data source
- **a.** Click the Mail Merge Helper button on the Mail Merge toolbar.
- **b.** Create a new data source by clicking Get Data, then clicking Create Data Source.
- **c.** In the Field names in header row list box, remove all the field names except FirstName, LastName, and JobTitle.
- **d.** Add a field called "MailStation" using the Add Field Name button, then click OK.
- **e.** Name the data source file "Ideas Data" and save it to your Project Disk.

3. Enter and edit records in a data source
- **a.** Click Edit Data Source to add records to the data source document.
- **b.** Enter the following records, clicking [Enter] or [Tab] to move from field to field, and clicking Add New between records:

FirstName	LastName	JobTitle	MailStation
James	Quirk	Marketing Manager	34
Elizabeth	Martinez	Customer Service Manager	18
Scott	Silver	Vice President of Sales	4
Peter	Hendry	Charter Sales Liaison	45
Miranda	Ortez	Vice President of Marketing	35
Monica	Sims	Director of Advertising	20
Lorraine	Crow	Director of Development	32
Isaac	Parsons	Human Resources Manager	22

- **c.** Click OK after entering the last record.
- **d.** Click the Edit Data Source button on the Mail Merge toolbar, then click View Source.
- **e.** Compare the data source table to the table in Step b, save your changes to the data source file, then close it.

4. Insert merge fields
- **a.** Display the non-printing characters in the main document, then click after the tab character that follows To:.
- **b.** Click the Insert Merge Field button on the Mail Merge toolbar, then click FirstName.
- **c.** Press [Spacebar], then insert the LastName merge field.
- **d.** Type (a comma), press [Spacebar], then insert the JobTitle merge field.
- **e.** Click after the tab character that follows MAILSTATION:, then insert the MailStation merge field.
- **f.** Save your changes to the main document.

5. Perform a mail merge
- **a.** Click the Merge to New Document button on the Mail Merge toolbar.
- **b.** Scroll through the merged memos to check for errors.
- **c.** Save the merged document with the file name "Ideas Merge" to your Project Disk.
- **d.** Print one page of the document, then close the Ideas Merge document and the Ideas Main document, saving any changes.

6. Create labels
- **a.** Open a new blank document.
- **b.** Click Tools on the menu bar, then click Mail Merge.
- **c.** Click Create, click Mailing Labels, then click New Main Document.
- **d.** Click Get Data, click Open Data Source, select the Ideas Data file on your Project Disk, then click Open.
- **e.** Click Set Up Main Document.

f. Click 5161–Address in the Product number list box in the Label Options dialog box, then click OK.

g. In the Create Labels dialog box, click Insert Merge Field, then click FirstName.

h. Press [Spacebar], then insert the LastName merge field.

i. Press [Enter], then insert the JobTitle merge field.

j. Press [Enter], type "Mail station", press [Spacebar], then insert the MailStation merge field.

k. Click OK, then click Close in the Mail Merge Helper dialog box.

l. Save the labels main document as "Ideas Labels Main" to your Project Disk.

7. Sort records

a. Click the Mail Merge Helper button on the Mail Merge toolbar.

b. Click Query Options, then click the Sort Records tab.

c. Click the Sort by list arrow, click LastName, then click OK.

d. Click Merge in the Mail Merge Helper dialog box.

e. In the Merge dialog box, make sure New Document is selected, then click Merge.

f. Select all the labels, then change the font size to 14.

g. Change the name in the first label to your name, then save the merged labels with the file name "Ideas Labels Merge" to your Project Disk.

h. Print the labels.

i. Close all open files, saving changes when prompted.

▶ Visual Workshop

Using the Mail Merge Helper, create the nametags shown in Figure H-19. Name the main document "Nametags Main", name the data source document "Nametags Data", name the merged nametags document "Nametags Merge", and save all the files to your Project Disk. Add a record to the data source that includes your name. Print the nametags after performing the merge. (*Hint:* Create a mailing label main document. In the Label Options dialog box, select the 5095 – Name Badge product number. In the main document, increase the font size of the label text to 18 points, center the text, and boldface the field names for the name.)

FIGURE H-19

<table>
<tr><td>Louis Benoit
Director of Marketing
Computer Solutions, Inc.</td><td>Meredith Campbell
Vice President of Sales
VirtualWorld, Inc.</td></tr>
<tr><td>Gabriel Lee
Creative Director
Cyber Games Enterprises</td><td>Hannah Wadlington
President
Online Marketing, Inc.</td></tr>
</table>

Formatting
with Styles

Objectives

- ▶ **Understand styles and templates**
- ▶ **Create and use paragraph styles** [MOUS]
- ▶ **Create and use character styles** [MOUS]
- ▶ **Modify styles** [MOUS]
- ▶ **Use AutoFormat and the Style Gallery**
- ▶ **Display style names in a document**
- ▶ **Move around with styles**
- ▶ **Replace styles**

Word includes a variety of features to help you format documents to improve their appearance. You already know how to apply format settings such as font, font size, and font color to text. Using styles, you can apply multiple format settings to your text in one easy step. A style is a set of format settings that is named and stored together. You can apply styles one at a time in a document, or you can use AutoFormat to apply styles automatically to an entire document at once. You can also format a document by choosing styles from Word's Style Gallery, which provides templates for many built-in, professionally-designed business documents. **Scenario▶** Alice Wegman has prepared a summary of a recent customer survey for the MediaLoft annual report. She has also written a memo to all MediaLoft managers detailing the results of the survey. She uses a variety of style formatting techniques to improve the appearance of the summary and the memo.

Understanding Styles and Templates

Using styles to format a document can save you a lot of time and help to ensure that your documents are formatted consistently. A **style** is a stored set of format settings that can be applied to text. The format settings for a style are stored together and given a style name, such as "Heading". Instead of applying each format setting to your text, you apply the style so that the text is automatically formatted with all the formats included in the style. Styles are closely related to templates. A **template** is a document that is used as a basis for creating other documents. Templates contain text or formatting that is the same in every document of the same type, such as a memo or a report. When you create a new blank document in Word, that document is based on Word's **Normal template**.

Details

It is important to understand the following about styles and templates:

 The Normal template is a simple, all-purpose template that contains only a few basic format settings, such as font, font size, margins, and line spacing.

 When you start typing in a new blank document, Word automatically uses the font, font size, line spacing, alignment and other format settings defined for the Normal template. The **Normal style** is the default paragraph style in the Normal template. Figure I-1 shows text formatted in the Normal style. Word applies this style to text unless you specify otherwise.

 The Normal template comes with a set of predefined styles that you can use when you create a new blank document. You can view the styles associated with the Normal style, as shown in Figure I-2, by clicking the Style list arrow on the Formatting toolbar. Figure I-3 shows a document formatted with several predefined styles from the Normal template.

 In addition to the Normal template, Word also includes templates for many other specific types of documents. When you select a template to create a document, its default styles are automatically assigned to that document. When you use a Word document, you can apply the predefined styles, create new styles, modify existing styles, or copy styles from existing templates to a new document.

Style names are used to identify each set of stored format settings. When you apply a style, the format settings associated with the style name are applied to the selected text or paragraph. When you modify a style definition, the formatting changes are automatically made to all text to which that style has been applied.

There are two types of styles: paragraph and character. Paragraph styles include character and paragraph format settings and are used to format entire paragraphs at once. Character styles include font format settings and are used to format selected text.

FIGURE I-1: New blank document in Word with Normal style applied

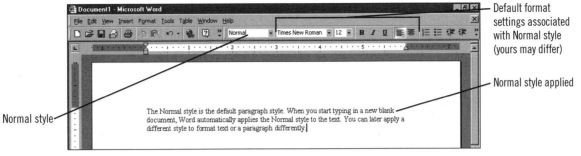

Normal style

Normal style

Default format settings associated with Normal style (yours may differ)

Normal style applied

FIGURE I-2: Predefined styles in Word's Normal template

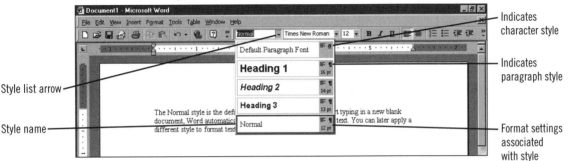

Style list arrow

Style name

Indicates character style

Indicates paragraph style

Format settings associated with style

FIGURE I-3: Document formatted with predefined styles from the Normal template

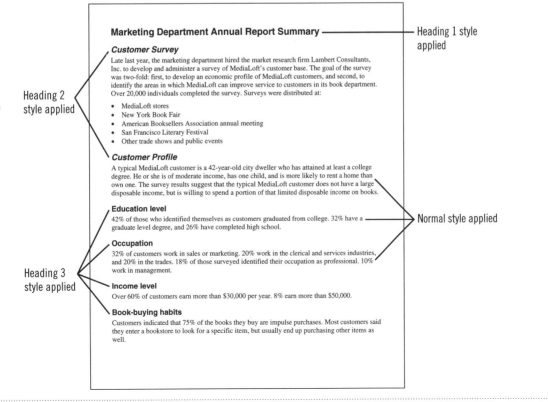

Marketing Department Annual Report Summary

Customer Survey

Late last year, the marketing department hired the market research firm Lambert Consultants, Inc. to develop and administer a survey of MediaLoft's customer base. The goal of the survey was two-fold: first, to develop an economic profile of MediaLoft customers, and second, to identify the areas in which MediaLoft can improve service to customers in its book department. Over 20,000 individuals completed the survey. Surveys were distributed at:

- MediaLoft stores
- New York Book Fair
- American Booksellers Association annual meeting
- San Francisco Literary Festival
- Other trade shows and public events

Customer Profile

A typical MediaLoft customer is a 42-year-old city dweller who has attained at least a college degree. He or she is of moderate income, has one child, and is more likely to rent a home than own one. The survey results suggest that the typical MediaLoft customer does not have a large disposable income, but is willing to spend a portion of that limited disposable income on books.

Education level

42% of those who identified themselves as customers graduated from college. 32% have a graduate level degree, and 26% have completed high school.

Occupation

32% of customers work in sales or marketing. 20% work in the clerical and services industries, and 20% in the trades. 18% of those surveyed identified their occupation as professional. 10% work in management.

Income level

Over 60% of customers earn more than $30,000 per year. 8% earn more than $50,000.

Book-buying habits

Customers indicated that 75% of the books they buy are impulse purchases. Most customers said they enter a bookstore to look for a specific item, but usually end up purchasing other items as well.

Heading 1 style applied

Heading 2 style applied

Heading 3 style applied

Normal style applied

Creating and Using Paragraph Styles

Using styles can save a lot of time and reduce formatting errors. A **paragraph style** is a stored set of character and paragraph format settings that you can apply to a paragraph. Paragraph styles can contain information on all aspects of a paragraph's appearance, such as fonts, alignment, tab stops, line spacing, and borders. You can apply an existing paragraph style to a paragraph, or you can create a new paragraph style that includes the settings you want. Remember, a paragraph is any text followed by a paragraph mark. A paragraph can even be a single word such as a heading. Scenario ► Alice has already written the text for the annual report, formatted it in columns, created a header for the document, and completed some of the formatting. She now creates paragraph styles so that she can quickly and consistently format the report headings.

Steps

QuickTip

To return personalized tool-bars and menus to the default settings, click Tools on the menu bar, click Customize, click Reset my usage data on the Options tab, click Yes, then click Close.

1. Start **Word**, open the file **WD I-1** from your Project Disk, then save it as **Annual Report**
   The document opens in Print Layout view. The text is formatted using the styles associated with the Normal template. The quickest way to create a new style is to format a paragraph and then base the new style on the paragraph you formatted.

2. Select the heading **Sampling**, click the **Font list arrow** on the Formatting toolbar, click **Tahoma**, click the **Font Size list arrow**, click **16**, then click the **Bold button** B
   Next you'll add spacing under the paragraph.

3. Click **Format** on the menu bar, click **Paragraph**, click the **Indents and Spacing tab**, click the **Spacing After up arrow** once so that 6 pt displays, click **OK**, then deselect the text
   You'll create a style based on the existing example.

QuickTip

To create a new style from scratch click Format on the menu bar, click Style, click New, click Format, then use the options on the Format button menu to define the style settings.

4. Select **Sampling**, click **Format** on the menu bar, then click **Style**
   The Style dialog box opens as shown in Figure I-4. You can use the Style dialog box to create and modify paragraph and character styles.

5. Click **New**
   The New Style dialog box opens, as shown in Figure I-5. In this dialog box you provide a name for the new style and specify the type of style you want to create. You name the style "AR Heading" to remind you that this is the style you used for the annual report headings.

6. Type **AR Heading** in the Name text box, click the **Style type list arrow**, click **Paragraph** if necessary, click **OK**, then click **Apply** in the Style dialog box
   When you create a style based on selected text, it is important to click Apply in the Style dialog box so that the style name is applied to the selected text. The dialog box closes. The style name "AR Heading" appears in the Style list box on the Formatting toolbar. Now you can apply the AR Heading style to other paragraphs in the document.

QuickTip

The format settings associated with a style are applied to the style name so you can see what each style looks like.

7. Scroll down, select **Customer profile results**, then click the **Style list arrow** on the Formatting toolbar
   The Style list opens. The Style list includes the AR Heading style you created as well as several other styles associated with this document.

8. Click **AR Heading**
   The format settings for the AR Heading style are applied to the paragraph.

9. Click **Service to customers** in the second column, click the **Style list arrow**, click **AR Heading**, then save your changes
   Notice that to apply a paragraph style, you can simply click in the paragraph to which you want to apply the style; you do not need to select a whole paragraph to apply a paragraph style to it. Compare your document with Figure I-6.

FIGURE I-4: Style dialog box

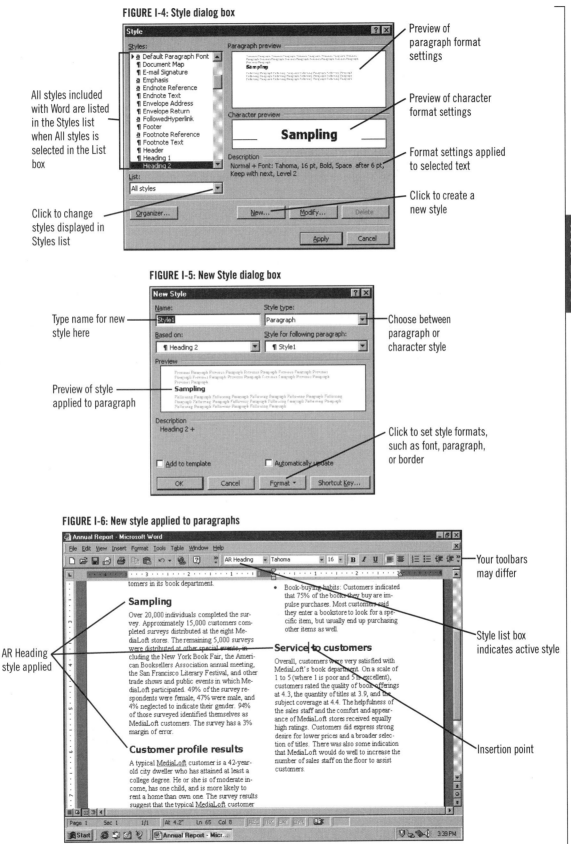

Preview of paragraph format settings

Preview of character format settings

Format settings applied to selected text

Click to create a new style

All styles included with Word are listed in the Styles list when All styles is selected in the List box

Click to change styles displayed in Styles list

FIGURE I-5: New Style dialog box

Type name for new style here

Choose between paragraph or character style

Preview of style applied to paragraph

Click to set style formats, such as font, paragraph, or border

FIGURE I-6: New style applied to paragraphs

Your toolbars may differ

Style list box indicates active style

AR Heading style applied

Insertion point

Creating and Using Character Styles

A **character style** is a stored set of font format settings that can be applied to words or characters within a paragraph. Text within a paragraph can have its own character style even if a paragraph style is applied to the whole paragraph. Using character styles to format text ensures consistent formatting. For example, you can create a character style that includes bold, small caps, and italic formatting. Then you can apply this style so all occurrences of a product name in a report are formatted the same. **Scenario** Alice wants all the bullet headings in the Customer profile results section of the annual report to stand out and to be formatted identically. She creates a character style and then applies it to all the bullet headings.

Steps

1. Scroll to the bottom of the page, select **Education level** in the first bullet, click the **Font list arrow** on the Formatting toolbar, click **Tahoma**, then click the **Bold button** B
   The text is formatted in 12-point Tahoma bold.

2. Click **Format** on the menu bar, click **Style**, then click **New**
   The New Style dialog box opens. Notice that the default style type is paragraph and that the description of the style includes settings for indents, bullets, and tabs. You want to save only the character format settings so that you can apply the style to text within any paragraph.

3. Type **AR Subhead** in the Name text box, click the **Style type list arrow**, then click **Character**
   When you select character as the style type, the font format settings appear in the style description as shown in Figure I-7.

4. Click **OK**, then click **Apply**
   The AR Subhead style is applied to "Education level".

5. Scroll to the top of the page, select **Occupation**, click the **Style list arrow** on the Formatting toolbar, then click **AR Subhead**
   The new character style is applied to the text. Notice that only the text you selected is formatted in the style. The other text in the paragraph does not change.

6. Apply the **AR Subhead** style to **Income level** and **Book-buying habits**, then deselect the text
   Compare your document with Figure I-8.

7. Save your changes to the document

FIGURE I-7: New Style dialog box showing character style

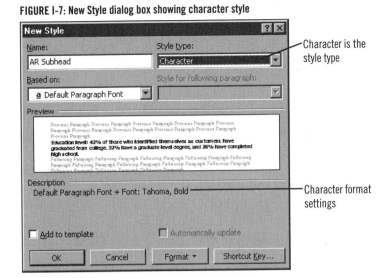

Character is the style type

Character format settings

FIGURE I-8: Character styles applied

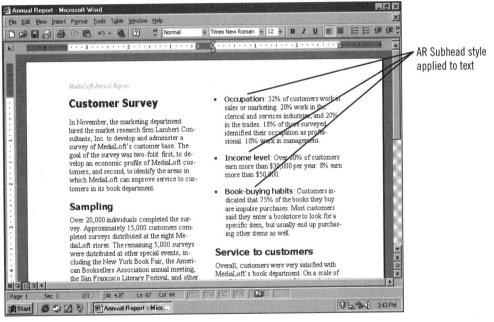

AR Subhead style applied to text

Changing the case of characters

When you are formatting a document, you may want to alter the way words are capitalized or the case in which text appears. For example, you may decide that every word in a heading should be capitalized. Rather than deleting the text you want to change and retyping it, you can quickly switch between uppercase and lowercase characters using the Change Case command on the Format menu. To change the case of text, select the text you want to change, click Format on the menu bar, then click Change Case. The Change Case dialog box opens and includes options for making all selected characters uppercase or lowercase, for capitalizing only the first character of a sentence (sentence case), for capitalizing each word in the selected text (title case), or for switching the case of all selected characters (toggle case).

Modifying Styles

When you use styles to format text and paragraphs, you can change the format of each occurrence of the style in the document quickly and consistently. When you modify a style, the new format settings associated with the style are applied automatically to all text formatted in that style. You can modify a style by changing the formatting of a selected example of a style and then reapplying the style, or by using the Style command on the Format menu. **Scenario** Alice thinks the document would look better if she added a border to the headings and italicized the subheadings in the bullets. She modifies the AR Heading and the AR Subhead styles so that the changes she makes are applied consistently throughout the document.

Steps

1. Select **Sampling**, click **Format** on the menu bar, click **Borders and Shading**, click the **Borders tab**, make sure the **first line style** is selected in the Style list, make sure **½ pt** is selected in the Width list box, click the **Apply to list arrow**, click **Paragraph**, click the **bottom border** in the Preview area, then click **OK**

   A ½-point border is added under the "Sampling" paragraph. You want to update the AR Heading style so that the border is applied to all instances of the style in the document. You can modify the style by reapplying it to the modified paragraph.

2. Make sure the "Sampling" paragraph is still selected, click the **Style list arrow** on the Formatting toolbar, then click **AR Heading**

   The Modify Style dialog box opens, as shown in Figure I-9. You can choose either to update the style based on the changes to the selected paragraph or reapply the original style settings to the selected paragraph. You want to update the style.

3. Make sure the **Update the style to reflect recent changes? option button** is selected, then click **OK**

   A border is added to all text to which the AR Heading style is applied in the document. Next you'll modify the AR Subhead style using the Style command.

4. Click **Format** on the menu bar, then click **Style**

   The Style dialog box opens.

5. Click **AR Subhead** in the Styles list, then click **Modify**

   The Modify Style dialog box opens. You can use this dialog box to change the format settings included in a style and to create keyboard shortcuts for styles.

6. Click **Format**, then click **Font**

   The Font dialog box opens.

7. Click **Bold Italic** in the Font style list, click **OK**, then click **OK** in the Modify Style dialog box

   The new format settings for the AR Subhead style appear in the Style dialog box as shown in Figure I-10. Notice that "Sampling" appears in the Character preview window. "Sampling" is formatted with the AR Heading style, but it is displayed in the Character preview window because it is selected in the document. When the modified AR Subhead style is applied, it will be applied only to text formatted with the AR Subhead style.

8. Click **Close**

   The style change is applied to all instances of the AR Subhead style, as shown in Figure I-11. When you use the Style command to modify a style, all instances of the style are automatically updated when you close the Style dialog box. You have finished formatting the summary for the annual report.

9. Type your name at the end of the document, save your changes, print the document, then close the file

FIGURE I-9: Modify Style dialog box

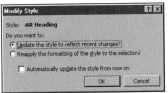

FIGURE I-10: Style dialog box with new format settings

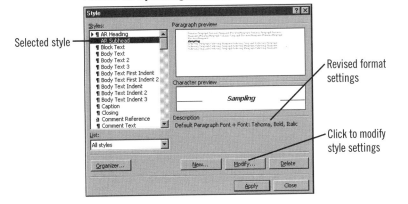

Selected style

Revised format settings

Click to modify style settings

FIGURE I-11: Style changes in the document

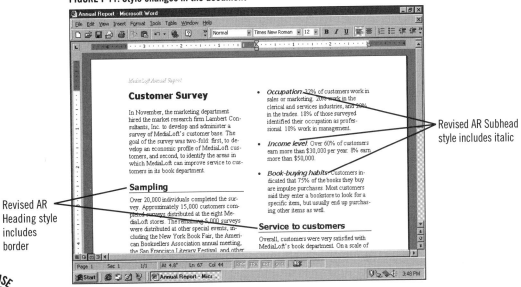

Revised AR Heading style includes border

Revised AR Subhead style includes italic

Assigning keyboard shortcuts to styles

To apply styles even faster, you can assign a keyboard shortcut to a style. In the Style dialog box, select the style to which you want to assign a keyboard shortcut, then click Modify. In the Modify Style dialog box, click Shortcut Key to open the Customize Keyboard dialog box. Press the combination of keys you want to use as a shortcut, verify that the correct combination appears in the Press new shortcut key text box, then click Assign. Take care not to assign a keyboard shortcut that has already been assigned to another command. Click the Save changes in list arrow to choose whether to save the shortcut as part of a template or as part of the document. If you are sharing your computer with other users, be sure to save the shortcut as part of the document. When you have finished, click Close, then close the other open dialog boxes. If you use a style often, it can save time to create a keyboard shortcut.

Using AutoFormat and the Style Gallery

With the AutoFormat feature, Word automatically applies paragraph styles to a document to improve its appearance. When you use AutoFormat, Word analyzes the paragraphs in your document and decides which type of paragraph style to apply to each—heading, body text, bulleted list, and so on. When you use AutoFormat, the paragraph styles applied to the document are styles from the Normal template. Once you have applied styles to a document—either by using AutoFormat or by applying styles individually—you can use the Style Gallery to select a different template and change the overall design of your document. When you choose a different template from the Style Gallery, Word applies the styles from that template to the current document. ▶Scenario◀ Alice has drafted a memo describing the results of the customer survey. She uses AutoFormat to apply styles to the memo and then selects a different template from the Style Gallery.

Steps 1234

1. Open the file **WD I-2** from your Project Disk, then save it as **Survey memo**

The document opens in Print Layout view. Notice the formatting of the memo header, the headings, and the hyphens in front of some of the paragraphs. These elements will be formatted differently when you AutoFormat the document.

2. Click **Format** on the menu bar, then click **AutoFormat**

The AutoFormat dialog box opens as shown in Figure I-12. This dialog box offers the option of formatting the entire document at once or of reviewing each AutoFormat change individually in order to accept or reject it. You'll format the entire document at once.

3. Make sure the **AutoFormat now option button** is selected, then click **OK**

Word automatically applies styles and other formatting changes to the document as shown in Figure I-13. As you scroll down the document, click in various parts of it to view what style is applied to that part of the document.

4. Click **Sampling**

Notice the style name that appears in the Style list box on the Formatting toolbar indicates that the Heading 1 style is applied to this paragraph. However, you want the "Sampling" heading to be a subheading under the memo title "MediaLoft Customer Survey".

5. Click the **Style list arrow** on the Formatting toolbar, then click **Heading 2**

The Heading 2 style is applied to the text.

6. Scroll down, click **Survey Results**, apply the **Heading 2** style, click **Customer profile**, apply the **Heading 3** style, click **Service to our customers**, then apply the **Heading 3** style

Now that styles are applied in the document, you can experiment with other templates.

7. Press **[Ctrl][Home]**, click **Format** on the menu bar, click **Theme**, then click **Style Gallery** in the Theme dialog box

The Style Gallery dialog box, which lists the templates that come with Word, opens. You can click the name of a template in the Template list to view a preview of the styles for that template applied to the current document.

8. Scroll down the list of templates, then click **Elegant Memo**

A preview of the current document formatted with the styles from the Elegant Memo template appears in the Preview of area, as shown in Figure I-14.

9. Click **OK**, then save your changes to the document

The Style Gallery closes. The styles you assigned to the Survey memo document are replaced with the styles from the Elegant Memo template. Notice that the style names applied to each paragraph in the document are the same, but the format settings associated with those style names have changed.

FIGURE I-12: AutoFormat dialog box

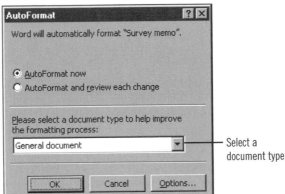

Select a
document type

FIGURE I-13: Formatting applied to document

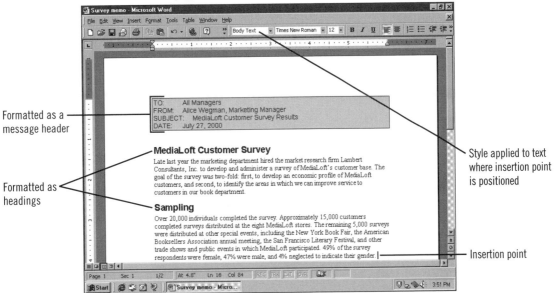

Formatted as a
message header

Formatted as
headings

Style applied to text
where insertion point
is positioned

Insertion point

FIGURE I-14: Style Gallery dialog box

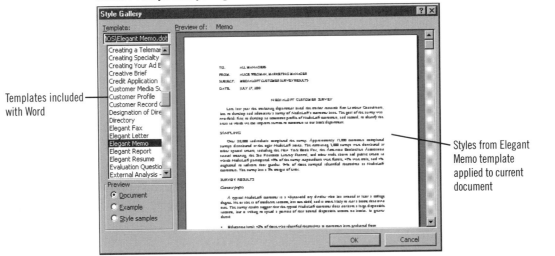

Templates included
with Word

Styles from Elegant
Memo template
applied to current
document

Displaying Style Names in a Document

When formatting with styles it is often useful to see the name of the style applied to a paragraph. In Normal view, you can display style names in the document window so that you can easily identify the styles applied to your document. You display the style names in the document window by displaying the Style area. With the style names displayed in the Style area, you can quickly select a paragraph by clicking its style name in the Style area, or you can modify a style by double-clicking its style name in the Style area and modifying the format settings. **Scenario** Alice displays the style names in her memo. She then uses the Style area to help her modify a style and change the formatting of some of the text.

1. Click the **Normal View button** ▣ on the horizontal scroll bar, click **Tools** on the menu bar, click **Options**, then click the **View tab** if necessary
   The View tab of the Options dialog box opens.

2. Click the **Style area width up arrow** until 1" appears, then click **OK**
   The names of the styles appear next to each paragraph on the left side of the document window, as shown in Figure I-15. You can adjust the width of the Style area by dragging the vertical line that separates the Style area from the document.

3. Scroll down to view the name of the style that is applied to each paragraph, then scroll up so that the "Survey Results" heading appears at the top of the document window
   You will change the formatting of the Heading 3 style to make the Heading 3 paragraphs more prominent.

4. Double-click **Heading 3** in the Style area next to "Customer profile"
   The Style dialog box opens with the Heading 3 style selected in the Styles list. You want to enlarge the font size and add bold formatting to the style.

5. Click **Modify**, click **Format**, click **Font**, click **Bold Italic** in the Font style list in the Font dialog box, click **12** in the Size list, click **OK**, click **OK**, click **Close**, then scroll down until you can see both paragraphs formatted in the Heading 3 style
   The paragraphs formatted in the Heading 3 style change to 12-point bold italic text. If you apply the Heading 3 style to other text, these new format settings will be applied. Next, you want to make the memo title, "MediaLoft Customer Survey", more prominent. You want to change the formatting of the title, but you do not want to change the Heading 1 style that is applied to the title.

6. Scroll up, then click **Heading 1** in the Style area next to "MediaLoft Customer Survey"
   Clicking the style name one time in the Style area selects the paragraph associated with that style.

7. Click **Format** on the menu bar, click **Font**, click **Bold** in the Font style list, click **20** in the Size list, click **OK**, then deselect the text
   The title of the memo is enlarged. Note that the formatting changes do not affect the Heading 1 style. If you apply the Heading 1 style to other text, the original format settings will be applied.

QuickTip
You can also close the Style area by setting the Style area Width to 0 on the View tab in the Options dialog box.

8. Position the pointer over the vertical line that separates the Style area from the document so the pointer changes to ◂‖▸, drag to the left until the Style area disappears, then click the **Print Layout View button** ▣ on the horizontal scroll bar
   Compare your document with Figure I-16.

9. Save your changes to the document

FIGURE I-15: Style names in Style area

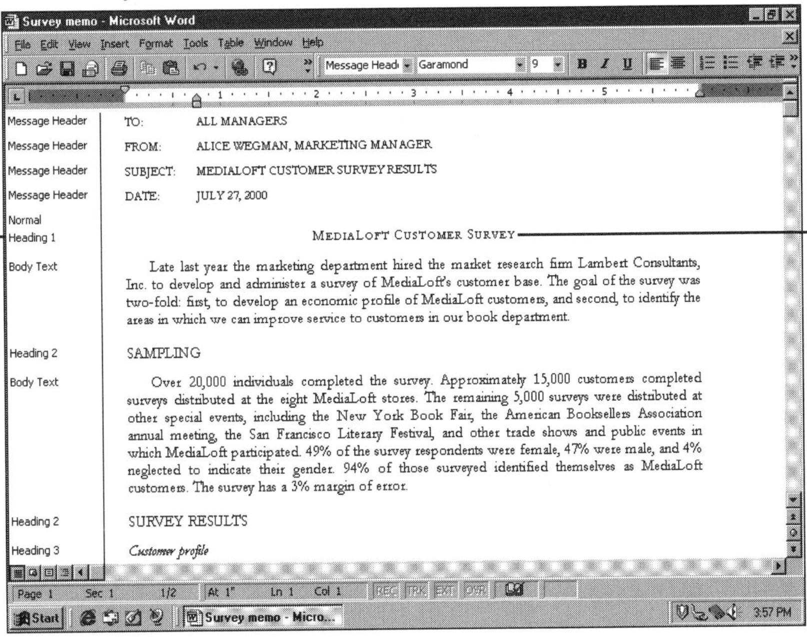

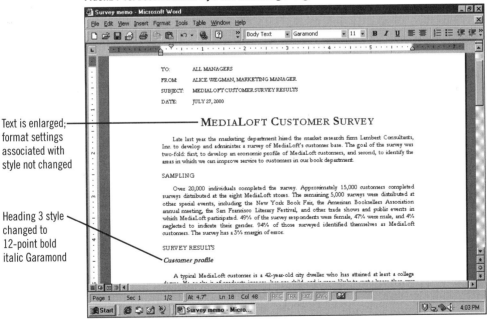

Style name in → Style area

Heading 1 style ← applied to this paragraph

FIGURE I-16: Document with style and formatting changes

Text is enlarged; format settings associated with style not changed

Heading 3 style changed to 12-point bold italic Garamond

Printing styles

Sometimes it is useful to print a hard copy document that includes the names of the styles available for a document as well as descriptions of the format settings associated with each style name. To print the style names and associated style formats for a

document, click File on the menu bar, click Print, click the Print what list arrow in the Print dialog box, click Styles, then click OK. The printed document will be a list of the styles available for the document and a description of each.

Moving Around with Styles

Styles can also play a valuable role in moving around longer documents because you can use styles to move quickly to different parts of a document. You can use the Browse by Object feature to scroll through a document by "paging" through its headings. You can also turn on the Document Map to display a document's headings on the left side of the screen and the document on the right side of the screen. By clicking a heading in the Document Map you can quickly navigate to that heading in the document. **Scenario** Alice checks the organization of the memo by reviewing each heading in the document. She takes advantage of the styles in the document to move quickly to the locations she wants.

Steps

1. Press **[Ctrl][Home]**, then click the **Select Browse Object button** at the bottom of the vertical scroll bar
   The Browse by Object menu appears as shown in Figure I-17. The menu includes a list of items you can use to move through a document. You want to browse by the headings.

2. Click the **Browse by Heading button**
   The insertion point moves to the first heading in the document, "MediaLoft Customer Survey", which is the first instance of text to which a heading style has been applied. Notice that the Previous and Next buttons on the vertical scroll bar are now blue. The blue color indicates that clicking these buttons will move the insertion point from item to item rather than from page to page.

3. Click the **Next Heading button** on the vertical scroll bar to move through all the headings in the document, then press **[Ctrl][Home]**
   To view all the headings in the document at once, you can use the Document Map.

QuickTip
You can adjust the width of the Document Map by dragging the vertical line that separates it from the document window.

4. Click the **Document Map button** on the Standard toolbar
   The window splits in two as shown in Figure I-18. On the left, the document headings appear in the Document Map. On the right, the document appears in the document window.

5. Click the **minus sign** next to "Survey results" in the Document Map
   The headings under "Survey results" disappear from the Document Map, and a plus sign appears next to "Survey results". Clicking a minus sign collapses a heading. In other words, the subheadings under the collapsed heading do not display in the Document Map. When you collapse a heading, a plus sign appears next to it to indicate that the heading can be expanded. When you expand a heading you display the subheadings under it. The ability to collapse and expand headings in the Document Map is useful if you are working with longer documents.

6. Click the **plus sign** next to "Survey results" in the Document Map
   The heading is expanded and the subheadings under it appear in the Document Map.

7. Click **Service to our customers** in the Document Map
   The insertion point moves to the "Service to our customers" heading in the document. You can now edit the text in this heading.

8. Select **Service to our customers** in the document, then type **Customer feedback**
   The heading is changed in both the document and in the Document Map.

QuickTip
You can also click View on the menu bar, then click Document Map to open and close the Document Map.

9. Click, press **[Ctrl][Home]**, then save your changes to the document
   Since the Document Map button is a toggle button, clicking the button again closes the Document Map.

FIGURE I-17: Browse by Object menu

Browse by Object menu
Browse by Heading button

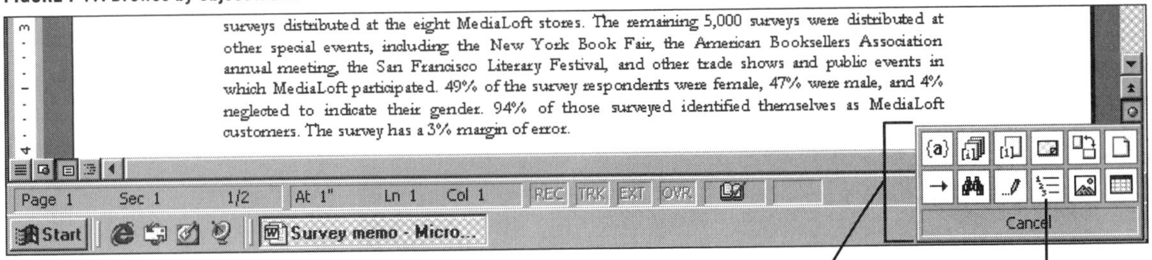

FIGURE I-18: Document Map

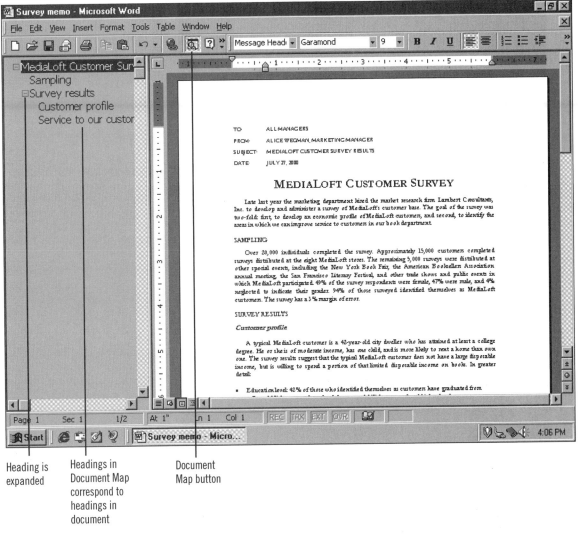

Heading is expanded
Headings in Document Map correspond to headings in document
Document Map button

Replacing Styles

Sometimes you may want to change all instances of a style to another style. Using the Replace command, you can locate and replace each instance of a style in a document in the same way you search for and replace text and other formatting. For example, you might want to replace all instances of the Heading 3 style with the Heading 2 style. With the Replace command you can instruct Word to search for text formatted in the Heading 3 style and format it in the Heading 2 style instead. **Scenario** Alice would like the message header to stand out more in the memo. She uses the Replace command to replace the Message Header style currently applied in the document with a different Message Header style that includes a border.

Steps 1234

1. **Click Edit on the menu bar, click Replace, then click More in the Find and Replace dialog box to expand it if necessary**
   The expanded Find and Replace dialog box opens. You want to replace the Message Header style with a different style. To replace a style, you use the Format button in the dialog box.

Trouble?

If a format setting already appears below the Find what text box, click the No Formatting button.

2. **Click in the Find what text box, delete any text in the Find what text box if necessary, click Format, then click Style**
   The Find Style dialog box opens. This dialog box lists the Word styles for all templates. You want to replace the Message Header style.

3. **Scroll down the Find what style list, click Message Header, then click OK**
   The Format area below the Find what text box in the Find and Replace dialog box indicates that Word will search for the Message Header style. Next you'll select a style to use instead.

Trouble?

If a format setting already appears below the Replace with text box, click the No Formatting button.

4. **Click in the Replace with text box, delete any text in the Replace with text box if necessary, click Format, then click Style**
   The Replace Style dialog box opens.

5. **Click Message Header Last in the Replace With Style list box**
   A description of the format settings in the Message Header Last style appears in the Description area of the Replace Style dialog box, as shown in Figure I-19. The style includes the original Message Header style as well as a border below the last line of text in the message header.

6. **Click OK**
   The Format area below the Replace with text box indicates that Word will replace the Message Header style with the Message Header Last style, as shown in Figure I-20. You are ready to replace the styles.

7. **Click Replace All**
   A message indicates the number of replacements made.

8. **Click OK, then click Close**
   Compare your document with Figure I-21.

9. **In the "From" line replace Alice Wegman with your name, save your changes to the document, print the document, then close the file and exit Word**

FIGURE I-19: Replace Style dialog box

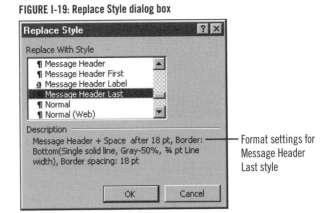

Format settings for
Message Header
Last style

FIGURE I-20: Find and Replace dialog box

Replace this
style . . .

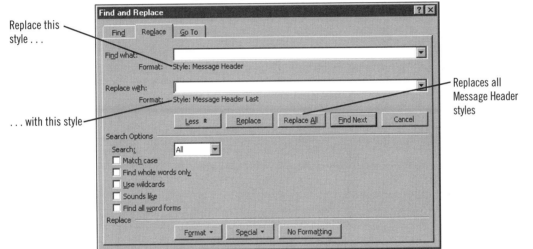

Replaces all
Message Header
styles

. . . with this style

FIGURE I-21: Completed memo

Message Header
Last is the new style

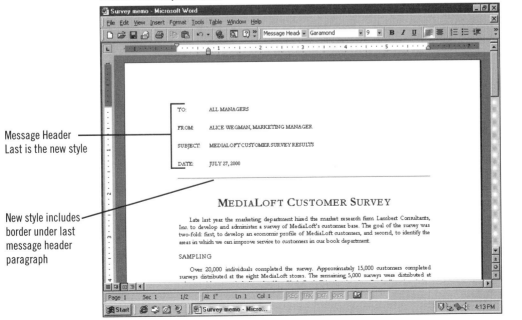

New style includes
border under last
message header
paragraph

Practice

► Concepts Review

Label each element shown in Figure I-22.

FIGURE I-22

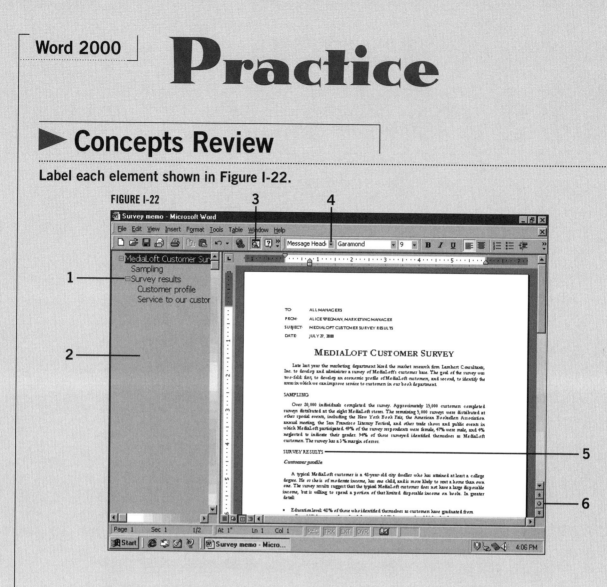

Match each term with the statement that describes it.

7. **AutoFormat**
8. **Paragraph style**
9. **Template**
10. **Style Gallery**
11. **Character style**
12. **Normal style**

a. A document used as a basis for creating other documents

b. A feature that allows you to preview and then apply styles from a different template to a document

c. The default paragraph style in the Normal template

d. A stored set of font format settings

e. A stored set of paragraph and character format settings

f. A feature used to apply styles to a document automatically

Select the best answer from the list of choices.

13. To create a new style you
   a. Click Format on the menu bar, then click Style.
   b. Click Format on the menu bar, then click Style Gallery.
   c. Select a different template in the Style Gallery.
   d. Apply a style from the Style list on the Formatting toolbar.

14. Which of the following is not a benefit of using styles?
   a. Using styles helps to keep a document's formatting consistent
   b. The AutoFormat feature organizes your document for you
   c. When you modify a style, every instance of the style is updated
   d. Applying a style applies format settings in one step

15. The default style for a new blank document is
   a. Heading.
   b. Body Text.
   c. Default Paragraph Font.
   d. Normal.

16. To display an outline of the headings in a document
   a. Click the Select Browse Heading button.
   b. Click View on the menu bar, then click Document Map.
   c. Open the Style area.
   d. Click View on the menu bar, then click Styles.

17. Unless you specify otherwise, a new memo you create will be based on the
   a. Normal template.
   b. Professional Memo template.
   c. Contemporary Memo template.
   d. Elegant Memo template.

18. A character style can include format settings for
   a. Font, font size, italic, and center alignment.
   b. Font, italic, shading, and borders.
   c. Font, font size, bold, and small caps.
   d. Font, font size, italic, and line spacing.

19. The fastest way to change a heading from uppercase to lowercase characters is to
   a. Type new lowercase characters.
   b. Click Format on the menu bar, then click Font.
   c. Modify the heading style.
   d. Click Format on the menu bar, then click Change Case.

20. The Style Gallery allows you to
   a. Create new templates.
   b. Create styles.
   c. Preview styles from different templates.
   d. Modify styles.

► Skills Review

1. **Create and use paragraph styles.**
   a. Start Word, open the file WD I-3 from your Project Disk, then save it as "Glacier report".
   b. Select the heading Milestones and format it in 16-point Tahoma bold.
   c. Use the Paragraph command on the Format menu to add 6 pt of spacing after the Milestones paragraph.
   d. Use the Borders and Shading command on the Format menu to apply a ½ pt border under the Milestones paragraph.
   e. Create a new paragraph style based on the Milestones paragraph. (*Hint*: Select Milestones, click Format on the menu bar, click Style, then click New.)
   f. Name the new style "Glacier Heading", be sure to select Paragraph in the Style type list box, click OK, then click Apply.
   g. Apply the Glacier Heading style to the other headings in the document.

2. **Create and use character styles.**
   a. Press [Ctrl][Home], click Edit on the menu bar, click Find, type "Glacier Adventures Ltd" in the Find what text box, click Find Next, then click Cancel. (*Note*: Click the No Formatting button if necessary to remove any format settings listed under the Find what text box.)
   b. Format the text "Glacier Adventures Ltd" in 12-point Tahoma bold.
   c. Create a new character style using the formatting you applied to Glacier Adventures Ltd. (*Hint*: Use the Style command on the Format menu, then click New.)
   d. Name the new style "Glacier Ltd", be sure to select Character in the Style type list box, click OK, then click Apply.
   e. Apply the Glacier Ltd style to all other occurrences of "Glacier Adventures Ltd" in the document.

3. **Modify styles.**
   a. Select the Milestones heading, click Format on the menu bar, click Font, then add a shadow to the text.
   b. Reapply the Glacier Heading style to the Milestones heading.
   c. Update the Glacier Heading style to reflect the change you just made.
   d. Use the Style command on the Format menu to open the Style dialog box.
   e. Select the Glacier Ltd style in the Styles list, then click Modify.
   f. In the Modify Style dialog box, click Format, click Font, change the font style to Bold Italic. Click OK, then click Close.
   g. Type your name at the bottom of the document, save the document, print a copy, then close the document.

4. **Use AutoFormat and the Style Gallery.**
   a. Open the file WD I-4 from your Project Disk, then save it as "Glacier memo".
   b. AutoFormat the document without reviewing each change.
   c. Apply the Heading 3 style to the following headings: Sales revenues, Performance on Wall Street, In-house publishing department, and New Director of Communications.
   d. Open the Style Gallery. (*Hint*: Use the Theme command on the Format menu.)
   e. Apply the Professional Memo template to the document.

5. **Display style names in a document.**
   a. Switch to Normal view, then display the Style area. (*Hint*: Click Tools on the menu bar, click Options, then click the View tab.)

b. At the top of the page, click Heading 1 in the Style area next to Glacier Adventures, apply the Company Name style, then deselect the text.

c. Apply the Message Header First style to the first line in the Message Header. (*Hint*: Scroll down the list of styles.)

d. Apply the Message Header Last style to the last line in the Message Header.

e. Replace "Your Name" with your name in the From line.

f. Double-click the Heading 1 style in the Style area, then modify the Heading 1 style to be 12-point italic text.

g. Close the Style area, then switch to Print Layout view.

6. Move around with styles.

a. Press [Ctrl][Home], click the Select Browse Object button on the vertical scroll bar, then browse the document by headings.

b. Press [Ctrl][Home], then open the Document Map.

c. Collapse and expand the headings in the Document Map.

d. Select "In-house publishing" department in the Document Map, type "New", press [Spacebar], press [Delete], then type "i".

e. Close the Document Map.

7. Replace styles.

a. Press [Ctrl][Home], click Edit on the menu bar, click Replace, then click More in the Find and Replace dialog box if necessary.

b. Replace all instances of the Heading 3 style with the Heading 2 style.

c. Replace all instances of the Body Text style with the Body Text First Indent style.

d. Save your changes to the document, print it, then close the document.

► Visual Workshop

Using the styles included in the Professional Memo template, format the file WD I-8 from your Project Disk as shown in Figure I-23. Save the file to your Project Disk with the file name "Write Staff". (*Hints:* AutoFormat the document, then use the Style Gallery to apply the Professional Memo template. Use the different heading and body text styles, then apply bullet, font, and paragraph formatting.)

FIGURE I-23

The Write Staff

Condensed General Writing Style Guidelines

To ensure that our work is uniform and consistent, writers must adhere to established criteria. This one page summary provides concise style guidelines for written text and forms. More detailed style information is contained in the writers' guide.

General Style

Titles, Headings, and Captions
- Capitalize the first letter of each word of a title, heading, and caption. Do not include any ending punctuation.

Formatting - Boldface/Italics
- Use boldface to designate a product name, unique product feature, discounted price, and special ordering instructions.

- Use italics to identify product sizes, color, special instructions, and product origin.

- Parentheses may be used to identify product sizes and special ordering instructions.

- Acronyms are not to be used without first spelling out the entire name followed by the acronym. Acronyms should be used only if necessary.

Writing Guidelines

Introductory Text
- The goal of the introductory text is to create a visual picture of the product using clear and concise language. The opening sentence should capture the essence of the product and generate the interest of the reader.

Pricing
- Clear definition of product pricing is essential.

Origin of Product
- The reader is interested in the product origin. The last item in the description should contain the point of origin. Use italics to increase reader awareness.

Sharing
Information with Other Programs

Objectives

- ► Understand linking and embedding objects
- [MOUS] ► Link an Excel worksheet
- [MOUS] ► Modify a linked object
- [MOUS] ► Use Paste Special to embed an object
- ► Create a PowerPoint presentation from a Word outline
- ► Insert a PowerPoint object
- [MOUS] ► Attach an Access data source
- [MOUS] ► Select records to merge

Sometimes the information you want to include in a Word document is actually stored in a file that was created in another Office program. For example, a list of names to whom you want to send a form letter might already exist in an Access database. Or, perhaps you want a financial summary document to include financial information that has already been entered in an Excel worksheet. Most Office programs can include information that was created in other programs so that you don't have to retype information that already exists in other files. This ability to share information with other programs is called **Object Linking and Embedding** (OLE). Scenario▶ Alice Wegman is preparing a proposal to include online author readings on the MediaLoft Web site. She saves time and effort by using Word's OLE features to include information already created in other Office programs.

Word 2000

Understanding Linking and Embedding Objects

There are a variety of ways you can insert information that is stored in files created in other Office programs into your Word documents. For example, you can use the Object command on the Insert menu to insert Excel worksheets or PowerPoint slides into a document, or you can use the Paste Special command to paste information from another program into a document. In addition, Office programs have the ability to convert information in a format that you can use in Word. A document that contains information created into two or more programs is called a **compound document**. The method you choose for creating a compound document depends on what you want to accomplish and the programs installed on your computer. Figure J-1 illustrates some of the options for creating compound documents. **Scenario** Alice explores some of the methods for using information stored in other Office programs in her Word documents.

Details

Copy and paste information from another program

If the information you want to include in your document is not being continually updated, you can copy information from another Office program to the Clipboard and then paste it into a Word document. The pasted information becomes part of the Word document and you can use Word features to edit and format the information. For example, if you copy an Excel worksheet and paste it in a document, it is pasted as a Word table.

Link information from another program as an object

When you insert information created in another program into a Word document (not copy and paste it), you insert the information as an object. An **object** is information that is exchanged between programs, for example, text, graphics, spreadsheets, charts, or sound and video clips. When you insert an object in a document, you have the option to create a linked object. When you create a **link**, you establish a connection between the Word document and the source file so that changes to the information in the source file are automatically made to the Word document. This connection is called a **dynamic data exchange** (DDE) link. For example, if you insert an Excel worksheet as a linked object in a Word document, when you edit the worksheet in Excel the change will occur automatically in the Word document the next time you open the file. Linked objects can also be edited in Word using the features of the **source program**, the program in which the information was created. You can link objects using the Object command on the Insert menu or the Paste Special command on the Edit menu.

Embed information from another program as an object

When you **embed** an object in a document, you use another program to create and edit the object, but the object is stored only in the Word document. You edit an embedded object using the features of the source program from within the Word window. For example, if you insert an Excel worksheet as an embedded object, you can edit the worksheet using the Excel menus and toolbars without ever leaving Word. Unlike a linked object, however, any change you make to an embedded object is saved only in the Word document. You can embed objects using the Object command on the Insert menu or the Paste Special command on the Edit menu.

Convert a file to another program

Some Office files can be converted to other programs. The Send to command on the File menu in each program displays a list of programs to which you can convert data from that program. For example, you can use the Send To command in PowerPoint to convert a PowerPoint presentation to a Word document.

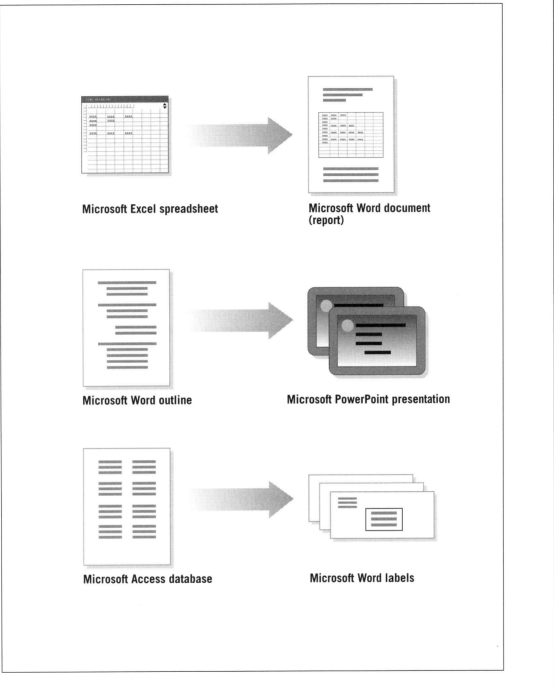

Word 2000

Word 2000

Linking an Excel Worksheet

Although tables in Word provide basic mathematical operations suitable for simple calculations, Excel is a full-featured spreadsheet program for performing sophisticated numerical analysis. If the data you want to include in a Word document is already stored in an Excel file, you can insert the worksheet into your document. If this file is continuously updated to reflect new information, you can create a link to the file so that the worksheet in your document is always up to date. **Scenario** Alice has created an Excel worksheet showing projected expenses for online author events. Now she inserts the Excel worksheet into a Word document.

Steps

QuickTip

Make a copy of your Project Disk before you use it.

1. Start **Word**, open the file **WD J-1** from your Project Disk, then save it as **Expense Summary**
   The document opens in Print Layout view.

2. Click the blank line under the second body paragraph, then press **[Enter]**
   You'll insert an Excel worksheet in the document at the location of the insertion point.

3. Click **Insert** on the menu bar, then click **Object**
   The Object dialog box opens. You can use the Create New tab in this dialog box to create a new object in another program, or you can use the Create from File tab to insert an object from an existing file.

4. Click the **Create from File tab**, then click **Browse**
   The Browse dialog box opens. You use this dialog box to select the Excel file you want to insert.

5. Make sure the location of your Project Disk is displayed in the Look in list box, click **WD J-2**, then click **Insert**
   The Object dialog box appears as shown in Figure J-2. Now that you have selected the file, you need to indicate how you want the file inserted in the document. Table J-1 describes the options for inserting objects using the Object dialog box. You want to link the document to the worksheet file so that the worksheet object will be automatically updated every time you open the document.

6. Click the **Link to file check box**, then click **OK**
   The worksheet is inserted in the document as a linked object, as shown in Figure J-3. It is formatted to look like a Word table, but to edit the worksheet you must edit it in its original (source) program.

7. Save your changes to the document

TABLE J-1: Options for inserting objects using the Object dialog box

option	how to activate option	description
Embed the object	Clear the Link to file check box to embed an object	Inserts the object so that it can be edited using the features available in the source program
Link the object to a file	Select the Link to file check box to link an object	Creates a DDE link to the source file so that whenever you open or save the document, the inserted object is updated to reflect the latest changes to the source file; also inserts the object so that it can be edited using the features available in the source program
Display the object as an icon	Select the Display an icon check box to display an icon	Inserts an icon that represents the object; double-clicking the icon in the document opens the object in the source program

FIGURE J-2: Object dialog box

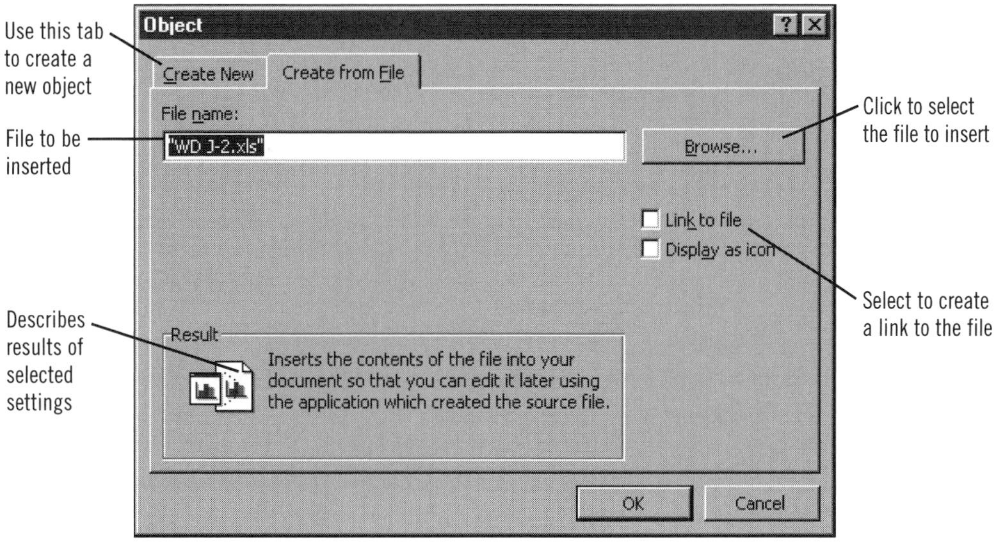

Use this tab to create a new object

File to be inserted

Describes results of selected settings

Click to select the file to insert

Select to create a link to the file

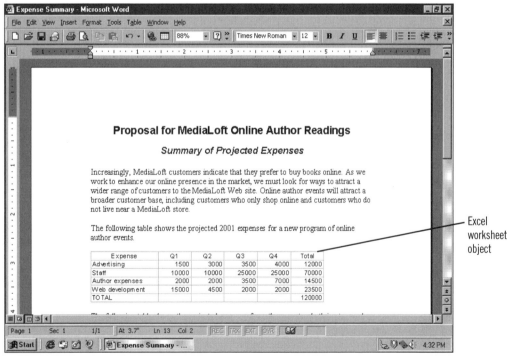

FIGURE J-3: Worksheet object inserted in a document

Excel worksheet object

Word 2000

Modifying a Linked Object

After inserting an object in a document, you can edit the object from within Word. By double-clicking a linked object in Word, you open the original source file in the program in which it was created. You then work in the source file. The changes you make and save to the source file are also made in the Word document. **Scenario** Alice edits the worksheet she inserted and changes its formatting.

Steps

QuickTip

You can also open the source file by selecting the object, clicking Edit on the menu bar, pointing to Linked Worksheet Object, then clicking Open Link.

1. Double-click the **worksheet object** in the Word document

The Excel program window opens from within Word, as shown in Figure J-4. If necessary you can resize the Excel program window by dragging a corner. You can now use Excel's editing and formatting features to edit the data and change the appearance of the worksheet object.

2. Click cell **B5**, type **12500,** press **[Tab]**, type **7000**, then deselect the cell

The changes are made in the Excel worksheet and in the Word document. Next you'll change the formatting of the data.

3. Select all the rows in the worksheet, click the **Currency Style button** 🔘 on the Formatting toolbar, click the **Bold button** 🔳 , then deselect the rows

The text in the worksheet is bolded and the number format changes to currency style, as shown in Figure J-5. Notice that the Word document is automatically updated as you change the format of the source file in Excel.

QuickTip

Links are automatically updated when you open a file that contains links.

4. Click the **Save button** 🔘 on the Excel Standard toolbar, then close the Excel program window

The changes to the Excel file are saved and you return to the Word program window. The changes you made in the Excel source file are automatically made in the document, as shown in Figure J-6.

5. Deselect the worksheet object, then save your changes to the document

Updating links manually

Word's default is to update linked objects automatically whenever the information in a source file changes. Word updates the links each time you open the file containing the links or whenever the source file changes while the document containing links is open. You can also create links that must be updated manually so that Word will update the links only when you decide. To create manual links or to update an existing manual link, click Edit on the menu bar, then click Links. In the Links dialog box, select the link you want to change or update in the Source file list box. To change the link to a manual link, click the Manual option button. To update a manual link, click Update Now. You can also use this dialog box to open or change the source file for a link and to break a link so that the information in the document is no longer associated with the source file. You can also update a linked object by selecting it and pressing [F9].

FIGURE J-4: Excel program window

Excel program window →

Word program window

Worksheet is the same in Excel and in Word →

→ Drag a corner of the window to resize it

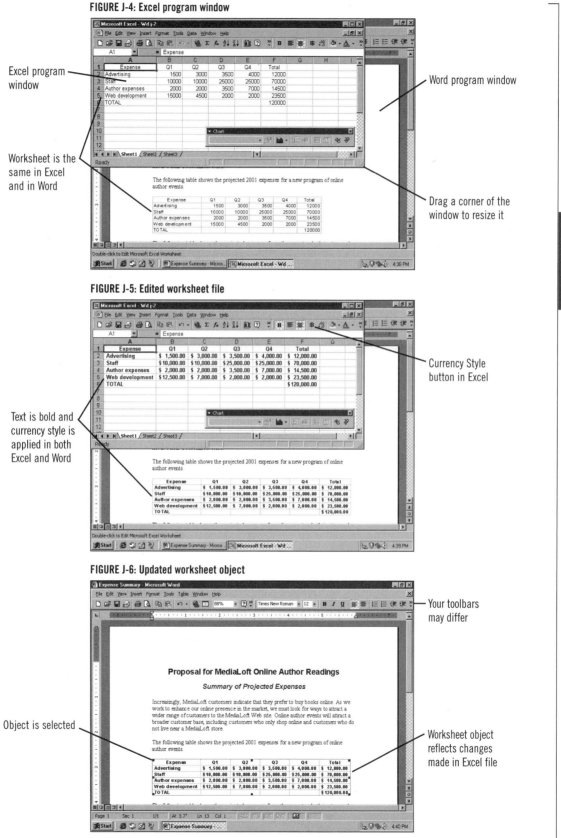

FIGURE J-5: Edited worksheet file

→ Currency Style button in Excel

Text is bold and currency style is applied in both Excel and Word →

FIGURE J-6: Updated worksheet object

→ Your toolbars may differ

Object is selected →

→ Worksheet object reflects changes made in Excel file

Word 2000

Using Paste Special to Embed an Object

Another way to insert information created in another program into a Word document is to copy the information from the source program to the Clipboard, and then use the Paste Special command either to link or to embed the object into a document. You can also select the format in which you want the information to be inserted, for example, as an object that can be edited in the source program or as formatted text that can be edited in Word. **Scenario** Alice uses the Paste Special command to embed information from an Excel worksheet into her summary document as a worksheet object. She then edits the worksheet information from Word.

Steps

1. Start Excel, then open the file **WD J-3** from your Project Disk
   The worksheet opens in Excel. You'll copy the data from the worksheet to the Clipboard.

Trouble?

Be sure to select only cells with values begining with cell A1.

2. Select all the cells in the worksheet, click **Edit** on the menu bar, then click **Copy**
   The data is copied to the Clipboard.

3. Click the **Expense Summary button** on the taskbar, press **[Ctrl][End]**, then press **[Enter]**
   You'll use the Paste Special command to insert the worksheet data at the location of the insertion point.

4. Click **Edit** on the menu bar, then click **Paste Special**
   The Paste Special dialog box opens, as shown in Figure J-7. In this dialog box you can choose between linking and embedding the object, and you can choose the format you want the pasted object to have. You'll embed the object as an Excel worksheet object.

QuickTip

You can also embed a new blank worksheet in a document by clicking the Insert Microsoft Excel Worksheet button [icon] on the Standard toolbar.

5. Make sure the **Paste option button** is selected, click **Microsoft Excel Worksheet Object** in the As list box, then click **OK**
   The worksheet is inserted in the document as an embedded object. When you embed an object it is no longer related to the source document. You want to change the format of the object to match the other worksheet object in the document. To edit an embedded object, double-click it to access the features of the source program but not the source program itself.

6. Double-click the **worksheet object** at the end of the document
   The worksheet object appears in an Excel object window and the toolbars change to Excel toolbars, as shown in Figure J-8. Because this object is embedded, the features available in Excel, such as those on the Excel Standard and Formatting toolbars, are available from within Word. You can now edit and format the object using the features available in Excel.

7. Click the **Bold button** [B] on the Formatting toolbar, select the cells in the **Cost/Event** and **Total Cost columns**, then click the **Currency Style button** [$]
   The text is bolded and the values in the two columns are displayed as currency.

8. Click outside the object to deselect it
   When you deselect the embedded object, the toolbars return to Word toolbars and the edited object appears, as shown in Figure J-9. The changes you make to an embedded object are only made to the Word document. The source file for the embedded object is not affected.

9. Press **[Ctrl][End]**, press **[Enter]** twice, type your name, save your changes to the document, print a copy, close the file, then click the Excel program button on the taskbar
   Note that the changes you made to the embedded Excel object in the document are not made to the source file in Excel.

10. Close Excel

FIGURE J-7: Paste Special dialog box

Select to embed the information from the Clipboard

Select to create a link to the source file

List of format options for inserting information

Describes results of selected settings

FIGURE J-8: Embedded Excel object

Title bar indicates that Word is the active program

Toolbars change to Excel toolbars

Worksheet in Excel object window

Sizing handles indicate the object is selected

FIGURE J-9: Formatted object in document

Toolbars return to Word toolbars

Changes to embedded object are saved in Word only

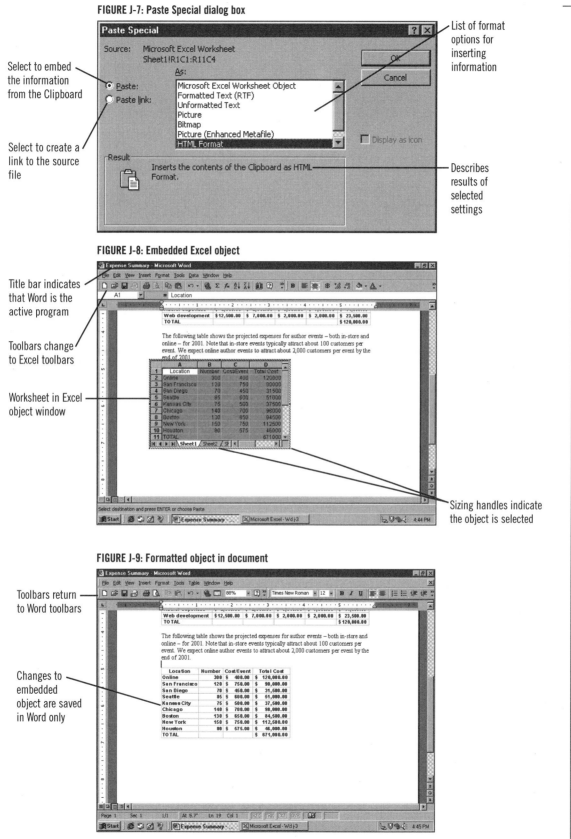

Creating a PowerPoint Presentation from a Word Outline

PowerPoint is a program for creating attractive slides for presentations. Because each slide can display only several lines of text (such as a heading and a few supporting ideas), each slide generally contains text related to a specific idea or topic. As a result, using a Word outline can be a great way to start creating a PowerPoint presentation. You can convert a Word outline to a PowerPoint presentation using the Send To command in Word. **Scenario** Alice will present her proposal at an upcoming company meeting. She has already created an outline for her proposal in Word. She uses the outline to create a PowerPoint presentation.

Steps 1234

1. Open the file **WD J-4** from your Project Disk, then save it as **Proposal Outline**
   The document contains the outline of the proposal. The outline was created by typing text into a new blank document in Print Layout view and applying styles from the Style list box to each paragraph. The bullets were created using the Bullets button on the Formatting toolbar. By default each paragraph that is formatted in the Heading 1 style will become a separate slide in the PowerPoint presentation.

2. Click **File** on the menu bar, point to **Send To**, then click **Microsoft PowerPoint**
   PowerPoint opens and the document appears in the PowerPoint program window formatted as slides, as shown in Figure J-10. You can edit the slide text and format the appearance of the slides in PowerPoint. You'll create a title slide for the presentation.

3. Click between the **slide 1 icon** and **The Features** in the Outline pane, press **[Enter]**, then click next to the slide 1 icon
   Pressing [Enter] creates a new blank slide. The blank slide appears in the presentation window.

4. Type **MediaLoft Online Author Readings**
   The text appears on the slide as you type. You can also change the formatting of the presentation.

5. Click **Format** on the menu bar, then click **Apply Design Template**
   The Apply Design Template dialog box opens. You can use this dialog box to preview and select formatting schemes for a presentation.

6. Click **Factory** in the list of design themes, then click **Apply**
   The design scheme is applied to the slides, as shown in Figure J-11. With the presentation complete you can view all the slides at once.

7. Click the **Slide Sorter View button** on the horizontal scroll bar
   All the slides appear in the PowerPoint window, as shown in Figure J-12.

8. Click **File** on the menu bar, click **Save**, then save the presentation with the file name **Proposal Presentation** to your Project Disk

FIGURE J-10: Word outline converted to PowerPoint

Slide 1 icon

Title of first slide

Word Heading 1 style

Word Heading 2 style

Text from Word outline in the Outline pane

Word Heading 3 style

Each paragraph formatted in Heading 1 style is a new slide

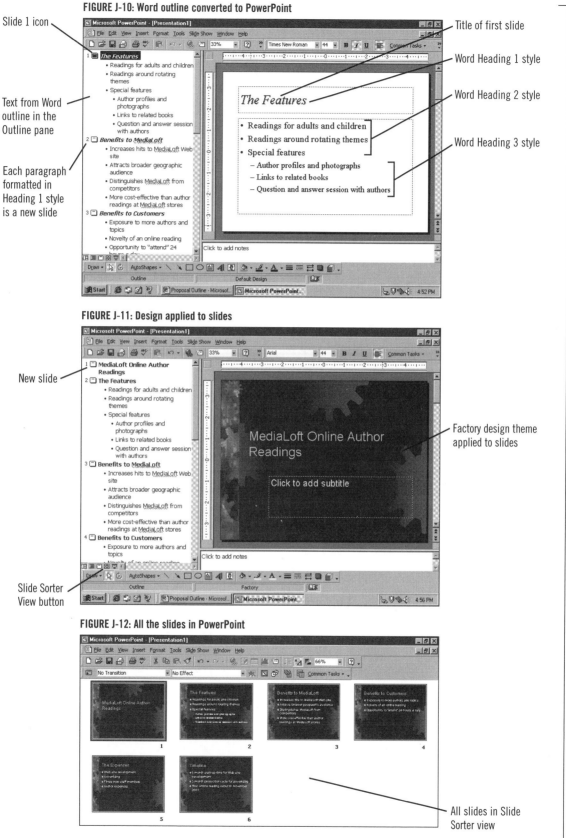

FIGURE J-11: Design applied to slides

New slide

Factory design theme applied to slides

Slide Sorter View button

FIGURE J-12: All the slides in PowerPoint

All slides in Slide Sorter view

Inserting a PowerPoint Object

To insert an entire PowerPoint presentation in a Word document, you use the Send To command in the PowerPoint program window. In PowerPoint, this command gives you the option of specifying how you want the slides and any accompanying notes to be laid out in the document. You also have the option of inserting the slides as graphic objects or of linking the presentation to the document. Once the presentation is converted to a Word document, you can use Word's familiar editing and formatting tools to change the document. Scenario▶ Alice wants to create a document that includes the slides as well as some notes. She converts the presentation to a Word document, edits some of the slides from Word, and types notes using Word.

Steps

1. Click **File** on the menu bar, point to **Send To**, then click **Microsoft Word**
   The Write-Up dialog box opens, as shown in Figure J-13. You use this dialog box to specify the layout you want for the slides and notes in a Word document.

2. Make sure the **Notes next to slides option button** is selected
   You can choose to simply paste the slides in a Word document as graphic objects or to create a link between the Word document and the PowerPoint presentation.

QuickTip

To better see the table, display the gridlines by clicking Table on the menu bar, then clicking Show Gridlines.

3. Click the **Paste link option button**, then click **OK**
   After a moment, the slides appear in a new Word document. The data from the presentation is formatted in a table in Word.

4. Press **[Ctrl][Home]**
   The document appears as shown in Figure J-14. The slides are inserted in the table as linked objects. You can double-click a slide to open the PowerPoint widow, where you can edit the slide text or formatting.

5. Double-click the **slide 1 object**
   The slide appears in PowerPoint.

6. Click the **Click to add subtitle placeholder**, type **A new event on the MediaLoft Web site in 2001**, click the **Save button** 🖫 on the PowerPoint Standard toolbar, then close the file and exit PowerPoint
   PowerPoint closes and you return to the converted Word document. Notice that the change you made to slide 1 in PowerPoint was automatically made in the Word document as well. Saving the change in the PowerPoint presentation automatically updated the Word document. Next you'll add notes to the document.

7. Click in the cell to the right of slide 1, type your name, scroll down, click in the cell to the right of slide 3, then type **Although we will continue to expand readings at MediaLoft stores, online readings will provide us with a broader audience, a more diverse program of events, and a cost-effective way to promote more authors.**
   Compare your document with Figure J-15.

Trouble?

PowerPoint presentations sent to Word documents create very large files that might not fit on a floppy disk. If you are saving your Project Files to a floppy disk, do not save this file, then close all open Word files.

8. Print a copy of the document, save the document with the file name **Proposal Notes** to your Project Disk, then close all open Word files
   The notes you added are saved in the Word document. Note that the changes you make to the Word document are not made to the PowerPoint presentation. Because you linked the presentation to the Word document, not visa versa, only the changes you make in the PowerPoint presentation are reflected in the Word document.

FIGURE J-13: Write-Up dialog box

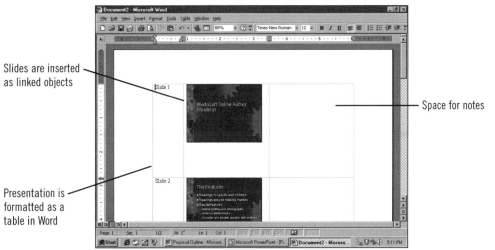

Layout options for slides and notes in document

Select to insert slides as graphic objects

Select to create a link to the source file

FIGURE J-14: Presentation sent to a Word document

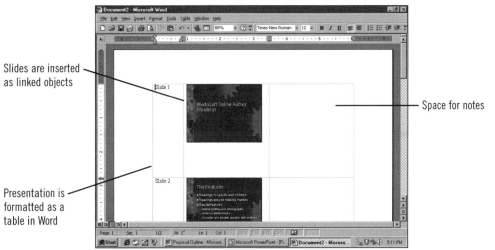

Slides are inserted as linked objects

Space for notes

Presentation is formatted as a table in Word

FIGURE J-15: Notes in the Word document

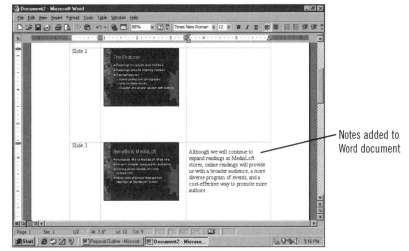

Notes added to Word document

Inserting a presentation with the Object command

If you use the Object command on the Insert menu to insert a PowerPoint object in a document, only the first slide of the presentation is inserted as a graphic object. You might choose to use this feature if you create a cover page for a document and want to use the first slide from the presentation as a graphic.

Attaching an Access Data Source

The Mail Merge feature in Word is a great way to create letters or mailing labels for many individuals at one time. When you create a main document, you also attach it to a data source that contains the name and address information for each recipient. If you don't wish to create a new data source in Word, you can use an existing file from another program as a data source. For example, if a mailing list that is being maintained in Access already contains the name and address information you want to use, you can specify the Access database as your data source. **Scenario** Alice will send the proposal to the department heads at MediaLoft. She uses mail merge to create the labels to mail the proposal. Because the names and internal mailing address information is already stored in an Access database, Alice uses this file as the data source for the mail merge.

Steps

1. Click the **New button** □ on the Standard toolbar, click **Tools** on the menu bar, then click **Mail Merge**

   The Mail Merge Helper dialog box opens. You'll create a main document for the mailing labels.

2. Click **Create**, click **Mailing Labels**, then click **Active Window**

   A temporary name for the main document appears in the Mail Merge Helper dialog box. Next, you'll specify the data source that has already been created in Access.

3. Click **Get Data**, click **Open Data Source**, click the **Files of type list arrow**, click **MS Access Databases**, then use the Look in list arrow to display the drive or folder that contains your Project Disk

   Access database files appear in the dialog box. You'll select the file you want to use.

4. Click **WD J-5**, then click **Open**

   A Microsoft Access dialog box that shows the names of the tables available in the database opens, as shown in Figure J-16. Database information is usually stored in tables within a database. You'll use the Department Heads table.

5. Make sure **Department Heads** is selected, then click **OK**

   A message on the status bar indicates that a dynamic data exchange (DDE) link with Microsoft Access is being created.

6. Click **Set Up Main Document**

   The Label Options dialog box opens. In this dialog box, you select the type of label you want to create.

7. Scroll to and click **5161 – Address** in the Product number list box, then click **OK**

   The Create Labels dialog box opens. In this dialog box you insert the merge fields for the labels. The available fields in the WD J-5 file are listed in the Insert Merge Fields list.

8. Click **Insert Merge Field**, click **First_Name**, press **[Spacebar]**, insert the **Last_Name merge field**, press **[Enter]**, insert the **Title merge field**, press **[Enter]**, type **Mail Box**, press **[Spacebar]**, then insert the **Mail_Box merge field**

   Compare your dialog box with Figure J-17.

9. Click **OK**

   The Mail Merge Helper dialog box appears, as shown in Figure J-18 and the label main document displays in the document window. You'll complete the merge in the next lesson.

FIGURE J-16: Tables tab in the Microsoft Access dialog box

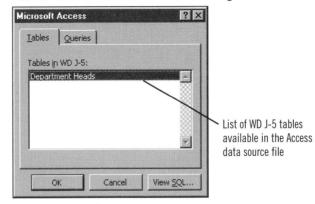

Microsoft Access
Tables
Queries
Tables in WD J-5:
Department Heads
OK
Cancel
View SQL...
List of WD J-5 tables available in the Access data source file

FIGURE J-17: Create Labels dialog box

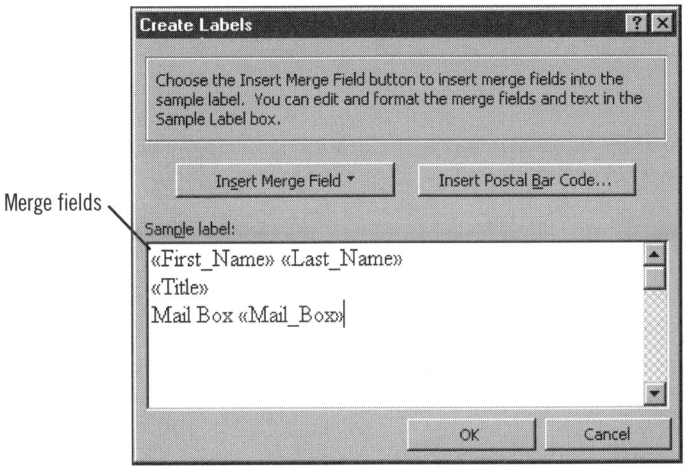

Create Labels
Choose the Insert Merge Field button to insert merge fields into the sample label. You can edit and format the merge fields and text in the Sample Label box.
Insert Merge Field
Insert Postal Bar Code...
Merge fields
Sample label:
«First_Name» «Last_Name»
«Title»
Mail Box «Mail_Box»
OK
Cancel

FIGURE J-18: Mail Merge Helper dialog box

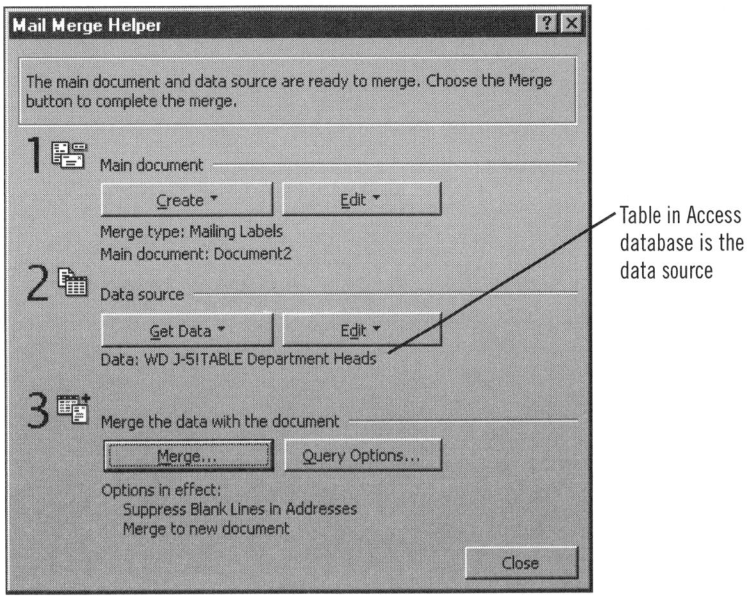

Mail Merge Helper
The main document and data source are ready to merge. Choose the Merge button to complete the merge.
1
Main document
Create
Edit
Merge type: Mailing Labels
Main document: Document2
2
Data source
Get Data
Edit
Data: WD J-5!TABLE Department Heads
Table in Access database is the data source
3
Merge the data with the document
Merge...
Query Options...
Options in effect:
Suppress Blank Lines in Addresses
Merge to new document
Close

Selecting Records to Merge

Sometimes you do not want to send a document to all the individuals in a data source. When you use the Mail Merge Query Options feature you can choose to sort or filter the records to be merged with the main document. When you filter records, you identify the contents of the fields that each record must match to be included in the merge. **Scenario** Alice does not need to send a copy of the proposal to herself, so she filters the data source by specifying criteria to exclude her name from the merge.

Steps

1. **Click Merge in the Mail Merge Helper dialog box**
The Merge dialog box opens.

2. **Click Query Options**
The Query Options dialog box opens. On the Filter Records tab, you specify the criteria you want to use to select the records to merge.

3. **Click the Field list arrow in the Field column, then click Last Name**
The Last Name field is the field to which you want to apply a filter.

4. **Click the Comparison list arrow in the Comparison column, then click Not equal to**
This selection specifies that the contents of the Last Name field in a record must not match the contents you will specify in the Compare to text box. You want to exclude Alice Wegman from the merge.

5. **Type Wegman in the Compare to text box**
Compare your dialog box with Figure J-19. If you wanted to narrow your criteria, you could specify additional selection criteria in the subsequent rows on the Filter tab. You'll continue with the merge process.

6. **Click OK, then click Merge**
The Merge dialog box opens.

7. **Click Merge**
The records that matched the query are merged to a new document, as shown in Figure J-20. Notice that Alice Wegman's information does not appear as a label in the document.

QuickTip

If you need your name on the printed solution, replace Maria Abbott's name with your name.

8. **Save the document with the file name Proposal Merge to your Project Disk, print a copy of the labels, then close the file**

9. **Save the main document with the file name Proposal Main to your Project Disk, then close the file and exit Word**

FIGURE J-19: Query Options dialog box

Field to which ——— filter is applied

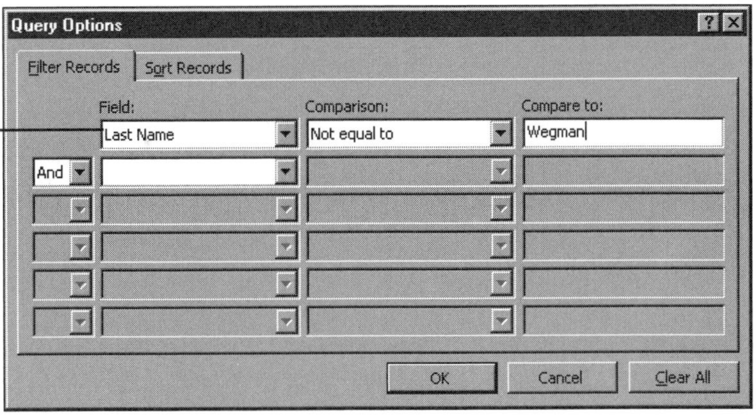

Field:	Comparison:	Compare to:
Last Name	Not equal to	Wegman

Query Options

Filter Records | Sort Records

And

OK   Cancel   Clear All

FIGURE J-20: Merged label document

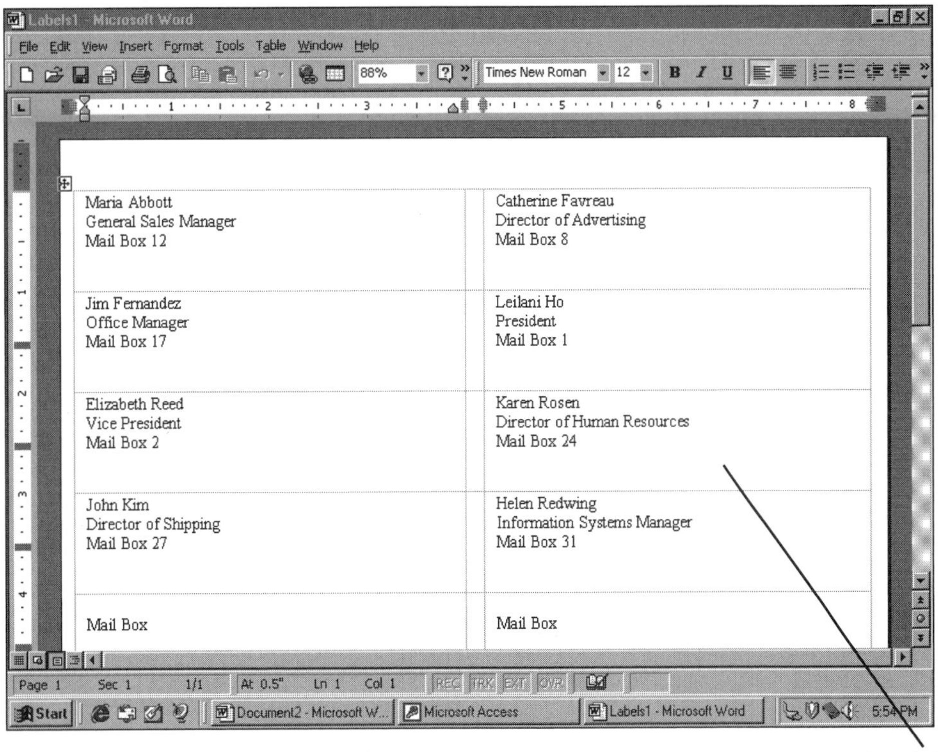

Labels1 - Microsoft Word

File Edit View Insert Format Tools Table Window Help

Times New Roman   12   B I U

Maria Abbott General Sales Manager Mail Box 12	Catherine Favreau Director of Advertising Mail Box 8
Jim Fernandez Office Manager Mail Box 17	Leilani Ho President Mail Box 1
Elizabeth Reed Vice President Mail Box 2	Karen Rosen Director of Human Resources Mail Box 24
John Kim Director of Shipping Mail Box 27	Helen Redwing Information Systems Manager Mail Box 31
Mail Box	Mail Box

Page 1   Sec 1   1/1   At 0.5"   Ln 1   Col 1   REC TRK EXT OVR

Start   Document2 - Microsoft W...   Microsoft Access   Labels1 - Microsoft Word   5:54 PM

Records from Access
data source merged
to a Word document

Practice

► Concepts Review

Label each element shown in Figure J-21.

FIGURE J-21

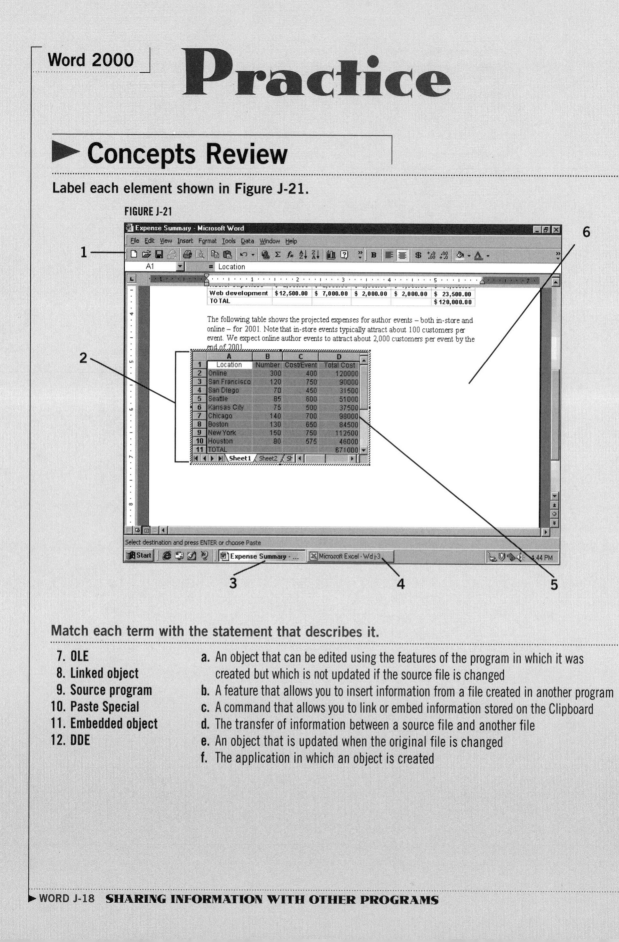

Match each term with the statement that describes it.

7. OLE

8. Linked object

9. Source program

10. Paste Special

11. Embedded object

12. DDE

a. An object that can be edited using the features of the program in which it was created but which is not updated if the source file is changed

b. A feature that allows you to insert information from a file created in another program

c. A command that allows you to link or embed information stored on the Clipboard

d. The transfer of information between a source file and another file

e. An object that is updated when the original file is changed

f. The application in which an object is created

Select the best answer from the list of choices.

13. To convert a file to another program use the _____ command.
   a. Link
   b. Send To
   c. Object
   d. Paste Special

14. Which of the following is not true of an embedded object?
   a. It can be edited using the features of the source program
   b. It is created using another program
   c. Changes made to an embedded object are not saved in the source program
   d. It is automatically updated when the source file is updated

15. Which of the following is not true of a linked object?
   a. It can be edited using the features of the source program
   b. It is created using another program
   c. Changes made to a linked object are not saved in the source program
   d. It is automatically updated when the source file is updated

16. Which of the following groups represents objects you can insert in a document?
   a. Commands, features, and buttons
   b. Spreadsheets, slides, and graphics
   c. Labels, merge fields, and records
   d. Page numbers, columns, and breaks

17. Which of the following is not a way to share information between Office programs?
   a. Insert a text box
   b. Insert a linked object
   c. Insert a hyperlink to a file
   d. Insert an embedded object

18. To create an embedded object in a document, click
   a. 🖼
   b. 🖼
   c. ⬜
   d. 🖼

▶ Skills Review

1. Link an Excel worksheet.
   a. Start Word, open the file WD J-6 from your Project Disk, then save it as "Telecommuting Expenses".
   b. Click the blank line under the first body paragraph, then press [Enter].
   c. Click Insert on the menu bar, click Object, click the Create from File tab, then click Browse.
   d. Make sure the location of your Project Disk is displayed in the Look in list box, click WD J-7, then click Insert.
   e. Click the Link to file check box, then click OK.
   f. Save your changes to the document.

2. Modify a linked object.

   a. Double-click the worksheet object in the document.

   b. Click cell E2, then enter the following values in the Q4 column, clicking the down arrow to move from cell to cell: 150, 75, 160, 60, 34, 18.

   c. Select all the cells in the worksheet, click the Currency Style button on the Formatting toolbar, click the Bold button, then deselect the rows.

   d. Click the Save button on the Excel Standard toolbar, then close the Excel program window.

   e. Deselect the worksheet object, then save your changes to the document.

3. Use Paste Special to embed an object.

   a. Start Excel, then open the file WD J-8 from your Project Disk.

   b. Select all the rows in the worksheet, click Edit on the menu bar, then click Copy.

   c. Click the Telecommuting Expense document button on the taskbar, press [Ctrl][End], then press [Enter] twice. Be sure there is one blank line between the last paragraph and the insertion point.

   d. Click Edit on the menu bar, then click Paste Special.

   e. Make sure the Paste option button is selected, click Microsoft Excel Worksheet Object in the As list box, then click OK.

   f. Double-click the newly inserted worksheet object.

   g. Click the Bold button on the Formatting toolbar, click the Currency Style button, then deselect the object.

   h. Press [Ctrl][End], press [Enter] twice, type your name, save your changes to the Word document, print a copy, then close the file.

   i. Click the Excel program button on the taskbar, then close Excel.

4. Create a PowerPoint presentation from a Word outline.

   a. Open the file WD J-9 from your Project Disk, then save it as "Telecommuting Outline".

   b. Click File on the menu bar, point to Send To, then click Microsoft PowerPoint.

   c. Click Format on the menu bar, then click Apply Design Template.

   d. Click Network Blitz in the list of design themes, then click Apply.

   e. Click the Slide Sorter View button on the horizontal scroll bar.

   f. Save the presentation as "Telecommuting Presentation" to your Project Disk.

5. Insert a PowerPoint object.

   a. Click File on the PowerPoint menu bar, point to Send To, then click Microsoft Word.

   b. Make sure the Notes next to slides option button is selected, click the Paste link option button, then click OK.

   c. Press [Ctrl][Home], click Table on the menu bar, then click Show Gridlines if necessary.

   d. Double-click the slide 1 object.

   e. Click after "Decentralized offices" on the slide, press [Enter], type "At home", press [Enter], then type "On the road".

   f. Save your changes, then exit PowerPoint.

   g. Click in the cell to the right of slide 1, type your name, click in the cell to the right of slide 2, then type "Depending on circumstances, workers value flexibility and choice over modest salary increases."

   h. Print a copy of the document.

   i. If you are saving your Project Files to a floppy disk, close all open Word files without saving changes. If you are saving to your hard drive, save the document with the file name "Telecommuting Notes" to your Project Disk, then close all open Word files.

6. Attach an Access data source.

   a. Open a new blank document in Word, click Tools on the menu bar, then click Mail Merge.

   b. Click Create, click Mailing Labels, then click Active Window.

   c. Click Get Data, click Open Data Source, click the Files of type list arrow, then click MS Access Databases.

   d. Open the Access database file WD J-10 from your Project Disk.

   e. Select the Attendees table, then click OK.

   f. Click Set Up Main Document.

   g. Scroll to and click 5161 – Address in the Product number list box, then click OK.

   h. Click Insert Merge Field, click Prefix, press [Spacebar], then continue inserting merge fields so that the name appears on the first line of the label, the street address appears on the second line, and the city, state, and postal code appear on the third line. Be sure to use proper spacing and punctuation.

   i. Click OK to return to the Mail Merge Helper dialog box.

7. Select records to merge.

   a. Click Merge in the Mail Merge Helper dialog box, then click Query Options.

   b. Click the Field list arrow in the Field column, then click State.

   c. Click the Comparison list arrow in the Comparison column, then click Not equal to.

   d. Type "CA" in the Compare to text box.

   e. Click OK, then click Merge.

   f. Replace Deborah Andersen's name with your name.

   g. Save the document with the filename "Attendees Merge" to your Project Disk, print a copy of the labels, then close the file.

   h. Save the main document with the filename "Attendees Main" to your Project Disk, then close the file and exit Word.

▶ Visual Workshop

Create an outline for the presentation shown in Figure J-23, convert it to a PowerPoint presentation, then convert it back to the Word document shown in the figure. (*Hint:* Apply the Lock and Key design template. Create the title slide – slide 1 – in PowerPoint, not in Word.) In the final document, type your name in the cell next to the first slide, add notes next to each additional slide, then print a copy of the document. Save the outline with the filename "EarthWear Outline". Save the presentation with the filename "EarthWear Presentation". Do not save the final Word document unless you are saving it to your hard drive. If you are saving to your hard drive, save the final Word document as "EarthWear Notes".

FIGURE J-22

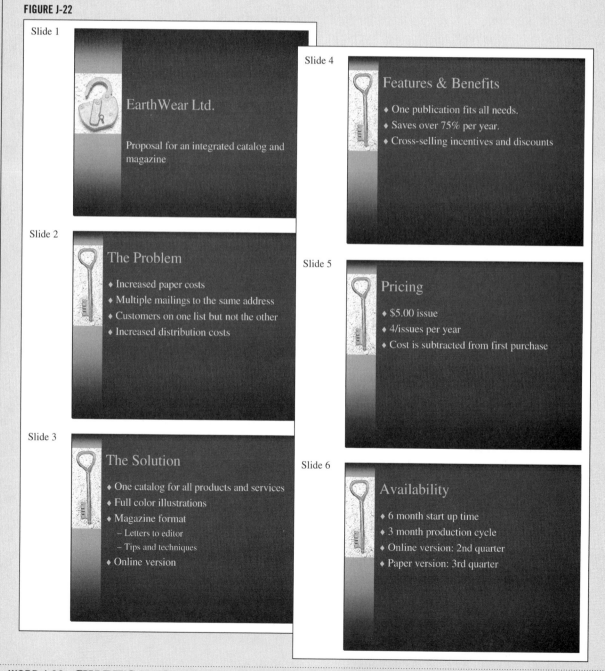

Word 2000

Working
with Larger Documents

Objectives

- ▶ **Create a document in Outline view**
- ▶ **Edit a document in Outline view**
- ▶ **Organize a document in Outline view**
- MOUS ▶ **Insert footnotes and endnotes**
- MOUS ▶ **Create a table of contents**
- MOUS ▶ **Format pages in multiple sections**
- MOUS ▶ **Create an index**
- MOUS ▶ **Create master documents**

Working with documents longer than two or three pages can involve a variety of new formatting and organizational challenges. You need to keep track of the sequence of topics, insert and modify footnotes and endnotes, create and manage a table of contents and perhaps even an index, handle formatting changes from section to section, and even incorporate subdocuments within master documents. You can work in Outline view, which provides the tools you need to organize long documents into headings, subheadings, and paragraphs. **Scenario** Jim Fernandez in the accounting department at MediaLoft's head office works in Outline view to create and organize a multiple-page document. He inserts footnotes, creates a table of contents page, an index, and a master document that contains one subdocument.

Creating a Document in Outline View

You work in Outline view in order to quickly and easily organize the topics and subtopics included in a multiple-page document such as an annual report or a proposal. In Outline view you establish the structure of a document by assigning levels to headings and subheadings, depending on their purpose in the document. For example, you identify the main headings in the document as Level 1 by assigning the Heading 1 style to them. Similarly, you assign lower levels and their corresponding heading styles to the headings for subtopics and even sub-subtopics. **Scenario** Jim needs to write the Quality Assurance section of the Financial Results report that will be included as part of MediaLoft's annual report. He begins by writing an outline.

Steps 1 2 3 4

1. Start Word, click the **New Blank Document button** 🔲 on the Standard toolbar, then click the **Outline View button** 🔳 on the horizontal scroll bar
   The program window opens in Outline view. Table K-1 identifies the buttons on the Outlining toolbar.

2. Type **Quality Assurance**
   See Figure K-1. Notice that the text, which is Level 1, is formatted in the Heading 1 style. The minus outline symbol ▭ indicates a line of text with no subheading or subordinate text.

3. Press **[Enter]**, then type **Product Testing Center Established**
   By default, this line of text is assigned the same heading style as the previous line of text, which is the Heading 1 style. However, this line of text should be at Level 2. To change the level of a heading, you can click the Promote and Demote buttons, press the keystrokes [Tab] and [Shift][Tab], or click the Style list arrow and apply a heading style.

4. Press **[Tab]**
   Notice the line of text is indented to show that the idea is subordinate to the previous heading, and the text is assigned the Heading 2 style. Also notice that the plus outline symbol ✚ appears to the left of the Level 1 text to indicate the addition of subheadings or subordinate text.

5. Press **[Enter]**, then type **New Alliances**
   Notice that the new line of text is assigned a Heading 2 style, which is the same heading style as the previous line. This line of text should be Level 3, which is assigned the Heading 3 style.

6. Click the **Demote button** 🔳 on the Outlining toolbar
   The text "New Alliances" is now Level 3 text formatted with the Heading 3 style.

7. Press **[Enter]**, click the **Demote to Body Text button** 🔳 on the Outlining toolbar, then type the paragraph of text shown below
   The testing results led to MediaLoft establishing partnerships with three other independent café/booksellers in the San Diego area. These companies will also sell the four coffee flavors tested by the student groups.
   Notice that the body text is indented below its heading and is assigned the Normal style.

8. Press **[Enter]**, click the **Promote button** 🔳 on the Outlining toolbar **twice**, type **Survey Results**, press **[Enter]** twice, then type your name
   The document appears, as shown in Figure K-2.

9. Save the file as **Quality Assurance Outline** to your Project Disk, print the document, then close it

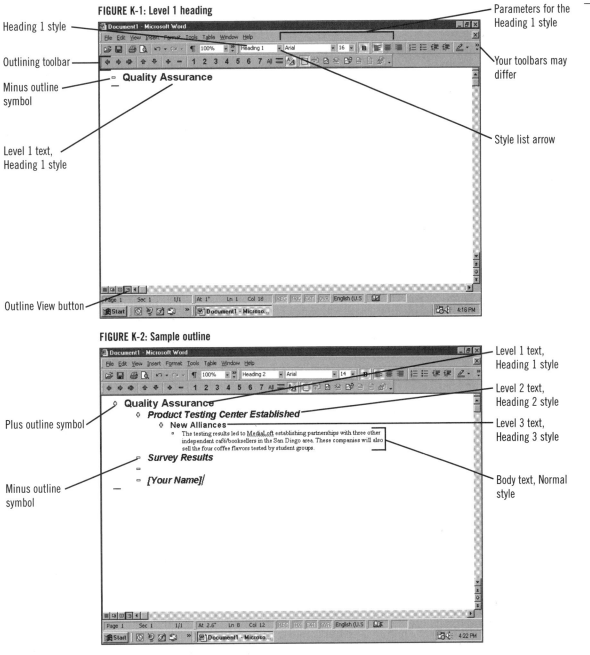

FIGURE K-1: Level 1 heading

Heading 1 style
Outlining toolbar
Minus outline symbol
Level 1 text, Heading 1 style
Outline View button

Parameters for the Heading 1 style
Your toolbars may differ
Style list arrow

Quality Assurance

FIGURE K-2: Sample outline

Plus outline symbol
Minus outline symbol

Level 1 text, Heading 1 style
Level 2 text, Heading 2 style
Level 3 text, Heading 3 style
Body text, Normal style

Quality Assurance
  Product Testing Center Established
    New Alliances
      The testing results led to MediaLoft establishing partnerships with three other independent café/booksellers in the San Diego area. These companies will also sell the four coffee flavors tested by student groups.
  Survey Results

  [Your Name]

TABLE K-1: Buttons on the Outlining toolbar

button	use to	button	use to
←	Promote text one level at a time	−	Collapse text under a heading one level
→	Demote text one level at a time	1 7	Display heading levels up to 7
⇒	Demote to Body text	All	Display all headings and text in a document
↑	Move a heading and its text up one line	=	Show first line only
↓	Move a heading and its text down one line	ᴬ𝐴	Show formatting
+	Expand text under a heading one level	▤	Master Document view

Word 2000

Editing a Document in Outline View

In Outline view you can choose to view document text based on the heading and body text styles you have applied to your document. For instance, when you want to focus on the overall organization of ideas, you can choose to view only the Level 1 headings in your document. Similarly, when you wish to focus on the detailed text, you can choose to view all the topics, subtopics, and paragraphs of text included in your document. The Outlining toolbar contains buttons that allow you to view as much or as little information as you like. **Scenario** Jim opens a draft version of the Financial Results report. He views the document in Outline view so he can examine its overall structure and organization of ideas. Jim then uses buttons on the Outlining toolbar to change the levels of selected headings.

Steps

1. Open the file named **WD K-1**, then save it as **Financial Results**

Trouble?

Make sure the Show First Line Only button is not indented.

2. On the horizontal scroll bar, click the **Outline View button**

   The document appears in the window in Outline view. Notice that subordinate headings and text appear indented under higher-level text. Text not formatted in a heading style is called body text and is identified by a small square ■. By default, body text is formatted with the Normal style.

3. On the Outlining toolbar, click the **Show Heading 3 button** 3

   The first three heading levels of the document appear, as shown in Figure K-3. This setting is useful when you want to see the basic structure of the document without being distracted by all the body text.

4. On the Outlining toolbar, click the **Show Heading 1 button** 1

   With only the top level listed, you can focus on the main ideas of your document. You can also use the keyboard to show heading levels in Outline view. Press [Alt][Shift][n] (where [n] represents the desired heading level) to show that level. For example, [Alt][Shift][2] shows the first two heading levels. You decide to show all the levels and all the text again.

5. On the Outlining toolbar, click the **Show All Headings button** All

   All the heading levels and subordinate text appear.

QuickTip

You can also press [Shift][Tab] to promote a heading.

6. Click the heading **Survey Results** in the Quality Assurance section, then click the **Promote button** on the Outlining toolbar

   Notice that the text moves up a level in the hierarchy from Level 3 to Level 2, and the Style box on the Formatting toolbar reflects the new heading style, which is Heading 2.

QuickTip

You can also press [Tab] to demote a heading.

7. Scroll down and click the subheading **Newsletter Sent to Customers**, then click the **Demote button** on the Outlining toolbar

   The text moves down a level in the hierarchy from Level 2 to Level 3 and is formatted in the Heading 3 style.

8. Scroll to the top of the document, click in the heading **See attached report for complete...** under the Financial Results 2000 heading, then click the **Demote to Body Text button** on the Outlining toolbar

   Notice that when you demote a heading to body text, the Normal style is applied.

9. Compare your screen with Figure K-4, then save the document

FIGURE K-3: Top three levels of the outline

Show Heading 3 button

Show First Line Only button

Show All Headings button

Level 1

Level 2

Level 3

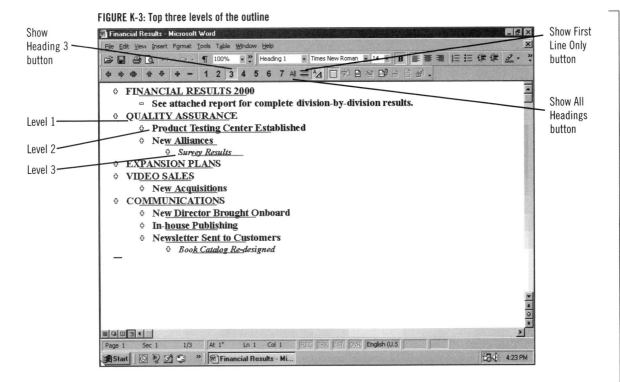

FIGURE K-4: Multilevel outline

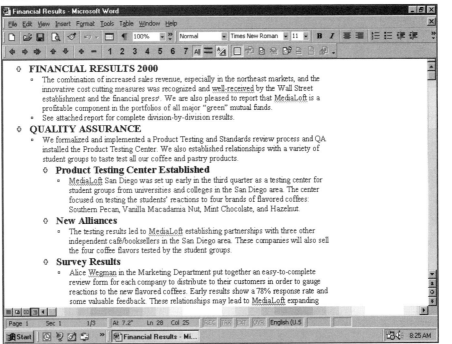

Organizing a Document in Outline View

Outline view is designed to let you quickly and easily rearrange text. You can use buttons on the Outlining toolbar or drag-and-drop mouse techniques to move any heading, along with its subordinate headings and paragraphs of text, quickly to another location. Table K-2 includes buttons and keyboard shortcuts for performing these operations. **Scenario** After reviewing his document, Jim realizes he needs to change the order of topics in his report. Jim decides to work in Outline view to reorganize his document.

Steps

1. Click the **Show Heading 1 button** 1 on the Outlining toolbar
   The five Level 1 headings in the document are listed in Outline view.

2. Click the heading **Video Sales**, then click the **Expand button** + on the Outlining toolbar
   The next level of text, which is Level 2, appears only for the Video Sales portion of the document.

3. Click + again
   Now all the subordinate body text for Video Sales appears under the appropriate Level 1 or Level 2 headings, as shown in Figure K-5.

4. Position the mouse pointer over the **plus outline symbol** ⊕ for the heading **Video Sales**; then, when the pointer changes to ⊕, double-click the mouse button
   With a heading completely collapsed, you can move (or delete) significant amounts of text, without selecting all the text first.

5. Click the **Move Down button** ⬇ on the Outlining toolbar
   The heading Video Sales, along with all its subordinate text, moves to the end of the document. If you want to see all the subordinate text for Video Sales, you can double-click the plus outline symbol to the left of the heading Video Sales.

6. Click anywhere in the **Communications** heading, then click the **Move Up button** ⬆ on the Outlining toolbar
   The selected heading Communications, along with all its subordinate text, moves above the Expansion Plans heading in the document organization.

7. Click ⊕ next to the **Quality Assurance** heading, then drag the heading above the Financial Results 2000 heading
   The Quality Assurance heading and its subordinate text are now the first topic in the document.

8. Click the **Show All Headings button** All on the Outlining toolbar, then deselect the text
   Compare your document with Figure K-6. All the text associated with the Quality Assurance heading has moved along with the heading.

9. Click the **Print Layout View button** ▣ on the horizontal scroll bar, then save your changes
   Once you have finished working in Outline view, you should return to Print Layout view where you can see how your document will appear on the printed page.

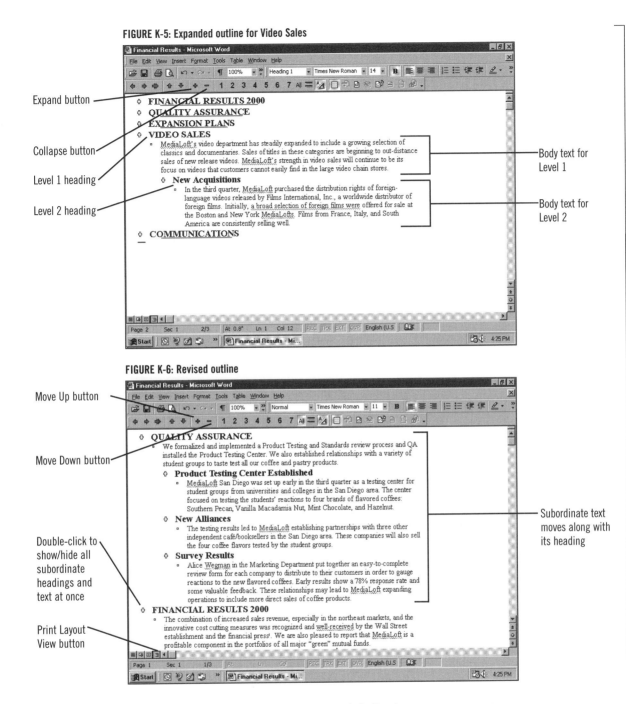

FIGURE K-5: Expanded outline for Video Sales

Expand button

Collapse button

Level 1 heading

Level 2 heading

Body text for Level 1

Body text for Level 2

FIGURE K-6: Revised outline

Move Up button

Move Down button

Double-click to show/hide all subordinate headings and text at once

Print Layout View button

Subordinate text moves along with its heading

TABLE K-2: Buttons and keyboard shortcuts for viewing and moving headings in Outline view

to	click	press
Expand text under a heading one level	+	[Alt][Shift][+]
Collapse text under a heading one level	−	[Alt][Shift][-]
Display all headings and text in the document	All	[Alt][Shift][A]
Move a heading and its text up one line	⬆	[Alt] [Shift] ↑
Move a heading and its text down one line	⬇	[Alt] [Shift] ↓

Inserting Footnotes and Endnotes

A footnote is text that appears at the bottom of a page. An endnote is text that usually appears at the end of a document. Usually, footnotes and endnotes provide acknowledgment of a source or additional information. To insert a footnote or endnote, you identify the text you want associated with it, then you select the Footnote command from the Insert menu. Next you identify the reference marker, which is the identifying mark that appears in the document text after the word the footnote or endnote references. Finally, you enter the actual footnote or endnote text. When you insert new footnotes or delete existing ones, Word automatically updates the reference markers for the remaining footnotes. **Scenario** Jim's report already includes some footnotes. He plans to insert a new footnote and delete an existing footnote.

Steps

1. **Click Edit on the menu bar, click Find, type division results, press [Enter], then close the Find dialog box**
   The words "division results" are highlighted. In Print Layout view, the footnote area appears at the bottom of the document window and is separated by a gray line from the body of the text.

2. **Click at the end of division results (before the period), click Insert on the menu bar, then click Footnote**
   In the Footnote and Endnote dialog box, you identify where you are inserting a footnote or an endnote. You also identify the format of the reference marker.

3. **Click Options, click the Number format list arrow, click a, b, c, ..., click OK, then click OK again**
   Notice that a superscript [b] appears after "results". The blinking insertion point in the footnote area indicates where you need to enter the text for the new footnote. The footnote text is too small to read in 100% view. You need to increase the Zoom percentage.

4. **Click the Zoom list arrow on the Standard toolbar, click 150%, scroll up to see the text of footnote [a], type The attached report also contains information about projected results for 2001.**
   Compare your screen to Figure K-7. You can remove a footnote after it has been entered.

5. **Click above the footnote dividing line to return to the text of your report, click Edit on the menu bar, click Go To, select Footnote in the Go to what list box, type a in the Enter footnote number text box, click Go To, then click Close**
   To remove a footnote, you just need to find it and then delete it within the text of your document. You can use the Go To command to find a footnote.

6. **Move the cursor over the superscript [a] that follows "press" and note how the wording for footnote [a] appears in a pop-up box**

7. **Select the superscript [a] following "press", then press [Delete]**
   Compare your screen with Figure K-8. The footnote reference marker in the text has been updated to footnote [a].

8. **Scroll down the page to view the footnote area**
   Notice that the text for the original footnote [a] no longer appears and that the original footnote [b] has been updated to footnote [a].

9. **Click the Zoom list arrow, select 100%, then save your document**

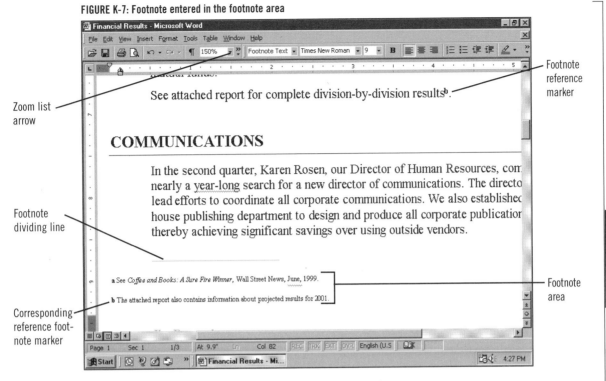

FIGURE K-7: Footnote entered in the footnote area

Zoom list arrow

Footnote reference marker

Footnote dividing line

Footnote area

Corresponding reference foot-note marker

FIGURE K-8: Footnote reference marker updated

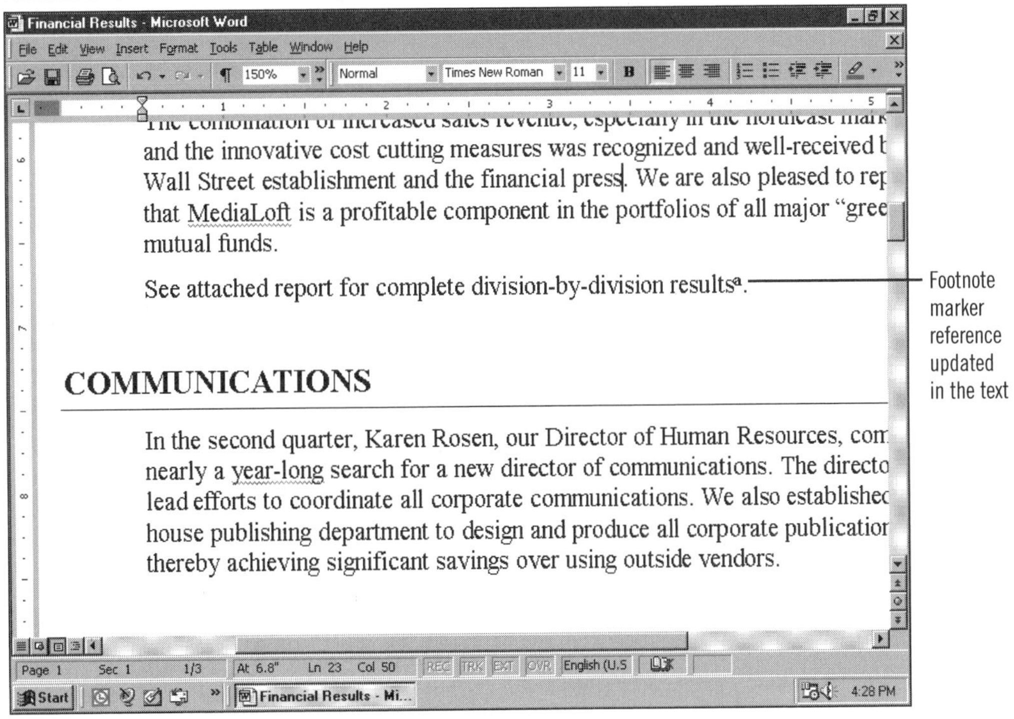

Footnote marker reference updated in the text

Creating a Table of Contents

When you have a large document that is divided into topics based on heading levels, you can easily create a table of contents. With the Index and Tables command on the Insert menu, you specify the heading levels you want to include in your table of contents. You can then automatically generate a table of contents that contains the heading levels along with the page numbers on which they occur. The entries in a table of contents are automatically made into hyperlinks. **Scenario** Jim decides to create the table of contents in a separate section. Later he can apply page numbering to the table of contents page that is different from the page numbering he applies to the body of the report.

Steps

1. Press **[Ctrl][Home]** to move to the top of the document, click **Insert** on the menu bar, click **Break**, click **Next page**, then click **OK**

   When you inserted the page break, the Heading 1 style was automatically applied to the blank space above the next page break. If you typed text above the page break, it would appear in the Heading 1 style.

QuickTip

Press "n" to move quickly to Normal in the list of styles.

2. Press **[Ctrl][Home]**, click the **Style list arrow**, scroll down and select **Normal**, click **Insert** on the menu bar, then click **Index and Tables**

3. Click the **Table of Contents tab**, verify that the **Show page numbers check box** is selected, then verify that **3** appears in the Show levels text box

4. Click the **Formats list arrow**, click **Formal**, note the Print Preview of the Formal format that appears as shown in Figure K-9, then click **OK**

   The table of contents appears at the beginning of the document, as shown in Figure K-10. The levels you identified in Outline view determine how the headings are treated in the table of contents. The line or dotted line that appears in front of the page number is called a tab leader. You can change the appearance of the tab leader.

5. Point to the left of the first line of the table of contents to display the ⟰, click ⟰ to select the entire table of contents, click **Format** on the menu bar, then click **Tabs**

   In the Tabs dialog box, you can specify the location of tab stops and the leader associated with the tab stop.

6. Click the **Clear All button** to delete any existing tab stops, type **6** in the Tab stop position text box, click the **Right option button** in the Alignment area, click the **4 option button** in the Leader area, click **Set**, click **OK**, then click below the table of contents to deselect it

   The page numbers continue to be right-aligned and the leaders appear as solid lines. You decide to remove the entire Quality Assurance section from the report and then update the table of contents.

7. Click the **Outline View button** ▤, click the **plus outline symbol** ✛ to the left of **Quality Assurance**, then press **[Delete]**

   After you delete text, you must update the table of contents.

8. Click the **Print Layout View button** ▣ on the horizontal scroll bar, then scroll up to the top of the document

   Notice the error messages that appear instead of page numbers. Error messages occur when the link between the heading in the table of contents and the corresponding heading in the document is broken. You broke the link when you deleted the Quality Assurance materials.

9. Right-click the table of contents, click **Update Field**, click away from the table of contents to deselect it, then save your document

   Compare your table of contents with Figure K-11.

FIGURE K-9: Index and Tables dialog box

Table of Contents tab

Preview of Formal format

Show page numbers check box

Formal format selected

Number indicates which heading levels to include in the table of contents

Formats list arrow

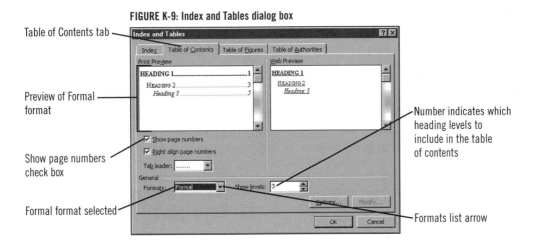

FIGURE K-10: Table of contents based on heading styles

Heading 1

Heading 2

Heading 3

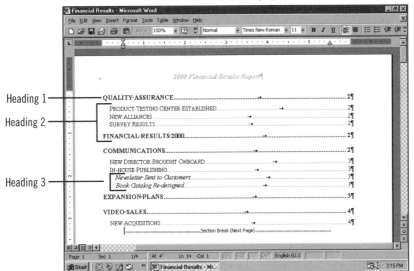

FIGURE K-11: Updated table of contents

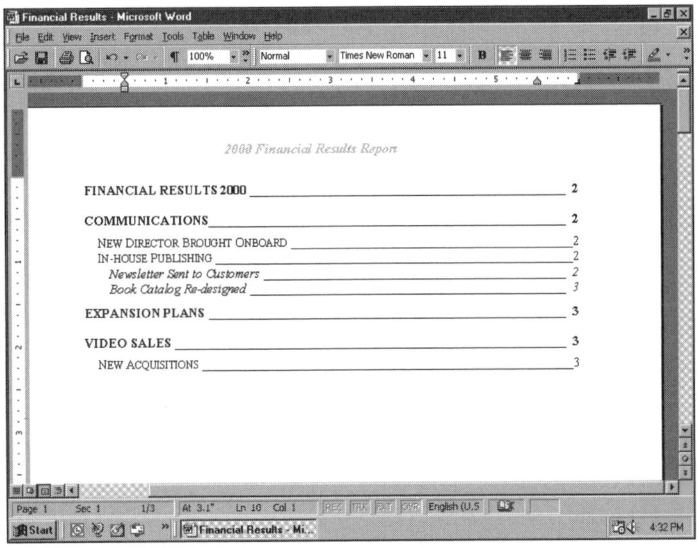

Word 2000

Formatting Pages in Multiple Sections

When you have multiple sections in a document, you can specify unique formatting for each section. For example, you can vary the text that appears in the headers and footers or use different page setup options in each section. **Scenario** Jim decides to change the page-numbering format and to modify the footer text that appears on his table of contents page. However, before Jim can change the footer that appears on the table of contents page, he needs to display the footer in Section 2 and then deselect the Same as Previous button on the Header and Footer toolbar. By doing this, Jim makes sure that the footer in Section 2 can display completely different text from the footer in Section 1. In this case, Jim wants the footer in Section 1, which is the table of contents, to display only the page number formatted in the lower-case Roman numeral style. He does not want the wording in the Section 2 footer to change, but he does want the page number in Section 2 to start on page 1.

Steps

1. Click **Communications** in the table of contents
   Notice that the Communications heading and subordinate text appears.

2. Click **View** on the menu bar, click **Header and Footer**, then click the **Switch Between Header and Footer button** 🖳 on the Header and Footer toolbar
   The footer text appears.

3. Click the **Same as Previous button** 🖳 on the Header and Footer toolbar to deselect it as shown in Figure K-12
   Now that you have deselected the Same as Previous button, you can modify the footer in Section 1 without affecting the footer in Section 2. If the Same as Previous button is not deselected, then changes you make to the Section 1 footer will also appear in the Section 2 footer.

4. Click the **Show Previous button** 🖳 on the Header and Footer toolbar
   The footer for Section 1 appears. Notice that the footer for Section 1 and the footer for Section 2 are the same.

5. Click to the left of the footer outside the footer area to select all the text in the footer, then press **[Delete]**

6. Click **Insert** on the menu bar, click **Page Numbers**, click **Format**, click the **Number format list arrow**, select **i, ii, iii, ...** as shown in Figure K-13, then click **OK**
   The Page Number Format dialog box closes.

7. Click the **Alignment list arrow** in the Page Numbers dialog box, select **Center**, then click **OK**
   The newly formatted page number appears in Section 1. Next you need to modify the starting page number for Section 2.

8. Click the **Show Next button** 🖳 on the Header and Footer toolbar to show the footer in Section 2, click **Insert** on the menu bar, click **Page Numbers**, click **Format**, click the **Start at option button**, verify that the starting number is **1**, click **OK**, then click **Close**
   Section 2 now starts with Page 1. Now that you have made changes to the document, you need to update the table of contents.

9. Click **Close** on the Header and Footer toolbar, press **[Ctrl][Home]**, press **[F9]**, click **OK** to accept Update page numbers only, then click away from the table of contents to deselect it
   The table of contents now reflects the revised page number format for the report, as shown in Figure K-14.

10. Save your document

FIGURE K-12: Same as Previous button deselected

Same as Previous button

Show Previous button

Header and Footer toolbar

Switch Between Header and Footer button

Footer text for Section 2

FIGURE K-13: Page Number Format dialog box

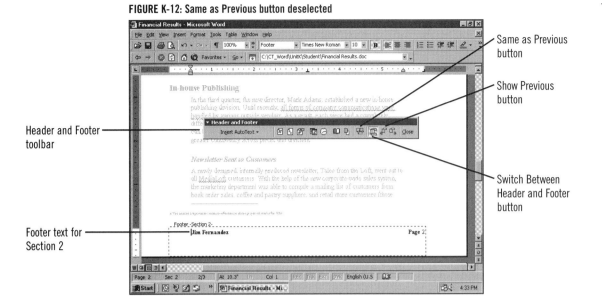

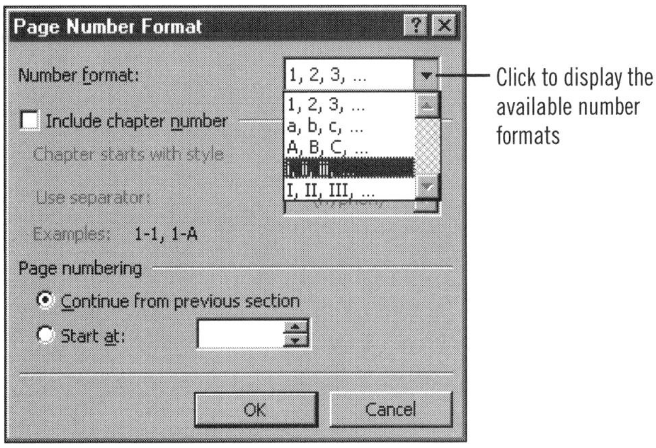

Click to display the available number formats

FIGURE K-14: Updated table of contents

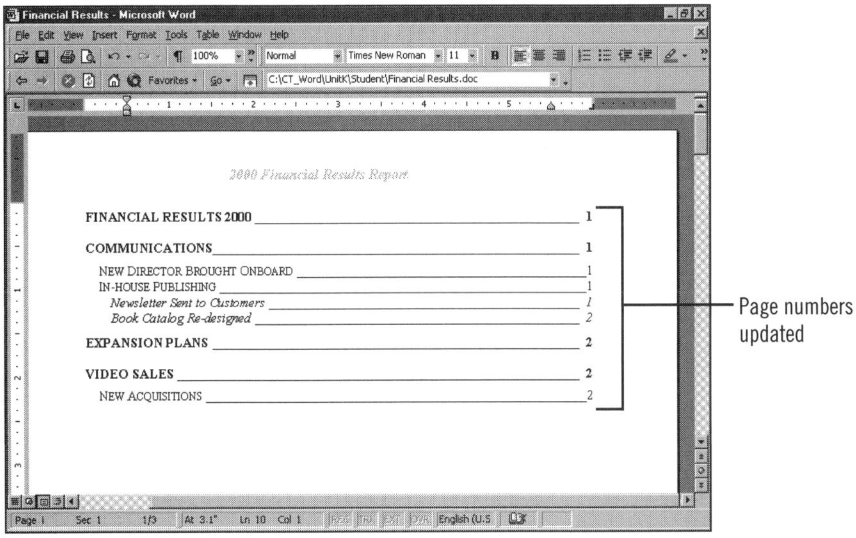

Page numbers updated

Creating an Index

You use an index to list key words and phrases that readers of your document may wish to look up. Most often you will create indexes for long documents such as books and reports that exceed 100 pages. To begin building an index, you must first mark the text entries you would like the index to include. After you have marked your entries, Word alphabetizes them and references their page numbers. The Index tab in the Index and Tables dialog box offers many formats and options for building an index. **Scenario** Jim has decided to include an index on the last page of his report so that his readers can quickly locate key information in it.

QuickTip

You can also press [Alt][Shift][X] to display the Mark Index Entry dialog box.

1. Click **Communications** in the table of contents, select the text **publications** in the body text under the heading Communications, click **Insert** on the menu bar, click **Index and Tables**, click the **Index tab**, then click **Mark Entry**
   The selected text "publications" appears in the Main entry text box. You want the title of the MediaLoft publication *Tales from the Loft* to appear as a subentry for the main entry "publications" in the index.

2. Click in the **Subentry text box**, type **Tales from the Loft**, then click **Mark**
   Compare your screen with Figure K-15. A field code appears following "publications", and the paragraph marks are visible.

3. Click the document, select the name **Mark Adams** under the heading "New Director…", click the Main entry text box, then click **Mark**

4. Click the document, select the text **MediaLoft** under the heading "New Director…", click the Main entry text box, verify that the Current page option button is selected in the Options area, click **Mark All**, click **Close**, then click the document to deselect the text
   Clicking the Mark All button marks the first occurrence of text in each paragraph of the document that matches the entry exactly. You modify the index so that every occurrence of "Mark Adams" in the document is included.

5. Click **Edit** on the menu bar, click **Find**, type **Mark Adams** in the Find what text box, click **Find Next**, click **Insert** on the menu bar, click **Index and Tables**, click **Mark Entry** in the Index tab, then click **Mark All**
   A field code is inserted after the first occurrence of "Mark Adams" in each paragraph that includes the words "Mark Adams".

6. With the Mark Index Entry dialog box still open, deselect the text "Mark Adams", click the Find and Replace dialog box, type **Toronto** in the Find what text box, click the **Find Next button**, click the Main entry text box, click after "**See**" in the Cross reference text box, type **Canada**, then click **Mark All**
   People looking for "Toronto" will now be directed to look under "Canada".

Trouble?

Be sure to deselect document text before conducting a new search.

7. Mark every instance of **sales revenue, Canada**, and **foreign-language videos** in the document, click **Close** in the Mark Index Entry dialog box, close the Find and Replace dialog box if it is open, then click to deselect the highlighted text

8. Press **[Ctrl][End]** to place the insertion point at the end of the document, click **Insert** on the menu bar, click **Break**, click the **Next page option button**, then click **OK**

9. Click **Insert** on the menu bar, click **Index and Tables**, click the **Formats list arrow** in the Index tab, select **Formal**, then click **OK**
   The index appears as shown in Figure K-16.

10. Save the document

FIGURE K-15: Marked index entry in the document

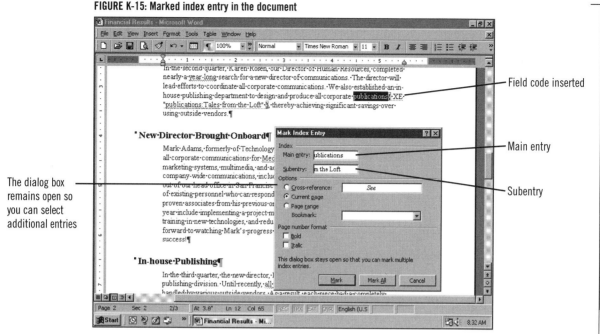

The dialog box remains open so you can select additional entries

Field code inserted

Main entry

Subentry

FIGURE K-16: Completed index

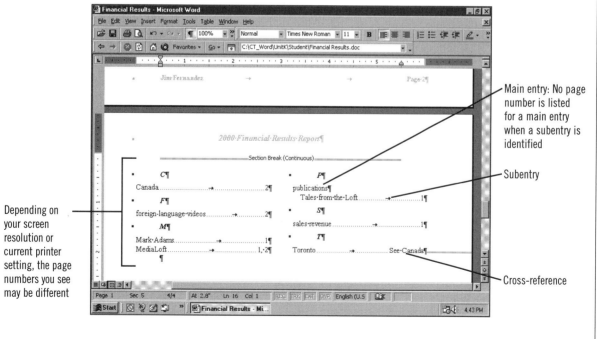

Depending on your screen resolution or current printer setting, the page numbers you see may be different

Main entry: No page number is listed for a main entry when a subentry is identified

Subentry

Cross-reference

Creating Master Documents

When you work with very large documents or in documents that contain many graphic objects, you may need quite a bit of time to scroll through the pages or preview the document. To save time, you can divide the large document into smaller documents, called subdocuments, which you then insert in a master document. Master documents open only the subdocument you wish to edit, so your computer responds quickly to your commands and you can work more efficiently. **Scenario** Jim will insert his Quality Assurance file into the Financial Results report as a subdocument. He will then adjust the text flow options to control how the text breaks across pages.

Trouble?

Be sure Financial Results is the active document.

QuickTip

If you make and save changes to the originating subdocument file, these changes will also be reflected in the master document because the subdocument is linked to the master document.

1. Open the file WD K-2, save it as **Quality Assurance**, then close it

2. Click to the left of the section break that appears just above the Index on the last page, then click the **Outline View button** 🗐 on the horizontal scroll bar

3. Click the **Insert Subdocument button** 🗐 on the Outlining toolbar, use the Look in list arrow to navigate to the location of the file **Quality Assurance**, then double-click **Quality Assurance** to open it

   Section breaks appear before and after the text of the subdocument as shown in Figure K-17. In addition a gray line surrounds the Quality Assurance document and a small disk icon appears in the upper-left corner. Both these elements remind you that this section of the master document is a subdocument.

4. Double-click **agreements** in the text under the "New Partnerships" subheading, then type **partnerships**

   Any changes you make to a subdocument and save to a Master document are saved to the originating subdocument file as well.

5. Click the **Collapse Subdocuments button** 🗐 on the Outlining toolbar, click **OK** to save the changes, then click the **Print Layout View button** 🗐

   When working with large documents, you sometimes need to adjust the text flow options in order to control how text flows between pages. Table K-3 describes the text flow options.

6. Click the heading **Newsletter Sent to Customers** in the table of contents

   You want the heading and the paragraph text to stay together.

7. Click **Format** on the menu bar, click **Paragraph**, click the **Line and Page Breaks tab**, click the **Keep with next check box**, then click **OK**

   Now the heading and its subordinate text will always appear as one block. You need to return to Outline view and expand the subdocuments before you can update the table of contents.

8. Click the **Outline View button** 🗐, click the **Expand Subdocuments button** 🗐, scroll to the top of the document if necessary, right-click the table of contents, click **Update Field**, click the **Update entire table option button**, click **OK**, switch to Print Layout view, then click to the left of the section break below the table of contents to deselect the table of contents

   The table of contents includes the headings from the subdocument, as shown in Figure K-18.

9. Type your name on the table of contents, save your document, print it, then close it

FIGURE K-17: Quality Assurance subdocument inserted in Outline view

Indicates the subdocument is a file

Contents of the subdocument is contained within the grayed borders

Collapse Subdocuments button

Insert Subdocument button

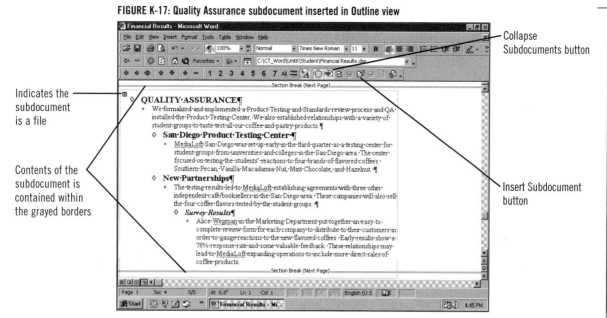

FIGURE K-18: Updated table of contents in Outline view

Subdocument headings included in the updated table of contents

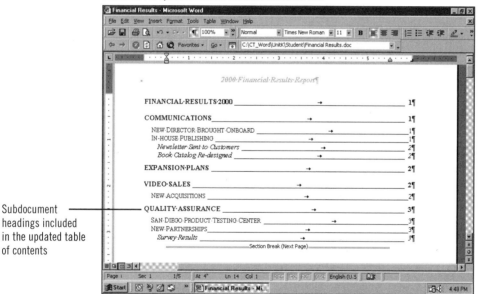

TABLE K-3: Text flow options

choose this option	to
Widow/Orphan control	Prevent the last line of a paragraph from printing at the top of a page (widow), and the first line of a paragraph from printing at the bottom of a page (orphan). Widow/Orphan control is a default setting in Word 2000.
Keep lines together	Prevent a page break within a paragraph
Keep with next	Prevent a page break between the selected paragraph and the paragraph after it
Keep break before	Position the selected text at the top of the next page

Practice

► Concepts Review

Label each element of the Word document window in Figure K-19.

FIGURE K-19

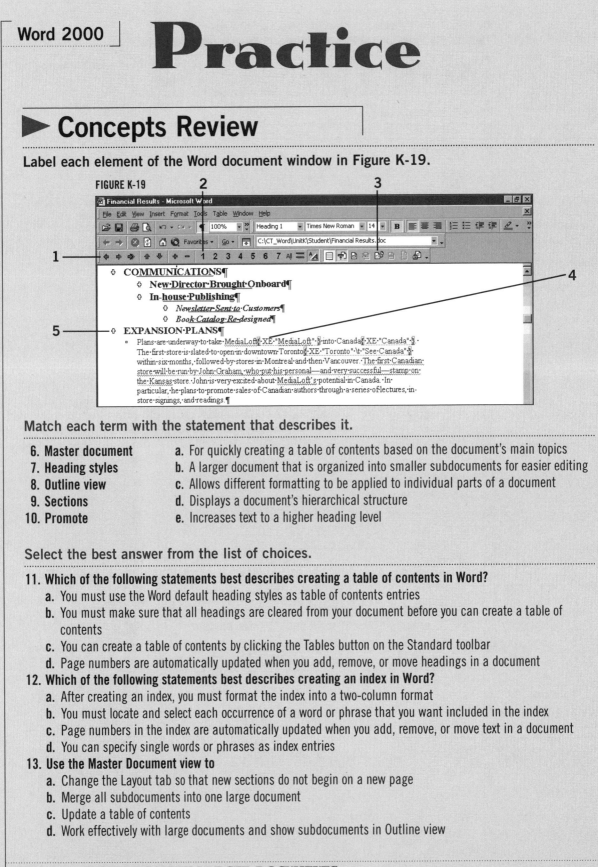

Match each term with the statement that describes it.

6. **Master document**
7. **Heading styles**
8. **Outline view**
9. **Sections**
10. **Promote**

a. For quickly creating a table of contents based on the document's main topics
b. A larger document that is organized into smaller subdocuments for easier editing
c. Allows different formatting to be applied to individual parts of a document
d. Displays a document's hierarchical structure
e. Increases text to a higher heading level

Select the best answer from the list of choices.

11. Which of the following statements best describes creating a table of contents in Word?
   a. You must use the Word default heading styles as table of contents entries
   b. You must make sure that all headings are cleared from your document before you can create a table of contents
   c. You can create a table of contents by clicking the Tables button on the Standard toolbar
   d. Page numbers are automatically updated when you add, remove, or move headings in a document

12. Which of the following statements best describes creating an index in Word?
   a. After creating an index, you must format the index into a two-column format
   b. You must locate and select each occurrence of a word or phrase that you want included in the index
   c. Page numbers in the index are automatically updated when you add, remove, or move text in a document
   d. You can specify single words or phrases as index entries

13. Use the Master Document view to
   a. Change the Layout tab so that new sections do not begin on a new page
   b. Merge all subdocuments into one large document
   c. Update a table of contents
   d. Work effectively with large documents and show subdocuments in Outline view

1. Create a document in Outline view.

a. Click the New Blank Document button on the Standard toolbar.

b. On the horizontal scroll bar, click the Outline View button.

c. Type "Investment Basics".

d. Press [Enter], press [Tab], then type "Identify long term and short term goals".

e. Press [Enter], press [Tab], then type "Identify current obligations".

f. Press [Enter], click the Promote button twice, type "Identify cost saving strategies", then press [Enter].

g. Demote the text that follows to body text, type "Determine how investors can use a variety of strategies to reduce their monthly expenses and increase their monthly investments".

h. Press [Enter], then click the Promote button.

i. Type "Identify income enhancing strategies".

j. Press [Enter], then type "Invest".

k. Press [Enter] two times, type your name, then save the document as "Strategy Outline".

l. Print the document, then close the document.

2. Edit a document in Outline view.

a. Open the document named WD K-3, then save it as "Investment Outline".

b. On the horizontal scroll bar, click the Outline View button, then show all the level 3 headings.

c. Promote the Fund Performance heading one level.

d. Demote the "Windlow Stock Fund" heading one level.

e. Demote the text that begins "The Class B Plan provides for payments by …" to body text.

3. Organize a document in Outline view.

a. On the Outlining toolbar, click the Show Heading 1 button.

b. Click the "Fund Description" heading.

c. Click the Move Up button once, then click the Expand button twice.

d. Click the "Growth Stock Fund" heading, then click the Collapse button.

e. Select the line with the heading "Common Stock Fund", then drag the heading above "Fixed Income Fund".

f. On the Outlining toolbar, click the Show All Headings button to verify that all subordinate text moved along with the "Common Stock Fund" heading, then deselect the text.

g. On the horizontal scroll bar, click the Print Layout View button.

4. Insert footnotes and endnotes.

a. Use the Find command to search for "Appendix A".

b. Close the Find and Replace dialog box, click after "A", click Insert on the menu bar, then click Footnote.

c. Change the footnote numbering style to A, B, C.

d. For the footnote text, type "Table 1 in Appendix A was compiled by Richard Walters in the Financial Investments Division".

e. Click in the text of the document, then use the Go To command to find footnote A.

f. Delete footnote A.

5. Create a table of contents.

a. With the insertion point at the top of the document, click Insert on the menu bar, then click Break.

b. Click the Next page option button, then click OK.

c. Press [Ctrl][Home] to move to the top of the document.

d. Change the current style from Title to Normal.

e. Click Insert on the menu bar, then click Index and Tables.

f. Click the Table of Contents tab.

g. Click the Options button, verify the Styles check box is selected, then click OK.

h. In the Formats section, click Fancy, then click OK.

i. Switch to Outline view, then show the Heading 2 entries.

    j. Delete the Common Stock Fund heading.

    k. Switch to Print Layout view.

    l. Right-click the table of contents, then click Update Field and update the page numbers.

6. Format pages in multiple sections.

    a. Scroll down the page and click anywhere below the document title (Investment Fund Fact Sheet), click View on the menu bar, then click Header and Footer.

    b. Click the Switch Between Header and Footer button.

    c. Click the Same as Previous button to deselect it.

    d. Click the Show Previous button to view the footer for Section 1.

    e. Delete the footer text.

    f. Click Insert on the menu bar, click Page Numbers, then click Format.

    g. Click the Number format list arrow, select i, ii, iii, …, then click OK.

    h. Click the Alignment list arrow in the Page Numbers dialog box, select Center, then click OK.

    i. Click the Show Next button.

    j. Click Insert on the menu bar, click Page Numbers, click Format, click the Start at option button, verify 1 is the number in the Start at text box, click OK, then click Close.

    k. Close the Header and Footer toolbar.

7. Create an index.

    a. Select the text "Omaha Investors Group" in the Introduction.

    b. Click Insert on the menu bar, click Index and Tables, then click the Index tab.

    c. Click Mark Entry.

    d. Click in the Main entry text box, then click Mark All.

    e. Use the Find command with the following text and repeat step d for each main entry.

    f. Be sure to deselect the text before you initiate each find. Close all open dialog boxes when the entries are completed.

main entry	subentry	main entry	subentry
Guaranteed Investment contracts	GIC	Standard & Poor's	
Bank Investment contracts	BIC	FDIC insurance	security

    g. Press [Ctrl][End], press [Enter] once, click Insert, click Break, select Next page, then click OK.

    h. Click Insert, then click Index and Tables, then click the Index tab.

    i. In the Formats section, select Modern, then click OK.

8. Create a master document.

    a. Press [Ctrl][Home] to move to the top of the document, then click Fund Performance in the table of contents to move to the Fund Performance heading.

    b. Click the paragraph below the Fund Performance heading, click Format on the menu bar, click Paragraph, then click the Line and Page Breaks tab.

    c. Click the Keep lines together check box, then click OK.

    d. Repeat steps a–c for the heading Growth Stock Fund and its paragraph.

    e. Click the Outline View button, expand Fund Performance, click between the last word "fund" and the paragraph mark.

    f. Click the Insert Subdocument button on the Outlining toolbar.

    g. Double-click Strategy Outline.

    h. Click in the second heading "Identify long term and short term goals", click the Demote button, select your name, then delete it.

i. Move to the top of the document, right-click the table of contents, click Update Field, click the Update entire table option button, then click OK.

j. Switch to Print Layout view, type your name at the bottom of the document, view the document in the Print Preview screen, then make sure that the pages appear attractively formatted over six pages.

k. Save the document, print it, then close it.

Word 2000

▶ Visual Workshop

As the marketing manager for Western Pacific Airlines, you need to present a short proposal regarding new travel destination opportunities to senior staff members at the upcoming annual meeting. Open the draft proposal named WD K-5 and save the document as "Airline Outline". Using Figure K-20 as a guide, reorganize the document in Outline view. Generate a table of contents in the Formal style, such as the one shown in Figure K-20. Include a footer starting on the first page of the document text that shows the centered page number starting at 1. Do not include a page number in the footer on the table of contents page. Using Figure K-21 as a guide, select and mark index entries and then create an index in the Formal style at the end of the document. Type your name at the end of the index, then save, print, and close the document.

FIGURE K-20

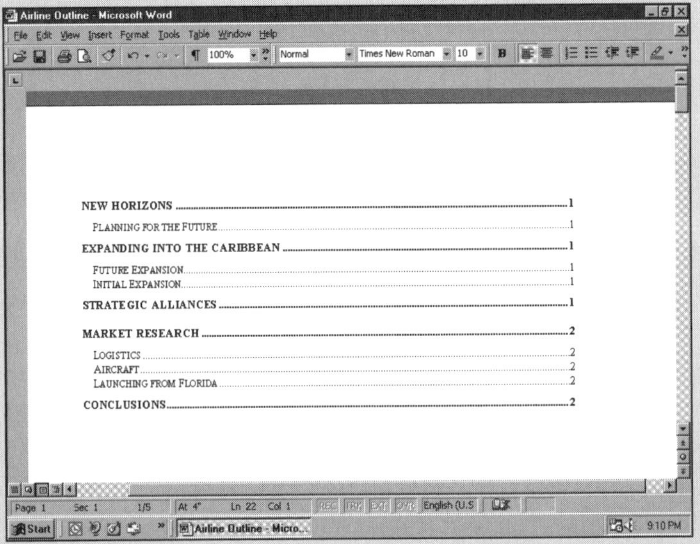

FIGURE K-21

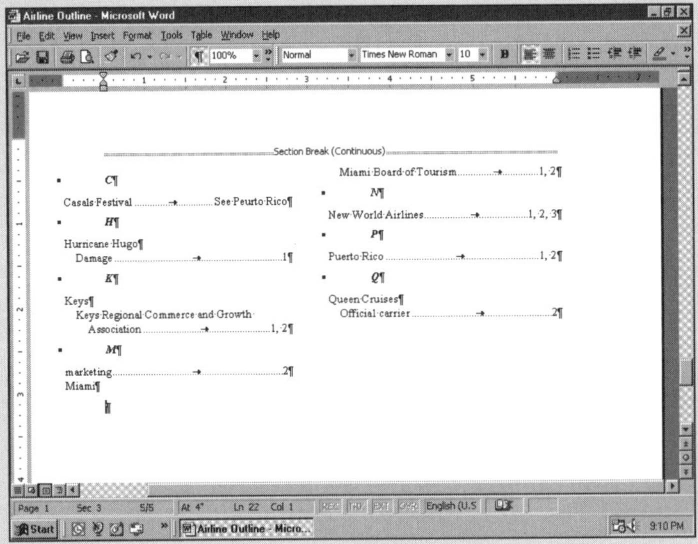

Collaborating
with Documents

Objectives

- ▶ Insert comments in a document
- ▶ Save versions of a document
- ▶ Track changes in a document
- ▶ Compare and protect documents
- ▶ Accept and reject changes
- ▶ Use advanced find and replace techniques
- ▶ Create a bookmark and cross-reference
- ▶ Understand Online Collaboration

Sometimes you need to create documents as part of a team. Word 2000 includes features that help you develop documents in collaboration with others. These features include the Comment feature, the Track Changes feature, and the Versions feature. In addition, you can use advanced search and replace techniques to find special characters and formatting, bookmarks and cross-references to jump quickly to different parts of a document, and the Online Collaboration feature to conduct a NetMeeting live over the Internet. Scenario▶ Jim Fernandez in MediaLoft's accounting department needs to customize a standard work agreement. He and Adam Ingraham, a legal adviser, will use Word's features that make collaboration easier as they work together to produce a final draft of the agreement.

Inserting Comments in a Document

Word 2000

If you are working on a document that other people will review, you can add comments directed to your reviewers. A **comment** is text you enter in a separate pane so that the comment does not appear with the document text. A **comment mark** is inserted in the document at the point where you add the comment. Comments and comment marks are formatted in hidden text, so by default, they do not print when you print the document. **Scenario** Jim starts with a standard document that was provided by Adam Ingraham, MediaLoft's legal adviser. Jim would like to add additional information about the changes he is suggesting, so he inserts comments for Adam to read as he reviews the document.

Steps

1. Start Word, open the document **WD L-1**, then save it with the name **Contract**

Trouble?

The initials you see will probably be different.

2. If necessary, click the **Show/Hide ¶ button** ¶ on the Standard toolbar to select it, click **Insert** on the menu bar, then click **Comment**

   A comment mark is placed in the document at the point where the comment is inserted, and the comment pane opens at the bottom of the window, as shown in Figure L-1. The letters at the start of the comment represent your initials, and the number after your initials identifies the comment number. Each comment is automatically numbered sequentially as you add comments. If you delete a comment, the numbers are automatically updated.

QuickTip

You cannot delete the comment mark that appears in the comment pane. To delete a comment, you must delete the comment mark in the document. Similarly, you cannot delete paragraph marks in the comment pane.

3. In the comment pane, type **Shouldn't this document have a title?**, then click **Close**

   The comment pane closes. You can easily identify document text that has a comment associated with it because the text before the comment mark is highlighted in color.

4. Move the pointer over the comment mark in the document until the pointer changes to

   The comment text appears in a pop-up window, as shown in Figure L-2.

5. After you have finished reading the comment, move the pointer away from the comment mark, then double-click the **comment mark** in the document

   The comment pane opens.

6. Click at the end of the text in the comment pane, press **[Spacebar]**, type **Please be as specific as possible.**, then click **Close**

7. Move the pointer over the **comment mark**

   Notice that the comment, as shown in Figure L-3, includes the new text.

8. Click the **Save button** on the Standard toolbar

Printing comments

When you print a document that contains comments, the comments do not print by default. If you want to print the comments, click the Print what list arrow in the Print dialog box, then click Comments to print a list of comments only. To print comments along with the document, click the Options button in the Print dialog box, then in the next Print dialog box, click the Comments check box in the Include with document area. The comment marks will be printed in the document and the comments will print after the last page of the document.

FIGURE L-1: Comment pane

Comment mark

Writer's initials

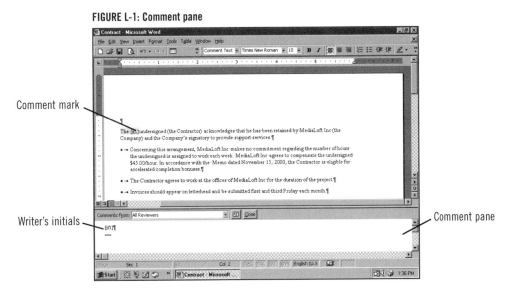

Comment pane

FIGURE L-2: Comment displayed

Move the pointer over the comment mark to display the comment

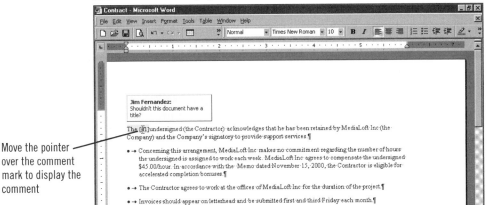

FIGURE L-3: Modified comment

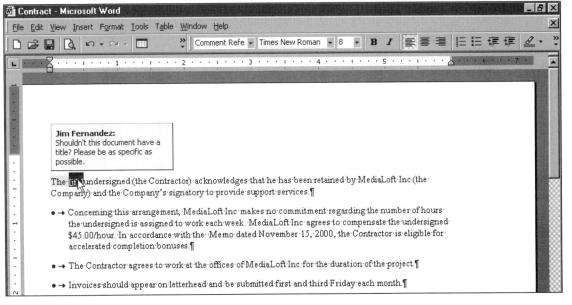

Saving Versions of a Document

Sometimes when you are drafting a document, you might want to pursue one line of thinking, while still retaining an earlier version of your ideas. Although you can always save the current document with a new name and make your changes in the new document, that method takes up unnecessary disk space and requires that you create and remember new file names for each separate copy. Instead, you can use the Versions feature to save a version of the document within the current document. A **version** is the saved changes stored with a document. If you want to return to an earlier version, you can select that version and open it. **Scenario** Jim is investigating the possibility of lending the contractor a special scanner to use. Because he is still not certain if a scanner is available for loan, Jim wants two versions of the contract to allow for the possibility of providing the scanner or not.

Steps 1 2 3 4

1. Click **File** on the menu bar, then click **Versions**
   The Versions in Contract dialog box opens.

2. Click **Save Now**
   The Save Version dialog box opens. When you save a document version, you should add a comment or a description that will help you identify that specific version.

3. Type **Contract without scanner**, then click **OK**
   The Save Version and the Versions in Contract dialog boxes close. All the changes you have made so far are stored in the version you just saved, which is the same as the currently open document.

4. Click after the **last bulleted item**, press **[Enter]**, then type **For the purpose of completing tasks for current assignments, the Company will provide a flatbed scanner to be returned to the Company upon completion of the Work.**
   You want this change to be saved as a separate version.

5. Click **File** on the menu bar, then click **Versions**
   The Versions in Contract dialog box opens and information about the document version you saved earlier appears in the Existing versions area.

6. Click **Save Now**, then in the Save Version dialog box, type **Before legal reviewer's comments, including scanner text**, compare your screen to Figure L-4, then click **OK**
   A second version of the contract document is saved. You can open the earlier version of the document to view it.

7. Click **File** on the menu bar, then click **Versions**
   The Versions in Contract dialog box opens, as shown in Figure L-5.

QuickTip

Use the date and time information listed in the Existing versions area to identify when a version was created.

8. Double-click **the older version of the document** (at the bottom of the list), then scroll to compare the bulleted lists in both versions
   The older version of the document appears in a separate document window with the version date and time in the title bar, as shown in Figure L-6. Notice that the scanner text appears in the current version but not in the older version.

9. Click the **Close button** in the document window of the older version of the document (without scanner text), click the **Maximize button** to maximize the newer version, then save the document

FIGURE L-4: Save Version dialog box

Name of document

Click to open the Save Version dialog box

Information about previously saved versions

Information about the new version that will appear in the Existing versions area of the Versions in Contract dialog box

Click to save the version and identifying information

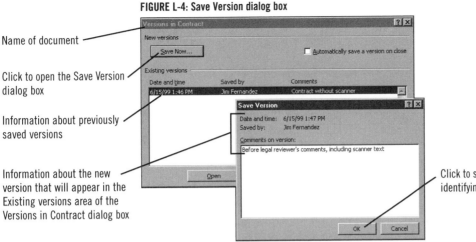

FIGURE L-5: Versions in Contract dialog box

Newer version

Older version

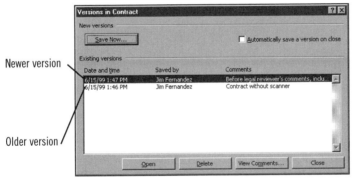

FIGURE L-6: Two versions of the same document

Newer version with scanner text inserted

Title bar contains version information

Older version before scanner text inserted

Maximize button for current version

Scroll bar for current version

Close button for older version

Scroll bar for older version

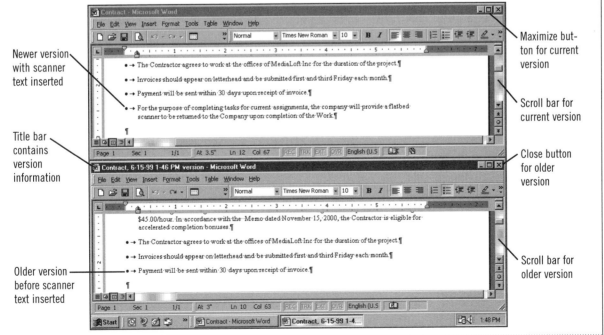

Tracking Changes in a Document

When you track the changes you make in a document, you can quickly identify the history of the modifications made. You use the Track changes while editing option when you want changes you made to a document to be clearly marked. For example, the Track changes while editing option automatically shows inserted text underlined and in a different color, and deleted text in **strikethrough** formatting. Strikethrough formatting ~~looks like this~~. Strikethrough formatting means you can see the deleted text, but it has a line through it to indicate that the text is marked for deletion. **Scenario** After further discussions with Adam, Jim realizes that he needs to make more changes to the second version of the Contract document. Jim will use the Track changes while editing option to make his changes. Using this option leaves the original text visible so that Adam, MediaLoft's legal adviser, can review Jim's changes.

Steps

1. Click **Tools** on the menu bar, point to **Track Changes**, then click **Highlight Changes**
   The Highlight Changes dialog box opens, as shown in Figure L-7.

2. Click the **Track changes while editing check box**, be sure the other two check boxes are checked, then click **OK**
   Now your changes are being tracked. Any changes you make to the document will appear specially formatted in the document window as you work.

3. Click after the **last bulleted item**, press **[Enter]**, then type **The Contractor will provide his or her own hardware and software. The Company will provide any proprietary material required for the final product.**
   Notice that the text you want to insert appears underlined and in a different color, as shown in Figure L-8.

4. Scroll to the top of the page, select the word **support** in the first sentence, then type **Web page and graphics design**
   Notice the word "support", which you want to delete, is marked in strikethrough format and the text you want to insert is underlined and in a different color, as shown in Figure L-9.

5. Type your name at the end of the document, save it, print it, then close it

Changing tracking options

By default, underlined text represents text that has been inserted and text with strikethrough formatting represents text that is marked to be deleted. Also by default, the vertical line in the left margin indicates that a change has been made to that line of text. You can change the tracking options to specify how you want each type of change formatted. For example, you might prefer double underlining for inserted text and deleted text simply to be marked with a symbol. You can also indicate how changes in formatting, such as boldface type, should be identified. To change tracking options, click Tools on the menu bar, click Options, click the Track Changes tab, then select how you want to highlight the changes in a document.

FIGURE L-7: Highlight Changes dialog box

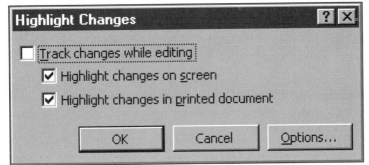

FIGURE L-8: New text inserted

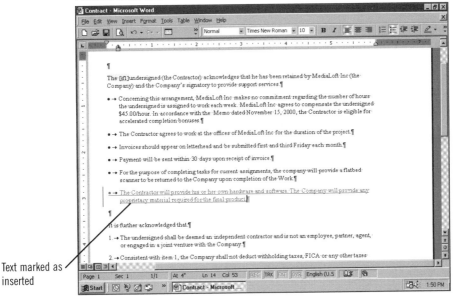

Text marked as inserted

FIGURE L-9: Tracked changes

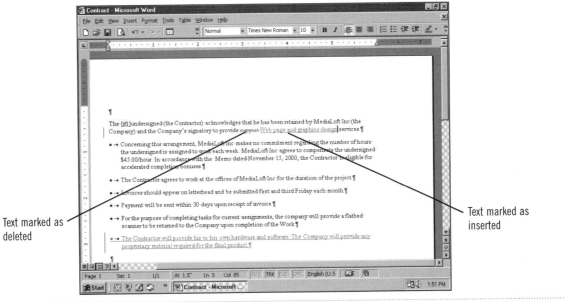

Text marked as deleted

Text marked as inserted

Comparing and Protecting Documents

You can use the Compare Documents option to identify deleted and inserted text in reviewed documents. As with the Track changes while editing option, the Compare Documents option uses strikethrough formatting to represent deleted text, underlining and color to represent inserted text. **Scenario** Jim submits his revised contract to Adam Ingraham, who makes additional changes, saves the document as WD L-2, then sends the document back to Jim. Jim compares Adam's completed document with the document he originally submitted and then protects the document.

Steps

1. **Open the document called WD L-2, scroll to the bottom of the document, type your name on the last line, then save the file with the name Designer Contract**

   This document, as shown in Figure L-10, contains the changes and comments made by Jim and comments made by Adam. One change Adam made was to add a title to the document. The title does not appear as a tracked change because Adam did not activate the Track changes while editing option. Before you review the changes that Adam made, you decide to save the current version of the document.

2. **Click File on the menu bar, click Versions, click Save Now, type Contract after Adam Ingraham's review in the Save Version dialog box, then click OK**

   You are ready to compare Adam's revised document with your edited contract version.

3. **Click Tools on the menu bar, point to Track Changes, then click Compare Documents**

   From the list provided, you identify the document you want to compare with the current document. When Word compares documents that have changes, a message box appears indicating that some changes may not be detected and asking if you want to compare the documents anyway. It is OK to continue.

4. **Click the file Contract, click Open, click Yes to answer the question "Compare anyway?", then click Yes again**

   Word compares the two documents and tracked changes between the documents appear in the document window, as shown in Figure L-11.

5. **Compare Figure L-10 with Figure L-11**

   The title as well as other changes that Adam made to the document appear as tracked changes in Figure L-11. For example, the title in Figure L-11 is marked as text to be inserted.

6. **Click File on the menu bar, click Versions, click Save Now, type Contract after comparison in the Save Version dialog box, then click OK**

   Jim decides to protect the document so that only he can accept or reject the final changes.

7. **Click Tools on the menu bar, click Protect Document, then type scanner as the password**

   While entering a password is optional, it does provide an extra measure of security. To ensure that no one else can see the password as you type it, a row of asterisks appears in place of "scanner" as shown in Figure L-12.

8. **Click OK, read the warning in the Confirm Password dialog box, type scanner again to confirm the password, then click OK**

   With the document protected, the tracked changes cannot be accepted or rejected unless the person making the changes uses the "scanner" password to unprotect the document.

FIGURE L-10: Document with reviewers' comments

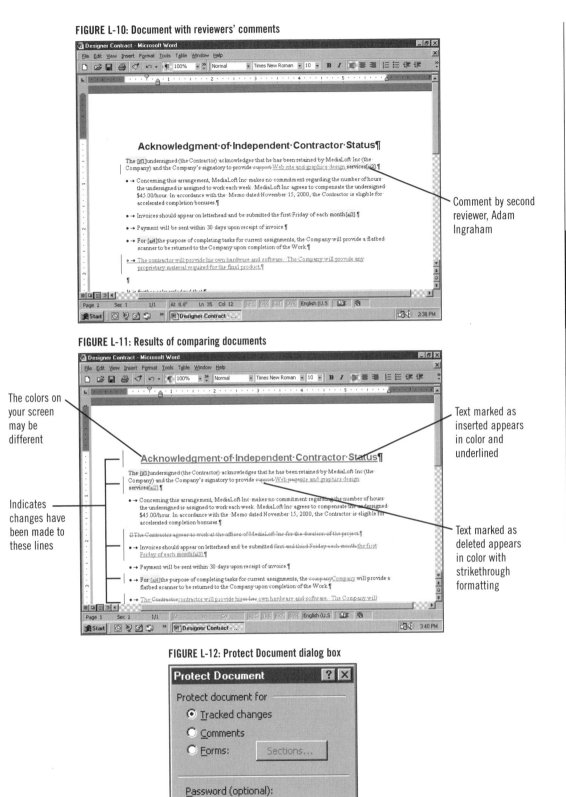

Comment by second reviewer, Adam Ingraham

FIGURE L-11: Results of comparing documents

The colors on your screen may be different

Indicates changes have been made to these lines

Text marked as inserted appears in color and underlined

Text marked as deleted appears in color with strikethrough formatting

FIGURE L-12: Protect Document dialog box

Accepting and Rejecting Changes

When you accept a change, the revised text becomes part of the document. When you reject a change, the original text is restored. You can use the Reviewing toolbar shown in Figure L-13 to review the changes in a document. **Scenario** Now that Jim has compared the revised document with his original, he will accept and reject changes.

Steps

1. Click **View** on the menu bar, point to **Toolbars**, then click **Reviewing**
   The Reviewing toolbar appears in the document window. You are ready to move to and select the first change in the document.

2. Press **[Ctrl][Home]**, click the **Next Change button** on the Reviewing toolbar, then click the **Accept Change button** on the Reviewing toolbar
   The first change, which is the title, is selected. However, because the document is protected against tracked changes, nothing happens when you click the Accept Change button. You need to unprotect the document before you can accept or reject the changes.

   Trouble?
Passwords are case sensitive. Be sure to type the word "scanner" as all lowercase letters.

3. Click **Tools** on the menu bar, click **Unprotect Document**, type **scanner**, then click **OK**

4. Click the **Accept Change button** on the Reviewing toolbar, then click the **Next Change button**
   The change is accepted and the title appears as regular text, as shown in Figure L-14.

5. Position the pointer over the **comment mark** at the end of the paragraph, read the comment, then click on the Reviewing toolbar to accept the change
   Next, you use the Accept or Reject Changes dialog box.

   Trouble?
If you accept the change to delete the second bulleted item, click Edit on the menu bar, then click Undo Change Accept.

6. Click **Tools** on the menu bar, point to **Track Changes**, click **Accept or Reject Changes**, click the **Find button**, click **Accept** to approve the insertion of "Web", then continue to click **Accept** until the second bulleted item is highlighted (contains all strikethrough text)

7. Click **Reject** to reject deleting the second bulleted item
   Notice in Figure L-14 that the second bullet is marked as deleted, but in Figure L-15 the change has been rejected and the second bullet appears as unmarked text.

   QuickTip
You can also use the buttons on the Reviewing toolbar to create, edit, move to, accept, or reject comments.

8. Press **[Ctrl][Home]**, click the **Next Comment button**, move the pointer over the comment, read the comment, click the **Delete Comment button**, use to move to each comment, read each comment, then use to delete remaining comments
   Once all comments are removed, the only comment button available is Insert Comment.

9. Click **Accept All** in the Accept or Reject Changes dialog box, click **Yes** to accept all remaining changes without reviewing them, then click **Close**
   Compare your screen with Figure L-16. Notice that all changes have been accepted.

10. Click the **Save Version button** on the Reviewing toolbar, type **Contract after final review**, click **OK** to save the version, click **View**, click **Toolbars**, click **Reviewing**, then save, print, and close the document

Previous Comment
Edit Comment
Insert Comment
Next Comment
Delete Comment
Track Changes
Previous Change
Next Change
Accept Change
Reject Change
Highlight (No Highlight)
Save Version
Send to Mail Recipient (as an attachment)
Create Microsoft Outlook Task

FIGURE L-13: Reviewing toolbar

FIGURE L-14: Accepted change

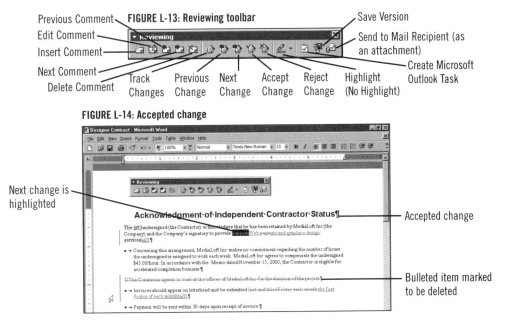

Next change is highlighted

Accepted change

Bulleted item marked to be deleted

FIGURE L-15: Rejected change

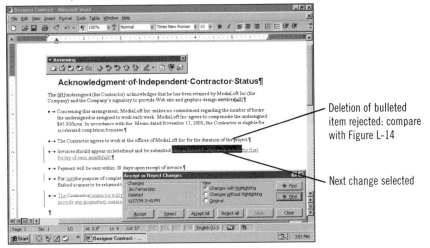

Deletion of bulleted item rejected: compare with Figure L-14

Next change selected

FIGURE L-16: Document after review

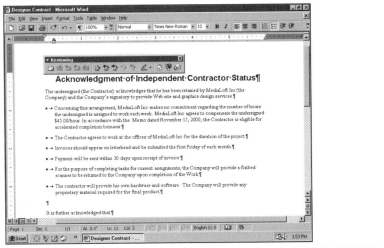

Using Advanced Find and Replace Techniques

You can use advanced find and replace features to search for and replace formats, special characters, and nonprinting elements. For example, you can search for every occurrence of bold-face type in a document and replace it with italic type. **Scenario** Jim receives a file from Maria Abbott in the marketing department that contains some of Jim's comments as well as some tracked changes. Maria has also added bold formatting to the company name. Jim knows that the issues raised in the comments have been addressed, and he wants to remove them from this file. He also wants to replace every instance of the company name that appears in bold with nonbold text.

Steps

1. Open the document called **WD L-3**, type your name at the end of the document, then save it with the name **Document Development Contract**

2. Click **Edit** on the menu bar, then click **Replace**

3. Click in the **Find what text box**, delete the contents if necessary, then click the **More button**

   The Find and Replace dialog box is expanded, as shown in Figure L-17. A variety of find and replace options are available.

4. Click the **Special button**, then select **Comment Mark**, as shown in Figure L-18

   A caret symbol (∧) and an "a" appear in the Find what text box. These characters represent a comment mark. You want to replace every instance of a comment mark with nothing, which will effectively delete each comment mark and its associated comment. Therefore you need to make sure that the Replace with text box contains nothing.

5. Click in the **Replace with text box** and delete all existing content if necessary, then click the **Find Next button**

6. Click **Replace All**, click **OK**, then click **Close**

   All the comment marks and their associated comments are removed. The words "MediaLoft Inc" appear in boldface type throughout the document. You decide to change the formatting from boldface type to regular type.

7. Press **[Ctrl][Home]**, press **[Ctrl][F]** to open the Find and Replace dialog box, click the **Replace tab**, delete the contents of the **Find what text box**, type **MediaLoft Inc**, click **Format**, click **Font**, click **Bold** as shown in Figure L-19, then click **OK**

8. Click in the **Replace with text box**, type **MediaLoft Inc**, click **Format**, click **Font**, click **Regular** in the Font style area, click **OK**, then compare your Find and Replace dialog box with Figure L-20

9. Click **Replace All**, click **OK**, click **Close**, scroll through the document to confirm that **MediaLoft Inc** has been replaced with MediaLoft Inc, then save the document

FIGURE L-17: Expanded Find and Replace dialog box

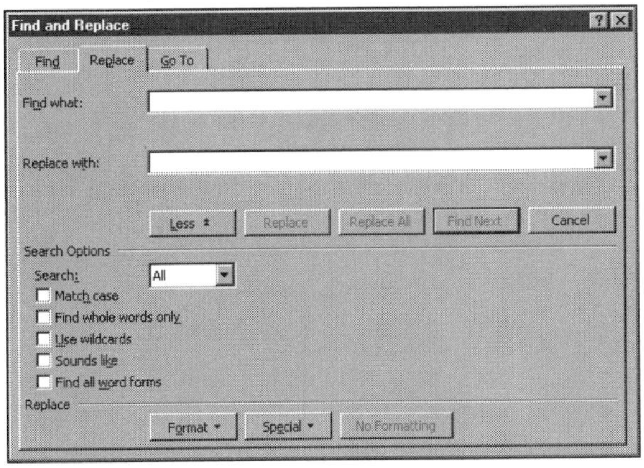

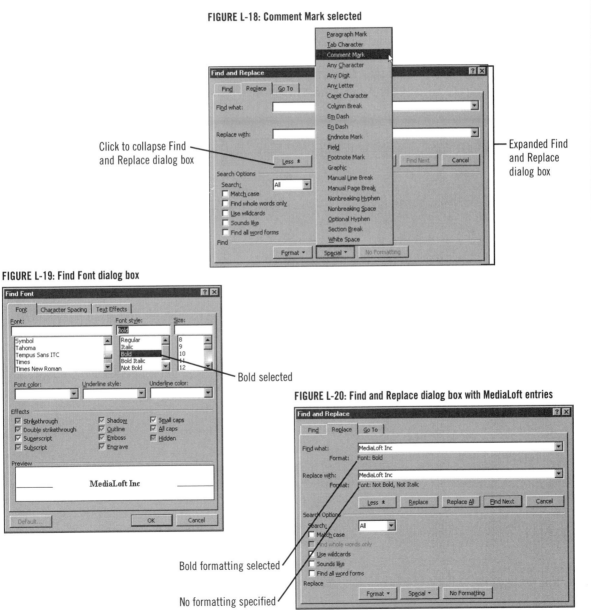

FIGURE L-18: Comment Mark selected

Click to collapse Find and Replace dialog box

Expanded Find and Replace dialog box

FIGURE L-19: Find Font dialog box

Bold selected

FIGURE L-20: Find and Replace dialog box with MediaLoft entries

Bold formatting selected

No formatting specified

Creating a Bookmark and Cross-Reference

Word 2000

A **bookmark** is a location that you name and save in your document. It can be as simple as a word, phrase, heading, or paragraph, or it can be a range of text that covers many pages. You cannot see bookmarks in your document text but you can locate them by using the Go To dialog box. A **cross-reference** is a statement in the document that refers the reader to another part of the document. For example, you can create a cross-reference from the text "See Video Sales" on page 2 of a report to a pie chart on page 10 of the same report. You can create cross-references to headings, footnotes, bookmarks, captions, and so on. Like bookmarks, cross-references may be hyperlinks. **Scenario** So that he can move quickly to the numbered items in the contract from any location in the document, Jim creates a bookmark next to item 1. He then creates a cross-reference from text in the first bulleted item to the numbered item 4, which appears toward the end of the document.

Steps

1. Scroll to item 1 and place the insertion point to the left of the word "The" in the text that begins "The undersigned shall be ...," click **Insert** on the menu bar, then click **Bookmark**
   The Bookmark dialog box opens, as shown in Figure L-21. In this dialog box you can create and delete bookmarks that are saved in your document. A bookmark must begin with a letter (not a number) and can have no spaces.

Trouble?

Type an underline _ between "numbered" and "items".

2. Type **numbered_items** in the Bookmark name text box, then click **Add**
   When the Bookmark dialog box closes, you see no change in the document, but your bookmark is saved.

QuickTip

You can also display the Go To dialog box by double-clicking anywhere in the left side of the status bar or by pressing [Ctrl][G].

3. Press **[Ctrl] [Home]**, click **Edit** on the menu bar, then click **Go To**
   In the Go To tab of the Find and Replace dialog box you can specify how you want to move from location to location in your document (including moving from page to page, section to section, comment to comment, etc.).

4. Click **Bookmark** in the Go to what list
   The Enter bookmark name list box on the right is updated to reflect the type of search, as shown in Figure L-22. In this case, the bookmark you just added appears in the Enter bookmark name text box. If you have more than one bookmark in a document, you can click the list arrow to display a list of bookmarks from which you can choose.

5. Click **Go To**, then click **Close**
   The insertion point moves to the first numbered item. Next you decide to create a cross-reference that will direct readers from the first bulleted item to numbered item 4.

6. Scroll to the top of the page, click at the end of the first bulleted item, press **[Spacebar]**, then type **"See item 4 for additional clarification."**, as shown in Figure L-23

7. Click after the words "item 4" in the text you just typed, press **[Spacebar]**, click **Insert** on the menu bar, click **Cross-reference**, click the **Reference type list arrow** to view the options available and make sure **Numbered item** is selected; make sure the Insert as hyperlink check box is checked, make sure **4. The undersigned further acknowledges that he shall** is selected in the For which numbered item area, click the **Insert reference to list arrow**, then select **Above/below** as shown in Figure L-24

8. Click **Insert**, click **Close**, move the mouse over **below** to show the 🖑, then click 🖑
   Item 4 appears.

9. Print, save, then close your document.

FIGURE L-21: Bookmark dialog box

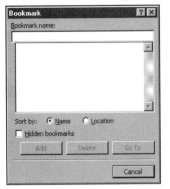

FIGURE L-22: Go To tab in the Find and Replace dialog box

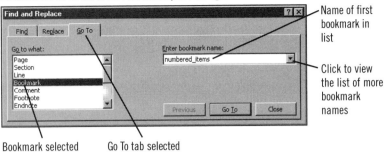

Name of first bookmark in list

Click to view the list of more bookmark names

Bookmark selected

Go To tab selected

FIGURE L-23: Cross-reference text

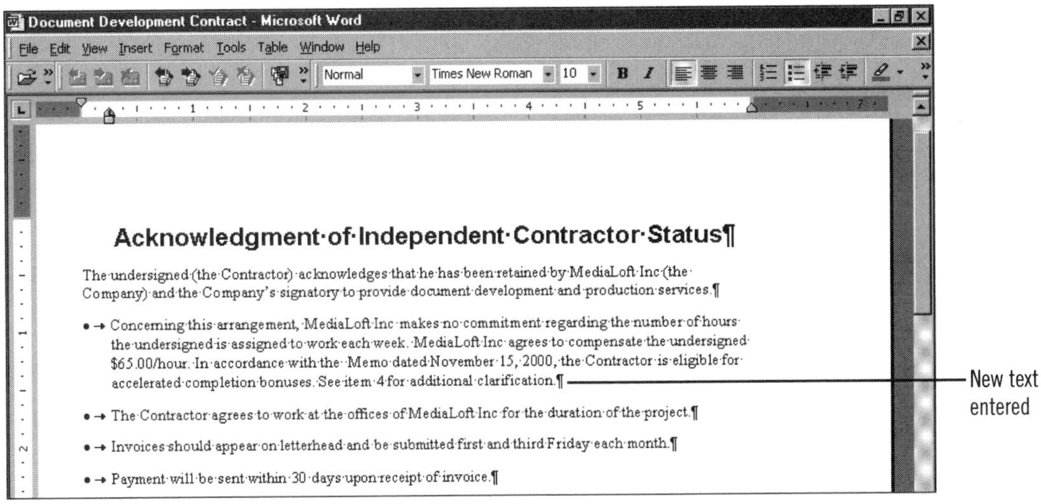

Document Development Contract - Microsoft Word

File Edit View Insert Format Tools Table Window Help

Normal   Times New Roman   10   **B** *I*

Acknowledgment·of·Independent·Contractor·Status¶

The·undersigned·(the·Contractor)·acknowledges·that·he·has·been·retained·by·MediaLoft·Inc·(the· Company)·and·the·Company's·signatory·to·provide·document·development·and·production·services.¶

● → Concerning·this·arrangement,·MediaLoft·Inc··makes·no·commitment·regarding·the·number·of·hours· the·undersigned·is·assigned·to·work·each·week.·MediaLoft·Inc·agrees·to·compensate·the·undersigned· $65.00/hour.·In·accordance·with·the··Memo·dated·November·15,·2000,·the·Contractor·is·eligible·for· accelerated·completion·bonuses.·See·item·4·for·additional·clarification.¶

● → The·Contractor·agrees·to·work·at·the·offices·of·MediaLoft·Inc·for·the·duration·of·the·project.¶

● → Invoices·should·appear·on·letterhead·and·be·submitted·first·and·third·Friday·each·month.¶

● → Payment·will·be·sent·within·30·days·upon·receipt·of·invoice.¶

New text entered

FIGURE L-24: Cross-reference dialog box

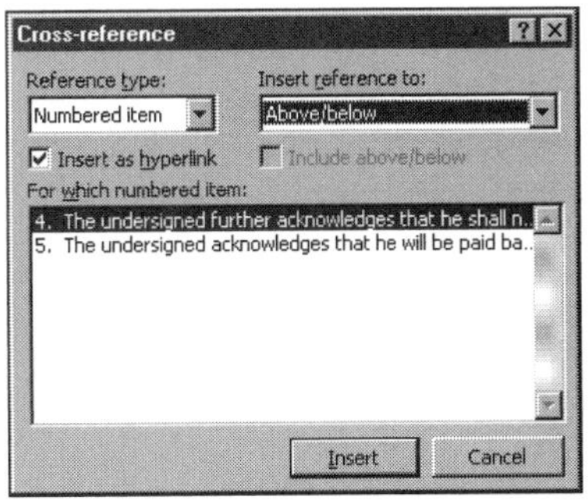

Cross-reference

Reference type: Insert reference to:
Numbered item   Above/below

☑ Insert as hyperlink   ☐ Include above/below

For which numbered item:
4. The undersigned further acknowledges that he shall n...
5. The undersigned acknowledges that he will be paid ba...

Insert   Cancel

Understanding Online Collaboration

You can use the Online Collaboration feature to schedule online meetings with your colleagues and to conduct Web discussions. The Online Collaboration feature allows you and your colleagues to chat online and to insert remarks into the same document at once. **Scenario** Jim is intrigued by the possibility of using the Online Collaboration feature to meet with other colleagues online and to work with several reviewers at once on a document. Before setting up a NetMeeting or a Web discussion, he decides to read more about the Online Collaboration feature.

Details

 NetMeeting Application

To conduct a NetMeeting in Word, you need to make sure that NetMeeting is running on your computer. To start NetMeeting, click Start on the menu bar, then click Programs and select NetMeeting. Before you can use NetMeeting, the Microsoft Office Server Extensions must be set up by your system administrator.

 Online Collaboration user profile

The first time you use NetMeeting, you will need to create a user profile that identifies your name and e-mail address and selects a server in the Server name list box, as shown in Figure L-25. Once you have completed your user profile, you can begin the process of connecting to the Internet and accessing the Online Collaboration options.

 Online Collaboration feature

The Online Collaboration feature is available on the Tools menu. When you select the Online Collaboration feature, a menu appears, as shown in Figure L-26. You select from the menu to meet with other colleagues connected to a common server, to schedule a new meeting online, or to participate in a Web discussion. In order to use any of the Online Collaboration options, you must be running NetMeeting. In addition, the person or persons with whom you meet online using the same Online Collaboration option also must be running NetMeeting. (*Note:* The system administrator at your college or place of work must set up the Microsoft Office Server Extensions, which include NetMeeting, before you can use any of the Online Collaboration options.)

 Online Collaboration tools

When you initiate an Online Collaboration NetMeeting you will use the Place a Call dialog box to identify NetMeeting participants. As you continue to work with the Online Collaboration options, you will use the floating Online Meeting toolbar shown in Figure L-27.

 Type of Web discussions

Another option of the Online Collaboration feature is Web discussions. Two types of discussions are available: **inline discussions** and **general discussions**. You conduct an **inline discussion** directly in a document and related to a specific paragraph, table, or graphic. You conduct a **general discussion** to relate to the entire document instead of just a specific part of it. When you select the Web Discussions option, you will be asked to identify a server (your system administrator must provide the server information). As you participate in a Web discussion you will use the Discussion toolbar to add, edit, accept, or reject discussion remarks. The Discussion toolbar is similar to the Reviewing toolbar and opens automatically when you initiate a Web discussion.

FIGURE L-25: Server selected in the Options dialog box in NetMeeting

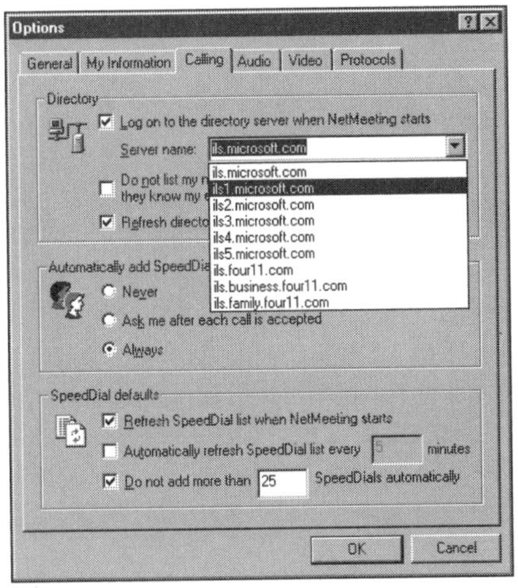

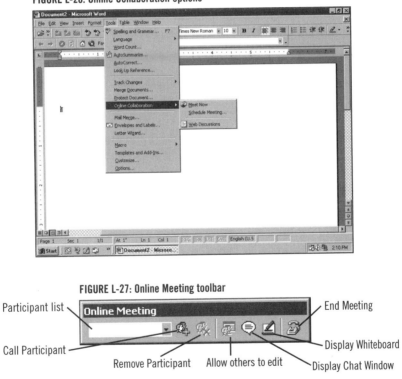

FIGURE L-26: Online Collaboration options

FIGURE L-27: Online Meeting toolbar

Participant list

Call Participant

Remove Participant

Allow others to edit

End Meeting

Display Whiteboard

Display Chat Window

CLUES TO USE

Round-trip documents from HTML

Microsoft Word 2000 is "Web-compatible," which means that you can save a Word document as an .htm file, view it in your Web browser, open it again in Word, make changes to it, then save it again as a Word document with the .doc extension or as an HTML document with an .htm extension. The process is referred to as **round-tripping** a document from HTML. It is useful when you receive an .htm document and want to convert it back to a Word document. To round-trip a document from HTML, open the .htm file in Word, select Save As from the File menu, click the Save as type list arrow, select Word Document, then click Save. You can modify the document just as you would any Word document.

Practice

► Concepts Review

Label each element of the Word document shown in Figure L-28.

FIGURE L-28

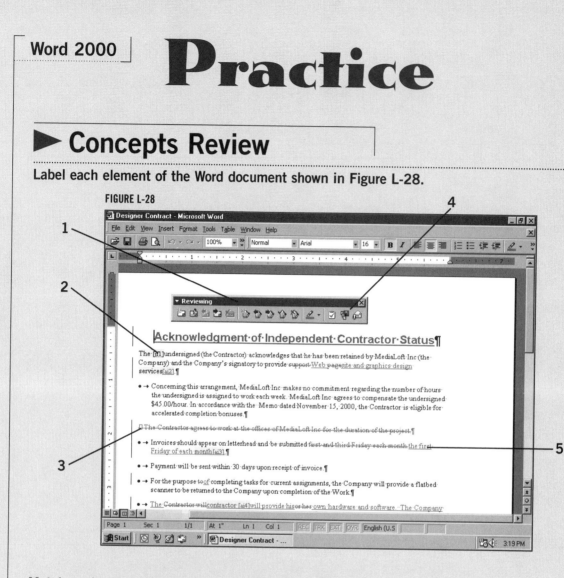

Match each term with the statement that describes it.

6. Special character
7. Bookmark
8. Comments
9. Strikethrough formatting
10. Versions command

a. A nonprinting symbol such as a paragraph mark or comment mark
b. Allows you to save only the changes made to a document without using a new file name
c. Identifies deleted text
d. A location that is named and saved in a document
e. A way to convey messages to the next editor through hidden text

Select the best answer from the list of choices.

11. **Which of the following statements is NOT a benefit of saving versions of a document?**
    a. When saving a version, you can add a comment or description to help you identify the version later.
    b. Saving a document using the Versions command uses less disk space.
    c. The Versions command allows you to return to the original documents or track edits from previous changes.
    d. The Versions command allows you to work in a document without seeing the comments displayed in earlier versions.

12. **Which of the following statements is NOT true about using comments in a document?**
    a. Comments are entered in a separate window pane.
    b. Comment text will be printed immediately following the text to which it refers.
    c. Comments can be edited by double-clicking on the comment mark.
    d. Comments can be viewed by positioning the pointer over the comment mark.

13. **To delete a comment, you**
    a. Cannot delete a comment once it has been inserted.
    b. Delete the text in the comment pane including the paragraph mark.
    c. Select the comment mark and press [Delete].
    d. Click Insert, Comments, then select the comment and press [Delete].

14. **You can alter the formatting for your tracked changes, using the**
    a. Modify tracking options on the Highlight Changes menu.
    b. Comments dialog box on the Reviewing toolbar.
    c. Formatting toolbar.
    d. Options dialog box on the Tools menu.

15. **To accept or reject changes made to a document,**
    a. Click the Accept or Reject buttons on the Reviewing toolbar.
    b. Click the Undo or Redo button on the Standard toolbar.
    c. Click the Accept or Reject buttons on the Standard toolbar.
    d. Use the Accept or Reject commands on the Edit menu.

16. **Which of the following is NOT a way to move quickly to a location in a document?**
    a. Cross-reference
    b. Go To command on the Edit menu
    c. Bookmark
    d. Arrow keys

17. **Which of the following statements regarding the Online Collaboration feature is NOT correct?**
    a. You need your system administrator to set up the Microsoft Office Server Extension feature before you can conduct a Web discussion.
    b. You do not need to be connected to the Internet in order to take advantage of the Online Collaboration feature.
    c. All participants must be running NetMeeting.
    d. Two types of discussions are available: inline and general.

▶ Skills Review

1. **Insert comments in a document.**
   a. Start Word, open the document WD L-4, then save it as "Report Edits".
   b. Make sure the Show/Hide ¶ button is selected, then click in the blank line above the tabbed text and type "Cost Comparisons".
   c. Click Insert on the menu bar, then click Comment.

    d. Type "Will this information be formatted using a preset style in the final copy?", then click Close.

    e. Position the pointer over the comment mark, then double-click.

    f. Press [End], press [Spacebar], then type "I added this title. Please edit as you wish."

    g. Click Close.

    h. Save your document.

2. Save versions of a document.

    a. Click File on the menu bar, then click Versions.

    b. Click Save Now, type "Cost Comparisons table included", then click OK.

    c. Select and delete the entire table including the title. (*Hint*: Use [CtrL] [X] to delete the table.)

    d. Click File, click Versions, then click Save Now.

    e. Type "No table", then click OK.

3. Track changes in a document.

    a. Click Tools on the menu bar, point to Track Changes, then click Highlight Changes.

    b. Click the Track changes while editing check box, then click OK.

    c. Scroll to the bulleted list under the heading "In-house Publishing".

    d. Place the insertion point at the end of the last bulleted item, then press [Enter].

    e. Type "Division Reports", press [Spacebar], then type "by [your name]".

    f. Select the text "Newsletter", then type "Tales from the Loft".

    g. Save your changes, print, then close the document.

4. Compare and protect documents.

    a. Open the document WD L-5, save it as "Second Edits".

    b. Click File, click Versions, then click Save Now.

    c. Type "Second Draft", then click OK.

    d. Click Tools on the menu bar, point to Track Changes, then click Compare Documents.

    e. Double-click the file Report Edits, then click Yes twice to continue.

    f. Click File on the menu bar, click Versions, then click Save Now.

    g. Type "After comparisons", then click OK.

    h. Click Tools on the menu bar, click Protect Document, make sure that Tracked changes is selected, then enter "no_table" as the password.

    i. Click OK, enter "no_table", then click OK.

5. Accept and reject changes.

    a. Press [Ctrl][Home].

    b. Click View on the menu bar, point to Toolbars, then click Reviewing.

    c. Click the Next Change button on the Reviewing toolbar, then click the Accept Change button.

    d. Click Tools, click Unprotect Document, type "no_table", then click OK.

    e. Click the Accept Change button.

    f. Use the Next Change and Accept Change buttons to accept changes to the document except the following:

        1. Bulleted item with your name: reject the deletion of your name and reject the insertion of [your name] so you are listed as the author of the Division Reports.

        2. Item IV. RECEPTION: reject the deletion of 3:00 and the insertion of 4:30 so the time remains 3:00.

    g. Click the Save Version button on the Reviewing toolbar, type "Final changes", then click OK.

    h. Hide the Reviewing toolbar.

6. Use advanced find and replace techniques.

    a. Press [Ctrl][Home] to move to the top of the document.

    b. Click Edit on the menu bar, then click Replace.

    c. Click in the Find what text box and delete the contents if necessary, click the More button, click the Special button, then select Comment Mark.

d. Click in the Replace with text box and delete any contents that may appear.

e. Click Find Next to highlight the first comment mark in the document, click Replace All, click OK, then click Close.

f. Move back up to the top of the document, then show the Find and Replace dialog box. Be sure the Replace tab is selected.

g. Enter "Tales from the Loft" in the Find what text box, then click the No Formatting button if the No Formatting button at the bottom of the dialog box is not grayed out.

h. Enter "Tales from the Loft" in the Replace with text box, click Format, click Font, select Italic, then click OK.

i. Replace all occurrences of "Tales from the Loft" with the same text formatted in italic, then click OK.

j. Close the Find and Replace dialog box.

k. Save the document.

7. Create a bookmark and cross-reference.

a. Scroll to and click in front of the heading "Shareholder Meeting".

b. Click Insert on the menu bar, then click Bookmark.

c. Type "meeting", then click Add.

d. Press [Ctrl][Home], click Edit on the menu bar, then click Go To.

e. Click Bookmark, select "meeting" in the Enter bookmark name list box, click Go To, then click Close.

f. Press [Ctrl][Home], then click after the last sentence of the first paragraph.

g. Type "See In-house publishing", then press [Spacebar].

h. Click Insert on the menu bar, then select Cross-reference.

i. Click the Reference type list arrow, then select Heading.

j. Click In-house publishing in the For which heading list box.

k. Click the Insert reference to list arrow, then select Above/below.

l. Click Insert, click Close, then type a period [.].

m. Test the cross-reference, be sure your name appears in the bulleted list as the author of the Division Reports, save the document, print a copy, then close it.

▶ Visual Workshop

As conference coordinator for an upcoming creativity conference, you have final responsibility for all conference communications. Your assistant has drafted a flyer and made some revisions she would like you to approve. Open the document named WD L-11 and save it as "Conference Edits". Use the Compare Documents command to compare the file Conference Edits with the file WD L-12, then save a version as "After comparisons". Review the changes. Accept all changes except the change to the word "specialty" in the first paragraph. Reject that change. Note that you will also need to accept changes to the header. Review and respond to the comments by inserting comments of your own. Use Figure L-30 as a guide for responding to the comments. (*Note:* The references to page numbers appear if you or another user has selected the Field codes check box in the View tab of the Options dialog box.) In addition, create a bookmark that goes to the Enlightened Massage section. Test your bookmark. Turn off the Track Changes feature. Type your name at the end of the document, then preview, save, print, and close the document.

FIGURE L-29

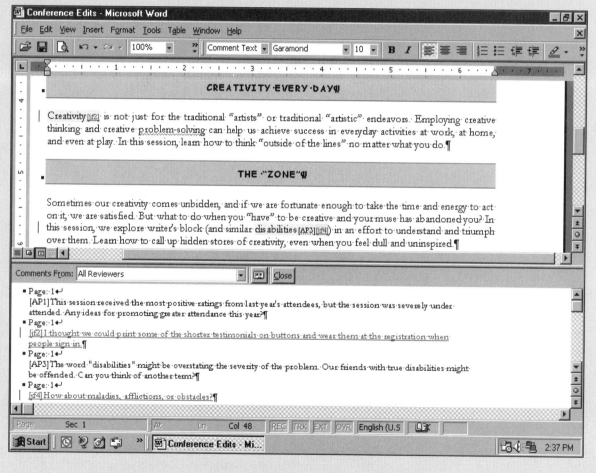

Working

with Graphics

Objectives

- ▶ **Create drop caps**
- ▶ **Group and ungroup graphics**
- ⌐MOUS⌐ ▶ **Position graphics**
- ▶ **Layer graphics**
- ⌐MOUS⌐ ▶ **Align and distribute graphics**
- ▶ **Add color effects to graphics**
- ▶ **Modify Shadow and 3-D Settings**
- ⌐MOUS⌐ ▶ **Add a watermark and page border**

In Word you can modify objects, including graphics, in many ways to add sparkle to even the most mundane document. You can add drop caps, group two or more objects into one object, and change the layering of overlapping objects. You can also position graphics anywhere on a page. You can change how text wraps around an object, and modify how objects are aligned relative to each other and to the page. Finally, you can achieve dramatic effects by enhancing graphics objects with gradient color fills, textures, shadows, and 3-D effects and by adding a watermark and page border. Scenario▶ Maria Abbott, the regional sales manager for MediaLoft, decides to use a variety of graphic features to enhance a one-page news flyer she wants to distribute at some of the MediaLoft stores and then to design an attractive scratch pad for use by MediaLoft employees.

Word 2000

Creating Drop Caps

A **drop cap** is the initial character of a paragraph that is formatted significantly larger than the surrounding text. When you select the Drop Cap command from the Format menu, the first character of the current paragraph appears three lines high and in its own text box. You can change the font style of a drop cap and the number of lines high it should be. You can also decide whether the drop cap appears within the paragraph or in the margin area to the left of the text. **Scenario** Maria has finished writing the text she wants to include in her news flyer. Now she wants to start enhancing its appearance. Her first step is to insert a Drop Cap in the first paragraph under each of the three headings included in the news flyer.

Steps

QuickTip

To return personalized toolbars and menus to the default settings, click Tools on the menu bar, click Customize, click the Reset my usage data on the Options tab, click Yes, then click Close.

1. **Start Word, open the document named WD M-1, save it as MediaLoft Spring News Flyer, then scroll through the document to get a feel for its contents**
   The file opens in Print Layout view. You can see the WordArt object at the top of the document and a variety of other graphics objects inserted at the end of the document. You will use these objects in later lessons to enhance the news flyer in a variety of interesting ways.

2. **Click in the paragraph that begins On March 18, ... under the Book Signings heading**
   You do not need to select the individual letter that you want to be a drop cap because Word automatically assigns the drop cap to the first letter of the paragraph in which you have placed the insertion point.

3. **Click Format on the menu bar, click Drop Cap, then click Dropped**
   The Drop Cap dialog box appears, as shown in Figure M-1. Notice that the In Margin option is not available when you are inserting dropped caps into a document formatted in columns. Next, you want to select a font style.

4. **Click the Font list arrow, scroll through the list of available fonts, then select Arial Black**
   You can specify how many lines deep the drop cap should appear.

5. **Click the Lines to drop down arrow once to reduce the lines to drop to 2, then click OK**
   The first letter of the paragraph appears in a text box, as shown in Figure M-2. The drop cap looks good, but you decide to format the next drop cap differently to see how it looks in the document.

Trouble?

If you do not have Arial Rounded MT Bold, select another font. If you use a different font, your document layout may not match the figures.

6. **Click in the paragraph that begins Starting in April,... under the Gourmet Coffee! heading, click Format, click Drop Cap, click Dropped, click the Font list arrow, select Arial Rounded MT Bold, verify 3 is entered in the Lines to drop text box, then click OK**
   You decide the format of the drop cap *S* is what you will use in the news flyer. You need to add one more drop cap using that format.

7. **Scroll down, click in the paragraph that begins The Seattle MediaLoft takes its role... under the Short Story Contest heading, click Format, click Drop Cap, click Dropped, click the Font list arrow, select Arial Rounded MT Bold, then click OK**
   You need to modify the drop cap in the first paragraph.

8. **Scroll up, click the drop cap in the first paragraph of the news flyer, then click the slanted border that indicates the drop cap has been selected**
   Black handles appear around the border to indicate that the drop cap is selected.

9. **Right-click the drop cap, click Drop Cap, change the font to Arial Rounded MT Bold, change the lines to drop to 3, click OK, click anywhere to deselect the drop cap, then click the Save button ⊞ on the Standard toolbar**
   Compare your screen with Figure M-3.

FIGURE M-1: Drop Cap dialog box

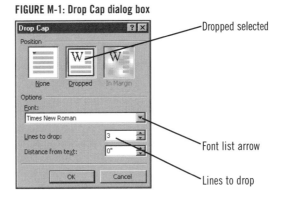

Dropped selected

Font list arrow

Lines to drop

FIGURE M-2: Drop cap inserted in the paragraph

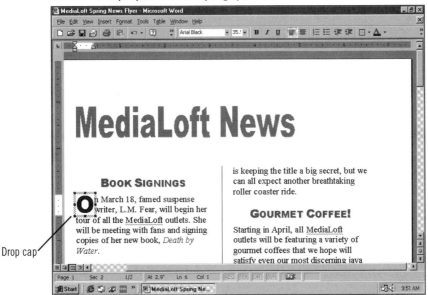

Drop cap

FIGURE M-3: News flyer with drop caps

Grouping and Ungrouping Graphics

You can use the Group and Ungroup features to group two or more graphics into one object. You can then easily size and position the new object you have created. If you decide that you want to remove one of the graphics in the group, you can just select the Ungroup option. The grouped object is then separated into its component parts. **Scenario** Maria has already inserted several AutoShapes and clip art graphics at the bottom of the news flyer. She plans to use these graphics in various ways to enhance the news flyer content. Her first task is to add an interesting graphic next to the news flyer heading at the top of the page. She decides to use the Grouping feature to make one picture out of the crescent moon, the star, and one of the suns.

Steps

1. Press **[Ctrl][End]** to move to the bottom of the document where you will see the crescent moon, the star, and the three suns, then click the **Show/Hide ¶ button** ¶ if necessary to show the paragraph marks
   When you are working with graphics, you should work with the paragraph marks visible so that you can more clearly see where to position each graphic.

2. Click one of the suns, drag it into position as shown in Figure M-4, then click away from it to deselect it
   Before you can group the star, the sun, and the moon into one object, you need to select all of them. You use [Shift] to select multiple objects.

3. Click the **star**, press and hold **[Shift]**, click the **moon**, click the **sun**, then release **[Shift]**
   Notice that sizing handles for the three graphics appear to indicate that all three graphics are now selected, as shown in Figure M-5. You are ready to group the three graphics into one object.

4. **Right-click** the star, point to **Grouping**, then click **Group**
   Now only one set of sizing handles appears around all three pictures to indicate that they are grouped into one object.

5. Drag the group to the right about two inches
   All three graphics move together. You decide that your new picture is a bit too crowded so you need to remove the sun from the group.

6. With the group still selected, **right-click** the group, point to **Grouping**, then click **Ungroup**
   Once again the sizing handles for all three graphics appear indicating that the three graphics are treated individually and not as a group. Although you could use the Grouping command by right-clicking selected graphics, you decide to access the Grouping command from the Draw menu on the Drawing toolbar. The Draw menu contains many of the commands you can use to modify a graphic object. First you need to show the Drawing toolbar.

7. Click **View** on the menu bar, point to **Toolbars**, then click **Drawing**
   The Drawing toolbar appears. This toolbar contains the buttons you use to create and modify drawing objects, WordArt objects, and clip art objects.

8. Click away from the selected graphics to deselect them, press and hold the **[Shift]** key, click the star and the moon graphics to select them, click **Draw** on the Drawing toolbar, then click **Group**
   The two graphics are grouped into one object, as shown in Figure M-6.

9. Save your document

FIGURE M-4: Sun graphic positioned

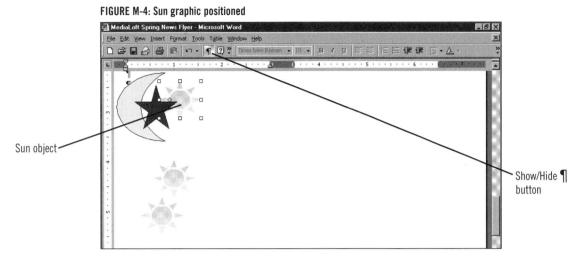

Sun object

Show/Hide ¶ button

FIGURE M-5: Sun, moon, and star graphics selected

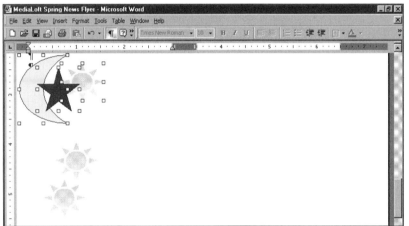

FIGURE M-6: Moon and star graphics grouped into one object

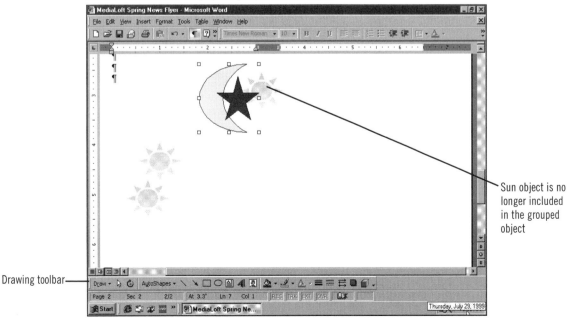

Sun object is no longer included in the grouped object

Drawing toolbar

Word 2000

Positioning Graphics

You can drag a graphic, such as the moon and star object, to position it on the page or you can position it precisely relative to the column, page, or margin. For example, you can precisely position a graphic so that its top left corner appears two inches from the left margin and two inches from the top margin. ▶Scenario◀ Maria wants to position the grouped moon and star object she created at the top of the flyer. First, she will use Cut and Paste to move the object to the top of the document.

Steps

1. Make sure the moon and star object is still selected, click the **Cut button** ✂ on the Standard toolbar, scroll to the top of the document, click the paragraph mark to the right of the MediaLoft News heading, then click the **Paste button** 📋 on the Standard toolbar
   The object appears in the middle of column 1. You've just discovered that Cut and Paste are not the features you should use to move a graphics object!

2. Drag the object up so that it appears to the right of the MediaLoft News heading
   You will position the object exactly.

   ▶ 3. Be sure the object is selected, click **Format** on the menu bar, click **Object**, click the **Layout tab**, click **Advanced,** then click the **Picture Position tab** if necessary
   The Picture Position tab of the Advanced Layout dialog box opens, similar to Figure M-7.

4. Click the **Alignment option button** in the Horizontal area, click the **Horizontal Alignment list arrow**, click **Right**, then verify that **Column** appears in the relative to text box

5. Click the **below list arrow** in the Vertical area, then click **Page**
   You specify the number of inches the picture appears below the top of the page.

6. Select the contents of the **Absolute position text box** in the Vertical area, type **.6**, click the **Lock anchor check box**, compare your Picture Position dialog box with Figure M-8, click **OK**, then click **OK** again
   The position of the object is set exactly .6" below the top of the page and aligned to the right margin. You selected the Lock anchor check box to ensure that the object always remains anchored to the same paragraph when you move the object. Next, you will use the wrapping and horizontal alignment features in the Layout tab to position the coffee bean bag graphic so that the text in the paragraph wraps tightly around it to the left.

   ▶ 7. Scroll to the bottom of the document, click the **coffee bean bag graphic**, drag it up so it appears in the first paragraph under the Gourmet Coffee heading, **right-click** it, click **Format Picture**, click the **Layout tab**, click **Tight**, click the **Right option button**, then click **OK**
   You decide to edit the wrap points of the graphic in order to control more precisely how the text wraps around it. **Wrap points** are black dots that outline a graphic, are connected by a dotted line, and can be dragged to change how text wraps around the graphic.

8. Be sure the coffee bean bag graphic is selected, click **Draw** on the Drawing toolbar, point to **Text Wrapping**, then click **Edit Wrap Points**
   The bag is outlined with a dotted line connected by small black handles, each of which is a wrap point that you can click on and drag.

9. Drag the center left wrap points as shown in Figure M-9, release the mouse button, then save the document
   The text repositions itself to adjust to the wrapping boundary drawn by the wrap point.

QuickTip

The numbers in the Absolute position text boxes indicate the current position of the object. Your numbers may differ.

QuickTip

If the Picture toolbar is not visible and you want to see it, click View on the menu bar, point to Toolbars, then click Picture.

FIGURE M-7: Picture Position tab in the Advanced Layout dialog box

Horizontal Alignment
option button

Vertical Alignment
option button

Horizontal Alignment
list arrow

Relative to list arrow

To the left of
list arrow

Below list arrow

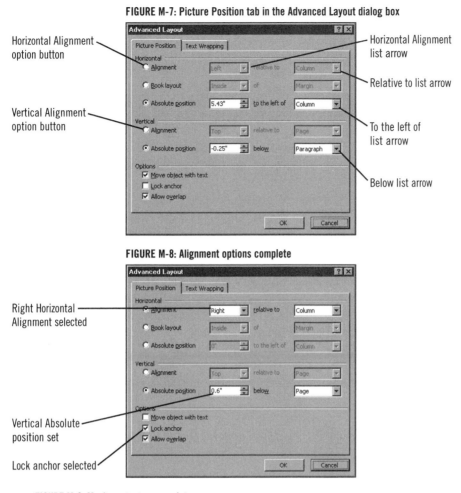

FIGURE M-8: Alignment options complete

Right Horizontal
Alignment selected

Vertical Absolute
position set

Lock anchor selected

FIGURE M-9: Moving a text wrap point

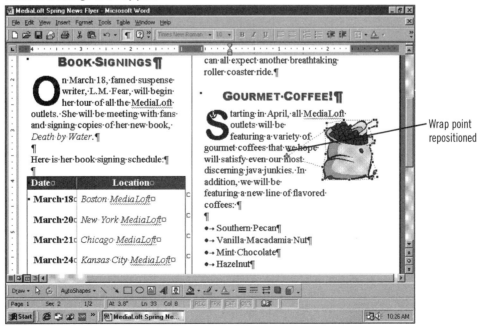

Wrap point
repositioned

Word 2000

Layering Graphics

You can choose how you want several graphic objects to appear relative to each other. For example, you can show one object on top of or half-way on top of another object and you can then show both objects behind the text. You layer graphics by selecting options such as "Send Back" and "Bring Forward" from the Order submenu on the Draw menu. **Scenario** Maria decides to layer differently the grouped object of the moon and star she created earlier. First, she will ungroup the two objects, then she will use one of the Order options to send the star behind the moon.

Steps

1. Scroll to the top of the page, **right-click** the star and moon object, point to **Grouping**, click **Ungroup**, then click away from the selected objects
   Now that you have ungrouped the objects into two separate objects, you can move the star behind the moon.

2. Click just the **star** to select it, then click **Draw** on the Drawing toolbar
   A selection of Draw options appears.

3. Point to **Order**, then click **Send to Back**
   The order of the objects changes and the star moves behind the moon.

4. Use **[Shift]** to select the moon object so that both the moon and star objects are selected, **right-click** them, point to **Grouping**, then click **Group**
   The modified object appears, as shown in Figure M-10. In addition to changing the order of how graphics relate to each other, you can change the order of how graphics and text relate. You decide to see how a graphic image placed behind text looks.

5. Scroll down until the image of the books below the table in column 1 appears in the document window, then click the image to select it
   Black sizing handles appear around the clip art image. These black handles signify that you can resize the clip art image. However, before you can modify the image's ordering options, you must modify the layout options for the image.

6. **Right-click** the image, click **Format Picture**, click the **Layout tab**, then click **Behind text** as shown in Figure M-11
   When you click Behind text, the options in the Horizontal Alignment area of the Format Picture dialog box become available, indicating that you can modify the position of the object relative to the left and right margins of the page or the left and right margins of the column. You are currently working in a two-column document so the object will be horizontally aligned between the left and right margins of column 1.

7. Click **OK** to exit the Format Picture dialog box
   A text wrapping style is applied, but the graphic is still in front of the text. Next, you must identify the order of the text and the graphic.

Trouble?

You may need to scroll down the document to see how the image appears behind the text.

8. Click **Draw** on the menu bar, point to **Order**, click **Send Behind Text**, then click away from the graphic to deselect it
   You decide the graphic behind the text is distracting. In a later lesson you will learn how to use image control options to create an image that appears very light and that can be placed behind text without distracting from the text. For now, you decide to change the text wrapping option for the graphic of the books. You first need to undo the Send Behind Text command.

9. Click the **Undo button** 🔄 on the Standard toolbar, right-click the graphic, click **Format Picture**, click the **Layout tab**, click **Square**, then click **OK**
   The text wraps to the right of the graphic, as shown in Figure M-12. Note that you clicked the Undo button in order to bring the image in front of the text. Once the image is in front of the text, you can select and format it. When the image is behind the text, you cannot select it.

10. Save the document

FIGURE M-10: Layering of star object modified

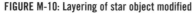

Star appears behind the moon

FIGURE M-11: Layout tab in the Format Picture dialog box

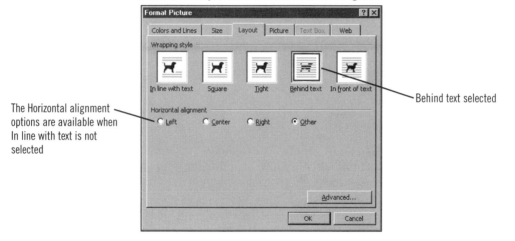

The Horizontal alignment options are available when In line with text is not selected

Behind text selected

FIGURE M-12: Clip art image square wrapped

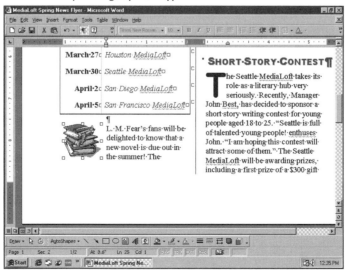

Aligning and Distributing Graphics

You use the Align and Distribute features on the Draw menu to modify how two or more objects appear relative to each other. For example, you can distribute a selection of graphics equally along an imaginary straight line or align them in relation to their left, right, top, or bottom edges. Scenario▶ Maria would like the three sun graphics, which are currently at the end of the document, to appear below the description of the short story contest. She would like these graphics to appear evenly distributed along the horizontal plane and aligned so that their top edges are even.

Steps

1. Press **[CTRL] [End]**, then click one of the sun objects
2. Press and hold the **[Shift]** key, then click the other two sun objects so that all three suns are selected

   You want an equal amount of space to appear between each sun so you distribute the three objects horizontally.
3. Click **Draw** on the Drawing toolbar, point to **Align or Distribute**, then click **Distribute Horizontally**, as shown in Figure M-13

   The three objects are now evenly spaced. However, they are not aligned horizontally.
4. Click **Draw** on the Drawing toolbar, point to **Align or Distribute**, then click **Align Top**

   Now the top edges of all three objects are aligned horizontally and are equally distributed. You group the suns into one object so you can more easily size and position the grouped object.
5. Be sure the three suns are selected, **right-click** one sun, point to **Grouping**, then click **Group**
6. **Right-click** the grouped object, click **Format Object**, click the **Size tab**, select the contents of the **Width text box** in the Size and rotate area, type **2.5** as shown in Figure M-14, then click **OK**

   Since you have changed only the width of the object, the suns appear slightly elongated. If you wanted to keep the correct proportions of the object, you would need to click the Lock aspect ratio check box to select it.
7. Drag the grouped object up so the three suns are placed just below the last line of the document, **right-click** the object, click **Format Object**, click the **Layout tab**, click **Tight**, click the **Center option button** in the Horizontal alignment area, then click **OK**

   The suns are centered at the end of the column, as shown in Figure M-15. At present, the document does not fit on one page. You will fix this problem just before you print the document in a later lesson.
8. Click away from the object to deselect it, then save the document

Using a grid

You can turn on the drawing grid to help you align two or more graphic objects. When you use the mouse to position an object over the grid, Word "snaps" the object into alignment with the nearest intersection of gridlines. To turn on gridlines, click Draw on the Drawing toolbar, then click Grid. In the Drawing Grid dialog box, make sure the Display gridlines on screen check box is selected. You then need to specify both the Vertical and Horizontal spacing in the Grid Settings section and you need to enter a number in the Vertical every and Horizontal every text boxes.

FIGURE M-13: Distribute Horizontally selected

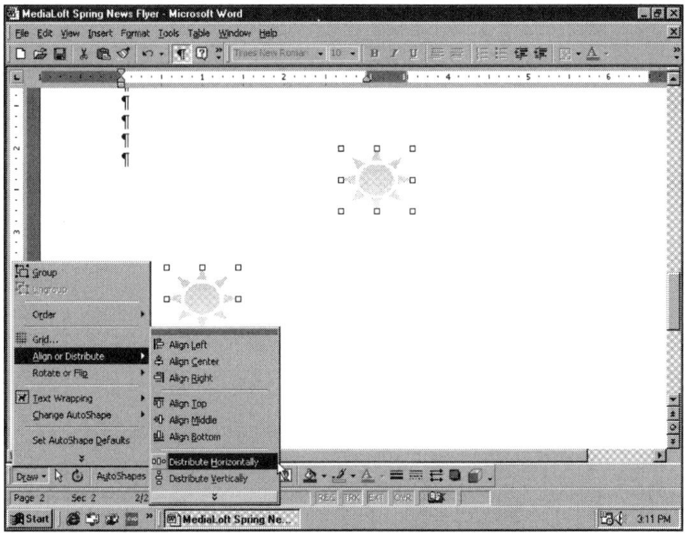

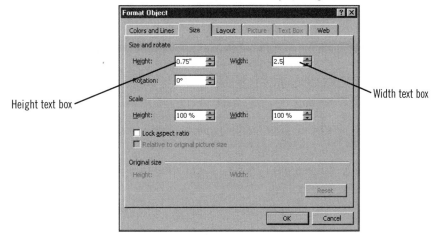

FIGURE M-14: Size tab in the Format Object dialog box

Height text box

Width text box

FIGURE M-15: Grouped object positioned

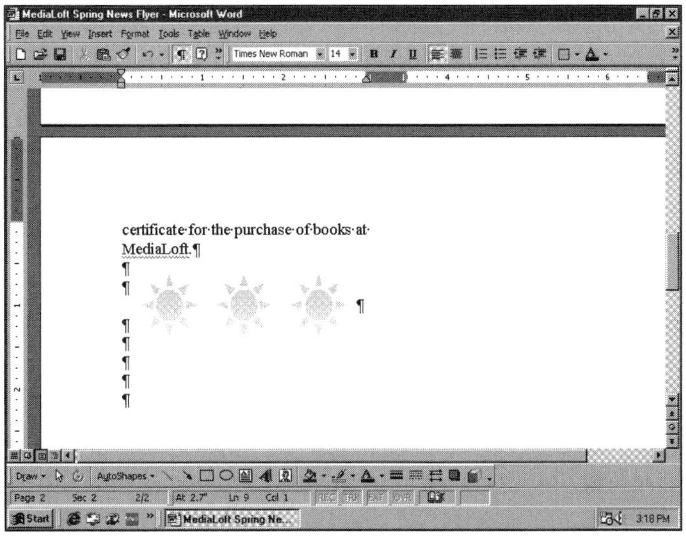

Adding Color Effects to Graphics

You can adjust the color and texture of any graphic. Word supplies many pre-set gradient fills or you can create your own gradient fill using a combination of one color and white or black or two colors that blend into each other in a variety of ways. You can also fill a graphic object with a texture such as granite or canvas, a pattern such as stripes or polka dots, and even a picture file. These options are available in the Fill Effects dialog box. **Scenario** Maria would like to draw more attention to the title of the news flyer. She decides to fill the WordArt object with one of Word's preset gradient fills. She will then modify the image of the coffee bean bag so that just the bag portion of the image is filled with the Woven Mat texture.

Steps

Trouble?

If the WordArt toolbar does not appear, right-click the WordArt object, then click Show WordArt toolbar.

▶ **1.** Scroll to the top of the page, then click the **WordArt object ("MediaLoft News")**
The WordArt toolbar appears.

2. Click the **Format WordArt button** 🖅 on the WordArt toolbar, then click the **Colors and Lines tab**
In this tab you can adjust the color of the text in a WordArt object.

3. Click the **Color list arrow** in the Fill area, then click **Fill Effects**
The Fill Effects dialog box opens. The tabs in this dialog box provide additional options for changing the gradient, texture, pattern, or picture fill effects.

4. Click the **Gradient tab** if necessary, click the **Preset option button**, click the **Preset colors list arrow**, then select **Late Sunset**
You can see a preview of the color pattern in the sample area.

5. Click the **Diagonal down option button** in the Shading styles area, then in the Variants area, click the option in the lower-left corner as shown in Figure M-16
The sample area shows the selected gradient fill pattern.

6. Click **OK**, click **OK** again, then click away from the WordArt object
Now you decide to modify the clip art image of the coffee bean bag so that just the bag is filled with the Woven Mat texture.

QuickTip

You may need to click Picture Object instead of Edit Picture.

▶ **7.** **Right-click** the coffee bean bag image, point to **Edit Picture**, then click **Open**
The clip art object appears in a new document window with the Edit Picture toolbar. In this window you can modify the individual components of the object. The coffee bean bag, for example, is made up of many images including the bag and each little bean. You can select all of the objects at once by clicking the Select Objects tool ⌖ on the Drawing toolbar and dragging the mouse across all of the objects to select them or you can select just one or two of the objects by clicking them.

8. Click just the bag to select it as shown in Figure M-17, click the **Fill Color list arrow** 🖌▾ on the Drawing toolbar, click **Fill Effects**, click the **Texture tab**, scroll down and click the **Woven mat** texture, then click **OK**
The clip art image is modified.

9. Click **Close Picture** on the Edit Picture toolbar, click away from the image to deselect it, close the Picture toolbar if it is open, then save the document
The modified coffee bean bag image and WordArt object appear, as shown in Figure M-18.

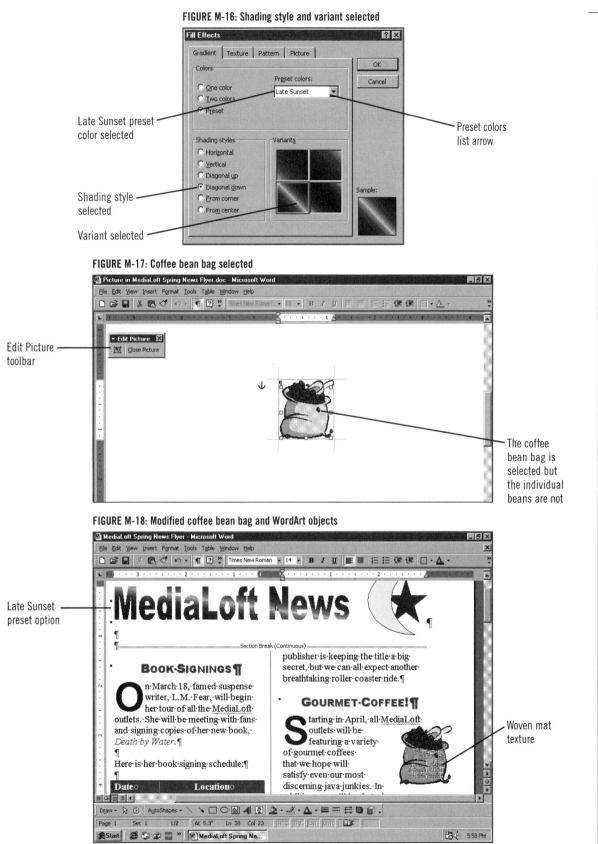

FIGURE M-16: Shading style and variant selected

Late Sunset preset color selected

Preset colors list arrow

Shading style selected

Variant selected

FIGURE M-17: Coffee bean bag selected

Edit Picture toolbar

The coffee bean bag is selected but the individual beans are not

FIGURE M-18: Modified coffee bean bag and WordArt objects

Late Sunset preset option

Woven mat texture

Unit
M

Modifying Shadow and 3-D Settings

You can use the shadow and 3-D buttons on the Drawing toolbar to create a wide variety of exciting effects. For example, you can change a 2-D object to a 3-D drawn object or you can add an attractive shadow to a clip art image. Once you have added a 3-D or shadow effect to an object, you can modify the shadow or 3-D settings in a wide variety of ways. **Scenario** Maria decides to apply a 3-D effect to the WordArt object she just modified. She then wants to add a shadow to the star object.

Steps

1. Click the **WordArt object** to select it, click the **3-D button** on the Drawing toolbar, then click **3-D Style 2**

   As you can see, the object now appears very dark. You decide to change the color of the 3-D effect.

2. With the object still selected, click, then click **3-D settings**

   The 3-D Settings toolbar appears, as shown in Figure M-19. The 3-D Settings toolbar contains a variety of options that you can use to change the look of an object enhanced with a 3-D style. For example, you can change the surface texture of the 3-D effect, the direction of the 3-D effect, and how the effect is tilted. You want to change the 3-D color.

3. Click the **3-D Color list arrow** on the 3-D Settings toolbar, then click the **Gold color box**

   Now you decide that the 3-D effect you've applied to the WordArt object is too deep. The depth of a 3-D effect is calculated in number of points—the same as font sizes.

4. Click the **Depth button** on the 3-D Settings toolbar, select the contents of the **Custom box**, type **18**, then press **[Enter]**

   The depth of the WordArt object changes. Finally, you decide to change the lighting on the 3-D object.

5. Click the **Lighting button** on the 3-D Settings toolbar, click the top left lamp icon, then close the 3-D Settings toolbar

   Now you decide to add a shadow to the moon and star object at the top of the news flyer.

6. Click the **moon/star object** to select it, click the **Shadow button** on the Drawing toolbar, then click **Shadow Style 1**

   You decide to change the color of the shadow.

7. Click, then click **Shadow Settings**

   The Shadow Settings toolbar appears, as shown in Figure M-20. You can use the buttons on this toolbar to modify the depth and position of the shadow as well as its color.

QuickTip

On the Custom tab in the Colors dialog box, you can use your mouse to select the shade you require or you can enter numbers in the Red, Green, and Blue boxes or in the Hue, Sat, and Lum boxes.

8. Click the **Shadow Color list arrow** on the Shadow Settings toolbar, click **More Shadow Colors**, click the **Custom tab**, complete the Red, Green, and Blue boxes, as shown in Figure M-21, click **OK**, then close the Shadow Settings toolbar

9. Press **[Ctrl][End]** to move to the bottom of the page, press **[Backspace]** to erase all but two of the extra hard returns under the suns, type your name at the last hard return, click the **Print Preview button** on the Standard toolbar, click the **Shrink to Fit button** on the Print Preview toolbar, then compare your completed news flyer to Figure M-22

10. Close the Print Preview window, save the document, print a copy, then close the document

    Depending on your printer capabilities, your printed copy may vary. You may need to delete the Word Art object and replace it with a text heading.

FIGURE M-19: 3-D Settings toolbar

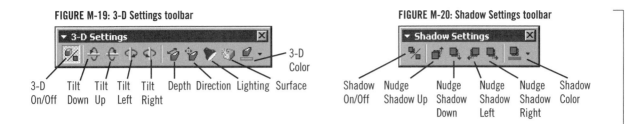

3-D On/Off   Tilt Down   Tilt Up   Tilt Left   Tilt Right   Depth   Direction   Lighting   Surface   3-D Color

FIGURE M-20: Shadow Settings toolbar

Shadow On/Off   Nudge Shadow Up   Nudge Shadow Down   Nudge Shadow Left   Nudge Shadow Right   Shadow Color

FIGURE M-21: Custom tab in the Colors dialog box

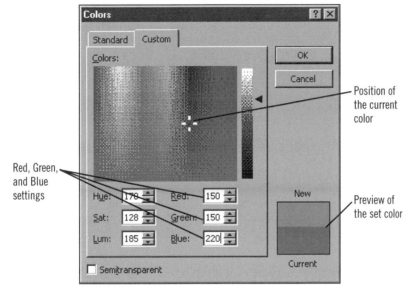

Position of the current color

Red, Green, and Blue settings

Preview of the set color

FIGURE M-22: Completed news flyer in Print Preview

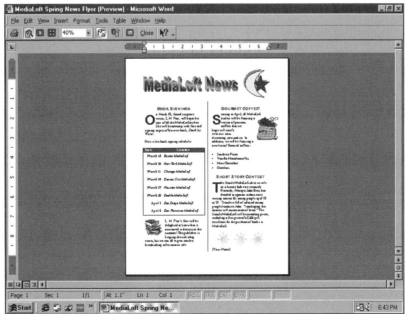

Adding a Watermark and a Page Border

A **watermark** is a picture or other type of graphic object that appears grayed out or lightly tinted behind text in a document. For example, a document could include a text box containing the word "DRAFT" formatted in very large letters that appear in gray behind the document text. Alternatively, a lightly tinted picture of a company logo could appear behind the document text. Another way to enhance a Word document is to include a page border. You can choose to insert a simple box border to enclose each page in the document and then you can modify the style, color, and thickness of the lines that make up the border. You can also insert one of Word's preset art borders. **Scenario** Maria decides to design a note pad for sales clerks to use at the San Diego MediaLoft store. She will insert a watermark of a stack of books that will appear behind the name and address of the MediaLoft store. She will also add an art page border.

Steps

QuickTip

If the Picture toolbar doesn't appear, right-click the picture, then click Show Picture toolbar.

1. Open the document named **WD M-2**, save it as **MediaLoft Note Pad**, then click the picture of the stack of books
   The Picture toolbar appears, as shown in Figure M-23. Next, you assign watermark properties to the picture.

2. Click the **Image Control button** on the Picture toolbar, then click **Watermark**
   The colors of the picture now appear very pale. You can make the colors more or less bright and adjust the contrast between light and dark shades by clicking the appropriate buttons, such as the More Brightness button, on the Picture toolbar. You decide that the default settings look good so now you need to change the text wrapping option so that the books appear behind both the WordArt object and the text.

3. Click the **Text Wrapping button** on the Picture toolbar, then click **Behind Text**
   The border enclosing the picture disappears and the sizing handles appear as plain white boxes, indicating that a text wrapping style is applied. Now that text wrapping is applied, you can size, position, and order the picture correctly.

4. Click the **Format Picture button** on the Picture toolbar, click the **Size tab**, click the **Lock aspect ratio check box** to deselect it, select the contents of the **Height text box** in the Size and rotate area, type **9**, select the contents of the **Width text box** in the Size and rotate area, type **6.5**, then click **OK**
   The picture of the book is resized based on the height and width specifications that you entered.

5. Click ▣, then click **Behind Text**

6. Drag the WordArt object ("Notes from the Loft!") so that it appears approximately one inch from the top of the page, add several hard returns above the company name and address so that it moves toward the bottom of the page, then click ¶ to hide the paragraph marks if necessary
   Now you decide to add an art page border.

7. Click **Format** on the menu bar, click **Borders and Shading**, then click the **Page Border tab**
   You can add a simple box, a shadow, or a 3-D border and you can modify the style of the border line along with its color and its width. In addition, you can apply one of Word's preset border patterns.

8. Click the **Art list arrow**, scroll down and select the row of **slanted pencils**, select the contents of the **Width text box**, type **15**, then click **OK**

9. Compare the completed note pad with Figure M-24, type your name at the bottom of the document, then save the document, print a copy, and close the document

FIGURE M-23: Picture toolbar

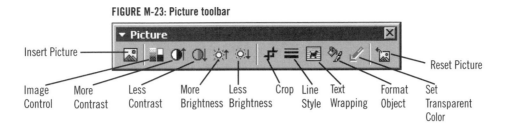

Insert Picture

Image Control

More Contrast

Less Contrast

More Brightness

Less Brightness

Crop

Line Style

Text Wrapping

Format Object

Set Transparent Color

Reset Picture

FIGURE M-24: Completed note pad in Whole Page view

Printing a page border

Sometimes a document that includes a page border will not print or only a portion of the border will print. If the document does not print at all then you will need to remove the page border because your printer does not have sufficient memory to print a document that includes a border. If a portion of the border does not print (for example, the bottom border), then you need to adjust the settings in the

Border and Shading Options dialog box. Click Format on the menu bar, click Borders and Shading, click Page Border, click Options, then increase the point size of the top, bottom, left, or right margins. You can also specify that the border be measured from the text and not from the edge of the page. You will need to experiment to find the settings that work with your printer.

Practice

► Concepts Review

Label each element shown in Figure M-25.

FIGURE M-25

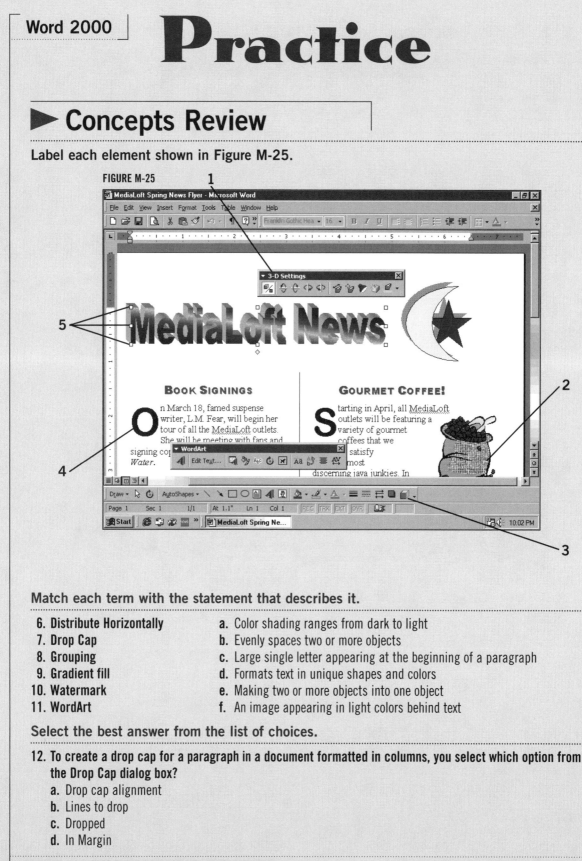

Match each term with the statement that describes it.

6. **Distribute Horizontally**
7. **Drop Cap**
8. **Grouping**
9. **Gradient fill**
10. **Watermark**
11. **WordArt**

a. Color shading ranges from dark to light
b. Evenly spaces two or more objects
c. Large single letter appearing at the beginning of a paragraph
d. Formats text in unique shapes and colors
e. Making two or more objects into one object
f. An image appearing in light colors behind text

Select the best answer from the list of choices.

12. To create a drop cap for a paragraph in a document formatted in columns, you select which option from the Drop Cap dialog box?
    a. Drop cap alignment
    b. Lines to drop
    c. Dropped
    d. In Margin

13. **Which of the following tasks can you not perform from within the Format Object or Format Picture dialog box?**
    a. Filling the object with a texture
    b. Setting the vertical alignment
    c. Editing wrap points
    d. Wrapping text

14. **How do you precisely set the position of an object within a document?**
    a. Modify the settings on the Picture Position tab in the Advanced Layout dialog box
    b. Select an alignment option on the Picture tab in the Format Object dialog box
    c. Use the Cut and Paste commands
    d. Select a wrapping option on the Layout tab in the Format Object dialog box

15. **You select the Edit Wrap Points feature when you want to**
    a. Change how two or more objects appear relative to each other.
    b. Modify the shape of an object or picture.
    c. Change the size of an object or picture.
    d. Change how surrounding text appears relative to an object or picture.

16. **To modify how two or more objects appear relative to each other, which option do you select from the Draw menu?**
    a. Align and Distribute
    b. Change AutoShape
    c. Nudge
    d. Distribute

17. **Which of the following is NOT a way to modify a WordArt object?**
    a. Click Format, then click WordArt
    b. Use the buttons on the Formatting toolbar
    c. Double-click the WordArt object
    d. Use the buttons on the WordArt toolbar

18. **Which button on the 3-D Settings toolbar would you select to change the size of the 3-D effect?**
    a. Tilt Down button
    b. Direction button
    c. Lighting button
    d. Depth button

19. **What fill effects are available in the Fill Effects dialog box?**
    a. Pattern
    b. Texture
    c. Gradient
    d. All of the above

20. **One way to manually adjust how the colors appear in a watermark is to click which button on the Picture toolbar?**
    a. Edit Color
    b. More Brightness
    c. Text Wrapping
    d. Reset Picture

▶ Skills Review

1. Create Drop Caps.
  a. Start Word.
  b. Open the document named WD M-3 and save it as "Square Peg Theater Newsletter".
  c. Click anywhere in the paragraph below the Overview heading.
  d. Click Format, click Drop Cap, then click Dropped.
  e. Change the font to Brush Script MT or a font of your choice, then click OK.
  f. Make the first letter of the first paragraph in the Shakespeare Festival section a drop cap in the Comic Sans MS font and dropped two lines.
  g. Make the first letter of the first paragraph in the Join Us section a drop cap in the Comic Sans MS font and dropped two lines.
  h. Edit the drop cap in the Overview section so that it is formatted in the Comic Sans MS font and dropped two lines.

2. Group and Ungroup.
  a. Scroll to the end of the document, click the heart object, press and hold the [Shift] key, then click the lightning bolt object.
  b. Right-click the selected objects, point to Grouping, then click Group.
  c. Click the object consisting of four stars.
  d. Ungroup the object, then delete the star appearing closest to the bottom margin.
  e. Save the document.

3. Position graphics.
  a. Right-click the picture of the two figures in the Julius Caesar section, click Format Picture, then click the Layout tab.
  b. Click Advanced, then in the Horizontal area set the Absolute position to 0 inches and to the left of Column.
  c. In the Vertical area set the Absolute position to 0 inches and below Paragraph.
  d. Click OK, then click OK again to exit the Format Picture dialog box.
  e. Click the picture of the two figures, click Draw on the Drawing toolbar, point to Text Wrapping, then click Edit Wrap Points.
  f. Drag one of the wrap points along the right side of the object so that the text moves a few spaces to the right. Experiment with various effects.

4. Layer graphics.
  a. Ungroup the heart and lightning bolt object at the bottom of column 2.
  b. Right-click just the heart object.
  c. Point to Order, then click Send to Back.
  d. Right-click the image of the two masks in the Join Us section.
  e. Click Format Picture.
  f. Click Behind Text on the Layout tab, then click OK.

5. Align and distribute graphics.
  a. Scroll to the bottom of the document, then use the [Shift] key to select all three of the star objects.
  b. Click Draw on the Drawing toolbar, click Align or Distribute, then click Distribute Vertically.
  c. With all three objects still selected, click Draw on the Drawing toolbar, point to Align or Distribute, then click Align Center.
  d. Group the stars into one object, then drag the stars object so that it appears along the right side of the Hamlet section with the top of the star aligned horizontally with the Hamlet heading. The stars will overlap the text.
  e. Right-click the stars, click Format Object, click Tight on the Layout tab, then click OK.

6. **Add color effects to graphics objects.**
   a. Press [Ctrl][Home], then right-click the WordArt object ("Square Peg Theater").
   b. Click Format WordArt, click the Colors and Lines tab, click the Color list arrow in the Fill area, click Fill Effects, then select the Nightfall preset gradient fill.
   c. Change the Shading style to Vertical.
   d. Select the top left Variant style, click OK, then click OK.
   e. Scroll down the document, then right-click the image of the two figures in the Julius Caesar section.
   f. Click Edit Picture.
   g. Click the Select Objects button on the Drawing toolbar.
   h. Point to the top left corner, then drag the mouse to select all the objects that make up the two figures.
   i. Click the Fill Color list arrow on the Drawing toolbar, click Fill Effects, then click the Texture tab.
   j. Select the Sand texture, then click OK.
   k. Click Close Picture.

7. **Modify Shadow and 3-D Settings.**
   a. Scroll to the top of the page, then click the Square Peg Theater WordArt object to select it.
   b. Click the 3-D button on the Drawing toolbar.
   c. Click 3-D Style 3.
   d. Click the 3-D button, then click 3-D settings.
   e. Change the depth of the 3-D setting to 25 point, click the 3-D Color list arrow, then select the light turquoise color box.
   f. Close the 3-D Settings toolbar.
   g. Select both the lightning bolt and heart objects at the bottom of the page, then group them into one object.
   h. Click the Shadow button on the Drawing toolbar, then click Shadow Style 5.
   i. With the grouped object still selected, click the Shadow button, click Shadow Settings, click the Shadow Color list arrow, click More Shadow Colors, then click the Custom tab.
   j. Change the Red to 200, the Green to 140, and the Blue to 200, then click OK.
   k. Center the object relative to the left and right margins of the column.
   l. View the document in Print Preview, then, if necessary, click the Shrink to Fit button to fit the enter newsletter on one page.
   m. Type your name at the bottom of the document, print a copy, then save and close it.

8. **Add a watermark and page border.**
   a. Open the document named WD M-4 and save it as "Baseball Flyer".
   b. Click the image of the baseball player to select it, then, if necessary, click View, Toolbars, Picture, to show the Picture toolbar.
   c. Click the Image Control button on the Picture toolbar, then click Watermark.
   d. Right-click the image, click Format Picture, click the Layout tab, then click Behind Text.
   e. Click the Size tab, select the contents of the Height box in the Size and rotate area, type 8.5, then click OK.
   f. Move the image as needed so it appears centered in the middle of the page.
   g. Right-click the image, point to Order, then click Send Behind Text.
   h. Add hard returns to move the text from "All Toronto Companies..." down so that the contact phone number appears at the bottom of the page.
   i. Click Format on the menu bar, click Borders and Shading, then click the Page Border tab.
   j. Click the Art list arrow, select the art border of your choice, set its width at 10 pt, then click OK.
   k. Type your name in place of Mary Jo Foster, delete hard returns where necessary so that the flyer fits on one page, print a copy of the flyer, then save and close it. *Note:* If the bottom border does not print, click Format on the menu bar, click Borders and Shading, click the Page Border tab, click Options, try other spacing options or delete the border.

▶ Visual Workshop

As conference coordinator for the Creative Consultants creativity conference, you are responsible for developing an attractive letterhead that will appear at the top of all the conference documents. Open WD M-8, then modify the document so that it appears, as shown in Figure M-26. You will need to change the image control settings of the light bulb to Watermark, reduce its size, then change its layout options so that it appears behind the text. In addition, you will need to fill the WordArt object with the Bouquet texture and the drawn arrows with the Calm Water preset gradient fill. Save the document with the name "Creative Art". Be sure your name is on the document. Print the document before exiting Word.

FIGURE M-26

Creating
and Modifying Charts

Objectives

- ▶ Understand charts and graphs
- MOUS ▶ Create a chart
- MOUS ▶ Modify chart objects
- MOUS ▶ Modify the chart type
- ▶ Change pie chart elevation and proportions
- MOUS ▶ Create area and line charts
- MOUS ▶ Modify values in a chart
- MOUS ▶ Import data into a chart

A **chart** is a graphical representation of data often used to illustrate trends, relationships, or patterns. You use the chart options in Word to specify the kind of chart you want to make, such as a line graph, a column chart, a pie chart, a three-dimensional chart, and so on. When you create or modify a chart in Word, you open Microsoft Graph 2000, a program included with Office 2000. In this program, you can work with a chart to change both its appearance and the data it illustrates. Scenario▶ Jim Fernandez in the Finance Department plans to include several charts in a presentation related to recent MediaLoft sales. The data Jim needs for the charts is already contained in several Word tables. Now he needs to convert these tables into a series of charts.

Word 2000

Understanding Charts and Graphs

A chart provides readers with a visual representation of numerical relationships. When you present numbers in a table, your reader may not always spot their significance in the rows and columns of values. Charts and graphs help your readers analyze numbers and draw conclusions by enabling them to visualize trends and make comparisons. The Microsoft Graph program provides many different kinds of charts and graphs from which to choose, as shown in Figures N-1 and N-2. **Scenario** Before he begins transforming the table data into charts, Jim decides to analyze the uses for the various charts available so he can be sure to choose the best chart for the data.

 You use **line graphs** to illustrate trends. Each value is connected to the next value by a line.

 Area graphs are similar to line graphs, except that the area under each line is filled with a unique color so you can distinguish different values from one another.

 XY (or **scatter**) **charts** are useful for identifying patterns or for recognizing clusters of values, because each value is represented as a single dot. Values for each item are represented in a unique color.

 Column charts are useful when you want to compare values for different items side by side. Each value is represented as a vertical bar, and values for each item are represented in a unique color. **Bar charts** are similar to column charts, except that the values are displayed as horizontal (rather than vertical) bars. **Pyramid**, **cylinder**, and **cone charts** are similar to bar and column charts except that data is displayed in pyramids, cylinders, and cones rather than rectangles.

 Combination charts combine bar (or column) charts with line (or area) charts.

 Pie charts are useful for showing values in relation to one another and as parts of a whole (as in a percentage). Values for each item are displayed in different colors to help you compare proportions. A **doughnut chart** is similar to a pie chart except that the center is not filled.

For a more dramatic effect, you can also select a **three-dimensional** format for most charts. In addition, you can create **custom charts** that combine elements of two or more of the standard charts, as shown in Figure N-2.

FIGURE N-1: Examples of types of charts and graphs available in Word

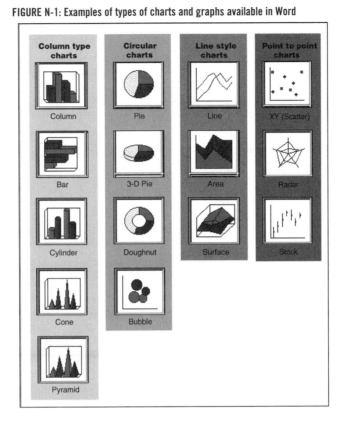

FIGURE N-2: Examples of custom charts available in Word

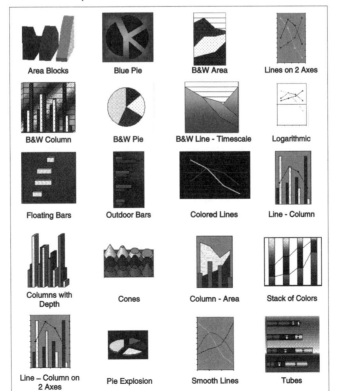

Creating a Chart

You can quickly display a table or selected table information as a chart by choosing the Chart command on the Insert menu. This command automatically inserts the default column chart based on the selected table information. You can then modify the chart type, color, text, placement, and other features. **Scenario** The first table Jim needs to chart compares how much money each of four age groups spends on fiction and nonfiction books.

1. Start **Word**, open the document named **WD N-1**, save it as **Finance Charts**, then click the **Show/Hide ¶ button** ¶ on the Standard toolbar
   You show the nonprinting characters so that you can easily see where paragraph breaks occur with relation to the charts you will create. To create a chart, your first step is to select the table data that you want the chart to show. You can select either part or all of a table.

2. Point anywhere in the first table, move the mouse over the top left corner to display the **Table Select icon** ⊞, then click ⊞
   The entire table is selected. You are now ready to create the chart.

3. Click **Insert** on the menu bar, point to **Picture**, then click **Chart**
   Because the default chart type is a column chart, a column chart is inserted in the document, as shown in Figure N-3. Once you have inserted a chart, the chart is selected for editing in the Microsoft Graph 2000 program. You can double-click different parts of the chart or use the Chart Objects list on the toolbar to change the color and appearance of chart elements. You can also modify the data in the datasheet and you can adjust the location of the **legend**, the key to the chart's data. Jim decides to move the legend to the bottom of the chart.

4. Right-click the **legend**, then click **Format Legend**
   The Format Legend dialog box opens. In this dialog box you can modify the font, placement, borders, and fill colors of a legend. On the Placement tab you can adjust the location of the legend in relation to the chart.

5. Click the **Placement tab**, click the **Bottom option button**, then click **OK**
   The legend appears below the chart. Just as you can size pictures and graphics, you can also adjust the size of a chart object to fit the document. Before you can work with a chart as an object, however, you need to exit Microsoft Graph 2000.

6. Click anywhere **outside the datasheet** to exit Microsoft Graph 2000, click the **chart** to select it, scroll down a few inches, then drag the **lower-right corner sizing handle** so it appears slightly to the left of the 6" mark on the horizontal ruler and slightly above the 5½" mark on the vertical ruler to increase the chart size so it appears as shown in Figure N-4
   You decide to move the chart about one inch below the table. However, the chart is currently formatted to be **in line with text**, meaning that it is positioned at the insertion point just like text in a document and can only be moved or aligned like a text selection. You need to first change the layout of the chart object so that you can position it freely using your mouse.

7. **Right-click** the chart, click **Format Object**, click the **Layout tab**, click **Behind Text**, click the **Center option button**, then click **OK**

8. Drag the chart to position it approximately one inch below the table as shown in Figure N-5

9. Click the **Save button** 🖫 on the Standard toolbar

FIGURE N-3: Inserted chart in the Microsoft Graph 2000 window

Standard toolbar in Microsoft Graph 2000

You can drag the title bar to move the datasheet

Y-axis

Data series

Indicates more chart buttons are available

Datasheet button

Datasheet

Chart

X-axis

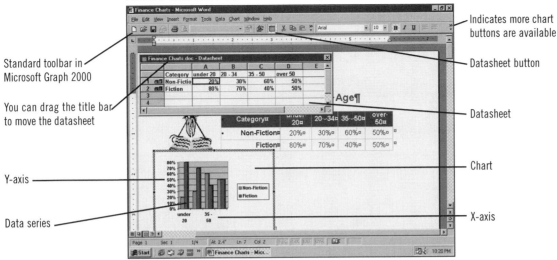

FIGURE N-4: Resized column chart

6" mark

Middle sizing handle

Legend repositioned

Lower-right sizing handle

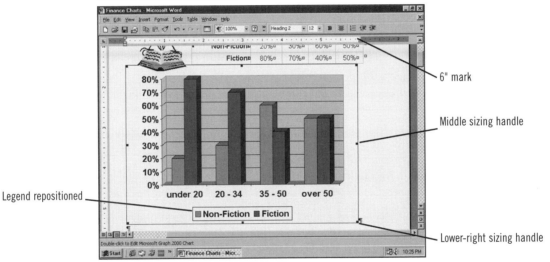

FIGURE N-5: Completed column chart

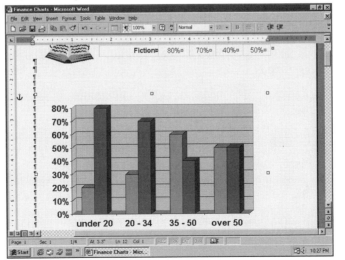

N
Word 2000

Modifying Chart Objects

You can improve a chart's appearance by making a variety of formatting changes. A chart is a graphic object in Word, so formatting it is similar to formatting a picture. The chart itself is composed of several individual graphic objects, each of which you can modify. For example, you can change the color of a **data series** (in a column chart, all the columns related to one category) or change the color of just one **data point** (one column). **Scenario** To make the chart more striking and easier to read, Jim decides to change the color of the Fiction columns to red and then to fill the Non-Fiction column that represents sales to the 35–50 age group with an interesting texture.

Steps

1. Right-click the **chart**, point to **Chart Object**, then click **Edit**
   Microsoft Graph opens and the chart appears in the Graph window.

2. Click one of the **maroon columns**, then, if necessary, click one of the columns again so that all the columns are selected
   All the maroon columns are selected when handles appear around each maroon column.

3. Click **Format** on the menu bar, then click **Selected Data Series**
   The Format Data Series dialog box opens, as shown in Figure N-6.

4. Click the **Red color box**, then click **OK**
   Each maroon column changes to red. Notice that the legend automatically changes to match the new color. You can also choose to fill just one of the columns in a chart.

Trouble?

If you double-click instead of clicking twice slowly, the Format Data Series dialog box opens. If this happens, click Cancel and then repeat Step 5.

5. Click the **blue column** above the **35-50** heading, then click it again so that only the 35-50 column is selected

6. With the column selected, right-click the **column**, then click **Format Data Point**
   The Format Data Point dialog box opens. In this dialog box you can modify the appearance of a single column.

7. Click **Fill Effects**, click the **Texture tab**, scroll down in the Texture list, click the **Denim texture** (the area below the list reads "Denim"), click **OK**, then click **OK** again
   Notice that the legend and the other columns attached to the Non-Fiction heading have not changed. If you wanted the legend to show the Denim texture, you would have needed to change the entire data series. Another chart formatting change you can make is removing the chart background, or **wall**.

8. Click the **Chart Objects list arrow** on the Chart toolbar, then click **Walls**, as shown in Figure N-7

9. Click **Format** on the menu bar, click **Selected Walls** to open the Format Walls dialog box, click the **None option button** in both the Border and Area sections, click **OK**, click away from the **chart area** to close Microsoft Graph, scroll down so that you can see the chart legend, then save the document
   The chart walls are removed, leaving only the gridlines, as shown in Figure N-8. Another way to do this is just click the chart walls to select them and then press [Delete] to remove them. Notice that the Non-Fiction color box in the legend is still blue because blue is still the color of the data series. Only one data point in the series is formatted with a different fill.

FIGURE N-6: Patterns tab in Format Data Series dialog box

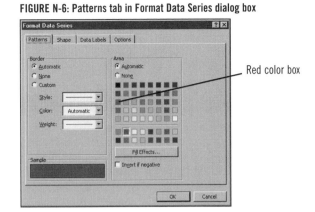

Red color box

FIGURE N-7: Selecting the Walls chart object

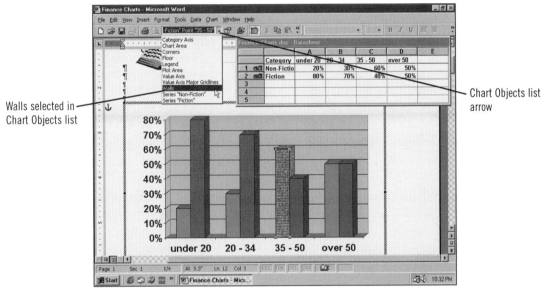

Walls selected in Chart Objects list

Chart Objects list arrow

FIGURE N-8: Modified chart

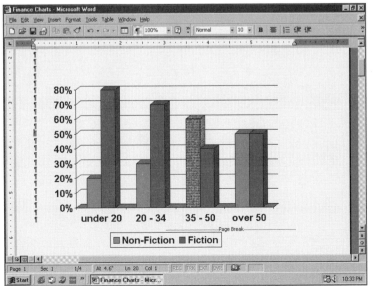

Word 2000

Modifying the Chart Type

Once you have created a chart, you can change the chart type as often as necessary until you find the one that best illustrates the information you want to convey. A pie chart is another kind of chart that is frequently used to compare values. It differs from a bar or column chart in that it compares values as part of a whole rather than across different data series. Each value is represented as a wedge of the pie. All of the wedges add up to 100 percent so that the entire pie reflects a total of all the values. Therefore you use a pie chart to display values for only one row or column in a table. **Scenario** Jim decides to use a pie chart to illustrate the breakdown of nonfiction book sales by category.

Steps

1. Press **[Ctrl][G]** to open the Go To dialog box, click **Table** in the **Go to what list box** (you will need to scroll down), click **Next**, then click **Close**

2. Point to the top-left corner of the **Non-Fiction Book Sales table**, then click the **Table Select icon** ⊕ to select the table
   With the table selected, you are ready to chart the data.

3. Click **Insert** on the menu bar, point to **Picture**, then click **Chart**
   By default, a column chart is inserted in the document. You can change the chart type by opening the Chart Type dialog box and then selecting a different type of chart.

4. Click **Chart** on the menu bar, then click **Chart Type**
   The Chart Type dialog box opens. In this dialog box you can choose from a wide variety of chart types. Once you have chosen a chart type, you can also choose a chart style.

5. In the Chart types list click **Pie**, click the **middle chart sub-type** in the top row of the Chart sub-type list as shown in Figure N-9, then click **OK**
   The chart type changes, but the chart now contains data from only one data point in the table, the Cookbook category, because by default Word charted the first row of data as the data series. You want to chart the data in the entire column, so you need to change the data source for the pie chart.

6. Click **Data** on the menu bar, then click **Series in Columns**
   Now the chart displays the correct data. You would like readers to be able to see at a glance exactly what portion of the pie each category represents. You can do this by formatting the **data labels**, the numbers that describe each data point in the chart, as percentages.

7. Right-click the **pie**, click **Format Data Series**, click the **Data Labels tab**, click the **Show percent option button**, then click **OK**
   The percentages appear next to the related pie wedges to clarify the data displayed in the chart. The overall size of the pie has become too small. You need to resize the chart object.

8. Click away from the **chart area** to close Microsoft Graph, with the chart selected drag the **sizing handles** so that the right edge of the chart reaches the 6" mark and the bottom edge reaches the 5" mark as shown in Figure N-10, then save the document

FIGURE N-9: Chart Type dialog box

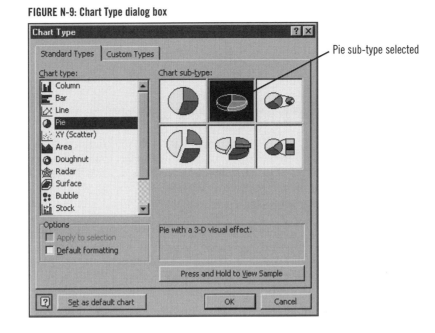

Pie sub-type selected

FIGURE N-10: Modified pie chart

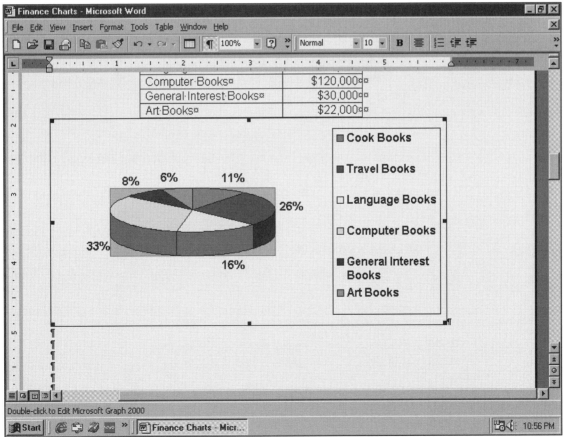

Changing Pie Chart Elevation and Orientation

Just as you modified the column chart earlier, you can change a pie chart by adjusting the position of the legend title and formatting the objects that comprise the chart. You can also adjust the **elevation** of a 3-D pie chart to better display the pie slices. The elevation of a 3-D chart is expressed in terms of the number of degrees the chart is tilted. A chart elevated to 15 degrees will appear almost two-dimensional. In a chart elevated to 45 degrees, however, some of the wedges will not be clearly visible. You can also change the **orientation** of a pie chart—that is, where the wedges are positioned—in order to emphasize specific slices. For example, you can choose to place a specific wedge at the bottom middle of the pie chart. Scenario ▶ Jim has decided his chart will have a better effect if it tilts farther forward so that the relative sizes of the pie slices are easier to distinguish, and if the pie slices appear against the white background of the page rather than the gray chart area. He also wants to change the orientation of the chart so that the Art Books slice appears at the front.

1. Double-click the **pie chart**
   The Graph window opens for you to modify the pie chart.

2. Click **Chart** on the menu bar, then click **3-D View**
   The 3-D View dialog box opens. In this dialog box you can adjust the elevation and height of the 3-D effect and modify the rotation angle.

3. Click the **up arrow** above the Elevation box until **35** appears, as shown in Figure N-11
   You can see the change in elevation in the view area as you click the degree arrows.

4. Click **OK**
   The elevation of the pie changes to 35 degrees. The 3-D effect will be enhanced if you remove the gray plot area that appears around the pie.

5. Click anywhere in the **chart area**, click the **Chart Objects list arrow**, click **Plot Area**, then press **[Delete]**
   You want to emphasize the Art Books slice. You can change the chart orientation so the Art Books slice is positioned at the front.

6. Right-click the **chart**, click **Format Data Series**, then in the Format Data Series dialog box click the **Options tab**

7. Click the **Up arrow** until the Degrees box reads **180** as shown in Figure N-12, then click **OK**
   You have changed to 180 degrees the angle at which the first slice, the Cookbooks slice, is positioned, thereby moving the Art Books slice to the front of the pie.

8. Click away from the **chart area**, then save the document
   The Graph window closes and the chart appears in the document window as shown in Figure N-13.

FIGURE N-11: 3-D View dialog box

Elevation up button

Elevation down button

Elevation box

Rotation box

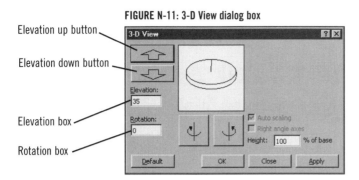

FIGURE N-12: Options tab in Format Data Series dialog box

Degrees box

Cookbooks slice now positioned 180 degrees from original position

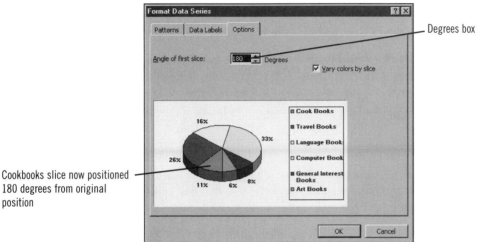

FIGURE N-13: Completed pie chart

Art Books slice now positioned at front of pie

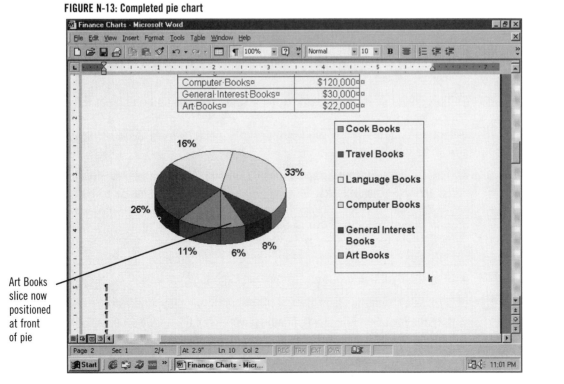

Creating Area and Line Charts

A line chart is similar to a column chart in that it shows how data changes over time or how one set of data compares to another set. An area chart is very similar to a line chart except that the space between the line and the base of the chart is filled with color. Most area charts also show each data point as a solid color stacked on the previous data point. **Scenario** Jim needs to create a chart to represent coffee sales information. He will first create an area chart and then he will change the chart to a line chart that illustrates the data by column instead of by row.

Steps

1. Press **[Page Down]** to reach the third table in the document, then select the **first five columns** in the table (do not select the Total column)
   Only the data in the columns you selected will appear in the chart.

2. Click **Insert** on the menu bar, point to **Picture**, then click **Chart**
   By default, a column chart is inserted.

3. Scroll down a few inches, then drag the **lower-right corner sizing handle** of the chart area down and to the right, so the right edge of the chart area reaches the **6" mark** on the horizontal ruler and the bottom edge of the object reaches the **5" mark** on the vertical ruler

4. Click **Chart** on the menu bar, click **Chart Type**, click **Area** in the Chart type list, then click **OK** to accept the default sub-type
   The chart changes to show stacked bands of color instead of columns. You can see at a glance that Cappuccinos are big sellers in Seattle but not in Dallas. You can also add titles to your chart.

5. Click **Chart** on the menu bar, click **Chart Options**, then click the **Titles tab**
   The Chart Options dialog box contains various options related to titles, labels, axes, gridlines, tables, and legends.

6. Click in the **Chart title text box**, type **Sales by Location** as shown in Figure N-14, then click **OK**
   The line chart highlights the overall popularity of each coffee drink by showing the daily sales volume of each drink in addition to comparing sales among locations.

7. Click the **More Buttons button** 🔲 on the Standard toolbar, click the **Chart Type button list arrow** 🔲▾ on the More Buttons toolbar, then click the **Line Chart button** 🔲
   The area chart changes to a line chart. This chart type more clearly compares the coffee sales from location to location than did the area chart. You decide to show the data by columns instead of by rows so that the emphasis of the chart is again on comparing the relative popularity of the various coffee drinks.

8. Click the **By Column button** 🔲 on the Graph toolbar

9. Click away from the chart to close Microsoft Graph, click the **chart** again to select it, drag the **lower-middle sizing handle** down to the 6" mark on the vertical ruler, compare your chart to Figure N-15, then save the document

FIGURE N-14: Chart Options dialog box

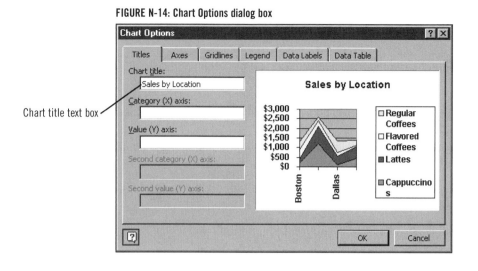

Chart title text box

FIGURE N-15: Completed line chart

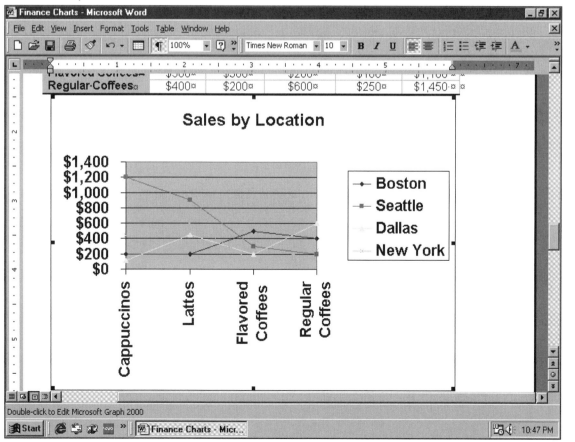

Modifying Values in a Chart

After you have created a chart from data contained in a table, you may decide to change the values entered in the table. When you do so, however, the chart is not automatically updated to reflect the new data entered in the table. Fortunately, you don't need to create a new chart; you can simply change the values in the datasheet to match the new values you've entered in the table. The datasheet is organized similarly to an Excel worksheet. Columns are lettered and rows are numbered. You can therefore use a **cell reference**, the intersection of the column letter and the row number, to locate data in a datasheet. Data in cell A2, for example, appears in the first column of the second row of the datasheet. Scenario ▶ Jim has received new sales data that he wants the chart to illustrate. He will enter the new data directly into the datasheet and then delete the table.

Steps 1234

1. Double-click the **line chart**, then click cell **C1** in the datasheet (contains $110)
   To enter new data in a datasheet, you simply type over the highlighted data.

2. Type **800**, then press **[Enter]**
   The value does not appear until you press [Enter]. Once you have entered the new value, the maroon color bar that represents Dallas changes to show the new value.

3. Make the following changes in the datasheet:

   | Boston | Flavored Coffee 1000 |
   | New York | Regular Coffee 1500 |

   Make sure you press [Enter] after typing each new value so that the chart is also updated. When you have entered the new values, the datasheet appears as shown in Figure N-16.

4. Click the **View Datasheet button** 🔲 on the Standard toolbar
   The datasheet is hidden. Clicking the View Datasheet button again will display the datasheet. Because the chart illustrates the information better than the table does, you can remove the table from the document.

5. Click outside the chart area, click in the **table** on this page, click **Table** on the menu bar, point to **Delete**, then click **Table**
   The table no longer appears in the document. However, the chart looks a bit lost floating on the page. A border would help.

6. Right-click the **chart**, click **Borders and Shading**, click **Box**, then click **OK**
   The text in the legend appears too large. You can reduce the font size of any text in a chart.

7. Double-click the **chart**, right-click the **legend**, click **Format Legend**, click the **Font tab**, click **10** in the Size box, then click **OK**
   The font size of the text in the Y-axis should also be reduced.

8. Right-click the **Y-axis**, click **Format Axis**, click **10** in the Size box, then click **OK**
   Finally, you decide to reduce the font size of the X-axis and rotate the labels 45 degrees.

9. Right-click the **X-axis**, click **Format Axis**, click the **Font tab**, click **10** in the Size box, click the **Alignment tab**, type **45** in the Degrees box as shown in Figure N-17, click **OK,** then save the document
   Your chart appears as shown in Figure N-18.

FIGURE N-16: Modified datasheet

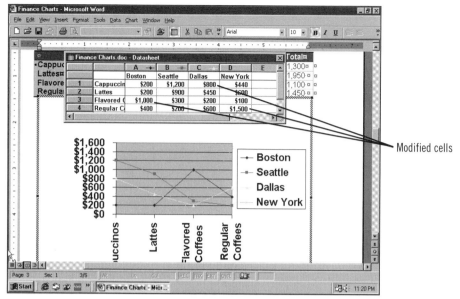

Modified cells

FIGURE N-17: Alignment tab in Format Axis dialog box

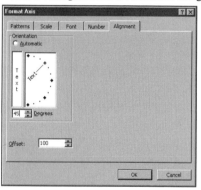

FIGURE N-18: Modified line chart

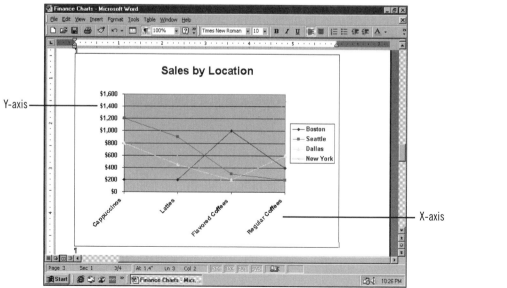

Y-axis

X-axis

Importing Data into a Chart

You can base a chart on table text, enter the data directly into a datasheet, or import data from sources such as an Excel worksheet into a chart you have created in Word. This last option is particularly useful when you have data that you wish to chart stored in an Excel worksheet. **Scenario** Jim has already created a cylinder chart that shows projected sales in three Canadian cities in which MediaLoft is considering opening stores. MediaLoft is also considering expanding to Europe. The data related to projected sales in three European franchises is stored in an Excel workbook. Jim needs to import the Excel worksheet into the chart so that the chart reflects the values in the worksheet instead of the values in the current datasheet.

Steps 1 2 3 4

1. Scroll to the **end of the document**, then double-click the **chart** on the last page
   This chart currently shows data related to projected sales in three Canadian cities where MediaLoft is considering opening franchises. You want to modify the chart to show projected sales in Europe. Instead of editing the datasheet, you can import the necessary information.

2. Click **Edit** on the menu bar, then click **Import File**

3. Navigate to your Project Disk, click **WD N-2**, then click **Open**
   The Import Data Options dialog box appears as shown in Figure N-19.

4. Click **OK** to accept Sheet1, then click **anywhere in the chart**
   The data related to projected sales in Paris, London, and Rome appears. You want to enter a title for the Z-axis to inform readers that the numbers represent millions. The axis is called the **Z-axis** because the cylinder chart is shown in 3-D view.

5. Click **Chart** on the menu bar, click **Chart Options**, click in the **Value (Z) axis text box** on the Titles tab, type **Millions**, then click **OK**
   You want to change the alignment of the Z-axis title so that it takes up less room.

6. Right-click **Millions**, click **Format Axis Title**, click the **Alignment tab**, type **90** in the Degrees box, then click **OK**

7. Click away from the chart to exit Microsoft Graph, select **Canadian** in the subtitle above the chart, then type **European**
   Compare your screen to Figure N-20.

8. Type your name at the bottom of the document, save the document, then print and close it

FIGURE N-19: Import Data Options dialog box

FIGURE N-20: Revised chart with imported data

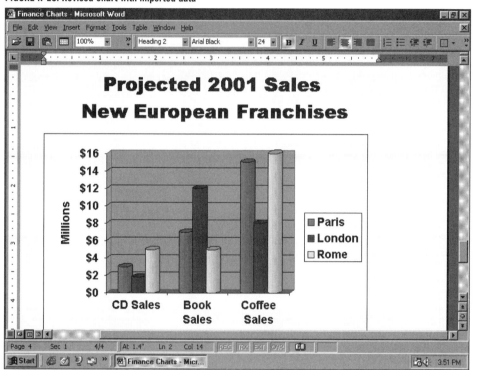

Using and adding custom chart types

Sometimes the standard chart types available in the Chart Type dialog box don't meet your needs for a particular chart. In these situations, you can choose from a variety of custom types that are built into Microsoft Graph or that have been added by other users. In the Chart Type dialog box, click the Custom Types tab, then click the Built-in option button to view and choose from built-in custom charts; or you can click the User-defined option button to choose from charts that have been modified and added by other users. You can also add your own custom styles to the dialog box. After customizing a chart in the

Microsoft Graph window, click Chart on the menu bar, click Chart Type, then click the Custom Types tab. In this tab, click the User-defined option button, then click Add. In the Add Custom Type dialog box, enter a name for the new type and a brief description. When you click OK, the chart type is added to the User-defined Chart Types list. You can also use the Custom Chart tab to change the default chart type. By clicking the Set as Default Chart option button on this tab, you can replace the currently selected chart style with the column chart as the default style.

Practice

▶ Concepts Review

Label each of the elements in Figure N-21.

FIGURE N-21

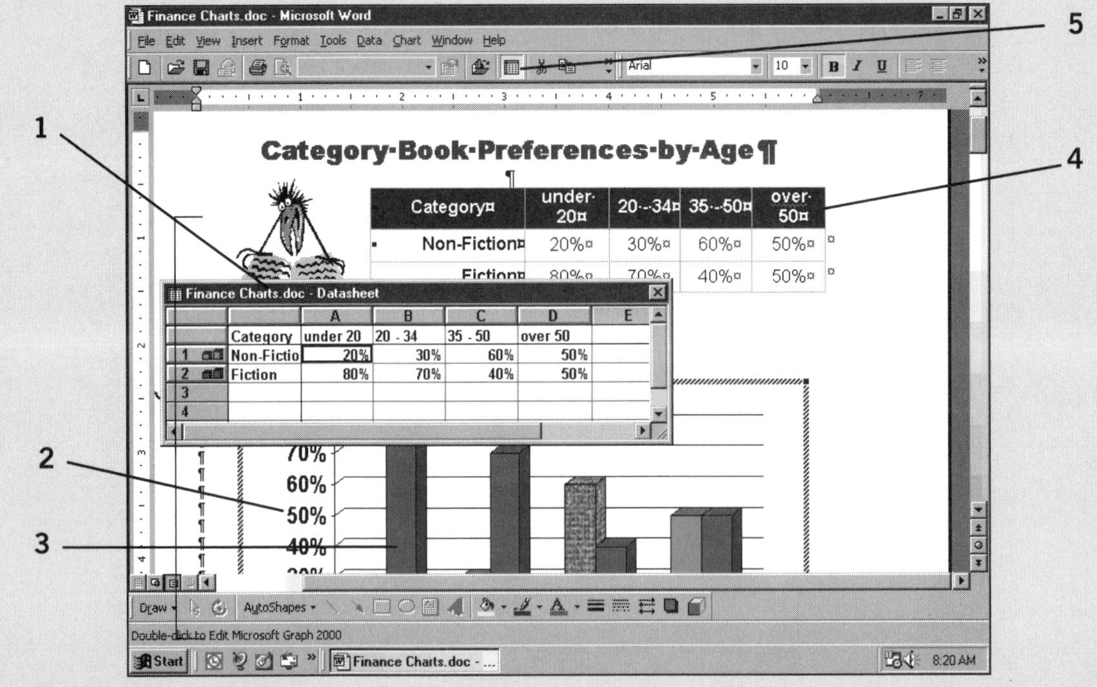

Match each term with the statement that best describes its function.

6. Datasheet
7. Column chart
8. Legend
9. Chart Type command
10. Pie chart

a. Contains the data for the chart
b. Used to change how the data is displayed
c. Shows how data changes over time
d. The key to the chart data
e. Shows values as parts of a whole

Select the best answer from the list of choices.

11. **The Insert Picture, Chart command inserts a chart and then displays the**
   a. Chart Wizard.
   b. Chart Type dialog box.
   c. Chart in the default style.
   d. Chart dialog box.

12. To modify a chart in Word, you
- **a.** Double-click the chart to start Microsoft Graph 2000.
- **b.** Click the View Datasheet button on the Graph toolbar.
- **c.** Click Format on the menu bar, then click Chart.
- **d.** Click Insert on the menu bar, then click Object.

13. Which of the following is *not* a way to modify the values displayed in a chart?
- **a.** Modify the values in the table in Word.
- **b.** Double-click the chart object in the Graph program.
- **c.** Double-click a column in the datasheet to exclude values.
- **d.** Edit values in the datasheet.

14. Which of the following chart or graph types is most useful when you want to illustrate a trend?
- **a.** Pie chart
- **b.** Line graph
- **c.** Column chart
- **d.** Scatter chart

▶ Skills Review

1. Create a chart.
- **a.** Start Word, then open the document named WD N-3 and save it as "Expense Chart".
- **b.** Select the table.
- **c.** Click Insert on the menu bar, point to Picture, then click Chart.
- **d.** Right-click the Legend.
- **e.** Click Format Legend, click the Placement tab, click the Bottom option button, then click OK.
- **f.** Click outside the datasheet, then drag the sizing handles to increase the size of the chart so that it is approximately 4" wide and 2" high.
- **g.** Right-click the chart, click Format Object, click the Layout tab, click Behind Text, click the Center option button, then click OK.
- **h.** Save the document.

2. Modify chart objects.
- **a.** Right-click the chart, point to Chart Object on the shortcut menu, then click Edit.
- **b.** Click any column in the Taxis data series to select the series. (*Note:* You will need to click a dark purple column.)
- **c.** Click Format on the menu bar, then click Selected Data Series.
- **d.** Click the Patterns tab if necessary, choose a bright green color, then click OK.
- **e.** Click the blue column above the April heading, then click it again so that only the April column is selected.
- **f.** With the column selected, right-click the column, then click Format Data Point on the shortcut menu.
- **g.** Fill the column with the Sand texture.
- **h.** Click the Chart Objects list arrow on the Chart toolbar, then click Walls.
- **i.** Click Format on the menu bar, click Selected Walls, click the None option button in both the Border and Area sections, then click OK.
- **j.** Click outside the chart area, then save the document.

3. Modify the chart type.

   a. Select the first two columns in the table.

   b. Click Insert on the menu bar, point to Picture, then click Chart.

   c. Click Chart on the menu bar, then click Chart Type.

   d. Click Pie, click the middle chart type in the top row, then click OK.

   e. Click the By Column button on the Graph toolbar. (*Note:* You may need to click the More Buttons button on the Graph toolbar to locate this button.)

   f. Right-click the pie, click Format Data Series, in the Format Data Series dialog box click the Data Labels tab, click the Show percent option button, then click OK.

   g. Save the document.

4. Change the elevation and orientation of a pie chart.

   a. Click Chart on the menu bar, then click 3-D View.

   b. In the 3-D View dialog box, change the chart elevation to 25 degrees.

   c. Click OK, then click anywhere in the chart area.

   d. Click the Chart Objects list arrow, click Plot Area, then press [Delete].

   e. Right-click the pie chart, click Format Data Series, then click the Options tab.

   f. Change the orientation of the first pie slice to 180 degrees.

   g. Click OK, click outside the pie chart, then increase the size of the chart object so it is approximately 4" wide and 2" high.

   h. Save the document.

5. Create area and line charts.

   a. Select the first four columns in the table.

   b. Click Insert on the menu bar, point to Picture, then click Chart.

   c. Click Chart on the menu bar, then click Chart Type.

   d. In the Chart Type list, scroll to and click Area, then click OK to accept the default area subtype.

   e. Increase the size of the chart so that it is approximately 5" wide and 3.5" high.

   f. Double-click the chart, click Chart on the menu bar, click Chart Options, in the Chart Option dialog box click the Titles tab if necessary, enter "Expenses" as the value (Y) axis title, then click OK.

   g. Click the More Buttons button on the Standard toolbar, click the Chart Type button list arrow, then click the Line Chart button.

   h. Click the By Column button on the Graph toolbar.

   i. Click away from the chart, click the chart again, then drag the bottom-middle sizing handle down to the 6" mark on the vertical ruler bar.

   j. Save the document.

6. Modify values in a chart.

   a. Double-click the line chart, then click cell A1 in the datasheet.

   b. Type "457.56", then press [Enter].

   c. Click the View Datasheet button on the Graph toolbar to close the datasheet.

   d. Click outside the chart area, click anywhere in the table, click Table on the menu bar, click Delete, then click Table.

   e. Double-click the line chart, right-click the legend, click Format Legend, click the Font tab, click 10 in the Size box, then click OK.

   f. Right-click the Y-axis, click Format Axis, click the Font tab if necessary, click 10 in the Size box, then click OK.

g. Right-click the X-axis, click Format Axis, click the Font tab if necessary, click 10 in the Size box, click the Alignment tab, enter 45 in the Degrees box, then click OK.

h. Click outside the chart, then save the document.

7. Import data into a chart.

a. Scroll if necessary and double-click the column chart.

b. Click the Import File button on the Chart toolbar.

c. Locate and open the Excel file WD N-4, then click OK to accept Sheet1 as the sheet to import.

d. Click the D label in the datasheet to select all of Column D, then press [Delete].

e. Click Chart on the menu bar, click Chart Options, click in the Value (Z) axis text box, type Expenses, then click OK.

f. Right-click Expenses, click Format Axis Title, change the alignment to 90 degrees, then click OK.

g. Increase the height of the chart as necessary so that all the lines are easy to see.

h. Click the Zoom Control list arrow, click Whole Page, then adjust the size of each chart as necessary so that all three charts fit on the page.

i. Click the pie chart to select it, then click the Center Align button on the Formatting toolbar.

j. Click the line chart to select it, then click the Center Align button.

k. Type your name at the bottom of the document, print the document, save the document, then exit Word.

▶ Visual Workshop

As the manager of the Footloose Travel Agency, you have created an Excel workbook that contains sales information about the various European tours you offer. In a blank Word document, insert a chart, then import the workbook WD N-7. Delete columns B and C in the imported datasheet, change the chart type to an exploded doughnut chart, then display the data by column. Modify the chart so that it appears as shown in Figure N-22. Save the document as "European Sales" to your Project Disk, type your name a few lines below the chart, preview the document, print a copy, then save and close the document.

FIGURE N-22:

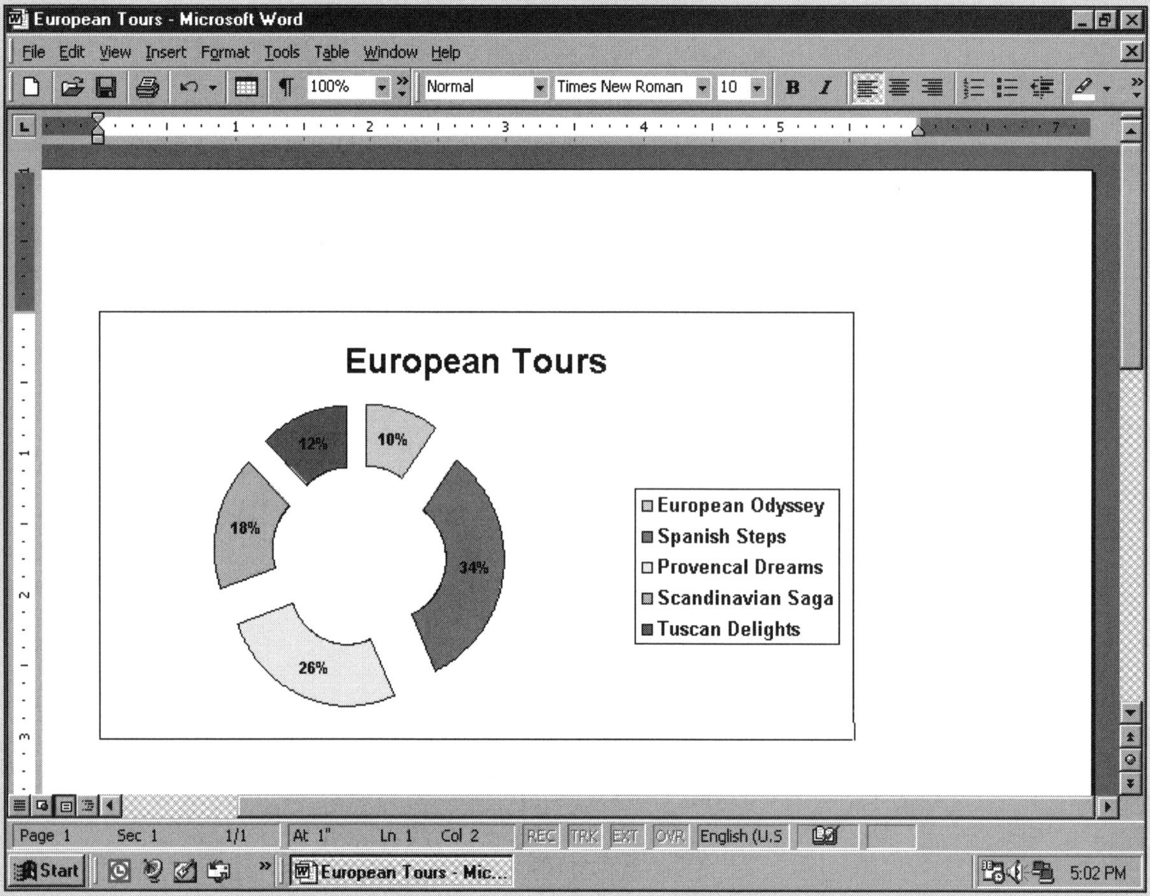

Creating
and Using Forms

Objectives

- [MOUS] ► **Create a form template**
- [MOUS] ► **Insert a text box form field**
- ► **Specify a calculation in a form field**
- [MOUS] ► **Insert a check box form field**
- [MOUS] ► **Insert a drop-down form field**
- ► **Add Help to a form field**
- ► **Prepare a form for a user**
- ► **Fill out a form as a user**

Just like the familiar paper forms you use every day, forms you create in Word include labeled blanks to be filled in and boxes to be checked. But unlike paper forms, the ones you create in Word can be completed in Word. Your online form can include check boxes, list boxes, and Help information that users can refer to as they complete it. You can even protect the form so that users can enter data but cannot change the form's structure. **Scenario** Sandra Barradas, general manager of MediaLoft's San Diego store, has decided to create an online version of the weekly time sheet form, to replace the paper form that employees currently complete. The handwriting on the paper forms is frequently undecipherable, and inconsistent responses have caused problems in the Payroll Department. Sandra is confident that an online form will provide more consistent data, and will make this timekeeping activity simpler and more accurate.

Creating a Form Template

Your first step when creating a form is to create a new template. A **template** is a special kind of document that contains standard text (also known as boilerplate text) and/or formatting that serve as a basis for new documents. A user opens a new document based on a form template and completes the form document without affecting the text, structure, or formatting of the template itself. Once you have created the new template, you insert and format the field labels and fields you want to include in the form. A **field label** is a word or phrase such as "Name" or "Street Address" that identifies the information users should enter in a given field. A **form field** is a special Word code you insert to hold the information users enter in the format you choose, such as a text field, check box, or drop-down list. ▶Scenario▶ Sandra has decided that her form should consist of two tables, one for employees to enter identifying information such as their name and employee number, another to record their hours. She begins by creating the form template.

Steps 1 2 3 4

1. **Start Word, click File on the menu bar, then click New**
   The New dialog box appears. In this dialog box you indicate the type of document you want to create. For example, you can use an existing template or wizard to create documents such as memos and fax cover sheets, or you can create a new blank document or a new blank template. You want to create a new template that will contain the form.

2. **Click the General tab, if necessary, click the Template option button in the lower-right corner of the dialog box, then click OK**
   A new document appears in the document window. The default name, Template1, appears on the title bar. To simplify the process of creating a form, you can display the Forms toolbar and quickly access the various form features.

QuickTip
If necessary, position the Forms toolbar so that it does not obscure the view of your work area in the document window by dragging its title bar to a different location.

3. **Click View on the menu bar, point to Toolbars, then click Forms**
   As shown in Figure O-1, the Forms toolbar contains buttons for creating and modifying a form. You are now ready to create a table to contain the fields required for the form. By containing fields within a table, you can more easily align them.

4. **Make sure the Show/Hide ¶ button ¶ is selected so that you can see nonprinting characters**

5. **Press [Enter] to allow room for text at the top of the page, click the Insert Table button 🔲 on the Standard toolbar, then click the fourth square in the second row**
   A table four columns wide by two rows long appears in the document window. This table will contain individual employee information. You need another table to contain information about the hours worked each week.

6. **Click below the table, press [Enter] to allow space before the next table, click 🔲, then click the fifth square in the third row**

Trouble?
If you press [Tab] in the last cell of the last row of a table, you will create a new row. If this happens, press [Ctrl]+[Z] to undo the action.

7. **Using Figure O-2 as a guide, type the text for the field labels in the cells as shown**
   Remember to press [Tab] to move from cell to cell within a table. Do not, however, press [Tab] in the last cell of the last row. When you are ready to enter the labels in the second table, click in the second cell of the second table. You will enter the form fields in the tables in the next lesson.

8. **Click the Save button 🔲 on the Standard toolbar, type San Diego Time Sheet in the File name box, then click Save**
   If you see a message asking if you want to override the existing template, click Yes. Word saves your document as a template in the Templates folder in the Microsoft Office folder. If you choose to save your template to another location, it may not appear in the New dialog box.

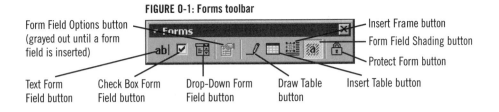

FIGURE O-1: Forms toolbar

Form Field Options button (grayed out until a form field is inserted)

Insert Frame button

Form Field Shading button

Protect Form button

Text Form Field button

Check Box Form Field button

Drop-Down Form Field button

Draw Table button

Insert Table button

FIGURE O-2: Tables completed with field labels

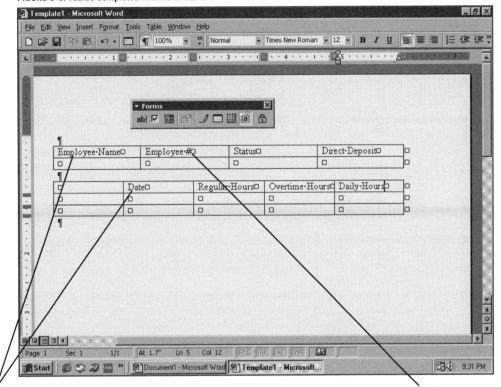

Type these field labels

Type a number sign here

CLUES TO USE

Setting the default file location for workgroup templates

Frequently you need to work with others to create and modify the templates you create for forms or other documents. A template that you want to make available to others to use is called a **workgroup template**. When you open a document associated with a workbook template or want to start a new document based on a workgroup template, you want to make sure that Word knows where to find the template. To check the location where Word saves and looks for workgroup templates, click Options on the Tools menu, click the File Locations tab, then read the path information for Workgroup templates. To set or change the path where workgroup templates are stored, click the path, click Modify, and then navigate to the desired location in the Modify Location dialog box. Once you have set the location, you can start a new document based on a workgroup template by clicking File on the menu bar, then clicking New. Workgroup templates are displayed in the General tab. To add a template to an existing document, open the document, click Tools on the menu bar, click Templates and Add-Ins, click Add, locate and select the template, then click OK. All the features included in the template will now be available to the current document.

Word 2000

Inserting a Text Form Field

An important step in creating a form is inserting the fields where users will enter information. You insert a **text form field** in any cell where you want users to enter text such as a name or an address. You use a text form field instead of simply leaving a space or a blank cell in the form so that you can monitor the kind of information users enter and inform users if they enter data incorrectly. For example, you can restrict the entry to a specific number of characters or specify that only numbers or dates are valid entries. A user will not be able to enter an invalid response. ▶Scenario▶ Sandra would like each employee to enter his or her name and employee ID number in the top table, and the starting and ending time for each day worked in the bottom table. She needs to insert text form fields for this information in the appropriate cells in the form.

Steps

1. In the top table, click in the **cell** directly beneath the Employee Name field label, then click the **Text Form Field button** abl on the Forms toolbar
   Five shaded dots appear in the cell that contained the insertion point, as shown in Figure O-3. Now you need to create fields for the employee number and the status of the employee.

2. Press **[Tab]** to move to the cell beneath the Employee # field label, then click abl
   You will enter the fields for the Status and Direct Deposit cells in a later lesson. For now, you need to enter text fields for the cells in the second table.

3. Click in the **cell** beneath the Date field label, click abl, then insert three text form fields in the cells beneath the Regular Hours, Overtime Hours, and Daily Hours field labels as shown in Figure O-4
   The cell under the Date field label will contain a date supplied by employees as they complete the form. You can format a text form field so that it will accept only dates. You can also ensure that the date is entered in a specific format. You specify such field options in the Form Field Options dialog box.

4. Click the **text form field** in the cell beneath the Date field label
   The gray shading darkens, indicating that the field is selected.

5. Click the **Form Field Options button** 🖼 on the Forms toolbar
   The Text Form Field Options dialog box opens. In this dialog box you can specify a variety of options that limit the kind of information a user can enter in a field and how this information should be formatted.

6. Click the **Type list arrow**, click **Date**, click the **Date format list arrow**, then click **M/d/yy**
   Your screen should match Figure O-5.

7. Click **OK**
   You will see no change in the form field. However, when you complete the form in a later lesson, you will be able to enter the date only in the correct format. Now you want to ensure that users enter the correct number of digits for their employee number in the Employee # field.

8. Click the **field** under the Employee # field label in the first table, click 🖼, in the Text Form Field Options dialog box click the **Maximum length up arrow** until **5** appears in the box, then click **OK**
   You will see no change in the form field, but the Maximum length option will ensure that the user enters the correct number of characters.

9. Click the **Save button** 💾 on the Standard toolbar

FIGURE O-3: Text form field inserted in table

Text Form
Field button

New text field

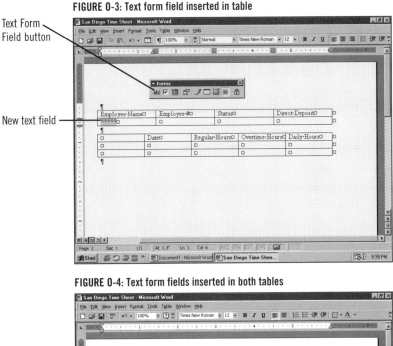

FIGURE O-4: Text form fields inserted in both tables

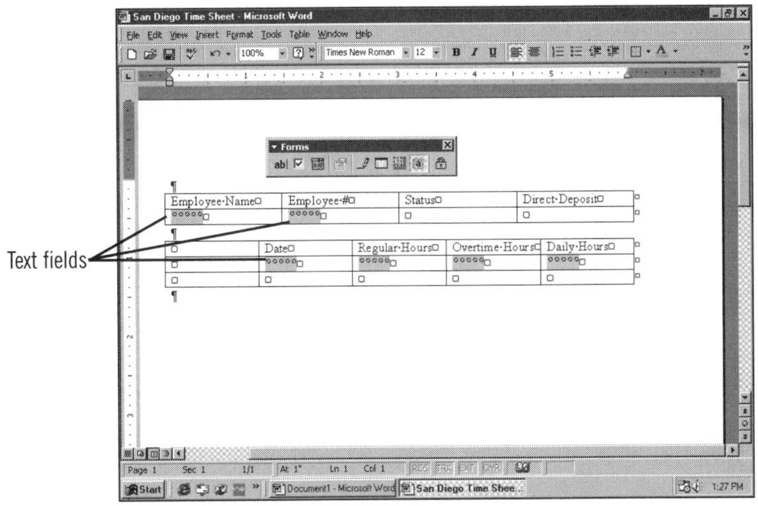

Text fields

FIGURE O-5: Setting date options for a text form field

Type list arrow

Date format
list arrow

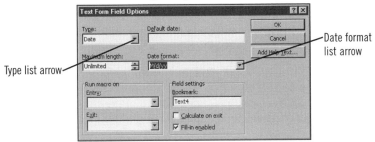

Using date formatting in a text form field

The key to a successful form is consistency. When you apply a specific date format to a text field, you ensure that the date will be entered consistently, no matter who uses the form. For example, if a user enters June 1, 2000 in a field formatted with the m/d/yy date format, the date will automatically be reformatted as 6/1/00.

Specifying Calculations in Form Fields

You can format form fields as calculation form fields. For example, you can enter a form field that will add up the numbers entered in selected fields in the form. You can also format a field with a Currency format so that every time a user enters a number in the field, it is formatted with the required currency symbol and decimal places. Scenario Sandra would like the form to calculate the total number of regular, overtime, and combined daily hours that each employee has worked in a given week. She needs to format specific fields to perform the calculations when users complete the form.

Steps

1. Click the **field** under the Regular Hours field label, then click the **Form Field Options button** on the Forms toolbar
   The Text Form Field Options dialog box opens. You need to apply the Calculate on exit option to the fields that will be used in the calculation so that the calculation is updated when the user makes the entry and exits the field.

2. In the Field settings area, click the **Calculate on exit check box**, then click **OK**

3. Click the **field** under the Overtime Hours field label, click, click the **Calculate on exit check box**, then click **OK**
   Now you can format the field that will contain the calculation.

4. Click the **last field** in the row under the Daily Hours field label, click, click the **Type list arrow**, then click **Calculation**
   With the Calculation option set, the box to the right becomes the Expression box, where you can enter a formula for the value you want to calculate. Formulas always begin with an equal sign, so this text (=) is already entered for you. You want the Daily Hours field to calculate the number of Regular Hours plus the number of Overtime Hours, so you need to insert a function for adding and specify the location of the cells to add.

5. In the **Expression box**, click after the equal sign, type **sum(left)** as shown in Figure O-6, then click **OK**
   Notice that "0" now appears in the field to indicate that it contains a formula (the result of which is 0 because no values have been entered in the calculated fields). In the bottom row of the table you need to create a "Total Hours" label and create fields that calculate totals for regular, overtime, and combined daily hours. First, you must merge two cells to create a new cell that is wide enough to accommodate the "Total Hours" label. Displaying the Tables and Borders toolbar will make it easier for you to format the cells.

6. Click **View** on the menu bar, click **Toolbars**, click **Tables and Borders**, in the second table select the **first two cells in the bottom row** as shown in Figure O-7, then click the **Merge Cells button** on the Tables and Borders toolbar
   Now you can enter the field label "Total Hours" in the merged cells and create a totals field for the regular hours worked in the next cell.

7. Type **Total Hours**, press **[Tab]**, click the **Text Form Field button** on the Forms toolbar, then click
   Now you need to enter an expression that adds the cells that are above the current cell.

8. In the Text Form Field Options dialog box, click the **Type list arrow**, click **Calculation**, click in the **Expression text box** after the equal sign, type **sum(above)**, then click **OK**

9. Repeat Steps **7** and **8** to insert a totals field in each of the next two cells, compare your screen to Figure O-8, then save the document

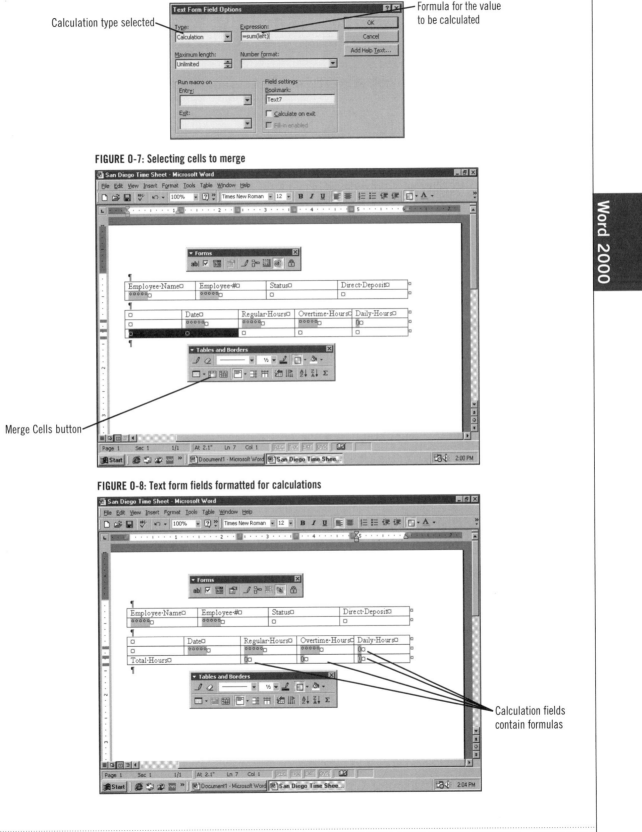

FIGURE O-6: Setting text form field calculation options

Calculation type selected

Formula for the value to be calculated

FIGURE O-7: Selecting cells to merge

Merge Cells button

FIGURE O-8: Text form fields formatted for calculations

Calculation fields contain formulas

Inserting a Check Box Form Field

Unit **O**

Word 2000

You insert a **check box form field** when you want a user to make selections from a set of options. You can also use check boxes to help users respond quickly to simple yes-or-no questions. **Scenario** The Payroll Department needs to identify quickly those employees who want their paychecks deposited directly into their bank accounts, because these checks are processed differently from the checks sent directly to employees. Sandra decides to insert a check box in the cell under Direct Deposit. If the box is checked, the Payroll Department will know immediately to process the employee's paycheck for direct deposit. In addition, Sandra needs to insert a series of check boxes below the tables for internal use by the Payroll Department.

Steps

1. In the **cell** beneath the Direct Deposit field label, click the **Check Box Form Field button** ☑ on the Forms toolbar

   A check box appears in the cell. If you anticipate that a check box is usually going to be checked by the user, you can specify that the check box be checked by default. Sandra knows that most employees have their checks directly deposited, so she wants the default to be checked.

2. Click the **Form Field Options button** ☑ on the Forms toolbar

   The Check Box Form Field Options dialog box opens. In this dialog box you can specify options for check boxes. For example, you can set the exact size of the check box. In this case, you will specify that this check box is checked by default.

3. In the Default value area, click the **Checked option button** as shown in Figure O-9, then click **OK**

   An "X" appears in the check box in the form. Users who do not want the direct deposit option can click the check box to deselect it when completing the form.

4. Double-click in the **blank line** below the second table, press **[Enter]**, type **For Payroll Use Only**, then press **[Enter]**

   You need to insert a series of check boxes and special codes that the Payroll Department will use to process the forms. These fields should not be checked by default.

5. Click the **Check Box Form Field button** ☑ on the Forms toolbar, press **[Tab]**, type **AB**, then press **[Enter]**

6. Click ☑, press **[Tab]**, type **CD**, then press **[Enter]**

7. Click ☑, press **[Tab]**, type **XW**, then press **[Enter]**

8. Click ☑, press **[Tab]**, type **YZ**, then press **[Enter]**

   Compare your document to Figure O-10.

9. Save your changes to the document

▶ WORD O-8 **CREATING AND USING FORMS**

FIGURE O-9: Check Box Form Field Options dialog box

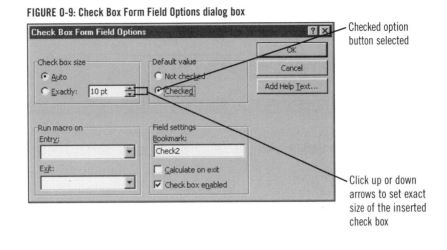

Checked option button selected

Click up or down arrows to set exact size of the inserted check box

FIGURE O-10: Check box fields inserted in the form template

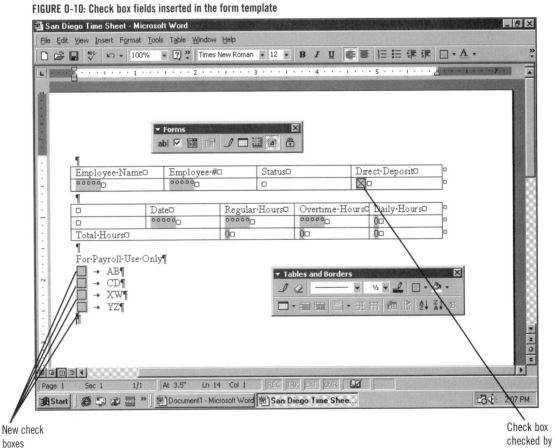

New check boxes

Check box checked by default

Inserting a Drop-Down Form Field

Unit O

Word 2000

When you want the user of a form to select from a list of several options, you insert a **drop-down form field**. This field provides a list of options without requiring a lot of space in a form. In the form document, a user sees an arrow next to a drop-down field. The user simply clicks the arrow to display a list of options from which to choose and then clicks the desired option. `Scenario` Sandra would like employees to provide information about their employment status. Because only one of several responses can be selected, Sandra creates a drop-down field.

Steps

1. **In the first table, click the cell below the Status field label, then click the Drop-Down Form Field button ⊞ on the Forms toolbar**
A blank drop-down field appears in the form. With the field created, you can enter the options that you want to appear in the list.

2. **Click the Form Field Options button ⊞ on the Forms toolbar**
The Drop-Down Form Field Options dialog box opens. In this dialog box you can specify the options you want to appear in the list. In this case, the list will contain employment status options.

3. **In the Drop-down item box, type contractor, then click Add**
The first item in the list appears in the Items in drop-down list box. You can continue adding items to this drop-down list.

Trouble?

If you make a spelling mistake, remove the item by selecting it in the Items in drop-down list box and clicking Remove. You can then type the item again.

4. **In the Drop-down item box, type the following items, and remember to click Add (or press [Enter]) after each item:**

temporary
part-time
full-time
intern
freelancer

The first item that appears in the Items in drop-down list box is the default item that appears in this field when the user fills out the form. You decide to rearrange the items in the list so that the "full-time" option appears as the default item.

5. **In the Items in drop-down list box, click full-time, then click the Move up arrow three times so that "full-time" appears at the top of the list, as shown in Figure O-11**
You can easily delete items if you decide you do not want them to appear in the drop-down field. Because a "freelancer" has the same status as a "contractor," you can remove the "freelancer" item from the list.

6. **In the Items in drop-down list box, click freelancer, then click Remove**
The item is removed from the Items in drop-down list box.

7. **Click OK**
The drop-down form field appears in the form and the "full-time" option appears in the field. When you open the form to complete it in a later lesson, you will see a drop-down list arrow next to "full-time". When you click the list arrow, the list of options you just entered will appear. Compare your form to Figure O-12.

8. **Click the Save button ⊞ on the Standard toolbar**

FIGURE O-11: Drop-Down Form Field Options dialog box

Type each item to be added to list

Click after typing an item to add it to list

Click to move selected item up in list

Click to move selected item down in list

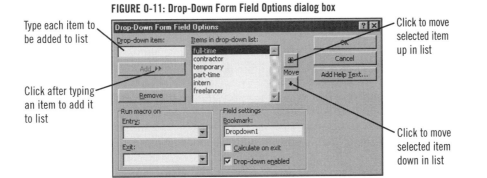

FIGURE O-12: Form template with drop-down field inserted

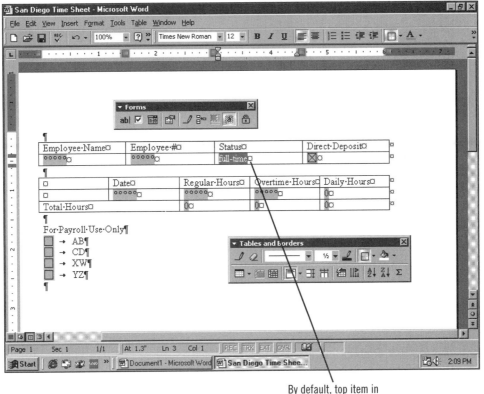

By default, top item in list appears in field

CLUES TO USE

Inserting additional form controls

Text, check box, and drop-down fields are three of several form controls (also called **Active X controls**) that you can use to create and modify a form. To see a complete selection of available controls, open the Control Toolbox toolbar by clicking View on the menu bar, pointing to Toolbars, then clicking Control Toolbox. This toolbar includes some of the buttons included on the Forms toolbar, such as the List Box

and Check Box controls. It also contains additional controls you can insert to design more sophisticated forms, such as toggle buttons, options buttons, and spin buttons. For example, instead of having users type numbers in a text form field, you can insert a **spin button control** that looks like this ⬦, so the user can click the arrows to specify a quantity.

Adding Help to a Form Field

In addition to using form fields to make a form easier to complete, you can provide the user with Help information and instructions. When a user selects a field for which Help information is available, instructions or other information appear on the status bar. You also have the option to provide more extensive information, which appears when the user presses the [F1] function key. **Scenario** Sandra wants to use the Help feature to provide employees with instructions for completing the form. In addition, Sandra needs to insert seven new rows in the second table to contain fields for each day of the week.

Steps

1. Click the **text form field** for the Employee # field label, then click the **Form Field Options button** on the Forms toolbar

2. Click **Add Help Text**, then click the **Status Bar tab** if necessary
The Form Field Help Text dialog box opens. In this dialog box you can enter text for two different kinds of Help information. In the Status Bar tab, you enter the text the user will see when the user selects the associated field.

3. Click the **Type your own option button**, then in the Type your own text box type **Enter your employee number.**, as shown in Figure O-13
You can enter up to 130 characters in the text box. In the Help Key (F1) tab, you can enter the information you want to appear when the user presses [F1] while the insertion point is in the field. You use (F1) help when you wish to provide more than a single line of information. You can enter up to 255 characters in the Help Key text box.

4. Click the **Help Key (F1) tab**, click the **Type your own option button**, then in the Type your own text box type **Your Employee Number is NOT the same as your Social Security number. In the Employee Number field, you must use the 5-digit number that appears in the Comments field on your pay stub.**
This text will appear in a message box when the user presses [F1] while the field is selected.

5. Click **OK** to return to the Text Form Field Options dialog box, then click **OK** to return to the form
You do not see any change in the form, but the Help information you entered has been applied to the field. You will see the Help information when you complete the form in a later lesson. With the fields in the form complete, you can now create additional rows of fields in the form so that the user can enter hours worked for up to seven days.

6. In the second table, select the **second row** (which contains the form fields), then click the **Copy button** on the Standard toolbar

7. Click the **Paste button** on the Standard toolbar, then click five more times so that you have a total of seven new rows containing form fields as shown in Figure O-14

8. Click in the first cell of row 2, type **Mon.**, press ↓, type **Tues.**, then enter the remaining abbreviations for the days of the week as shown in Figure O-14

9. Click the **Save button** on the Standard toolbar

QuickTip
Click to the left of the row to select the entire row at once.

FIGURE O-13: Status Bar tab of the Form Field Help Text dialog box

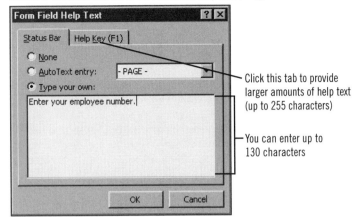

Click this tab to provide larger amounts of help text (up to 255 characters)

You can enter up to 130 characters

FIGURE O-14: Additional rows inserted in the form

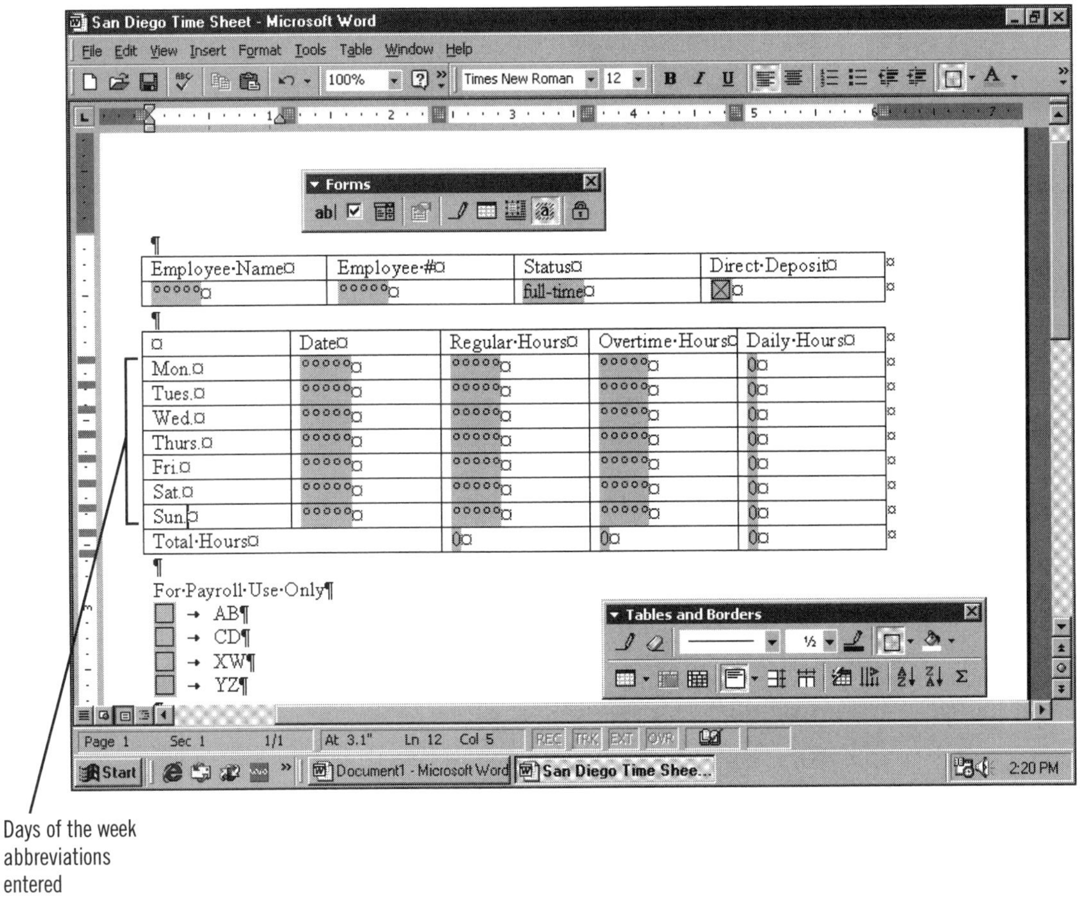

Days of the week abbreviations entered

Preparing a Form for a User

Before distributing a form template, you should enhance its appearance and protect the data so that users can complete it easily and safely. You can save the form with a specific magnification setting, hide the field shading in a form, and use the Table AutoFormat command to apply a preset table format, so the form is attractive and easy to follow. Most important, you can protect the form so that the user cannot change its structure. All the user can do is enter the required information. **Scenario** Sandra wants to prepare the form so that employees can use it online. First she will hide the shading in the form fields.

Steps 1 2 3 4

1. Click anywhere in the **first table**, then click the **Form Field Shading button** 📷 on the Forms toolbar
   The Form Field Shading button is deselected and the fields in both tables are no longer shaded. You can use the Tables and Borders toolbar to add lines and shading to the form.

2. Click anywhere in the **second table**, click the **Table AutoFormat button** 📷 on the Tables and Borders toolbar, click **3D effects 3** (you will need to scroll down), make sure the AutoFit check box is *not* selected, then click **OK**
   The table is attractively formatted with lines and shading, as shown in Figure O-15. To make the form look more interesting, you decide to change the text direction of the days of the week.

3. Select the **cells containing the days of the week**, right-click in the **selected area**, click **Text Direction**, click the **left box** in the Orientation area, then click **OK**
   With the text oriented vertically, you can specify how it should be aligned in each cell.

4. With the text still selected, click the **Align Top Left list arrow** 📷 on the Tables and Borders toolbar, click the **Align Center button** 📷, move the mouse over the upper-left corner of the table to display the **Table Select icon** 📷, click 📷 to select the table, click the **Font Size list arrow**, then click **14**

5. Adjust the width of each of the columns by dragging the **column dividers** to match the table shown in Figure O-16
   Now that you have reduced the column widths, you decide the table would look better if it was centered between the left and right margins of the page.

6. With the table still selected, click **Table** on the menu bar, click **Table Properties**, click **Center**, then click **OK**
   Now you need to format the top table.

7. Click anywhere in the top table, click 📷, click **3D effects 3**, deselect the **AutoFit option button**, click **OK**, then change the font size for the entire table to **14 pt**
   So that the user sees the entire width of the form when he or she opens it, you decide to display the form in the page width magnification.

8. Click the **Zoom list arrow** on the Standard toolbar, then click **Page Width**
   This information is saved when you save the form. In order to make sure the user does not make any changes to the form when completing it, you need to protect it.

9. Click the **Protect Form button** 📷 on the Forms toolbar, click the **Close button** on the Forms toolbar, click the **Close button** on the Tables and Borders toolbar, compare the completed form to Figure O-16, then save and close the document

FIGURE O-15: 3D effects 3 AutoFormat applied to table

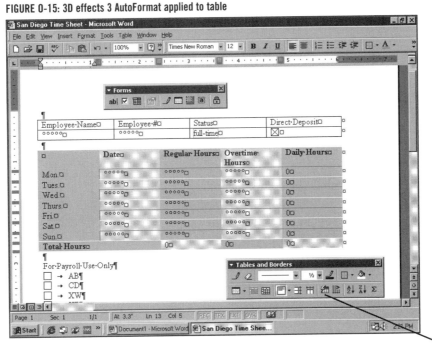

Table
AutoFormat
button

FIGURE O-16: Completed form template

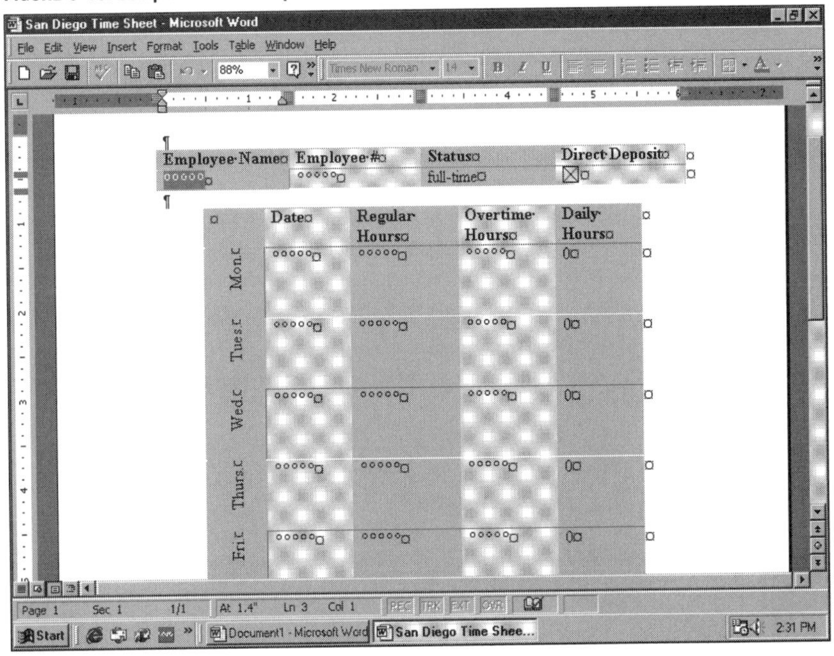

Filling Out a Form as a User

Unit O

Word 2000

After you have created a form template, you can test your form by attempting to complete it as a user would. To begin using a form, you create a new document based on the form template you created. **Scenario** Sandra is ready to test the form before she shares it with her employees.

Steps

1. Click **File** on the menu bar, then click **New**
   The New dialog box appears. You want to create a new document using the form template you created in this lesson.

2. Double-click **San Diego Time Sheet**, click the **Save button** 🖫 on the Standard toolbar, navigate to the location of your Project Files, type **Test Time Sheet** in the File name box, then click **Save**
   You have opened and then saved a new document that is based on the San Diego Time Sheet template. You have not opened the template itself. (For information on how to open a template so that you can make changes to its structure, see Clues below.) Notice that the field under the Employee Name field label is selected, ready for you to type your name.

3. Type your name
   Your name appears in the form. Notice that the text wraps to the next line if necessary to accommodate the information. Now you can move to the next field.

4. Press **[Tab]** to move to the next field, Employee #, then type **123434**
   As you can see, you are not able to enter the final "4" because when you created the template, you set this field to accept only five numbers. Notice the text that appears on the status bar. You can also press [F1] to display the Help information you entered in an earlier lesson.

5. Press **[F1]**
   The Help information appears in a Help window, as shown in Figure O-17.

6. Click **OK** to close the Help window, press **[Tab]** to move to the next field, click the **Status list arrow** next to **full-time**, then click **temporary**
   When you click the Status list arrow, a list of the options you can select appears. Once you select an option, it appears in the cell in place of the default option.

7. Press **[Tab]** twice, type **June 5**, then press **[Tab]**
   As you can see, 6/5/00 appears in place of June 5 and your cursor moves to the next cell. Note that a different year designation may appear in your form.

8. Type **6**, press **[Tab]**, type **2**, then press **[Tab]**
   The eight hours worked on Monday is automatically calculated.

9. Complete the remaining fields in the form according to the information provided in Figure O-18, save the document, print a copy, then close it

Trouble?

If the San Diego Time Sheet template does not appear in the New dialog box, check with your instructor or technical support person. You may need to move the template to the default template folder on your system or change the path where Word looks for the template in the File Locations tab in the Options dialog box.

Editing a form template

You protect a form so that users cannot make changes to its structure. However, sometimes you, as the creator of the form, may wish to make changes. You need to open the form template and then unprotect it before you can work on it. By default, the form template is stored in the Templates folder. To find the Templates folder, you need to navigate to WINDOWS/Application Data/Microsoft/Templates. If the form template is not stored in this folder, check the C:/Program Files/Microsoft Office/Templates/1033 folder or another folder as directed by your instructor or technical support person. Sometimes you need to search for the name of the form template in Windows Explorer in order to find the location where Word has saved it. When you have located the template, open it, then open the Forms toolbar (click View on the menu bar, point to Toolbars, then click Forms), and then click the Protect Form button to deselect it. You can then make changes to the form's structure. Once you have finished making changes to the form, you can protect and then save it again.

FIGURE O-17: Help information in a form

Help Key (F1)
help

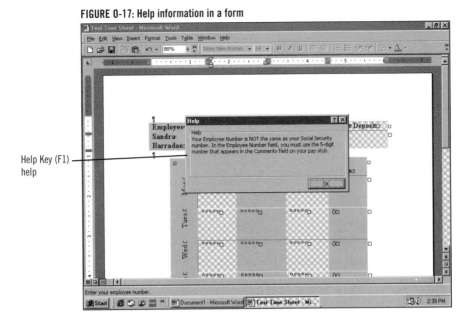

FIGURE O-18: Completed form

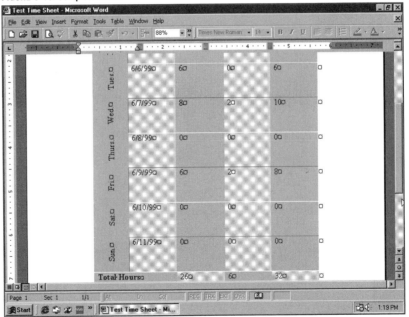

Practice

▶ Concepts Review

Label and describe each of the parts of the toolbar shown in Figure O-19.

FIGURE O-19

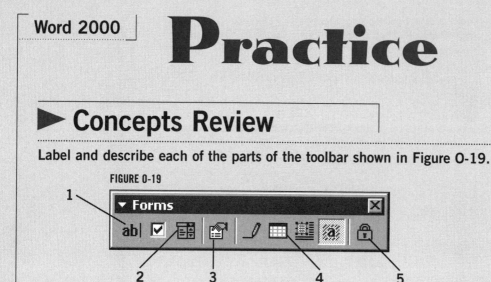

Match each term with the statement that describes it.

6. Template
7. Drop-down form field
8. Table AutoFormat
9. Text box form field
10. Protect Form

a. A feature that protects a form from changes
b. Preset formatting that can be applied to a table
c. A type of document that contains standard text and formatting that is a basis for new documents
d. An area to enter information in a form
e. An area in a form where you can choose from a list of options

Select the best answer from the list of choices.

11. Which of the following statements is true about drop-down form fields?
   a. A drop-down field provides a list of options from which you can choose
   b. Items in the drop-down list cannot be removed after you've entered them
   c. The order in which items appear in the list cannot be changed
   d. Until the user makes a selection in a drop-down form field, the field appears blank

12. To create a template:
   a. You first must have created a form.
   b. You click File on the menu bar, click New, then click the Template option button.
   c. You click the New button on Standard toolbar.
   d. You click File on the menu bar, then click Template.

13. **Which statement is true about the Protect Form function?**
    a. Once the form is protected, you must enter a password to unprotect it
    b. A form must be protected before it displays any Help information
    c. You can use the Protect Form button instead of the Save button
    d. You must always enter a password before you can enter information into a protected form

14. **You can use the Forms toolbar to**
    a. Change text direction.
    b. Save your changes.
    c. Add check boxes.
    d. Merge cells.

► Skills Review

1. **Create a form template.**
   a. Start Word. Click File on the menu bar, then click New.
   b. Click the Template option button in the lower-right corner of the dialog box, then click OK.
   c. Click View on the menu bar, point to Toolbars, then click Forms.
   d. If necessary, click the Show/Hide ¶ button on the Standard toolbar to show the paragraph marks.
   e. With the insertion point at the top of the page, type "Office Automation", then press [Enter].
   f. Type "Needs Assessment Form", then press [Enter] twice.
   g. Select the two lines of text, increase the font size to 24 pt, click the Bold button on the Formatting toolbar, then click the Center button.
   h. Click at the last paragraph mark below the title, then click the Insert Table button on the Standard toolbar and create a table that is two columns wide and three rows high.
   i. Enter the following items in the three cells in the first column: "Employee Name:", "Department Number:", and "Category:".
   j. Drag the column divider to reduce the width of column 1 to approximately 2".
   k. Click below the table, press [Enter], click the Insert Table button, then create a table that is four columns wide and 12 rows high.
   l. Enter text in the cells according to the table below.

I create or edit the following document types:	Check all that apply:	Frequency each week:	Hours to create or edit:
Interoffice memos			
Single letters			
Merge letters			
Internal reports			
Financial summaries			
Charts and graphs			
Flyers or newsletters			
Presentations			
Web pages			
Other:			
		Total Hours:	

m. Drag the column dividers to increase the width of column 1 to approximately 3" and decrease the width of columns 2, 3, and 4 to approximately 1" each.

n. Save the form with the name "Office Survey".

2. Create text box form fields.

a. Click in the cell next to the label "Employee Name" in the first row, then click the Text Form Field button on the Forms toolbar.

b. Repeat step 2a for the cell next to the Department Number field.

c. In the second table, insert text form fields in each cell in the Hours to create or edit column.

d. Click the form field next to the Department Number label, then click the Form Field Options button on the Forms toolbar.

e. Click the Maximum Length up arrow until 2 appears in the box, then click OK.

f. Click the Save button on the Standard toolbar.

3. Specify calculations in form fields.

a. Select the first field under the "Hours to create or edit" label, then click the Form Field Options button on the Forms toolbar.

b. Click the Type list arrow, then click Number.

c. In the Field settings area, click the Calculate on exit check box, then click OK.

d. Repeat steps 3a through 3c for all cells in the column except for the last cell (next to the Total Hours label).

e. Click the last field in the Hours to create or edit column (next to the Total Hours label), then click the Form Field Options button.

f. Click the Type list arrow, then click Calculation.

g. Click in the Expression box, type "=sum(above)", then click OK.

4. Create check box form fields.

a. In the first cell under the heading "Check all that apply", click the Check Box Form Field button on the Forms toolbar.

b. Repeat step 4a for each cell in column 2 of the table, excluding the last row.

5. Create drop-down form fields.

a. Click in the cell next to the Category label in the first table, click the Drop-Down Form Field button on the Forms toolbar, then click the Form Field Options button.

b. In the Drop-Down item box, type "supervisor", then click Add.

c. Type the following items, remembering to click Add after each item: "paralegal", "analyst", "administrative assistant", "office manager".

d. Click OK to close the dialog box.

e. In the second table, in the first cell under the Frequency each week label, click the Drop-Down Form Field button on the Forms toolbar, then click the Form Field Options button on the Forms toolbar.

f. In the Drop-down item box, type "twice/week", then click Add.

g. Type the following items, remembering to click Add after each item: "daily", "three/week", "once/week", "daily", "once/month", "none".

h. In the Items in drop-down list box, select the "none" item, then click the Move up arrow until it appears at the top of the list.

i. In the Items in drop-down list box, move the "once/week" item to above the "twice/week" item.

j. In the Items in drop-down list box, click the "three/week" item, click Remove, then click OK.

k. Click the Copy button on the Standard toolbar, click in the cell below, click the Paste button, then continue to paste the field into the remaining cells in this column, excluding the last two cells (the cell next to the Other label and the cell that contains the Total Hours label).

l. Click the Save button on the Standard toolbar.

6. **Add Help to form fields.**
   a. In the second table, click the first check box field under the Check all that apply label, then click the Form Field Options button.
   b. In the Form Field Options dialog box, click Add Help Text, then click the Status Bar tab if necessary.
   c. Click the Type your own option button, then in the Type your own text box, type "Click the check box for each type of document you create."
   d. Click the Help Key (F1) tab, click the Type your own option button, then in the Type your own text box, type "You can check as many document types as you wish. If a document type you use is not included on this form, click the Other check box, then enter the name of the document type in the field next to Other."
   e. Click OK to return to the Form Field Options dialog box, then click OK to return to the form.
   f. Save your changes to the form.
7. **Prepare a form for a user.**
   a. Click the Form Field Shading button on the Forms toolbar to turn field shading off.
   b. Click in the second table, click Table on the menu bar if necessary, then click Table AutoFormat.
   c. Click Grid 8, then click OK.
   d. Click anywhere in the first table, apply the Columns 5 AutoFormat, then increase the width of the second column so that its right edge is approximately even with the right edge of the second table.
   e. Click the Zoom list arrow on the Standard toolbar, then click Page Width.
   f. Click the Protect Form button on the Forms toolbar.
   g. Click the Save button on the Standard toolbar, then close the template.
8. **Fill out a form as a user.**
   a. Click File on the menu bar, click New, then double-click Office Survey.
   b. Save the form as "Analyst Survey" to your Project Disk, then in the Employee Name field enter your name.
   c. Press [Tab], in the Department Number field type "33", then press [Tab], click the Category arrow, then click administrative assistant.
   d. Click the first check box, read the text that appears on the status bar, then press [F1] and read the message.
   e. Click OK to close the Help window, press [Tab] to move to the next field, click the list arrow, click once/week, then press [Tab] and enter 4 in the last column.
   f. Complete the form as shown in Figure O-20.
   g. Save the document, print a copy, then close the document and exit Word.

FIGURE O-20

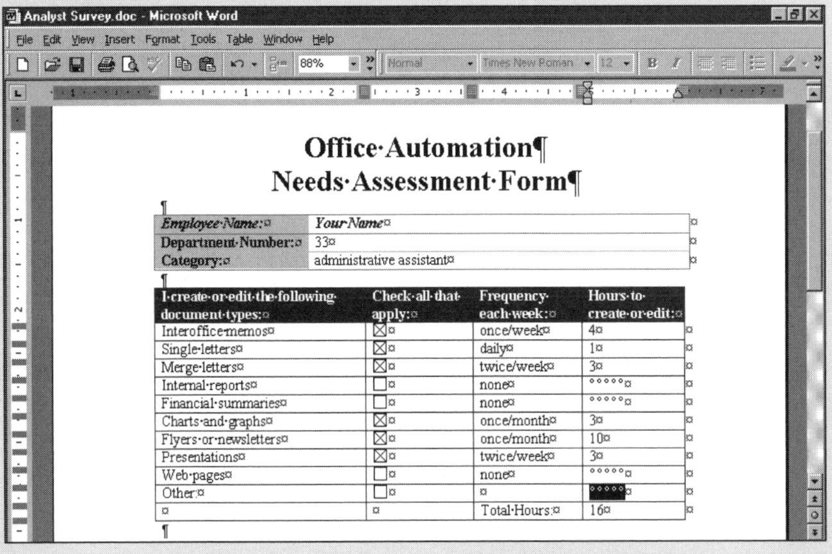

Office·Automation
Needs·Assessment·Form

Employee·Name:	*YourName*
Department·Number:	33
Category:	administrative assistant

I·create·or·edit·the·following·document·types:	Check·all·that·apply:	Frequency·each·week:	Hours·to·create·or·edit:
Interoffice·memos	☒	once/week	4
Single·letters	☒	daily	1
Merge·letters	☒	twice/week	3
Internal·reports	☐	none	° ° ° ° °
Financial·summaries	☐	none	° ° ° ° °
Charts·and·graphs	☒	once/month	3
Flyers·or·newsletters	☒	once/month	10
Presentations	☒	twice/week	3
Web·pages	☐	none	° ° ° ° °
Other:	☐		° ° ° ° °
		Total·Hours:	16

► Visual Workshop

As the compensation administrator in a company that provides financial and accounting consulting, you want to make it easy for the consultants to complete their travel expense forms so that they can get reimbursed promptly. By providing the consultants with a form they can complete online, you give them the ability to complete the form while they are out of the office. They can then e-mail you their completed forms. Create a form template that looks like the form shown in Figure O-21. Save the form to your Project Disk as "CPA Group". Type your name at the bottom of the document, save it, print a copy, and then close the document.

FIGURE O-21

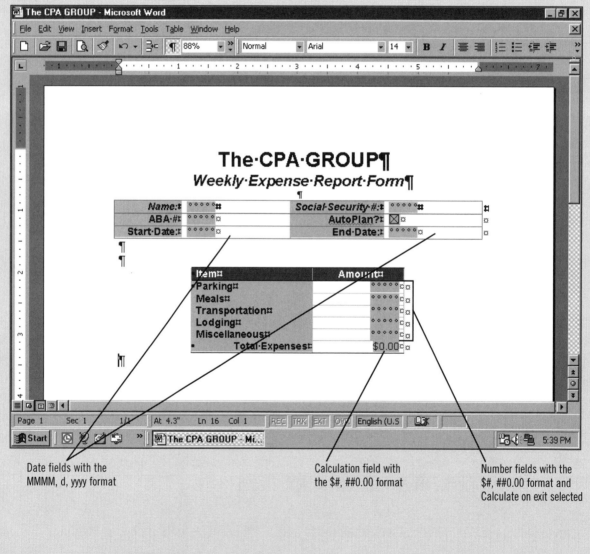

Date fields with the MMMM, d, yyyy format

Calculation field with the $#, ##0.00 format

Number fields with the $#, ##0.00 format and Calculate on exit selected

Customizing
Word with AutoText and Macros

Objectives

► **Create and insert an AutoText entry**
[MOUS] ► **Create a macro**
[MOUS] ► **Apply a macro**
[MOUS] ► **Edit a macro**
[MOUS] ► **Copy, rename, and delete macros**
[MOUS] ► **Customize a toolbar**
[MOUS] ► **Use a custom toolbar**
► **Modify options**

Word offers many features that you can use to automate the tasks you perform repeatedly. You can create AutoText entries for words and phrases that you use frequently, and you can create macros to automate Word procedures that you need to perform quickly. You can also create a custom toolbar to which you can add the buttons you use most, and change the default options related to a variety of Word functions, such as measurement units, saving methods, and spell checking options. Scenario► Each week, Maria Abbott in the marketing department receives book reviews of new novels from freelance reviewers. When Maria receives a review, she formats it consistently, then prints and distributes it as a handout at MediaLoft stores. She decides to use AutoText, macros, and custom toolbars to help her streamline the formatting process. She also wants to modify default options to more efficiently work with the reviews.

Unit P

Word 2000

Creating and Inserting an AutoText Entry

You can use the AutoText feature to store text selections you frequently insert in documents. An **AutoText entry** can consist of a standard closing to a letter, a request for information, a company name, or any word, phrase, or longer text selection. Once you've created an AutoText entry, you can insert it at the insertion point in a document either by using the Insert menu or by typing the name of the AutoText entry and then pressing [F3]. For example, you could create an AutoText entry called mlb that displays the text MediaLoft Boston when you type mlb and then press [F3]. Scenario Maria decides to create an AutoText entry for the paragraph of standard text she normally types above each of the book reviews she chooses for a particular week. Her first step is to type the text for which she will create the AutoText entry.

Steps 1 2 3 4

1. Start Word, in a new document type **Each week, MediaLoft provides its customers with an in-depth review of our best-selling work of fiction. If you are interested in writing your own book review, please contact Maria Abbott at mabbott@medialoft.com**., then press **[Enter]**
   You don't want Maria's e-mail address to appear in blue text and underlined because you plan to distribute the document in print form.
2. Right-click **mabbott@medialoft.com**, point to **Hyperlink**, then click **Remove Hyperlink**
   Now that you have the text you want to designate as an AutoText entry, you are ready to create the entry.
3. Select the entire **paragraph**, click **Insert** on the menu bar, point to **AutoText**, then click **New**
   The Create AutoText dialog box opens, as shown in Figure P-1. Word provides a suggested name for the AutoText entry based on the text selection. You decide to change the default name "Each week" to a shorter name, **mlr**, which stands for MediaLoft review. The default name is selected so you can simply begin typing to replace it.
4. Type **mlr**, then click **OK**
   The entry is created and the dialog box closes. You can close the current document without saving it because the AutoText entry is saved as part of the Normal template, not as part of the current document. Word saves AutoText entries as part of the Normal template so that they are available in any document you create. You are ready to insert the AutoText entry into the first review Maria has chosen for the second week of March.
5. Close the document without saving it, open the document named **WD P-1** on your Project Disk, then save it as **March Week 2 Reviews**
   You want the AutoText entry you just created to appear above the first review.
6. Click **Insert** on the menu bar, point to **AutoText**, point to **Normal**, then click **mlr**
   The text appears in the document. You can also insert an AutoText entry by typing its name and pressing [F3]. This method saves you time when you have assigned a short, easy-to-type name to the AutoText entry.
7. Scroll down to the first line of the next review ("*Darkling Dawn* by David Dread"), click in the blank line above the review, then press **[Enter]** twice
8. Type **mlr**, then press **[F3]**
   The entire paragraph of text appears as shown in Figure P-2.
9. Save the document

QuickTip

You can triple-click to select an entire paragraph at once.

FIGURE P-1: Create AutoText dialog box

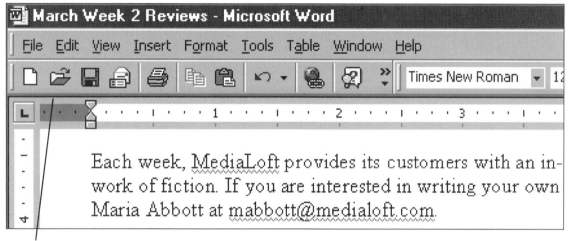

To name an AutoText selection, you can use the default name that appears or you can type a different name

FIGURE P-2: AutoText entry inserted

Each week, MediaLoft provides its customers with an in-
work of fiction. If you are interested in writing your own
Maria Abbott at mabbott@medialoft.com.

mlr AutoText entry

Creating AutoCorrect exceptions

In addition to creating your own AutoText entries, you can save time by using the hundreds of AutoCorrect entries included with Word. AutoCorrect entries help ensure your documents are error free. For example, when you type a period after a word, the AutoCorrect feature automatically capitalizes the next word you type, because a period usually identifies the end of a sentence. AutoCorrect also corrects common mis-spellings. For example, when you type "recieve", Word automatically corrects the spelling to "receive". One of the ways in which you can customize Word to match your working style is to create your own list of AutoCorrect exceptions. For example, suppose you want to use the abbreviation "Mass." for Massachusetts in your documents but you do *not* want Word to auto-matically capitalize the next word after the period. To create an AutoCorrect exception, click Tools on the menu bar, point to AutoCorrect, then click Exceptions. In the AutoCorrect Exceptions dialog box, type the word (including the period) in the Don't capitalize after box, click Add, then click OK.

Word 2000

Creating a Macro

When you find you are executing the same series of commands on a regular basis, such as a procedure like saving, printing, and closing a document, you have a good reason to create a macro. A **macro** is a series of Word commands that you assign to a single command. When you invoke this command, the series of tasks you recorded in the macro are performed automatically. Since Word can execute commands faster than you can, macros save time. Also, Word will never make an error when you run the macro. Each macro you create is stored in the Normal template, which means you can run the macro from any document. To minimize errors, you should record your macros in a blank document where you can experiment with them without being concerned about making changes that you might not be able to reverse later. **Scenario** When Maria formats a review, she double-spaces the entire document and formats the text with the Arial font and 14-point font size. She decides to create her macro in a blank document to make sure the steps work.

Steps

QuickTip

Click the More Buttons button on the Standard toolbar to show the Show/Hide ¶ button, if necessary.

1. Click the **New Document button** 🗋 on the Standard toolbar, click the **Show/Hide ¶ button** ¶ on the Standard toolbar to display paragraph marks if necessary, then press **[Enter]** three times
   You show the paragraph marks so that you will be able to see the formatting changes you are about to record. Now you are ready to record the macro.

2. Click **Tools** on the menu bar, point to **Macro**, then click **Record New Macro**
   The Record Macro dialog box opens, where you can name and begin recording a macro. A macro name can be up to 25 characters long and cannot include spaces. See the Clues to learn more about working in the Record Macro dialog box.

3. In the Macro name box, type **FormatReview**, select the contents of the Description box, type **This macro selects all the text, applies 1.5 spacing, and then formats the text in Arial and 14-point.**, compare the Record Macro dialog box to Figure P-3, then click **OK**
   The dialog box closes and the macro toolbar appears in the document window as shown in Figure P-4, along with the Macro pointer 🖰, which indicates you are recording. The first step you want to record is selecting all the text in the document. You cannot select text with the mouse when you are recording a macro because Word cannot record mouse selections. You therefore need to use a keyboard or menu command.

QuickTip

You can also select all the text in a document by clicking Edit on the menu bar, then clicking Select All.

4. Press **[Ctrl][A]**
   Word records the Select All command in the macro. Now you can apply 1.5 line spacing to the selection.

5. Click **Format** on the menu bar, click **Paragraph**, click the **Indents and Spacing tab** if necessary, click the **Line spacing list arrow**, click **1.5 lines**, then click **OK**
   The formatting change is applied and the command is recorded in the macro.

QuickTip

You can click the Pause button on the Macro Record toolbar to temporarily stop recording. You can then perform steps to see if they work without recording them. When you are ready to continue recording the macro, click the Pause button again to resume recording.

6. Click the **Font list arrow** on the Formatting toolbar, click **Arial**, click the **Font Size list arrow**, then click **14**
   Now you need to deselect the text. You cannot use the mouse to deselect text while you are recording a macro.

7. Press **[Down Arrow]** ↓ once
   You have completed all the steps that you want the FormatReview macro to perform.

8. Click the **Stop button** ■ on the Macro Record toolbar
   The pointer returns to the default pointer shape and the Macro Record toolbar closes.

9. Close the document without saving it
   By default, the macro is stored in the Normal template so you don't need to save the document in which you created the macro.

FIGURE P-3: Record Macro dialog box

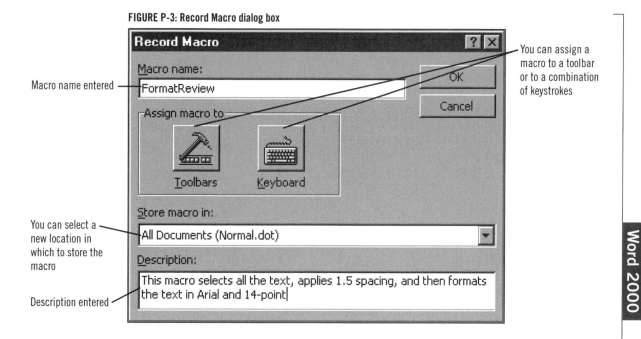

Macro name entered → Macro name: FormatReview

You can assign a macro to a toolbar or to a combination of keystrokes

Assign macro to — Toolbars   Keyboard

You can select a new location in which to store the macro → Store macro in: All Documents (Normal.dot)

Description entered → Description: This macro selects all the text, applies 1.5 spacing, and then formats the text in Arial and 14-point

FIGURE P-4: Recording the macro

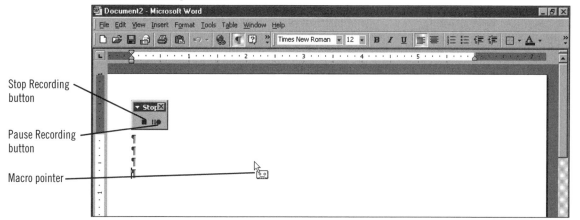

Stop Recording button

Pause Recording button

Macro pointer

Working in the Record Macro dialog box

In the Record Macro dialog box, you give a new macro a name and a description. A macro description should list all the tasks the macros will perform both to help you remember the macro contents and to help other users who might use the macro. In this dialog box you can also determine how you want to apply the macro. For example, you can choose to use a keyboard combination to apply a macro, to run the macro from the Macros dialog box, or to assign the macro to a toolbar. Finally, you can designate where you want to store the macro. For example, you can choose to store the macro only in the current document or you can store it in the Normal template. When you store a macro in the Normal template, it is available to all documents.

Word 2000

Applying a Macro

Once you have recorded a macro, you **apply**, or run the macro, and then the commands you recorded are performed. How you apply a macro depends upon the choices you made when creating it. You can run a macro by selecting it in the Macros dialog box, by clicking a button you have assigned to a toolbar, or by pressing a keyboard combination. You can also select additional methods for applying a macro once you have created it. [Scenario] Maria is ready to apply the FormatReview macro to the March Week 2 Reviews document. She also wants to be able to run the macro using a keyboard shortcut, so she needs to open the Keyboard Shortcuts dialog box and assign one.

Trouble?

Additional macros may appear in the Macros dialog box on your system if you or other users have already created macros.

1. With the March Week 2 Reviews document open on your screen, click **Tools**, point to **Macro**, then click **Macros**
   The Macros dialog box opens, as shown in Figure P-5. As you can see, the description provides information about the selected macro. This description is particularly useful if you have several macros listed in the Macros dialog box.

2. In the Macro name list, click the **FormatReview** macro, then click **Run**
   The macro you recorded selects all the text in the document, applies 1.5 spacing, formats the text with the Arial font and 14-point, then deselects the text. Because Maria prefers keyboard shortcuts to menu commands, she decides to assign a keyboard shortcut to the macro. You can assign a keyboard shortcut in the Record Macro dialog box when you create a macro, or in the Customize Keyboard dialog box any time after creating a macro.

3. Click **Tools**, click **Customize**, then click **Keyboard**
   The Customize Keyboard dialog box opens. In this dialog box, you can assign a keystroke combination to a macro or any other command. When assigning a keystroke combination to a macro, you should select a combination that is not already assigned to another command.

4. In the Categories list, scroll to and click **Macros**
   A list of the macros currently stored with your default template appears in the Macros box. Depending on the macros already stored on your computer system, your list might look different.

5. Make sure the **FormatReview** macro is selected
   The keyboard combination you enter will be applied to the selected macro, so if several macros are stored on your computer, make sure that you select the correct macro before proceeding.

6. Click in the **Press new shortcut key text box**, press **[Alt][R]** as shown in Figure P-6, click **Assign**, click **Close**, then click **Close** to return to the document
   Since you have already applied the FormatReview macro to the March Week 2 Reviews document, you decide to test the new keyboard shortcut on another review.

7. Close the **March Week 2 Reviews** document, save it, open the **WD P-2** document, then save it as **March Week 3 Review**

8. Press **[Alt][R]**
   The FormatReview macro runs.

9. Scroll to the top of the document, compare it to Figure P-7, then save the document

FIGURE P-5: Macros dialog box

Only macros in the active templates and documents are listed

The description provides useful information about the tasks performed by the macro

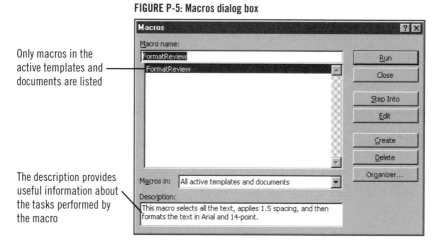

FIGURE P-6: Customize Keyboard dialog box

FormatReview macro selected

Macros selected in the Categories list

[Alt][R] shortcut keys entered

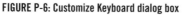
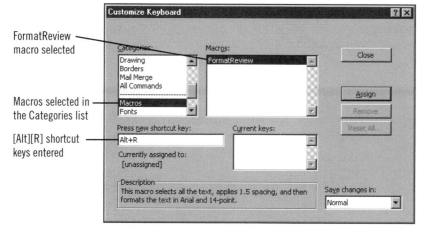

FIGURE P-7: Text enhanced with FormatReview macro

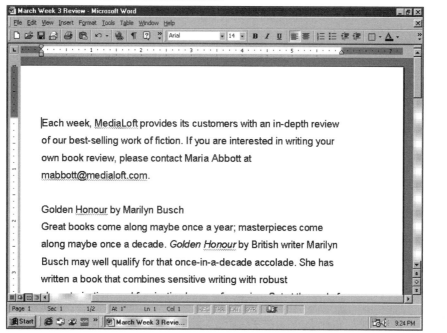

Editing a Macro

After you have recorded a macro, you might discover that you want to make changes to it. You edit a macro in the Microsoft Visual Basic window. Visual Basic is the programming language in which macros in Word are recorded. When you record a macro, Word assigns a Visual Basic code to each task performed by the macro. You can view and edit these codes in the Visual Basic window. Suppose, for example, that you've created a macro that contains a step for increasing the font size of selected text to 12-point, but you now want the font size increased to 14-point. You can open the macro for editing in the Visual Basic window, find the code related to font size, and then change 12-point to 14-point. **Scenario** Maria wants to edit the FormatReview macro to apply double spacing, the Arial Rounded MT Bold font, and 12-point font size instead of the current formatting attributes.

Steps 1 2 3 4

1. **Click Tools on the menu bar, point to Macro, then click Macros**
   The Macros dialog box opens and the FormatReview macro appears in the list of available macros.

2. **Click FormatReview to select it, if necessary, then click Edit**
   In a few moments, Microsoft Visual Basic opens. In the main pane, you see a list of codes. These codes were inserted as you performed the steps included in the FormatReview macro. The text to the left of the equals sign represents the code for a specific attribute such as LeftIndent or SpaceBefore. As you can see, these codes do not include spaces. The text to the right of the equals sign represents the attribute setting. For example, the space before a paragraph setting is set to 0 while WidowControl is currently turned on. While you would need to study programming in order to work extensively with the codes in the Visual Basic window, you can quickly learn how to make simple changes and even add new lines of code. For now, you will change the line spacing from 1.5 to Double.

3. **Click at the end of the line LineSpacingRule = wdLineSpace1pt5 as shown in Figure P-8**

4. **Press [Backspace] to delete just the characters 1pt5, then type Double**
   The macro has been changed to format the document with double spacing. Now you can change the font and font size specifications.

   Trouble?

   If you make an error, the line will turn red and a message will appear. Make sure you type the required text exactly as shown.

5. **Scroll down the page to the line Selection.Font.Name = "Arial", replace the text Arial with the text Arial Rounded MT Bold (keep the quotation marks), then replace the text Arial in the next line with the text Arial Rounded MT Bold**

6. **Select 14 in the line Selection.Font.Size = 14, then type 12**
   The three revised lines of code appear as shown in Figure P-9. Now you need to save your work and then switch to the Word document to test the results of your edits.

7. **Click the Save button 🖫 on the Standard toolbar, then click the View Microsoft Word button 🔟 on the Standard toolbar**

8. **Press [Alt][R] to run the macro, then press [Ctrl][Home] to move to the top of the document**
   The document is formatted in double spacing, Arial Rounded MT Bold, and 12-point. Now that you are sure that the revised macro works, you can close Microsoft Visual Basic.

9. **Click Microsoft Visual Basic on the taskbar, click the Close button in the Microsoft Visual Basic window, compare your document to Figure P-10, type your name at the bottom of the document, save it, print a copy, then close the document**

FIGURE P-8: Macro code in Microsoft Visual Basic window

Properties window displays the list of macros you can edit

Name of the macro being edited

In Step 3, click here

Attribute codes (to left of equals signs)

Attribute settings (to right of equals signs)

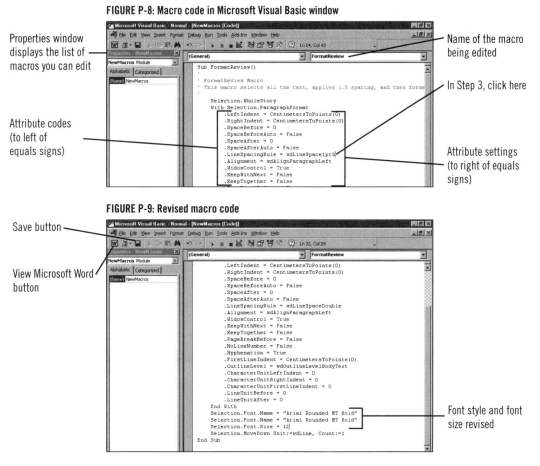

FIGURE P-9: Revised macro code

Save button

View Microsoft Word button

Font style and font size revised

FIGURE P-10: Edited macro applied to document

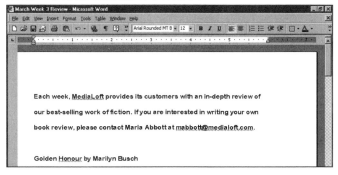

Each week, MediaLoft provides its customers with an in-depth review of our best-selling work of fiction. If you are interested in writing your own book review, please contact Maria Abbott at mabbott@medialoft.com.

Golden Honour by Marilyn Busch

Finding Visual Basic codes

Even if you are not a Visual Basic programmer, you can learn how to enter simple codes into the Visual Basic window. To find these codes, open Microsoft Visual Basic, click Help on the menu bar, then click Microsoft Word Visual Basic Help. You then type a brief description of the action you want to perform. For example, suppose you want the FormatReview macro to include a command for enclosing the document with a page border. You would type "page border", press [Enter], select the description related to page borders from the list of actions that appears, then copy the lines of code provided. You would then paste the lines in the Microsoft Visual Basic window in the location where you want the action to be performed. Always make sure that you insert new lines of code above the "End Sub" code and not between lines of codes related to other tasks.

Word 2000

Copying, Renaming, and Deleting Macros

Sometimes you may receive a document that contains a macro you would like to run in one of your own documents. You can copy macros stored in a document to another document or template—even to the Normal template where the macro will then be available to any document you open. You use the Organizer dialog box to copy macros and to rename and delete them. **Scenario** Barry Gray, one of the book review authors, has sent Maria a document that contains the macro he used to format his book review. Maria wants to copy the macro from Barry's document to a Word document that contains the review she wants to use for the last week in March. She will then run the macro to see if she wants to use it.

Steps

Trouble?

If the dialog box containing the Enable Macros option does not appear, see the Clues for information about setting the macro security level to medium.

1. Open the document **WD P-3**, click **Enable Macros**, then save the document as **March Week 4 Review**
   Now you are ready to copy a macro from the March Week 4 Review document to the March Week 2 Reviews document.

2. Click **Tools** on the menu bar, point to **Macro**, click **Macros**, then click **Organizer**
   The Organizer dialog box appears as shown in Figure P-11. By default, the macros in the current document are listed in the left side of the dialog box and the macros in the Normal template are listed in the right side of the dialog box. Before copying a macro, the following files need to be open in this dialog box: the **source file**, the file that contains the macro you are copying, and the **target file**, the file to which you want to copy the macro. The source file is already open. You now need to open the target file.

3. Click **Close File** under the right-hand list in the Organizer dialog box, click **Open File**, navigate to the location of the March Week 2 Reviews document, click the **Files of type list arrow**, click **All Word Documents**, click **March Week 2 Reviews**, then click **Open**
   Since only templates are listed by default, you need to specify that you want to open a Word document instead of a template.

4. Click **Copy** as shown in Figure P-12, click **Close**, then click **Yes** to save the document

5. Close the **March Week 4 Review** document, open the document **March Week 2 Reviews**, click **Enable Macros**, click **Tools** on the menu bar, point to **Macro**, click **Macros**, click **BookReviewFormat**, then click **Run**
   The BookReviewFormat macro formats the March Week 2 Reviews document with double spacing, the Garamond font, a 14-point font size, and a 2¼ page border. You decide that you don't really like Barry's macro and would prefer to format all your documents with the FormatReview macro you've already created. You can close the document without saving these changes; then, since you won't be using Barry's macro, you can delete it.

6. Close the document without saving it, open **March Week 2 Reviews** again, then click **Enable Macros**

7. Click **Tools** on the menu bar, point to **Macro**, click **Macros**, click **BookReviewFormat**, click **Delete**, then click **Yes**
   You decide that the FormatReview macro name is too long. You will change its name to Review.

8. Click **FormatReview**, click **Edit**, select **FormatReview** following **Sub** at the top of the New Macros (Code) window as shown in Figure P-13, type **Review**, close Microsoft Visual Basic, click **Tools** on the menu bar, click **Macro**, then click **Macros**
   The Review macro name appears in place of the FormatReview macro.

9. Close the Macros dialog box, insert a hard page break below the first review, type your name at the bottom of the document, save the document, print a copy, then close the document

FIGURE P-11: Organizer dialog box

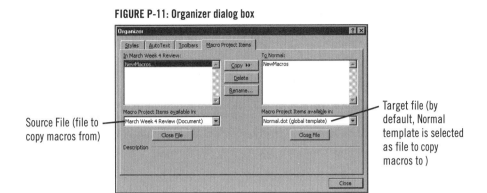

Source File (file to copy macros from)

Target file (by default, Normal template is selected as file to copy macros to)

FIGURE P-12: Copying a macro

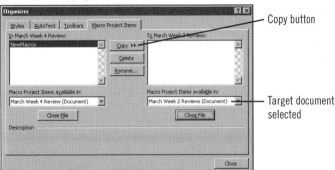

Copy button

Target document selected

FIGURE P-13: Macro name selected

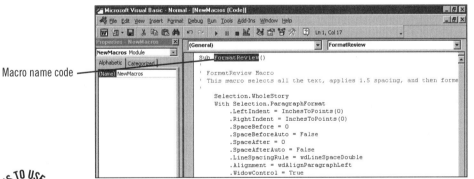

Macro name code

Changing security levels

When you open a document containing a macro, you run the risk of introducing a macro virus into your system. To safeguard against viruses, you can choose from three security levels in Word. A **High** security level allows you to run only macros that have been digitally signed and that you know originated from a trusted source. Unsigned macros are automatically disabled, and Word opens the document without any warning. For more information about how to digitally sign a macro, consult the Help files in Word. A **Medium** security level is the default setting. Word displays a warning whenever it encounters a macro from a source that is not on your list of trusted sources. You can choose whether to enable or disable the macros when you open the document. If the document might contain a virus, you should choose to disable macros. A **Low** security level turns off macro virus protection in Word. At this security level, macros are always enabled when you open documents. To change the security level, click Tools on the menu bar, click Macro, click Security, then select the security level you require. The recommended level is Medium, which allows you to choose whether to enable or disable macros contained in a document when you open it.

CUSTOMIZING WORD WITH AUTOTEXT AND MACROS WORD P-11 ◀

Customizing a Toolbar

As you've worked with Word, you have seen how it automatically customizes the Standard and Formatting toolbars to suit your personal working style. You can also customize any toolbar yourself by adding and removing buttons so that the toolbar always contains exactly the buttons you use most. You can also create your own custom toolbar that contains buttons for your favorite features, including your own macros and even hyperlinks to other documents or to pages on the World Wide Web. **Scenario** Maria would like to create a toolbar that contains buttons for the features and commands she uses most when preparing and printing the book reviews. The toolbar will contain the Spelling and Grammar button, a button linked to the Amazon.com Web site where Maria frequently checks for additional book reviews, and a button to run the Review macro.

Steps

1. Click **View** on the menu bar, point to **Toolbars**, click **Customize**, click the **Toolbars tab**, then click **New**

   The New Toolbar dialog box appears. In this dialog box, you enter a name for the new toolbar and designate where the toolbar should be stored. By default, the toolbar will be stored in the Normal template and therefore available to all documents.

Trouble?

If your toolbar is partially obscured by the dialog box, drag it to a clear area of the screen.

2. In the Toolbar name box, type **Book Review**, then click **OK**

   The new toolbar appears without any buttons, as shown in Figure P-14. In the Customize dialog box you can select the buttons and commands you want to appear on your custom toolbar.

3. Click the **Commands tab**, then in the Categories list, click **Tools**

   Once you have located the button you want to include on your toolbar, you just click on it and drag it to the toolbar.

4. Click and drag the **Spelling and Grammar button** 🔲 to the **Book Review toolbar** as shown in Figure P-15

   You can also place a button containing a hyperlink on a toolbar.

5. In the Categories list, click **Web**, scroll down the Commands list, click and drag the **Hyperlink button** 🔲 to the **Book Review** toolbar, click **Modify Selection** in the dialog box, point to **Assign Hyperlink**, then click **Open**

   The Assign Hyperlink: Open dialog box appears. In this dialog box you designate where the hyperlink should point to by selecting from one of four options in the Link to: column.

6. Make sure the **Existing File or Web Page browse button** is selected, type **www.amazon.com** in the Type the file or Web page name text box, then click **OK**

   The http:// preface automatically appears when you start typing the Web page URL.

7. In the Categories list, scroll to and click **Macros**, click **Normal.NewMacros.Review**, then drag it to the custom toolbar

   The macro name includes the location where the macro is stored (the Normal template), the Project Name assigned to the macro (NewMacros), and the name of the macro (Review).

8. Click the **Modify Selection button**, point to **Change Button Image**, then click the first button in the first row as shown in Figure P-16

9. Click the **Modify Selection button**, click **Text Only (in Menus)**, then click **Close** in the Customize dialog box

   Compare your toolbar to Figure P-17. Your toolbar will appear somewhere in the middle of your screen. You will use the new toolbar in the next lesson.

FIGURE P-14: New Book Review toolbar

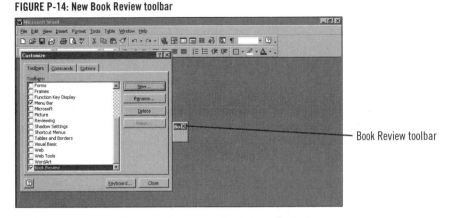

— Book Review toolbar

FIGURE P-15: Spelling and Grammar button dragged to Book Review toolbar

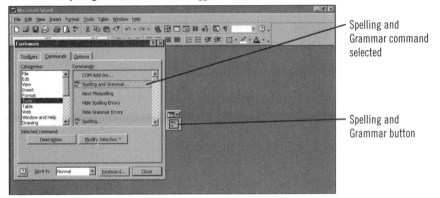

— Spelling and Grammar command selected

— Spelling and Grammar button

FIGURE P-16: Icon selected for the Macro button

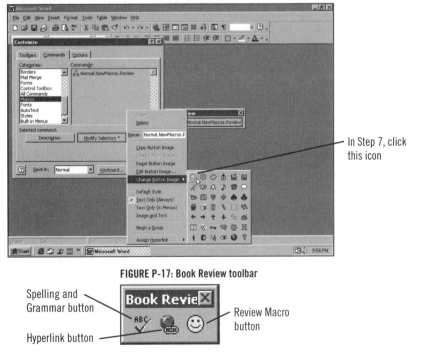

— In Step 7, click this icon

FIGURE P-17: Book Review toolbar

Spelling and Grammar button —

Hyperlink button —

— Review Macro button

Using a Custom Toolbar

You use a custom toolbar in the same way you use other toolbars in Word, by simply clicking the button you want. You can also position your custom toolbar anywhere in the document window or you can **dock** it, or move it to the top of the document window, below the other Word toolbars. Scenario▶ Maria decides to try out her new toolbar by formatting the review she plans to use for the first week in April. She will check the spelling of the document, center the review title, apply the Review macro, then check the Amazon.com Web site for additional reviews. She will also insert the mlr AutoText entry she created earlier.

Steps 1 2 3 4

1. Open the document **WD P-4**, save it as **April Week 1 Review**, drag the **Book Review toolbar** to the top of the document window (just above the ruler), then release the mouse button
When you release the mouse, the toolbar is docked below the Standard toolbar, as shown in Figure P-18.

2. Click the **Spelling and Grammar button** 📝 on the Book Review toolbar, ignore the suggested spelling for MediaLoft and Maria's e-mail address, accept the corrected spelling of "enough", "unforgettable", and "enjoyment", then click **OK**

3. Click the **Review Macro button** 😊 to format the review using the Review macro
While you like the current review, you decide to check out other reviews of the book on the Amazon.com Web site just to make sure that the author of the book review is on the right track.

Trouble?

If you inadvertently clicked the Insert Hyperlink button on the Standard toolbar, click Cancel, then click the Hyperlink button on the Book Review toolbar.

4. Click the **Hyperlink button** 🖳 on the Book Review toolbar
You may be prompted to connect to the Internet. In a few moments, the Amazon.com Web site appears in your Web browser similar to Figure P-19. Note that the page will look different on your system because Amazon.com updates its Web site frequently. In the future, Maria can use this button whenever she wants to conduct a search for a book on the Amazon.com Web site and find current reviews.

5. Close your Web browser and disconnect from the Internet if necessary, then maximize the Word window containing the April Week 1 Review document
Now that you have finished using the Book Review toolbar, you can close it.

6. **Right-click** the Book Review toolbar, then click **Book Review** to deselect it
You can also delete a custom toolbar. If you are working on a computer that other users access, you should delete your custom toolbars so that they don't interfere with how other users wish to work.

7. Click **View** on the menu bar, point to **Toolbars**, click **Customize**, click the **Toolbars tab**, click **Book Review** to select it, make sure the check box next to **Book Review** is also selected, click **Delete**, click **OK**, then click **Close**

8. Click the **Save button** 💾 on the Standard toolbar

FIGURE P-18: Book Review toolbar docked above the Ruler bar

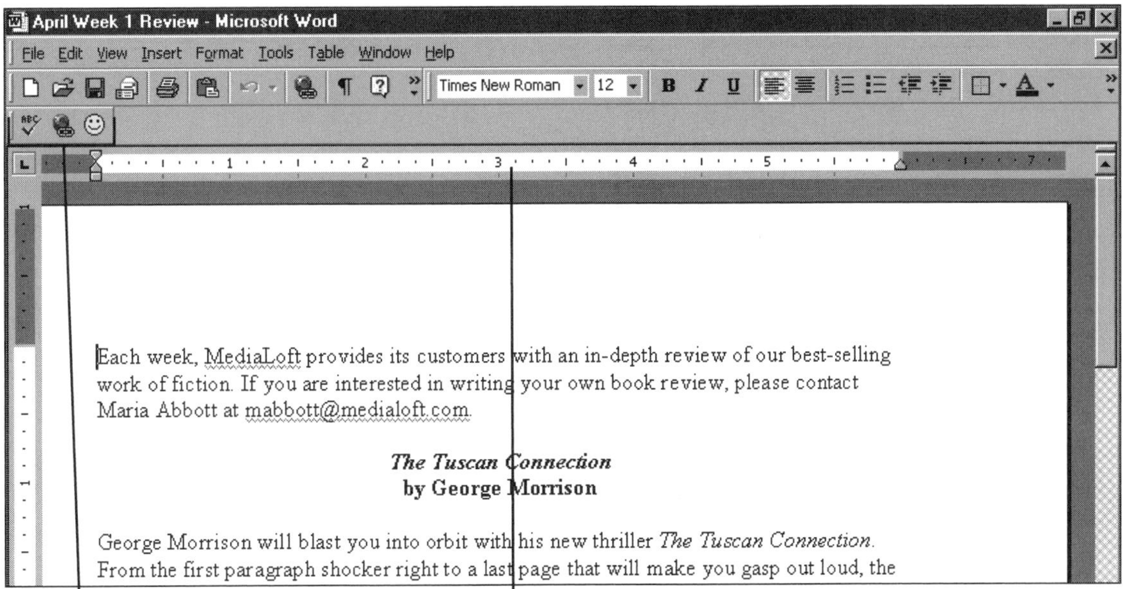

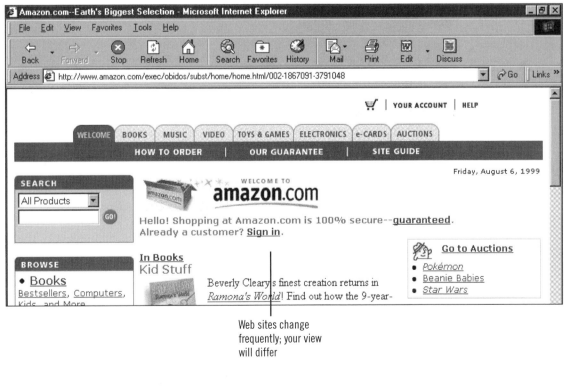

Book Review toolbar

Ruler bar

FIGURE P-19: Amazon.com Web site

Web sites change frequently; your view will differ

Word 2000

Modifying Default Settings

Word 2000 — Unit P

Word operates within a variety of default settings designed to meet the needs of most users. For example, the default measurement unit is inches and AutoCorrect exceptions are set to correct words containing two initial capital letters by making the second letter lowercase. Using the Options dialog box, you can change the default settings for a variety of options including viewing options, editing options, tracking options, and saving options. **Scenario** Maria decides to change some of the settings in the Options dialog box to better suit her working style. First, she needs to change the default measurement unit to centimeters so that the reviews conform to new company style guidelines requiring all in-house publications to have 2-centimeter margins. She also wants to modify the Spelling and Grammar feature so that the readability statistics of the document are displayed following the spell check; she can then determine if the reading level of the document is suitable for MediaLoft clientele. Finally, she will activate the fast saves option because she wants to make sure that her documents are automatically saved every five minutes.

Steps 1 2 3 4

1. Click **Tools** on the menu bar, then click **Options**
   The Options dialog box appears. In this dialog box you can change settings in a broad range of categories. To change the measurement unit, you need to look in the General tab, which also contains settings related to such options as sound and animation effects and file list entries.

2. Click the **General tab**, click the **Measurement units list arrow**, then click **Centimeters** as shown in Figure P-20
   Next, you want the readability statistics for a document to appear following the spell checking process. You need to select the required option from the Spelling & Grammar tab, which contains options related to how Word checks your documents for spelling and grammar errors.

3. Click the **Spelling & Grammar tab**, then click the **Show readability statistics check box** as shown in Figure P-21
   Finally, you want to set Word to perform fast saves. In the Save tab you can also set password options, and choose which prompts related to saving you want Word to display.

4. Click the **Save tab**, click the **Allow fast saves check box**, then click **OK**
   You are returned to the document. Note that the numbers on the Ruler bar now represent centimeters instead of inches. You need to change the left and right margins to 2 centimeters.

5. Click **File** on the menu bar, click **Page Setup**, change the **Left margin** to **2 centimeters**, change the **Right margin** to **2 centimeters**, then click **OK**
   Now you can test the readability level of the April Week 1 Review and determine how many words it contains.

6. Click **Tools** on the menu bar, click **Spelling and Grammar**, then ignore all the suggested changes until the readability statistics appear as shown in Figure P-22

7. Click **OK**
   The options you have changed will remain in effect until you or another user changes them. If you are the sole user of your computer, you don't need to change the options back to their default settings. However, if you are working on a computer that other users access, you need to restore the original options.

8. Click **Tools** on the menu bar, click **Options**, click the **General tab**, click the **Measurement units list arrow**, click **inches**, click the **Spelling & Grammar tab**, deselect the **Show readability statistics check box**, click the **Save tab**, then deselect the **Allow fast saves check box**

9. Click **OK** to exit the Options dialog box, type your name at the bottom of the document, preview it, print a copy, then save and close the document

FIGURE P-20: Changing the Measurement Units option

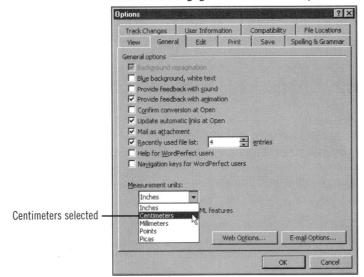

Centimeters selected ——

FIGURE P-21: Spelling & Grammar tab in the Options dialog box

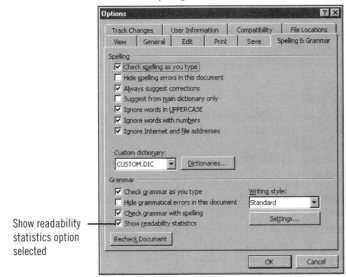

Show readability
statistics option
selected

FIGURE P-22: Readability statistics

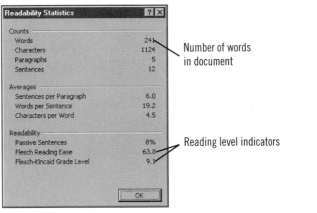

Number of words
in document

Reading level indicators

Practice

► Concepts Review

Label each of the elements of the screen shown in Figure P-23.

FIGURE P-23

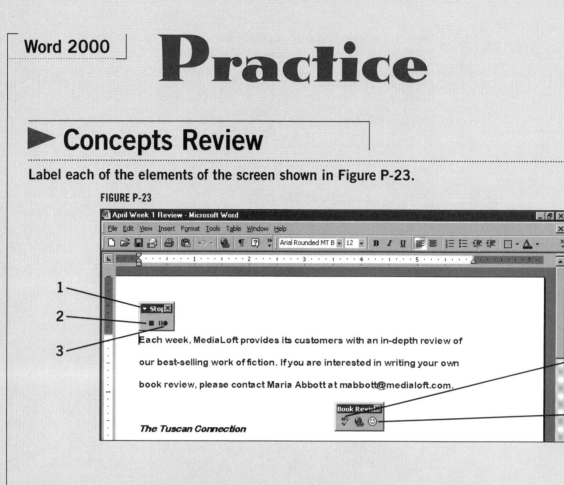

Match each of the following terms with the statement that best describes it.

6. LineSpacingRule = wdLineSpaceDouble
7. Microsoft Visual Basic window
8. Macro
9. Organizer dialog box
10. Macro toolbar
11. Options dialog box

a. Visual Basic code
b. Contains Stop and Pause buttons
c. Allows you to copy macros from one document to another
d. Contains user-controlled default settings for Word
e. Allows you to view and edit macro codes
f. Series of tasks performed automatically

Select the best answer from the list of choices.

12. Which of the following is an example of a possible AutoText entry?
   a. Your name.
   b. Complimentary closing to a letter.
   c. Company name.
   d. All of the above.
13. Which of the following describes the steps required to create a new macro?
   a. Double-click "REC" on the status bar.
   b. Click Tools on the menu bar, click Macro, then click Edit.
   c. Click Tools on the menu bar, then click Record Macro.
   d. Click Tools on the menu bar, click Macro, then click Record New Macro.
14. Which of the following Visual Basic codes represents the font style setting?
   a. Selection.Name = "Arial".
   b. Font.Name: "Arial".
   c. Selection.Font.Name = "Arial".
   d. Selection Name Font = Arial.

15. **In the Organizer dialog box, which macros are listed by default in the left side of the dialog box?**
    a. Macros contained in recently-opened documents.
    b. Macros contained in the Normal template.
    c. Macros contained in the target document.
    d. Macros contained in the source document.

16. **To which of the following locations can you assign a hyperlink?**
    a. An e-mail address.
    b. A place in the current document.
    c. A page on the World Wide Web.
    d. All of the above.

17. **Which tab in the Options dialog box do you click in order to set new measurement units?**
    a. General tab.
    b. View tab.
    c. Edit tab.
    d. Settings tab.

► Skills Review

1. **Insert an AutoText entry.**
   a. Start Word, turn on paragraph marks if necessary, then type "MediaLoft Boston."
   b. Select just the text without also selecting the paragraph mark, click Insert on the menu bar, point to AutoText, then click New.
   c. In the Create AutoText dialog box type "mlb", then click OK.
   d. Close the document without saving it, open the document named WD P-5, then save it to your Project Disk as "Book Review Contest".
   e. With your cursor positioned before "is" at the beginning of the first paragraph, click Insert on the menu bar, point to AutoText, point to Normal, click mlb, then press [Spacebar] once.
   f. At the end of the next sentence, click after "then drop it off at", to the left of the period type mlb, then press [F3].
   g. Save the document.

2. **Create a macro.**
   a. Click the New Document button on the Standard toolbar, click Table on the menu bar, point to Insert, click Table, accept the default table size, then click OK.
   b. Click Tools on the menu bar, point to Macro, then click Record New Macro.
   c. In the Macro name box, type "FormatTable", select the contents of the Description box, then type "This macro selects the table, applies 6 pt spacing above and below the text, then adds a solid line border to the entire table.", then click OK.
   d. Click Table on the menu bar, point to Select, then click Table.
   e. Click Format on the menu bar, click Paragraph, click the Indents and Spacing tab if necessary, change both the Before and After Spacing to 6 pt., then click OK.
   f. Click Format on the menu bar, click Borders and Shading, click the Borders tab if necessary, click the All box, then click OK.
   g. Press [Down Arrow] once to deselect the text.
   h. Click the Stop Recording button on the Macro Record toolbar, then close the document without saving it.

3. **Apply a macro.**
   a. With the Book Review Contest document open, click Tools, click Customize, then click Keyboard.
   b. In the Categories list, scroll to and click Macros.

   c. Make sure the FormatTable macro is selected, click in the Press new shortcut key box, press [Alt][C], click Assign, then click Close.

   d. Close the Customize dialog box, click in the table, press [Alt][C] to run the macro, then save the document.

4. **Edit a macro.**
   a. Click Tools on the menu bar, point to Macro, then click Macros.
   b. Click FormatTable to select it, then click Edit.
   c. Change the SpaceBefore to 3, and change the SpaceAfter to 18.
   d. Click the Save Normal button on the Standard toolbar, then click the View Microsoft Word button on the Standard toolbar.
   e. Make sure the insertion point is positioned in the table, then press [Alt][C] to run the macro.
   f. Click Microsoft Visual Basic on the taskbar, then click the Close button in the Microsoft Visual Basic window.
   g. Save and close the document.

5. **Copy, rename, and delete macros.**
   a. Open the document WD P-6, click Enable Macros, then save the document on your Project Disk as "San Diego Book Review Contest".
   b. Click Tools on the menu bar, point to Macro, click Macros, then click Organizer.
   c. Click Close File under the right-hand list in the Organizer dialog box, click Open File, navigate to the location of the Book Review Contest document, click the Files of type list arrow, click All Word Documents, click Book Review Contest, then click Open.
   d. Click Copy, click Close, click Yes to save the document, then close the document.
   e. Open the document "Book Review Contest", then click Enable Macros.
   f. Click on the table, click Tools on the menu bar, point to Macro, click Macros, click SanDiegoTableFormat, then click Run.
   g. Close the document without saving it, open the document again, then click Enable Macros.
   h. Click Tools on the menu bar, point to Macro, click Macros, click SanDiegoTableFormat, click Delete, then click Yes.
   i. In the Macros dialog box, click FormatTable, click Edit, select the text "FormatTable" following "Sub" at the top of the New Macros (Code) window, type "Table", then close the Microsoft Visual Basic window.
   j. Type your name at the bottom of the document, print a copy, then save and close the document.

6. **Customize a toolbar.**
   a. Click View on the menu bar, point to Toolbars, click Customize, click the Toolbars tab, then click New.
   b. In the Toolbar name box, type "Contest", then click OK.
   c. Click the Commands tab, then in the Categories list, click Web.
   d. Click and drag the Hyperlink button to the Contest toolbar.
   e. Click Modify Selection, point to Assign Hyperlink, then click Open.
   f. Make sure that Existing File or Web Page is selected, type "www.course.com/illustrated/MediaLoft" in the Type the file or Web page name text box, then click OK.
   g. In the Categories list, click Macros, then click and drag the Normal.NewMacros.Table macro to the custom toolbar.
   h. Change the button image to the red heart, and specify the Text Only (in Menus) option, then click Close in the Customize dialog box.

7. **Use a custom toolbar.**
   a. Open the document WD P-7, save it as Houston Book Review Contest, then drag the Contest toolbar to just above the Ruler bar.
   b. Click in the table, then click the Contest Macro button to format the table.
   c. Click the Hyperlink button on the Contest toolbar, connect to the Internet if necessary, click the About link on the MediaLoft site, then click the MediaLoft Houston link.

d. Select and copy the name of the General Manager of the MediaLoft Houston store, close your Web browser, disconnect from the Internet if necessary, then maximize the Word window containing the Houston Book Review Contest document.

e. Paste the name of the General Manager after the words "General Manager" in the second sentence of the Houston Book Review Contest document.

f. Right-click the Contest toolbar, then click Contest to deselect it.

g. Click View on the menu bar, point to Toolbars, click Customize, click the Toolbars tab, click Contest, click the check box next to Contest if necessary, click Delete, click OK, click Close, then save the document.

8. Modify options.

a. Click Tools on the menu bar, then click Options.

b. Click the General tab, then click the Blue background, white text check box to select it.

c. Click the Edit tab, then click the Allow accented uppercase in French check box to select it.

d. Click the Save tab, then click the Prompt for document properties check box to select it.

e. Click OK to exit the Options dialog box.

f. Click below the table, press [Enter] once, turn on Caps Lock, then type "SPONSORED IN PART BY THE CAFÉ PARIS."

g. Click the Save button on the Standard toolbar, enter "Houston Book Review Contest" as the Subject of the document, then click OK.

h. Click Tools on the menu bar, click Options, click the General tab, click the Blue background, white text check box to deselect it, click the Edit tab, click the Allow accented uppercase in French check box to deselect it, click the Save tab, then click the Prompt for document properties check box to deselect it.

i. Click OK to exit the Options dialog box.

j. Type your name at the bottom of the document, preview it, print a copy, then save and close the document.

► Visual Workshop

As the owner of Going to the Sun Tours, a small agency that conducts tours to Provence and Tuscany, you have hired a designer to create a new letterhead for the company. The designer has sent you a document containing the macro he used to create the letterhead. You decide to change the macro so that the sun picture in the letterhead is filled with a different color and the company name is formatted in a different font size and color. Open the document WD P-11, enable macros, then save the document as "Going to the Sun Tours Letterhead" to your Project Disk. In Visual Basic, modify the macro so that the codes appear as shown in Figure P-24. Note that you will need to change the font size to 24, the font color to DarkBlue, and the color of the sun object to 255, 180, 0. Run the SunTours macro on the document (make sure your cursor is positioned at the beginning of the document). Compare the modified letterhead to Figure P-25. Type your name a few lines below the letterhead, print a copy, then save and close the document.

FIGURE P-24

FIGURE P-25

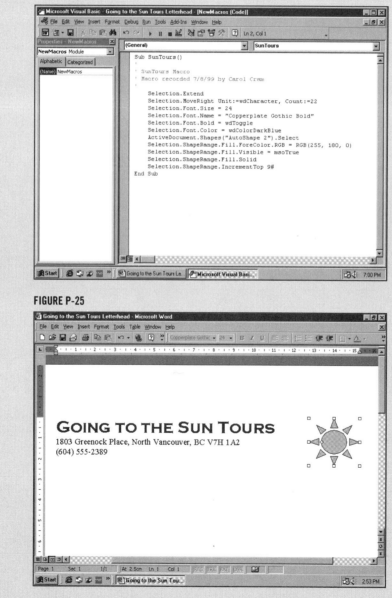

Glossary

ActiveX control A control or form element that you can insert in an online form. Text form fields, check boxes, and drop-down fields are all examples of ActiveX controls.

Alignment The horizontal position of text relative to page margins or tab stops; for example, left, center, or right.

Anchor Formatting feature that attaches a graphic object to a paragraph so that it moves with the paragraph if the paragraph moves.

Application See *program*.

Ascending order The sequence in which items are sorted from smallest to largest, or from A to Z.

AutoCorrect A feature that automatically corrects a misspelled word. Word provides several entries for commonly misspelled words, but you can add your own.

AutoFit A table formatting feature that automatically adjusts the width of a table to fit to the document margins.

AutoRecover A feature that automatically saves document changes in a temporary file at specified intervals, so you can recover some changes if power to your computer is interrupted.

AutoShape A drawing object, such as a circle, rectangle, triangle, or callout that is created using the Drawing toolbar.

AutoText entry A stored text or graphic you want to use again.

Bitmap A file format for graphics that is composed of pixels.

Boilerplate text Text that appears in every version of a merge document.

Bold Formatting in which text appears thicker and darker.

Bookmark A named location in a document. Bookmarks allow you to jump to specific locations, create hyperlinks, and include ranges of pages in an index.

Border A vertical or horizontal line you can add to the top, bottom or sides of paragraphs; also the line that divides cells in a table. You can format borders with different styles and colors.

Bullet A small graphic symbol, usually a round or square dot, often used to identify items in a list.

Callout A graphic object that calls attention to something in a document; contains text and a line that points to the item to which you want to call attention.

Cell The intersection of a row and a column in a table.

Cell reference Identifies a cell's position in a table. Each cell reference contains a letter (A, B, C, and so on) to identify its column and a number (1, 2, 3, and so on) to identify its row.

Center A form of paragraph alignment in which the lines of text are centered between the left and right margins.

Character spacing A form of character formatting that allows you to expand or condense the amount of space between characters, adjust the width (or scale) of characters, raise or lower characters, and adjust kerning.

Character style A stored set of font format settings that can be applied to words or characters within a paragraph.

Chart A visual or graphical representation of data. You generally create a chart to illustrate trends, relationships, or patterns.

Check box form field A field entered in an online form in a location where you want users to select or deselect a check box. You can insert a check box form field that contains a check box already selected or a blank check box.

Click To press and release a mouse button in one motion.

Click and Type A feature that allows you to insert text, graphics, and other items in a blank area of a document without having to apply formatting such as alignment.

Clip art A collection of pictures, sound clips, and motion clips that you can insert into a document.

Clipboard A temporary storage area for cut or copied items that are available for pasting. See *Office Clipboard*.

Clipboard toolbar A toolbar that shows the contents of the Office Clipboard; contains buttons for copying and pasting items to and from the Office Clipboard.

Column A vertical arrangement of cells in a table.

Column break A break inserted manually to force text to move to the top of the next column.

Comment Text that appears in a pop-up window when you position the pointer near a comment identifier. Double-clicking the comment identifier allows you to edit the comment text. In earlier versions of Word this feature was called "annotations."

Comment mark Identifying text that is inserted in the document at the point where you add a comment. The identifying text is the initials of the person who inserts the comment.

Compound document A document that contains an object created in another program.

Copy A command that copies a selected part of a document and places it on the Clipboard.

Cross-reference A statement in the document that refers the reader to another part of the document. When a user clicks on the statement, the insertion point jumps to the location. You can create cross-references to headings, footnotes, bookmarks, and other objects such as charts and tables.

Cut A command that removes a selected part of a document and places it on the Clipboard.

Data point The chart element that represent one set of data. In a column chart, a single column is a data point. In a pie chart, a single pie wedge is a data point.

Data series The chart element that represents the data represented by the chart. In a column chart, the columns are the data series. In a pie chart, the pie itself is the data series.

Data source In a mail merge, the document that contains the variable information to be merged with the boilerplate text of the main document.

Default   The original setting, such as page margins or tab spacing, set by the program.

Delete   To remove selected text or a graphic from a document.

Descending order   The sequence in which rows are sorted from Z to A or from largest to smallest.

Dialog box   A window that opens when more information is needed to carry out a command.

Document window   The rectangular area of the Word program window where you view and work on a document.

Drag   To hold down the mouse button while moving the mouse.

Drop cap   The initial character of a paragraph that is formatted significantly larger than the surrounding text. Only the first character of a paragraph may be formatted as a drop cap. You can modify the font, determine the number of lines deep that the drop cap should be, and set the placement of the drop cap as within the paragraph or in the margin to the left of the paragraph.

Drop-down form field   A field entered in an online form that provides users with a list of options. In the form document, the user clicks the arrow next to the drop-down field to display a list of options and then clicks the option required to select it.

Dynamic data exchange   The connection between a document and an object's source file that ensures that changes to information in the source file are automatically made to the document.

Edit   To add, delete, or change text and graphics.

Elevation (chart)   In a 3-D chart, the elevation is expressed in terms of the number of degrees the chart is tilted.

Embedded object   An inserted object that is created and edited using the features of another program but is stored as part of the document into which it has been inserted.

Endnote   Text that appears at the end of a document. Similar to a footnote, an endnote usually acknowledges a source stated in the text or provides additional information.

Facing pages   The left and right pages in a two-page spread of a double-sided document, such as a book or a magazine.

Field   An instruction or code inserted into a document that serves as a placeholder for information that changes, such as a date or a page number.

Field label   A word or phrase such as "Zip Code" or "Age" that identifies the information users should enter in a given field.

Field name   In a mail merge, the names of the data fields in the header row of a data source.

File   An electronic collection of information that has a unique name, distinguishing it from other files. In Word, all documents are stored as files.

Filename   The name assigned to a file; the name you assign to a document when you save it to a disk.

Filter   To isolate a set of records that meet certain criteria; used to select a specific set of records to merge.

Floating graphic   A graphic object that has text wrapping applied to it and can be placed anywhere on a page.

Folders   Subdivisions of a disk that work like a filing system to help you organize files.

Font   The typeface or design of a set of characters (letters, numerals, symbols, and punctuation marks).

Font effects   Enhanced formatting you can apply to text, such as bold, italics, shadows, or all caps.

Font size   The size of text, measured in points (pts). The larger the number of points, the bigger the font size.

Footer   Text that appears at the bottom of each page in a document.

Footnote   Text that appears at the bottom of a page. Like an endnote, a footnote usually acknowledges a source stated in the text or provides additional information.

Form   A special document in which you can create blanks and controls so that a user can complete a form online.

Form field   A special Word code inserted to hold the information users should enter in a specific area of a form. You can enter a text field, a check box, or a drop-down list.

Format   The appearance of a document, including color, font, attributes, borders, and shading.

Format Painter   A feature used to copy the formatting applied to one set of text to another.

Formatting toolbar   A toolbar that contains buttons for the most frequently used formatting commands.

Formula   A set of instructions used to perform numeric calculations (adding, multiplying, averaging, etc.).

Frame   A bordered area on a Web page that contains hyperlinks and other elements to help users navigate a Web site.

General discussion   A Web discussion related to an entire document instead of just a specific part of it.

Global replace   Replacing all occurrences of specific text in a document without having to review and change each occurrence individually.

Graphics   A picture, chart, or drawing in a document.

Gridlines   The dotted lines that separate cells in a table. Gridlines do not print. You can alternately hide and display gridlines with the Gridlines command on the Table menu.

Gutter   Extra margin space left for a binding at the top or on the left side of a page.

Hanging indent   A paragraph format in which the first line of a paragraph starts farther to the left than the subsequent lines.

Hard page break   A page break inserted manually to force text to begin on a new page.

Header   Text that appears at the top of each page in a document.

Header row   In a mail merge, the first row of the data source table that contains the names of data fields.

Home page   The first page that a visitor to a Web site usually sees. The home page usually links to other pages in the Web site, and other pages link back to the home page.

Horizontal ruler   A graphical bar across the top of the document window that you can use to place and align text.

Hyperlink   Text or an object in a document that, when clicked, opens another site or Web page.

Hypertext Markup Language (HTML) The language used to describe the content and format of Web pages.

Hyphens Short dashes used to break words that appear at the end of a line.

Indent The distance between the beginning or end of a line of text and the page margins. A paragraph can have left, right, first-line, and hanging indents.

Indent markers Movable buttons on the horizontal ruler that determine the indent settings for the selected paragraph.

Index Lists key words and phrases that readers of a document may wish to look up.

Inline discussion A Web discussion that is conducted directly in a document and related to a specific paragraph, table, or graphic.

Inline graphic A graphic object that is part of a line of text; the default setting for a graphic before text wrapping is applied.

Insertion point A blinking vertical line in the document window that indicates where text will appear when you type.

Internet A communications system that connects computers and computer networks located around the world using telephone lines, cables, satellites, and other telecommunications media.

Intranet A computer network that connects computers in a local area only, such as computers in a company's office.

Italics Formatting in which the text appears slanted.

Justify A form of paragraph alignment in which both the left and right edges of a paragraph are flush with the margins.

Kerning A form of character formatting that allows you to adjust the space between standard combinations of characters, such as "W" followed by "a".

Keyboard shortcut A combination of keys or function keys you can press to perform an operation in Word. Using keyboard shortcuts is often faster than using the menus and commands.

Landscape orientation Horizontal page orientation; a page that is wider than it is tall.

Left-align A form of paragraph alignment in which the left edge of a paragraph is even, usually flush with the left margin.

Legend A key to the symbol or colors used to represent data in a chart or graph.

Line spacing The amount of space between lines of text, measured in lines or points.

Link A connection established between a document and an object's source file that allows dynamic data exchange.

Linked object An inserted object that is created, edited, and stored in another program; changes made to a linked object in the source program are automatically made to the document to which the object is linked.

Lowercase The small letters of a character set (a, b, c, d...).

Macro A collection of commands and keystrokes performed in a sequence that you record and store to perform repetitive tasks.

Mail merge A feature that combines a main document, such as a form letter, with a data source, such as recipients' names and addresses, to create a set of customized documents.

Main document In a mail merge, the document that contains the merge fields and the boilerplate text.

Margin The empty space between the edge of the text, or the printed area, and the edge of the page. A document's margins are visible in Print Preview or Print Layout view.

Master document A document that contains a set of related documents, called subdocuments. You create a master document to organize and maintain a long document that you have divided into smaller, more manageable subdocuments.

Menu bar A bar beneath the title bar that contains menus that list the program's commands.

Merge Combining two or more cells in a table to form a single cell.

Merge field In mail merge, a placeholder that indicates where in the main document the data from each record should be placed when the main document and data source are merged.

Mirror margins Inside and outside margins that mirror each other in a document with facing pages.

More Buttons button The button you click to display toolbar buttons that are not currently visible.

Newspaper columns Columns of text in which text flows from the bottom of one column to the top of the next column.

Non-printing characters Marks displayed on the screen to indicate characters that do not print, such as tab characters or paragraph marks. You can control the display of non-printing characters with the Show/Hide ¶ button on the Standard toolbar.

Normal style The default paragraph style in the Normal template.

Normal template The template used as the basis for a new blank document.

Normal view The document view in which you do not see the edges of the page; useful for most editing and formatting tasks.

Object Information that is created in another program and inserted in a Word document; for example, graphics, spreadsheets, charts, or sound and video clips.

Object Linking and Embedding (OLE) A feature that allows you to use information stored in other Office programs in your Word documents.

Office Assistant An animated character that offers tips, answers questions, and provides access to the program's Help system.

Office Clipboard A temporary storage area shared by all Office programs to cut, copy and paste multiple items within and between Office programs. The Office Clipboard can hold up to 12 items. See also *Clipboard toolbar*.

Open The operation of retrieving and displaying a document in the document window.

Orientation (chart) In a pie chart, how the pie wedges are positioned. You can rotate a chart so that a specific wedge is foremost.

Outline view The view you work in to quickly and easily organize the topics and subtopics included in a document. You assign levels to headings and subheadings and identify body text.

Overtype mode A feature that lets you replace, or overwrite, existing text as you type.

Page break A separator that forces all text after the break to appear on the next page of a document.

Paragraph spacing The amount of space between paragraphs, measured in points.

Paragraph style A stored set of character and paragraph format settings that you can apply to a paragraph.

Paste A command that inserts cut or copied items into a document from the Clipboard.

Pixels Small dots that comprise a bitmapped graphic image and contain information about color and intensity.

Point The unit of measurement for fonts and space between paragraphs and text characters. There are 72 points per inch.

Portrait orientation Vertical page orientation; a page that is taller than it is wide.

Print Layout view A view that mimics the look of a printed page; useful for viewing margins, alignment, and text flow.

Print Preview A command you can use to display the document as it will look when printed.

Program Task-oriented software (such as Excel or Word) that enables you to perform a certain type of task such as data calculation or word processing.

Pull quote Decorative text in a document that is set off by wrapping document text around it.

Record In a mail merge, a complete set of data for one individual or one item, such as one person's first name, last name, address, city, state, and zip code.

Redo A command that repeats a reversed edit or formatting change; only reversed changes can be repeated with the Redo command.

Replace The command you use to locate and change a specific occurrence of text. Also, refers to the operation of selecting and typing over existing text to replace it.

Reset usage data An option that allows personalized toolbars and menus to be returned to their default settings.

Right-align A form of paragraph alignment in which only the right edge of a paragraph is even, usually flush with the right margin.

Row A horizontal arrangement of cells in a table.

Sans serif font A font whose characters do not include serifs, the small strokes at the ends of the characters. Arial is a sans serif font.

Save The command used to permanently store your document and any changes you make to a file. See also *filename*.

ScreenTip A pop-up label that appears when you point to a button. It provides descriptive information about the button.

Scroll To move within a window to display parts of a document that are not currently visible.

Scroll bars Bars at the right and bottom edges of the document window used to view different parts of a document not currently visible in the document window.

Scroll box The movable box in the scroll bars that you drag to move around in a document.

Search To use the Find command to locate specific text in a document.

Section A part of a document that is separated from the rest of the document by section breaks.

Section break A separator that divides a document into sections that can be formatted differently from other sections.

Security levels Safeguards to protect you from opening documents that may contain macro viruses. You set the security level at High, Medium, or Low. The default security setting is Medium.

Select To highlight text with the mouse. Most formatting and editing commands in Word require that you select the text.

Selection bar An unmarked column at the left edge of a document window that can be used to select text. In a table, each cell, row, and column also has its own selection bar.

Serif font A font that has small strokes (called serifs) at the ends of the characters. Times New Roman and Palatino are serif fonts.

Shading A background color or pattern you can apply to text, tables, or graphics.

Sizing handle Squares that appear on the corners and sides of a selected object and are used to resize an object.

Soft page break An automatic page break that Word inserts at the bottom of a page.

Sort An operation that arranges rows in a table (or paragraphs of text) in a sequence, such as chronological, alphabetical, or numerical order.

Sort criterion The detail of a table or list by which rows or paragraphs are sorted, for example, last name.

Source program The program in which an object is created.

Spin button control An ActiveX control that you insert in an online form when you want users to specify a quantity.

Split cells A command used to divide a cell in a table into two or more cells.

Standard toolbar The toolbar containing buttons that perform some of the most frequently used commands.

Status bar A bar at the bottom of the Word window that indicates the current page number and section number, the total number of pages in the document, and the vertical position (in inches) of the insertion point.

Strikethrough formatting Text formatted with strikethrough formatting appears with a line through it ~~like this~~. The Track changes while editing option automatically shows deleted text in strikethrough formatting.

Style A predefined set of character and paragraph format settings that you can apply to text to format it quickly and easily.

Subdocument A document contained within a master document. To work in a subdocument, you first open it from the master document and then add and edit text.

Superscript Formatting in which the text is raised above and is several points smaller than adjacent text. Copyright and trademark symbols are often superscripted.

Symbols Special characters such as bullets and foreign language characters that you can insert into a document.

Tab A key you press to position text so that it is located at a specific horizontal position in a document.

Tab leaders A solid or dotted line that appears in front of tabbed text.

Tab stop A measured position used for placing and aligning text horizontally at a specific location in a document. Word has five kinds of tab stops, left-aligned (the default), centered, right-aligned, decimal, and bar.

Table A grid of rows and columns divided by borders; commonly used to display text, numbers, or other items for quick reference and analysis.

Table AutoFormat A feature that includes preset formats to apply to format a table with shading, fonts, and borders.

Table of contents Lists the headings and subheadings included in a document along with the appropriate page numbers.

Tags HTML codes that describe how each element on a Web page should appear when viewed with a browser.

Template A special kind of document that provides basic tools and text for creating a document. Templates can contain styles, AutoText items, macros, customized menu and key assignments, and text or graphics that are the same in different types of document.

Text box A graphic object that is a container for text and graphics.

Text flow Refers to paragraph formatting which controls the flow of text across page breaks. Controlling text flow prevents awkward breaks within paragraphs, or ensures that related paragraphs appear together on the same page.

Text form field A field entered in an online form in a location where you want users to enter text such as a name or an address.

Text wrapping Formatting that forces text to flow around a graphic object rather than over it and changes an inline graphic to a floating object.

Theme A predefined set of Web backgrounds, bullets, horizontal lines, colors, and styles that you can apply to Web pages and e-mail messages to give documents a common visual look.

Title bar The bar at the top of a window that displays the program name and the filename of the current document.

Tone The feeling of a document, affected by its content and visual appearance.

Toolbar A bar that contains buttons that give you quick access to the most frequently used commands. For example, the Tables and Borders toolbar contains buttons that are useful when you create tables.

Undo A command that reverses previous edits or formatting changes you made to a document; you can undo up to 100 previous actions.

Uppercase The capital letters of a character set (A, B, C, D…).

Version The saved changes stored with a document. By saving versions of a document you can revert a document to an earlier stage of editing.

Vertical alignment The placement of text on a page or in a cell in relation to the top, bottom, or center of the page or cell.

Vertical ruler A graphical bar at the left edge of the document window in Print Layout view.

View A format for displaying a document in the document window that offers features useful for working on different types of documents. Word includes four views: Normal, Outline, Print Layout, and Web Layout.

View buttons Buttons on the horizontal scroll bar that allow you to switch between views.

Visual Basic A programming language in which Word macros are recorded. When you record a macro, Word assigns a Visual Basic code to each task performed. You open the Visual Basic window to edit the steps contained in a macro.

Watermark A picture or other graphic object that appears grayed out or tinted behind text in a document. You can make any picture into a watermark by clicking the Image Control button on the Picture toolbar, then selecting Watermark.

Web browser A software program used to access and display Web pages.

Web page A document that is stored on the World Wide Web or an intranet and viewed on a computer using a Web browser.

Web site A group of associated Web pages that are linked together with hyperlinks.

Wizard An interactive set of dialog boxes that guides you through the process of creating a document; it asks you questions about document preferences and creates the document according to your specifications.

Word processing program A software application used to create documents efficiently.

WordArt A graphic object that contains text formatted in unique shapes, special colors, and patterns.

Wordwrap A feature that automatically moves the insertion point to the next line of a paragraph as you type.

Workgroup template A template that you want to make available to other users. To determine where Word has stored a workgroup template, you need to check the File Location tab in the Options dialog box.

World Wide Web (Web or WWW) A part of the Internet containing Web pages that are linked together.

Index

Index

Index

in Word 2000, WORD A-14—15
Help Key (F1) tab
    of Form Field Help Text dialog box, WORD O-12—13
Highlight button, WORD C-4
Highlighter pointer, WORD C-4
Highlighting Changes dialog box, WORD L-6—7
High security level
    for documents containing macros, WORD P-11
home page, WORD G-2
horizontal lines
    in Web pages, WORD G-6
horizontal ruler, WORD A-6, WORD A-7
horizontal scroll bar, WORD A-6, WORD A-7
HTML, WORD G-2, WORD G-3. *See also* Web pages
    creating Web pages with, WORD G-4
    opening and saving documents in Word, WORD L-17
    tags, WORD G-4
    viewing tags, WORD G-16—17
Hyperlink button, WORD G-12
    on custom toolbars, WORD P-12—13, WORD P-14
Hyperlink command, WORD G-12
hyperlinks
    bookmarks and cross-references as, WORD L-14—15
    defined, WORD G-12
    editing, WORD G-14—15
    inserting in Web pages, WORD G-12—13
    navigation with, WORD E-15
    ScreenTips for, WORD G-14—15, WORD G-16
Hypertext Markup Language. *See* HTML
hyphenation, WORD E-16
hyphenation zone, WORD E-16

►I

I-beam, WORD A-4
icons
    displaying objects as, WORD J-4
Image Control button, WORD M-16
images. *See* clip art; graphics
Import Data Options dialog box, WORD N-16—17
importing
    data into charts, WORD N-16—17
indenting
    hanging indents, WORD C-9
    paragraphs, WORD C-8—9
indent markers, WORD C-8—9
Index, of Help system, WORD A-14
Index and Tables dialog box, WORD K-10—11,
    WORD K-14
indexes
    creating, WORD K-14—15
    purpose of, WORD K-14
inline discussions, WORD L-16
inline graphics, WORD F-2
    moving, WORD F-7
Insert Clip button, WORD G-8
Insert Date button, WORD E-9
Insert Hyperlink dialog box, WORD G-12—13
inserting rows and columns, WORD D-6—7
insertion point
    placing on a page, WORD A-8
    in Word, WORD A-4, WORD A-5
Insert Merge Field button, WORD H-10

Insert mode, WORD A-8
Insert Picture dialog box, WORD F-8
Insert Rows button, WORD D-6
Insert Table button, WORD D-2, WORD D-3
    of Forms toolbar, WORD O-2—3
Insert Time button, WORD E-9
Internet, WORD G-3
Internet Service Providers (ISPs), WORD G-17
intranets
    defined, WORD G-3
    publishing Web documents to, WORD G-17
italic text, WORD C-4—5

►J

JPEG graphics, WORD G-9
justified text, WORD C-6—7

►K

Keep break before option, WORD K-17
Keep lines together option, WORD K-17
Keep with next option, WORD K-17
keyboard shortcuts
    for adjusting line spacing, WORD C-10
    assigning to styles, WORD I-9

►L

Label Options dialog box, WORD H-14—15
labels
    creating for mail merge documents, WORD H-14—15
    formatting, WORD H-16
landscape orientation, WORD E-3
large documents, WORD K-1—17. *See also* documents
    creating documents in Outline view, WORD K-2—3
    editing documents in Outline view, WORD K-4—5
    endnotes in, WORD K-8—9
    footnotes in, WORD K-8—9
    formatting pages in multiple sections, WORD K-12—13
    indexes for, WORD K-14—15
    master documents for, WORD K-16—17
    organizing documents in Outline view, WORD K-6—7
    table of contents for, WORD K-10—11
Last Record button
    on Mail Merge toolbar, WORD H-11
layering graphics, WORD M-8—9
layout, of documents, WORD B-2—3
left-aligned text, WORD C-6—7
Left Indent marker, WORD C-8—9
Left Tab icon, WORD C-14
Left tabs, WORD C-15
legends, for charts
    adjusting location of, WORD N-4—5
Line button
    on Drawing toolbar, WORD F-14
line charts
    creating, WORD N-12—13
    defined, WORD N-2—3
    modifying values in, WORD N-14—15

Line Color list arrow
    on Drawing toolbar, WORD F-10—11
lines. *See also* gridlines
    adding to headers and footers, WORD E-4—5
    curved, WORD F-15
    drawing, WORD F-14—15
    formatting, WORD G-6
    freeform, WORD F-15
    horizontal, in Web pages, WORD G-6
    scribble, WORD F-15
line spacing, WORD C-10—11
    in paragraph styles, WORD I-4
Line Style button, WORD D-8
    on Drawing toolbar, WORD F-14
Line Style list arrow, WORD C-18
    on Drawing toolbar, WORD F-10—11
Line Weight button, WORD D-8
linked objects
    modifying, WORD J-6—7
    updating manually, WORD J-6
linking
    worksheets to documents, WORD J-4—5
links
    defined, WORD J-2
Links dialog box, WORD J-6
List Box control, WORD O-11
lists
    bulleted, WORD C-16—17
    numbered, WORD C-16—17
Lock aspect ratio check box, WORD F-8—9
    Low security level
    for documents containing macros, WORD P-11

►M

Macro pointer, WORD P-4
Macro Record toolbar, WORD P-4—5
macros
    applying, WORD P-6—7
    copying, WORD P-10—11
    defined, WORD P-1, WORD P-4
    deleting, WORD P-10—11
    descriptions of, WORD P-5
    editing, WORD P-8—9
    naming, WORD P-5
    organizing, WORD P-10—11
    recording, WORD P-4—5
    renaming, WORD P-10—11
    security levels for documents containing, WORD P-11
    storage location, WORD P-4, WORD P-5
Macros dialog box, WORD P-6—7
magnification
    of forms, WORD O-14
Magnifier button, WORD A-14
mail merge, WORD A-2, WORD H-1—17
    attaching an Access data source, WORD J-14—15
    basics, WORD H-2—3
    creating data source for, WORD H-2, WORD H-6—7
    creating labels for, WORD H-14—15
    creating main document for, WORD H-2, WORD H-4—5
    defined, WORD H-1
    entering and editing records for, WORD H-8—9
    filtering records for, WORD H-16—17

Index

Index